Mikell, Gwendolyn.

Cocoa and chaos in Ghana.

$29.95

DATE			

Cocoa and Chaos In Ghana

COCOA AND CHAOS IN GHANA

Gwendolyn Mikell

A PWPA Book

Paragon House
New York

First edition, 1989

Published in the United States by

Paragon House
90 Fifth Avenue
New York, NY 10011

A Professors World Peace Academy Book

Library of Congress Cataloging-in-Publication Data

Mikell, Gwendolyn.
Cocoa and chaos in Ghana / Gwendolyn Mikell. -- 1st ed.
p. cm.
"A PWPA book."
Includes index.
ISBN 0-943852-39-0
1. Cocoa trade--Ghana.
2. Ghana--Economic conditions-- 1979–
3. Ghana--Social conditions. I. Title.
HD9200.G62M55 1988
338.1'7374'09667--dc19 87-25795
CIP

Manufactured in the United States of America

Contents

Preface

It is impossible to accomplish worthwhile things without also accumulating significant debts along the way. This project has taken shape gradually over the years, so that it is only now that I can begin to appreciate how many people contributed to making this book a reality. My mother must be credited with cultivating my love of books, such that I had determined from quite early that I too would write some. With the generous supply of African nationalism which my father contributed to our household as I was growing up, it is probably not surprising that I adopted Nkrumah as my hero and that I became determined in the 1970s to understand why Ghanaians had ousted him. Had I written this book in 1974 when I was newly returned from the field and first wanted to write it, it would have been an entirely different, and perhaps a less satisfying work. During the intervening years, the exchanges with my professors, with colleagues, with Ghanaians both inside and outside of Ghana, and with friends and family, have sharpened my ideas and allowed me to focus them in ways which I think have strengthened this book.

During my various field trips and visits to Ghana, many Ghanaians shared with me their information, ideas and hopes about the country. Professor A. Adu Boahen took me under his wing during my first trip to Ghana in 1971, introduced me to other scholars, such as K.B. Dickson and I.M. Ofori, within the university, and helped arrange my relationship with the sociology department at Legon. Through Mr. Asiedu, then the Registrar at Legon, I met and interviewed Nana Asiedu Agyemfra V, Ohene of Kubease, Larteh, and began to feed my intellectual curiosity about cocoa farming. Jonas Adjei, nephew of Mr. Asiedu, was my first dedicated research assistant when I conducted exploratory research in Akwapim, Dampong-Ashanti and Sunyani. At the Sunyani Cocoa Marketing Board, I met enduring friends such as Daniel and Felicia Dosoo, who gave encouragement and shared their home, family and information with me over the years.

In Sunyani, Mr. F.W. Amankwa, Mr. Bedi and Mr. Boateng, made it possible for me to work with the Ghana Cooperative Societies; Mr. H.O. Kissi and Mr. Kofi Adu facilitated my work with the Produce Buying Agency of the Cocoa Marketing Board; Mr. Asare-Mensah made available the data from B/A Cooperative Food Farming and Marketing Association; and Elizabeth Adoma Kyeremah, my witty and insightful research assistant, helped conduct 233 survey interviews during 1972 and 1973. Hundreds of cocoa farmers were willing informants, but a few names deserve special mention: Nana Kodjoe Ntow, Stephen Ocrah, and Kwaku Kumah were farmers as well as local activists, and they helped me understand the connection between research facts and social realities. Ohene Kwesi Henneh of Nsuatre and the chiefs of Odumasi and Sunyani enlightened me about the relations between traditional leaders and the people. Personal friends like Quincy Hickson Baku and Jacqueline Long, and distinguished acquaintances like Judges Coussey and Sekyi were willing to talk over developments in Sunyani and Brong-Ahafo, or new discoveries about traditional Akan political allegiances. In assessing changes in the cocoa sector since 1983, Mr. R.K. Brittwum of the Cocoa Services Division-Sunyani came to my assistance; and as my focus shifted to the changing role of the Ghanaian state in family affairs, other colleagues such as Chief Justice E.K. Sowah and Judge George Beneh of the High Court in Accra were continually gracious and helpful. More recently, staff at the Ghana Embassy were helpful in confirming ethnic designations for family data; and they provided some of the photographs of Ghanaian heads of state.

The intellectual debts are among the greatest, but they are sometimes difficult to sort out as the contributions of Columbia University mentors merge with ideas that are instinctively my own. My interest in hierarchical relations between parts of the state is a legacy from the late Dr. Mort Fried; Elliott Skinner kept in touch with me in the field, and constantly asked questions that made me focus on the importance of structures and processes which mediate between global, national and local levels of culture; and Conrad Arensberg's ideas about regularities within communities stimulated my own notions of Sunyani town as the center of a regional community, structuring relations with surrounding villages. At a much later point, the late Eleanor Burke Leacock provided the stimulus for the investigation of historical change in Akan familial and women's roles; and Kwame Arhin insisted upon defining phenomena in ways that made me reexamine Akan historical data, and draw new conclusions.

A host of people were instrumental in the production of the manuscript. Research assistants Carol Oursler, Janet Redley, Diana Chung and Noreen Polk diligently searched library and archival sources, programmed and ran computer analyses of Ghana data, and organized background material; Samantha Hawkins provided technical advice in producing drafts of the manuscript; and W. Ofuatey-Kudjoe graciously read the manuscript, challenged ideas whenever necessary, helped sharpen various political arguments, and corrected my spelling of various Akan terms. Robert Brooks and the editorial staff have been patient and encouraging in all phases of producing the manuscript. Most importantly, my husband Elliott has provided me with constant intellectual challenge; consistently, he has been my sounding board, my critic and adviser. He, as well as our daughter Luce, deserve special credit for their support, especially in moments when being a writer and anthropologist competed with being a wife and mother.

Introduction

Cocoa has been a major source of wealth as well as one of the major causes of chaos in contemporary Ghana. In the late nineteenth and early twentieth century, cocoa replaced gold and slaves as the commodity which integrated the Gold Coast into the modern world economy. But, whereas the task of producing gold and slaves led to the preeminence of noble and merchant classes within a regionally linked economy,[1] the production of cocoa was to penetrate deeply into the society, changing the kin-based and political institutions of peasant cultivators. Cocoa, as distinct from any agricultural crop which preceded it, would link these basic food producers to the British imperial system, and through it to the global economy. In the process, traditional systems of stratification became indelibly marked; and the social and political institutions of Gold Coast societies, especially the cocoa-producing ones, would be radically transformed.

The production of cocoa made the Gold Coast a valuable colony, and facilitated the consolidation of social classes whose livelihood depended upon articulation with the global economic system. It should not have been surprising that crises within the world capitalist economy stimulated social unrest in the Gold Coast in the 1930s and 1940s,[2] and ultimately encouraged local economic initiatives by which elite groups clamored for greater control over the colony's resources. Inevitably, the social mobilization continued until (as Apter and Austin have shown)[3] it became transformed into demands for national political parties and independence. The conflict over cocoa resources punctuated the larger political struggle; it created socio-economic, ethnic and political unrest which was the basis of divisions within the colonial Gold Coast and the later state of Ghana. Cocoa continued to dominate Ghana's attempt to industrialize and the fate of cocoa in a troubled capitalist world economy has been a major cause of instability in that early "model" African state.[4] The link between cocoa, its rural peasant producers and an urban-oriented state is one that continues to haunt Ghanaian leaders in the 1980s.

When former colonial territories such as Ghana achieved national independence, their great expectations led many lay persons as well as scholars to underestimate the ramifications of the intense resource and capital extraction from rural producers. The initial focus of Nkrumah and others was on the "political kingdom"—the development of democratic institutions—rather than on the way in which these primarily agricultural and underdeveloped economies were linked to the world capitalist system. Moreover, as African countries moved out of the 1960s, the decade of independence, and created plans for the decade of the 1970s, they tended to ignore the rural base of their existence as well. Both Little and Mabogunje have described the rush of peasants to the cities, the growth in numbers of African elites.[5] These complicated factors appeared to give validity to the thesis that the urban classes, as linkage points between the Third World and the global system,[6] would provide the dynamic energy for African countries to move forward. It seemed logical, in the light of such thinking, to focus on issues of modern technology and development, on sophisticated educational, communications and production systems. Development was to begin at the top and trickle down to the rural masses. However, leaders such as Nkrumah were among the first to witness the brutal confrontation between rural economics and the "political kingdom"—a confrontation which was to transform African national politics.

The rash of political violence, coups and civil wars which broke out in Africa during the late 1960s and the early 1970s in states such as Ghana, Uganda, Nigeria and others,[7] halted the earlier optimism and demanded a more thorough examination of the links between internal socio-economic structures and political unrest. The revolutionary conflicts in Congo-Zaire, Angola and Mozambique between colonial and indigenous groups highlighted the difficulties in truly decolonizing Africa.[8] Young has reminded us that irrespective of whether many of these states were capitalist or socialist oriented, the economic realities were harsh.[9] There were drops in export commodity prices and rural exodus, high birth rates and population pressures exacerbating rural problems, compounded by food shortages in many African states. All these factors caused political unrest as well as starvation in many areas.[10]

Central to many of these African problems was the impact of a declining rural economy in the face of ever increasing urban and national demands. The multiplicity of politico-economic problems has necessitated a reanalysis of the difficulties facing under-developed nations as a result of their dependence for survival on kin-based small-scale rural communities. As Amin anticipated, the rural rather than the urban areas now appear to be the loci of attempts at positive systemic changes;[11] and the key to national regeneration may in fact lie in the African nation-state's readjustment to the realities and traditions of rural people.

Despite numerous studies, the processes by which African societies changed during earlier historical periods, and particularly how rural-urban disjuncture and disintegration occurred during the late nineteenth and early twentieth centuries, are still not clearly understood. Accustomed as anthropologists have been to making synchronic studies of the lives of people living in small-scale societies, they are still reluctant to use new paradigms when they analyze the trauma of people caught up in a revolutionary change as the societies in which they live move from autonomy to colonial rule to independence. The fault must not be laid solely on anthropologists, however, for they as well as other social scientists had participated in creating the disciplinary boundaries which isolated the study of social structures and processes from the study of power and bureaucracies, and from the study of markets and systems of exchange as well. The kind of analysis which is now needed is one which reintegrates these various aspects of social life; one that assists us in charting the movement of rural peoples caught up in a whirlwind of often violent, revolutionary political and economic forces emanating from the nation-state and global levels. Historically, these conflicts and contradictions were staggering as the people, especially the peasants, became chessboard pieces in the struggle between African societies desiring to retain their autonomy, and the intrusive demands of the expanding western economic system.

The primary problem is to assess which paradigm is effective in explicating social change within both rural-traditional societies and the larger states of which they are a part.[12] To be effective, the paradigm must deal with historical factors, so as to permit us to see the changes in all the factors relevant to the cohesive functioning of a traditional African society. It must also allow for the explication of such factors and forces of production which create links between small-scale peasant and global societies; and it must permit an examination of the changing cultural factors as they mediate between the micro- and macro-societies involved. Harris has pointed out that in order to avoid evolutionary and diffusionist speculation, many earlier anthropologists insisted upon structural-functionalism in their analysis of African societies, and stressed the integration and reintegration of all the institutions within the society.[13] Although there was justifiable concern with social and familial structures, these were not seen in terms of their linkages to the dynamic and sometimes cataclysmic developments in political economy as African and colonial groups interacted. While the functionalist analysis of these African colonial societies provided some useful models of social interaction, it also proved problematic in that it often stressed unity and "cross-cutting ties" between indigenous and colonizing groups, rather than seriously assessing evident schisms and conflicting interests between them. To this extent, the structural-functional paradigm was too static, and not sufficiently holistic to be utilized in understanding long term change in African societies.[14]

It seems that a more valuable paradigm would be one that placed special emphasis on the economic and political structures as pivotal points for change as well as for social disjuncture. However, all these things (change, integration as well as disjuncture) must be viewed in multi-level terms which reflect the interplay between African dynamics and that of other global players as well. Approaches such as those of Wallerstein, Curtin and Wolf[15] have focused our attention on the intense dialogue (often exploitative as well as integrative) which occurred between western and non-western political economies as capitalist development took place. These approaches have obviously differed. Leaving aside Wallerstein's approach for the moment, Curtin's focus on cross-cultural trade demonstrated the less well-known exchanges and similarities in socio-economic structures and practices which inevitably occurred across centuries as the desired economic exchange was carried out. What becomes clear is that the basis was being laid for global exchange at a much earlier point than many would have anticipated. Wolf's focus on pre-capitalist and capitalist socio-economic history has also been especially fruitful, because it has drawn back "into history" those peoples whose societies and materials provided the fuel for European development, and it allows us to further examine their contributions to the capitalist world economy.[16] It is this kind of inclusive and comprehensive paradigm that is being systematically attempted in the present analysis of change in Ghana, the difference being that the major concern is with presenting a detailed analysis of lower-level structural articulation with these higher level changes in national and global political economy.

The forces making for social change in Ghana have been long in operation and, while not recognized as such until recently, they have been as dramatic as the rural social transformations in Asia which have so concerned such social scientists as Wittfogel and Lattimore.[17] Long before sea-borne Europeans contacted the societies in the western forest area, these societies of the interior had been in contact with forces emanating from eastern and northern Africa. As Kea and Arhin have shown,[18] the Akan (who had been on the peripheries of empires even before 1600) had used their natural resources and agricultural products to establish trade and cultural contact with their mighty neighbors. As a consequence, they were becoming centralized and increasingly stratified, as they organized production and distribution in such a way as to consolidate their critical roles as suppliers of gold for the trans-Saharan trade and resources for regional needs. Through the recruitment of unfree labor, the basis for stratification and inequality between peasant producers and elites was laid in this early period.[19] Nevertheless, it is to the more dynamic period of European contact, capitalist expansion, and Ashanti state growth, that we must look for the roots of social distortion in Ghana.

Historians, sociologists and political economists looking at the origin of the capitalist world system have emphasized the relations between core areas and peripheral, semi-peripheral, and external areas. Wallerstein, in particular, has applied this paradigm to Africa's changing articulation with the capitalist world economy.[20] Wallerstein stresses that with the consolidation of the capitalist world economy in the 1700s, British mercantilist hegemony permitted them to transform Africa's limited involvement with Europe. Africa moved from absorbing luxury goods and exporting raw materials necessary for British production to the export of slave labor. Later, Africa became further entrenched in this periphery as a result of this extraction of labor potential.[21] However, during the stage of industrial capitalism, Africa's position shifted from peripheral to semi-peripheral, and Africa's agricultural products became more significant as exports in exchange for the manufactured products from Britain. The capitalist core thus increased the economic and political stability of the West, at the cost of great social and economic dislocation within the peripheral and semi-peripheral countries.

The relevance of Wallerstein's macro-analysis to the specific experiences of Third World countries has been a major source of discussion among Nash, Mintz and others.[22] Many of the criticisms of the world systems approach deal with its unitary view of the capitalist mode of production,[23] with implicit assumptions of the passivity of the peripheral countries during capitalist exploitative relationships. Alternatively, the criticisms deal with the failure to recognize the dynamic quality of pre-capitalist African and Asian economic and political systems.[24] In many cases, the "world systems" approach omitted a clear explication of the intense relationship between core and periphery during the eighteenth and nineteenth centuries, and of the impact of some African resistance movements on the penetration of the capitalist system in certain parts of the continent. It is these kinds of omissions which are partially rectified by the work of Wolf and Curtin.

The concern in this study is to get beneath the generalizations of the dependency versus world systems debate, to examine the process of social restructuring which took place as the ties between the core and one of its semi-peripheral areas were affected from the early 1700s to the 1960s, and to describe the tragic results of this process. While there is no denying the value of the world systems approach, the object will be to show how local and economic sociocultural factors conditioned the way these global factors created chaos in the lives of the people involved. So specific have these reactions been that in the short run at least, they appear *sui generis*. Nevertheless, it is in looking at this specificity that the larger issues of contemporary socio-cultural change can be explicated.

Despite the valuable work done on Latin American development,[25] there has been an astonishing ignorance of how capitalist development affected African social structures, particularly the kinship system and the productive units of the rural and agrarian segments of those societies.[26] The outstanding exceptions are the work of Rodney, which explored in great depth the western and capitalist economic impact on Upper Guinea Coast societies;[27] and the work of Dike and Daaku on African trade and capitalist articulation in the Niger Delta and the Gold Coast.[28] However, few others rose to the challenge; therefore, the social and cultural parameters within which trade, natural resource extraction, and commodity production took place in other parts of the African continent have been relatively underexplored. The result is that when the world systems approach is applied to Africa, the missing information distorts any understanding of the impact of global economic relationships on the indigenous structures and lives of rural groups. Any prognostication based on such flawed analysis further confuses the issues, rendering such global paradigms of doubtful utility.

The situation in West Africa is highly instructive. Most of these societies utilized relationships that Wolf has described as a "kin-ordered mode of production:"[29] and they maintained their cohesiveness in the face of external contact. Despite early rural production for the local, regional and trans-Saharan trades, the Akan forest societies of the Gold Coast (Ghana) did not experience intense social upheavals until the 1800s, and most particularly until the later years of the nineteenth century when cocoa was introduced into the Gold Coast. One obvious reason was that, until this period, the rate and amount of internal trade fluctuated only within a limited range, was relatively consistent, and that local Africans (by various means) resisted external control of their economies and societies.[30] The predominance of barter and special-purpose money was also a reflection of the relatively low level of complexity in economic transactions in local areas. Some local monarchs used their capital towns as trading centers, or "ports of trade" as Polanyi and others have called them,[31] and could therefore mediate between outside traders (mostly Muslim) and their own people. In Akan trading towns, the merchants often occupied distinct quarters or sections, and were thus more easily regulated.[32] In the process of mediating trade, rulers appropriated to themselves some of the surplus wealth that would have flowed to the outside, and regulated the concentration of wealth among subordinate groups within their own societies.

In contrast, as Rodney, Dike and Daaku have amply demonstrated,[33] European contact and commercial involvement was of a different order. Among the common people, barter began to be replaced by the use of general purpose money such as gold. New patterns of economic organization arose as mulatto middlemen and Africans using wage labor "organized themselves to meet European demands."[34] In the search for profits, elites often betrayed other elites and sold commoners as slaves. By the 1800s, when the slave trade was declared to be at an end in Africa, few aspects of traditional social structure remained untouched by the economic assault.[35] The use of stockpiled slaves for African plantation production in the 1800s, after the end of the slave trade,[36] further transformed rural social structures and set the stage for the monocrop production of cocoa. Thus began the process by which the Gold Coast society became "geared to serve the capitalist system."[37] Rodney's thesis of the underdevelopment of Africa is seen to have greater applicability when the importance of these processes is recognized. Yet, it must also be understood that there was a specific and older reality in those African societies that were subjected to this process.

African societies were not simply passive in the face of global pressures. They were often resilient even as they were transformed.[38] Moreover, since not all areas or institutions of these societies experienced the same impact of the global economy, they reacted differently. In some areas, traditional patron-client relationships were ruthlessly enforced, in opposition to emerging economic and political mobility for commoners.[39] In other areas, aspects of traditional kinship patterns were emphasized in ways that selectively allowed males rather than females to take advantage of new economic opportunities.[40] It is this differentiated incorporation of parts of African societies into the world system that has made for a great deal of indeterminacy. It has been difficult to predict how all or parts of these societies would react to changes stimulated both from the global system and increasingly from within the society. Thus, even well-intentioned attempts at change have often foundered on the shoals of surviving, transformed, or even recrudescent African institutions and values. National models of politico-economic change have recently been questioned as people reassessed the vibrancy of traditional culture despite the general integration of African societies into the capitalist economy.[41] It is now clear that within indigenous African societies, chaos can often be perceived as coming again and again, if the foot of the wave of local socio-cultural change is mistaken for its crest.

Many of the more recent questions about changes in the traditional as well as modern African society concern the relationship between social change and the state. With the current cycles of military-civilian power fluctuations, coups and politico-economic instability in post-1960 Africa, many political scientists began raising questions about the viability of the African state.[42] Today, sociologists and anthropologists are contributing to our understanding of this question by focusing on the ways in which institutionalized social relations are manipulated by national leaders supposedly in the interest of the state. The political scientists have focused on political fragmentation, competition between constituencies and lack of consensus about who should control power in the modern African state.[42] In such analyses, the Ghanaian state is viewed as handicapped by the colonial legacy of fragile local-national linkages, weak political institutions, corrupt politicians and a dependent relationship to the world economy. This instability is pinpointed as furthering an environment in which economic development cannot take place, and where economic collapse must occur.[43] The sociological and anthropological approaches which I use here suggest that the links between the global economic manipulation of the means and modes of production, national patterns of stratification, and the local political responses, may be the more important variables in the instability. Global economic changes have elicited many local responses and much rural economic initiative, as peasants struggle to make legal or sometimes illegal profits from their labor. Likewise, in response to global economic change, African states have often applied more radical and exploitative approaches to peasant resource extraction, sometimes with negative political repercussions.

My analysis of the processes by which cocoa became the dominant economic product in twentieth-century Ghana throws into bold relief the reactions of regional, local, and primarily rural populations to the developments in the late nineteenth and early twentieth century. Second, my analysis seeks to demonstrate the interplay between global economic penetration, the growth of peasant leadership in towns throughout the cocoa belt, and the dynamic anticolonial and nationalist sentiment in the 1940s and 1950s. Third, it will be shown how the attempts of various Ghanaian heads of state to control the resources from the cocoa belt in the interest of the national economy were frustrated by forces emanating from the western marketplace on one hand, and conflict between peasant decision-making and ethnic-elite power struggles on the other. Not only had the Gold Coast been under pressure to meet national needs as well as global economic needs, but the global and local developments had also deeply affected the lives of Akan people.

There were contradictions during the early period when the peoples of what became Ghana were drawn into the nexus of the world economy. At the *global* level, European administrators, producers and merchants struggled to bypass African middlemen and achieve strategic penetration of Ashanti and the North. This would allow more lucrative contracts, interior markets and Islamic trades, as well as access to labor, raw materials and commodities. Moreover, they also sought to limit the scope of the middleman classes, and obtain for Europeans the positions as linkage figures. At the *national* level, Ashanti tightened its military and administrative control over smaller states and recalcitrant Akan bureaucrats and middlemen who, by seeking political autonomy and economic mobility, could aid colonial penetration.[44] However, they set in motion smaller ethnically- and economically-based resistance movements which grew and became significant elements in the political economy of the mid-twentieth century. At the *local* level, both former slaves, freemen and elites redefined concepts of community, kinship group and social strata, as these entities were altered by the development of wage labor flowing from the penetrating capitalist economy. Henceforth, the emerging social groups began to interpret local realities in terms of the modern socio-economic benefits to each. This was especially true when cocoa became the crucial element in the capitalist-generated social transformation taking place in the Gold Coast over the past 100 years.

We shall see how conflict over cocoa resources fueled the monumental upheavals that took place in Ghana over the past thirty years, against the background of competition between capitalist-oriented peasants, regional ethnic groups, and a national government which sought to control export production given the global economic linkage. This book will show how these macro- and micro-changes are reflected in contemporary Ghanaian life. At the *local* level, the production of cocoa too allowed upward mobility, which intensified the antagonisms between traditional elites and ordinary people; it exaggerated differential, sex-linked mobility patterns and altered production dynamics of rural communities; and it generated domestic tensions between husbands, wives and children, and contributed to the fragmentation of lineages and other kinship/community groups. At the *regional* and *national* levels, cocoa production led to emergence of ethnicity and regional political alliances as strategies for gaining control of cocoa resources; and to the attempts of various national elites to control the economic and political life of Ghana, whether through economic policies or coups. At the *global* level, monocrop production of cocoa drew Ghana into an unavoidable economic dependence, such that the external manipulation of cocoa revenue produced periodic convulsions affecting all classes within Ghana; these convulsions have elicited shifts in national ideology which remain the subject of controversy.

This study seeks to go beyond the earlier ones which used the world systems paradigm by examining the articulation between local, national and global levels as cocoa became paramount in Ghana. Without undue emphasis upon "ideology" or definitional distinctions which can loom large in ideological analyses, this study intends to delineate how the mode of production, and relationships of rural people to the state, changed among the Akan as they began to produce one crop, cocoa, for the global economy. This important development greatly affected not only the larger Akan polities, such as the Asante empire and their component agrarian communities, but also rural areas such as Sunyani, where I did anthropological field work. The deep tensions between local level Akan communities and the centralizing polity, and the attempt to exploit rural producers in the interest of maintaining the political whole, were a recurring theme throughout most of the twentieth century. This study therefore uses Gold Coast/Ghana as one major point of articulation with the global economy and western political system; it uses the Brong-Ashanti polities as regional units; and uses Sunyani as an example of the local community.

Finally, this study demonstrates that regardless our level of analysis, the repercussions of the cocoa economy have been severe. Today, our attention tends to be focused on the decisions which Rawlings must make about the national political economy. However, we should not ignore that the crisis-ridden cocoa economy has exaggerated regional and ethnic conflicts, urban and rural competition for resources, and on the domestic level has differentiated interests between males and females, making it necessary for the state to take actions on behalf of the family. A holistic analysis of such continuous social, economic and political changes is critical to understanding the economic collapse and national chaos which occurred in the wake of cocoa production in Ghana, and to understanding the contemporary attempts to reverse it.

Notes

1. T.J. Lewin, *Asante Before the British: The Prempean Years, 1875–1900*, Lawrence: The Regents Press of Kansas, 1978, 9–12; Ray A. Kea, *Settlements, Trade and Politics in the Seventeenth Century Gold Coast*, Baltimore: Johns Hopkins University Press, 1982, 1.
2. Sam Rhodie, "The Gold Coast Cocoa Hold-Ups of 1930–31," *Transactions of the Historical Society of Ghana*, 1968, 105–118.
3. David Apter, *The Gold Coast in Transition*, 1965; Dennis Austin, *Politics in Ghana, 1946–1960*, New York: Oxford Paperbacks, 1970.
4. Tetteh Kofi, "The International Cocoa Agreements," in John Simmons (ed.) *Cocoa Production: Economic and Botanical Perspectives*, 1976: 82–109; and T. Kofi, "M.N.C. Control of Distributive Channels: A Study of Cocoa Marketing," in *Stanford Journal of International Studies*, vol. XI, Spring 1976, 70–95. See also, J. Fitch and M. Oppenheimer, *Ghana: End of An Illusion*, Monthly Review Press, 1966, 54, 91, 94–96.
5. Peter C. Lloyd, *Africa In Social Change*, London: Penguin, 1966, 109–142. Also, Akim L. Mabogunje, *Urbanization in Nigeria*, New York: Africana Publications, 1968. Mabogunje (pp. 313–317) has described the massive migration and over-urbanization in Nigeria, with accompanying unemployment as the economy was unable to keep pace with population expansion.
6. Thomas Kerstein, *The New Elites of Asia and Africa: A Comparative Study of Indonesia and Ghana*, New York: Praeger, 1966, 119–140 and 220–222; Kenneth Little, *West African Urbanization: A Study of Voluntary Associations and Social Change*. Cambridge University Press, 1965, 7–23.
7. For an analysis of factors in African coups, see Samuel DeCalo, *Coups and Army*

Rule in Africa: Studies in Military Style, New Haven: Yale University Press, 1976. On ethnic factors in economic and political instability, see Crawford Young, *The Politics of Cultural Pluralism*, Madison: University of Wisconsin Press, 1966; and A. Mabogunje, *Regional Mobility and Resource Development in West Africa.* Montreal: McGill University, Queens University Press, 1972.

8. Richard Gibson, *African Liberation Movements*, 1972; deBraganca and I. Wallerstein, *African Liberation Reader*, vol. 3, Zed Press, 1982.
9. Crawford Young, *Ideology and Development in Africa*, New Haven: Yale University Press, 1971.
10. G. Mikell, "Ghanaian Females, Rural Economy and National Stability," *African Studies Review*, vol. 29, no. 3, 1986.
11. Samir Amin, "Self-Reliance and the New Economic Order," in A. W. Singham, (ed.), *The Non-Aligned Movement in World Politics*, Washington, DC: Howard University Press, 1977, 145–157.
12. Marvin Harris, *Cultural Materialism: The Struggle for a Science of Culture*, New York: Random House, 1979: 19–21.
13. Marvin Harris, *The Rise of Anthropological Theory*, New York: Thomas Crowell, 1968: 514–524.
14. Particularly noteworthy of some of the contradictions within the early structural-functional analysis has been the inability to predict long-range social unrest and political violence in the Southern African context. B. Malinowski, "Dynamics of Culture Change," in I. Wallerstein (ed.), *Social Change: The Colonial Situation*, 1945; Max Gluckman, "Malinowski's Functional Analysis of Social Change," in I. Wallerstein (ed.), Op. Cit., 1945; also Gluckman, *Custom and Conflict in Africa*, Glenco Ill: The Free Press, 1955: 27–53, 105–130.
15. Immanuel Wallerstein, *The Modern World System: Capitalist Agriculture and the Origins of the European World Economy in the Sixteenth Century*, New York: Academic Press, 1974; Philip D. Curtin, *Cross-Cultural Trade in World History*, Cambridge University Press, 1984; Eric Wolf, *Europe and the Peoples Without History*, Berkeley: University of California Press, 1982.
16. Eric Wolf, 1984: 3-23.
17. Karl Wittfogel, *Oriental Despotism*, New Haven: Yale University Press, 1955. Owen Lattimore, *Inner Asian Frontiers of China*, 2nd ed, NY: American Geographical Society, 1951.
18. Ray A. Kea, *Settlement, Trade and Politics in the Seventeenth-Century Gold Coast*, Baltimore: Johns Hopkins University Press, 1982.
19. Ivor Wilks, "Land, Labor and Capital in the Forest Kingdom of Asante," in Friedland and Rowland (ed.), *The Evolution of Social Systems*, London:Ducksworth Publishing Co., 1977: 487–534.
20. Peter Gutkind and Immanuel Wallerstein, *The Political Economy of Africa*, Beverly Hills, CA: Sage Publications, 1976; I. Wallerstein, 1974, *The Modern World-System: Capitalist Agriculture and the Origins of the European World Economy in the Sixteenth Century*, New York: Academic Press, 1974; I. Wallerstein, *The Capitalist World Economy*, 1979.
21. Gutkind and Wallerstein, 1976: 30–37.

22. June Nash, "Ethnographic Aspects of the World Capitalist System," *Annual Reviews in Anthropology*, vol. 10, 1981: 393–423. Sidney Mintz, 1979, "Time, Sugar and Sweetness," *Marxist Perspectives* 2: 56–73.
23. K.E. Trimberger, "World Systems Analysis: The Problem of Unequal Development," *Theory and Society*, 1979: 101–106.
24. Samir Amin, Underdevelopment and Development in Black Africa: Historical Origins, *Journal of Peace Research*, 2, 1972: 105; and J. Schneider, "Was There a Pre-Capitalist World System?" in *Journal of Peasant Studies*, vol. 6, 1977: 20.
25. Andre Gunder Frank, *Capitalism and Underdevelopment in Latin America*, New York: Monthly Review Press, 1969: 122–142.
26. Captain R.S. Rattray, *Ashanti*, 1923; and *Ashanti Law and Constitution*, 1929. Early ethnologists such as Rattray made excellent observations on the nature of lineage and personal ownership of land and other property (1929: 330–366), although they were sometimes speculative on historical detail. Rattray, in particular, was conscious of recent changes in traditional patterns, but was not necessarily cognizant of the impact of the colonial system on Akan culture.
27. Walter Rodney, *A History of the Upper Guinea Coast*. Oxford: Clarendon Press, 1969. See also, *How Europe Underdeveloped Africa*, Washington DC: Howard University Press, 1970.
28. K. Onwuka Dike, *Trade and Politics on the Niger Delta*, Oxford: The Clarendon Press, 1956. K.Y. Daaku, *Trade and Politics in the Gold Coast, 1600–1720*, London, 1970.
29. Eric Wolf, *Europe And the Peoples Without History*, Berkeley & Los Angeles: University of California, 1982: 88–96.
30. Dike, 1956: 8 and E.P. Skinner, *The Mossi of Upper Volta*, Stanford University Press, 1964: 77–97.
31. Karl Polanyi, Conrad Arensberg, and Harry Pearson, T*rade and Markets in the Early Empires: Economies in History and Theory*, Glencoe Ill: The Free Press, 1957: 154–217.
32. Ivor Wilks, "The Northern Factor in Asante History," Institute of African Studies, University of Ghana-Legon, 1961; and "The Position of Muslims in Metropolitan Ashanti in the Early Nineteenth Century," in I.M. Lewis (ed.), *Islam in Tropical Africa*, 1966: 318–41.
33. Walter Rodney, *How Europe Underdeveloped Africa*, 1970: 258-60, 264–5; Dike, 1956; Daaku, 1970.
34. Rodney, *Op. Cit.*, p. 221.
35. Eric Wolf, 1984: 208–212.
36. *Rodney* pp. 268–9.
37. Rodney, 1970: 199.
38. I. Wilks, *Ashanti Government*, in D. Forde and P. Kaberry (ed.), *West African Kingdoms in the Nineteenth Century*, London: Cambridge University Press, 1967: 207–223, and 1975. Norman Miller, "The Political Survival of Traditional Leadership," in *African Politics and Society*, Glencoe Ill: The Free Press, 1970: 118–133.
39. I. Wilks, *Asante in the Nineteenth Century*, 1975: 666–671.

40. Ester Boserup, *Woman's Role in Economic Development*, New York: St. Martins Press, 1970. Kwame Arhin, "Peasants in Nineteenth Century Asante," *Current Anthropology*, vol. 24, 1984: 473–4. G. Mikell, "Filiation, Economic Crisis, and the Status of Women in Rural Ghana," *Canadian Journal of African Studies*, 1984: 195–218.
41. Samir Amin, "Self Reliance and the New Economic Order," 1977.
42. T.J. Lewin, *Asante Before the British: The Prempean Years, 1875–1900*. Lawrence: The Regents Press of Kansas, 1978: 41–2. Naomi Chazan, *An Anatomy of Ghanaian Politics: Managing Political Recession, 1969–1982*. Boulder, CO: Westview Press, 1983: 1–19.
43. Chazan, *Op. Cit*, 1983; also Chazan, "The Anomalies of Continuities: Ghanaian Elections Since Independence," African Studies Association Paper, 1984.
44. Kwame Arhin, "Rank and Class Among the Asante and the Fante in the Nineteenth Century," *Africa*, vol. 53 #1, 1983: 2–22. Wilks, 1975: 717–720 and 1979.

1

The Pre-Captialist Economy

When Gold Coast scholars chose "Ghana" as the name of the new nation born in the 1950s, they intended to encapsulate over thirteen centuries of documented trade and interaction between the northern Sudanic empires and the savannah-forest regions of west Africa. They chose to ignore the fact that cocoa was an important factor in their daily lives, and thought instead of a golden past, even if only speculatively connected with their own. Ghana was the name of the first great Sudanic empire which arose along the trans-Saharan trade routes which linked north Africa with west Africa.[1] Symbolically, the name spoke of the enormous role which the forest region had played in contributing gold and kola to the north African, Mediterranean, and Arab economies from A. D. 300 until the mid-twentieth century. Yet, the hinterlands of the Guinea, Grain, Ivory, Gold and Slave coasts—from Senegal through the Cameroon—had been linked in relationships of population migration and exchange of produce and conquest for an even greater time than indicated. Historians and anthropologists have recorded the nature of this regional system.

The rain forest region had not only been a major participant in a regional, continental and transcontinental economy long before the Portuguese ships reached the Gold Coast port of Nkran (Accra) in 1482,[2] but as the cocoa-producing areas replaced gold in importance, it would continue to play this role. It is this economic fact, among others, which makes an analysis of hinterland relations within Ashanti so crucial to this book; for the nature of these relations, both historically and contemporarily, has influenced the stability of states in this area. The Gold Coast economy was by no means isolated, but was part of a regional economy. Despite this fact, it was not until the mid-eighteenth century that the Akan forest area of the Gold Coast was fully integrated into the emerging capitalist global economy[3] which was binding Europe, Africa and the Americas into a precarious triadic relationship.

With the exception of the provocative work of Meyerowitz and Danquah[4] few scholars of Ghanaian history have attempted to use oral traditions to prove the links between the Gold Coast and the ancient Ghana empire. Meyerowitz cites oral accounts which she believes refer to the coming of ancestors of the Brong from "beyond the white sands,"[5] but these accounts have been subjected by scholars to great criticism and skepticism. Arab historical accounts have proven to be more reliable in providing information about a period for which there is scant documentation. These documents reveal a history of mediated contact between west Africa and the Mediterranean from about A.D. 300 with ancient Ghana controlling the trade routes between the two areas. Muslim historians also recorded how Islam expanded over Berber areas of Mauritania, and how Muslim Almoravids eventually conquered the Ghana empire in the eleventh century. Thereafter, the Mali empire in the thirteenth century replaced Ghana's early influence in western Africa.

Like Ghana, Mali depended upon a trading and bureaucratic superstructure to control the traditional village system, the exaction of peasant surplus from subsistence agriculture in outlying areas, and the use of slave labor on agricultural plantations and in salt mining.[7] Although the Malian king was given homage as the center of authority in the empire, the system of delegated authority meant that peasants were immediately responsible to their local chief or member of the elite. At base, village peasants had usufruct rights to plots of land on which subsistence crops were grown, and peasants were responsible for contributing labor to the growth of crops on the land of the traditional aristocracy which was linked to the trade in the area.[8] What surprised the Muslim chroniclers of life in ancient Ghana and Mali was the existence of matriliny in association with this complex state organization. In the mid-fourteenth century, Ibn Battuta sought to reassure his readers that this was possible when he declared of ancient Iwalatan in present-day Mali:

> The state of affairs amongst these people is indeed extraordinary. Their men show no signs of jealousy whatsoever; no one claims descent from his father, but on the contrary from his mother's brother. A person's heirs are his sisters' sons, not his own sons.[9]

What the ancient chroniclers also documented was the gradual acculturation of the west African elite to the Islamic culture. Their sources provide hints of the increase in patricentricity as Islamic control over the trade increased, but their accounts also reflect the persistence of traditional culture. Drawing on oral traditions, Ibn Khaldun writes of Sundiata, King of Mali:

"They made him king according to the custom of the non-Arabs, who gave the kingship to the sister and the son of the sister (of a former king)."[10]

While Danquah, among others, has speculated that the presence of matrilineality and the love of gold among the ancient Ghanaians and Malians is indicative of early links to the Akan on the Gold Coast, there is little doubt that the two regions and peoples were connected through trade and migrations. The early periods of west African history were extremely dynamic ones in which small secondary states fought for preeminence. Mali's emergence after the fall of Ghana was followed by the emergence of Songhai, and the development of each of these core states in turn influenced political change within their own peripheries.

Small-scale peasant agriculture was at the base of their political economies, but the prerogatives of royal control over servile and slave agriculturalists and over raw materials and other resources were well documented from Arab sources.[11] In addition to collecting taxes on wide-ranging caravans of goods which moved both south and north, Malian kings owned all nuggets of gold over one ounce in weight, thus keeping the value of their currency high and providing revenue for supporting the enlarged state bureaucracy and military.[12] The political and military shifts occurring as empires rose and fell led to the migration of the vanquished and must have exerted pressures on smaller societies on the peripheries. For example, the problems in Mali encouraged the emerging Mossi to raid and plunder Timbuktu and other Mali towns in the fourteenth century,[13] thus further endangering non-Malian groups. By the 1400s, migrations down into the savannah-forest regions of west Africa were evident.

Early Agriculture and Economy of the Akan Region of the Gold Coast

There is still considerable speculation about the population movements and the processes of production which occurred within the Gold Coast and other parts of west Africa. Many scholars debate the popular explanation that the Akan peoples of Ghana and the Ivory Coast began moving south in successive waves at the decline of the Mali empire, and were settling into the area above the forest in contemporary Ghana by the 1400s, where they met with the aboriginal inhabitants in the area around ancient Begho.[14] The ancestors of the Ashanti, Fanti and to a certain extent the Brong, would have been part of these dispersed and continuous early migrations of cultivators who brought with them knowledge of crops grown around the northern areas and knowledge of iron processing. From Ibn Battuta's descriptions of the Sudanese villages which were tied into the northern trade, we know that millet, milk, chickens, rice and beans were produced in the 1300s in Mali, and this knowledge would have been transmitted with southward migrations.[15] The indigenous inhabitants whom they would have met upon arrival in the savannah-forest area of the Gold Coast were primarily hunters and gatherers, but they also practiced proto-cultivation of kola nut trees, baobab and oil palm trees, as well as the processing of shea butter from indigenous plants.[16] Despite the fact that there were endogenously developed crops during the neolithic period, developed agriculture was not yet a part of the indigenous savannah-forest economy.[17] Yams, for example, exist in many varieties throughout savannah-forest areas of west and east Africa, and the ease of cultivation would have allowed it to coexist with hunting and gathering in a subordinate form for centuries.[18] There was rudimentary plant cultivation, but virtually no animal domestication in central and southern Ghana. As late as A.D. 1000, there was likely to be neolithic stone tool manufacturing in upper parts of Brong Ahafo in what is today Ghana.[19] This mesolithic culture possibly did not include fire, but emphasized hunting—a fact which may account for the role of the hunter in the myths of origin of the Akan people in general, and more specifically in the accounts of the people of Bono Mansu (Brong) and Gyaman.[20]

It is quite possible that the mesolithic hunters and gatherers were already mining gold when the Akan arrived. This would account for the stories of gold-mining "troglodytes" described for the area by several early accounts.[21] While many dispute the claim that the Phoenician trade with west Africa may have included gold exporting as early as the first millennium, there is some evidence that an early gold trade existed. Perhaps this was not unique, since archaeological evidence from other parts of west Africa suggest a pre-A.D. 1000 importation of beads and other worked articles into the rivers area of Nigeria.[22] Given such possibilities, there may yet be further explications of the nature of the ancient trade in gold and other items along the coasts of west Africa.[23]

The arrival of Akan cultivators in the Gold Coast introduced a new factor into the political economy of the region, but did not immediately replace the local stone tool industry or gold mining. The fact that iron was not immediately used for agricultural implements may be due to the low population density in the forest zone, and the efficiency of proto-cultivation and hunting-gathering. It was not until the subsequent larger migrations of the Akan and the settling of the Brong people at Bono-Manso, Begho, Nkranza and Techiman, above the forest in the Gold Coast, that metallurgy became significant in the culture of the Akan.

The emergence of the empire of Bono Manso as the first centralized kingdom within the confines of modern Ghana set the stage for the greater articulation of societies of the region with the north. Scholars originally believed that the state arose between 1300 and 1400[24] because interpretations of oral traditions and listings of kings and queen mothers of Bono suggested a date of about 1295. However, on the basis of archaeological evidence, later scholars have argued that Bono, Begho and other centers may in fact date from the fifteenth century.[25] What is significant is that pottery fragments and other culture items of Bono-Manso and Begho in the 1400s display both the importance of agriculture and the significance of metalworking as well as gold-weighing in the life of Akan peoples of the pre-colonial Gold Coast.

The location of Bono Manso and Begho in the region above the forest made them important centers for the trans-Saharan trade, and critical for the accumulation and distribution of goods from the coastal and northern African areas. These were likely to have been central points from which caravans and traders diverged along more southern routes into the Ivory Coast or the Gold Coast. Posnansky's work on Begho in the Banda state of modern Ghana has revealed that the layout of the town included four quarters housing an indigenous Akan population, an artisan metal-working population, as well as Islamicized merchants and heterogenous Mande-speaking Dyula, Nefana, and Ligby groups, which today inhabit much of the Ivory Coast.[26] There is archaeological evidence of pottery from diverse northern areas and of grain storage depots in Begho. More importantly, there is evidence that the Akan system of gold weights, so vital in the southern gold trade, was derived from the Islamic weighing system which was utilized at Jenne and at Begho.[27] Recognized as a center of culture and knowledge, it also appears that the art of weaving diffused from this area throughout the Gold Coast. Ashanti oral traditions, in fact, relate that during the reign of Asantehene Osei Tutu, the art of weaving was brought from Bono, as well as knowledge of how to make certain golden emblems indicating royal status.[28] The existence of centers such as Begho and Bono Mansu indicated that the small states of the southern Gold Coast were becoming more complex and heterogenous, both expanding and extending their links with external societies. It becomes necessary, however, to understand the nature of small-scale relations which made such macro-developments possible.

Pre-Colonial Production and Reproduction

The manner in which the people of Begho and Bono organized their agricultural production and conducted their social lives provided the basis for their political economy, and later served as the groundwork upon which global contact through cocoa production was introduced. Initially, the early Gold Coast economy was based on local peasant production and (given the importance of domesticating the forest environment) was heavily dependent upon labor importation to meet production needs.[29] There was rather early a steady importation of slaves from Moshi, Gurunsi and other northern groups to work large farms and plantations. Thus, the Akan political economy bore some similarities to the large labor-demanding empires which preceded it. By the 1500s in central and southern Gold Coast, local level societies were primarily composed of small village communities, with persons of both freeborn and slave origins, for whom matrilineal relationships defined the individual's relationship to the larger world. Elite and commoner distinctions existed, with urban areas generally as the centers for elite activity. However, urban areas were also primary areas for coordinating the north-south trade which had for centuries penetrated the savannah and upper forest zone. These urban centers would increasingly become oriented toward the coast, where from the 1500s onward, the initial activities of Portuguese merchants or "factors" were being felt.

The northern trade had brought Islamic agents and culture in contact with an indigenous one, particularly in the west-central area of Ghana. The nature of the amalgam of Islamic culture with that of the aboriginal people (originally unknown, but increasingly Akan over time) is still speculative and the subject of much research. It is known that Gur-speaking (Nefana, Koulango, and Mo) as well as Mande-speaking (Ligby, Huela and Numu) people resided in this area, but their traditions were subordinate to the Akan ones.[30] While there is much evidence that by the 1500s indigenous cultures both influenced and were influenced by Islam in the area, Akan culture and social structures predominated, being reflected in agrarian and village social relations of the central and western communities.

Historical evidence suggests that before the 1700s, production and social organization of labor among commoners was primarily within clan-based communities controlled by the elite. However, this *abusua* or matri-clan group was primarily a production unit, and was further developed as the importation of slave labor for plantation agriculture caused both slaves and commoners to be integrated into these structures. Kea suggests that the early clan groups were likely to have been amorphous but exogamous functional units, which are thought to have lived on land belonging to the elite.[31] However, by the early 1700s, the changing mode of production was encouraging a dispersal of these matrilineal groups, and the sub-divisions (plural *mmusua-kese*) became critical socio-political units related to their upper-class *abirempon* founders. These *mmusua-kese* were thus at the base of the evolving political unit, the *oman*.

At a local domestic level, the *abusua*, or corporate matrilineage, was normally under the control of a senior male or occasionally a female, and it traced descent through female progenitors over a period of three or more generations.[32] Mothers were the primary reference figures, with all children born of one woman together with her male and female siblings constituting a social group with obligations to support each other in social as well as economic activities.[33] Thus, small-scale family and household production was becoming the classic economic pattern.

Whether localized, or inhabiting several villages, these clearly defined matrilineages were the hub of sixteenth century Akan social life. As the social organization of production shifted, each *abusua* was usually allotted sufficient land by the chief of the community on which to grow subsistence crops. The amount of land was reasonably small (a few acres), but allowed for each family to observe a fallow season during which another part of the land was used for subsistence crops. The *abusua* members usually performed all the necessary agricultural labor, with males requesting the assistance of affines (usually brothers-in-law) at critical points in the crop cycle.[34] In most of Akan areas, ordinary individuals seldom owned (as individuals) the valuable factors of production such as land. Rather, each individual inherited, by virtue of *abusua* membership, certain usufruct rights to resources under lineage control, or the right to expect maintenance/subsistence from the proceeds of group resources. Where the allotted land was insufficient to satisfy *abusua* needs, additional allocations might be made by the chief, allowing land to be used temporarily by an *abusua*, later to be surrendered.[35]

Households within Akan villages were heterogenous extended social units, which included lineage members and others linked to them by polygamous marriages. However, the family house built by a husband for his wife, or by a brother for his mother or sister, might become the major residential reference point for future *abusua* generations. Both the brother and his sister might continue to reside within this household despite marriage.[36] There appears to be a traditional tendency within Akan households for a married female to continue to reside matrilocally, especially if her husband was from the same village; or she might return to her matrilineal compound after a few years of residence with her husband. Even in cases where women joined their husbands in his matrilineal compound or in his autonomous residence, they often maintained partial residence in their *abusua* compound; and this dual residence reflected the social and financial obligations which women incurred to members of their natal households, since their children would normally return to this household as adults.[37]

Adult males of the *abusua* were often given separate rooms where they might be joined by wives. When wives did not join them, these men established a visiting relationship with the wife or wives resident within other households. Therefore, residence patterns were flexible, and could be influenced by other economic responsibilities: for a man involved in trade, dispersed residences of wives was an asset. High rates of matrilocal residence for rural males and females naturally played a major role in holding the *abusua* together as a social unit. Since economic contribution by each adult household member was a normal expectation, where they were unable to contribute labor, they might give money, food or other economic assistance to the household. Thus, despite an individual's primary economic responsibility to the lineage, varying residential patterns could result in variance in economic or productive units within Akan society.[38]

The division of labor between the sexes was reflected in the production process of most Akan societies. Men generally cleared the land needed for planting crops (an arduous task for the primary forests of the 1600s), leaving fruit or kola nut trees and large boulders as markers. After males burned the fields, women performed such work as weeding, planting of most crops on *abusua* farms or on husbands' farms to grow vegetables such as tomatoes, okra, peppers, beans, cocoyams and yams. There is speculation that where farms required additional labor, permanent workers might have been utilized (even at this early period, just as they would later be in cocoa production), receiving a share of the crop as payment.

Either slaves or women therefore performed most of the labor in agriculture. In towns and villages, women also sold cooked food to travelers; female potters made cookware, water jugs or ceremonial pottery and, in some cases, funerary statues. Male agricultural tasks were seasonally concentrated at the beginning and end of the growing cycles, when they would burn or prepare the soil for the next fallow period or the next crop. However, since these tasks were seasonal, men also engaged in hunting to supplement the diet, or specialized in the production of gold, palm wine, local gin, collecting kola nuts or weaving.[39] If men possessed such skills, they generally passed these on to their nephews or sons. Nephews, in particular, were groomed to take over *abusua* farms from their uncles when they came of age.

The economic activities of traditional Akan societies, although organized around familial or lineage groups, was sufficiently prosperous to generate a surplus that supported Akan social and political organization, and that was sold in local periodic markets or exported to the coast. The lineage has often been described as a corporate structure within which individuals had economic responsibilities, and one sees this both with males and females. Male responsibilities to the nephew indicated this; although an adult female's agricultural labor tended to be concentrated on food farms which fed her children and conjugal family, proceeds of her nonagricultural labor (market sales or wages) often went to benefit her matrilineal relatives. Portions of certain commodities might also be claimed by the chiefs of communities as a tax-in-kind, in order that the proceeds of sale be used to maintain public buildings, roads, community events or royal paraphernalia. In this way, surplus items fed a regional and royal trade throughout the southern area.

Arab records indicate that the primary commodities for which northern Islamic traders had for centuries entered the edge of the Gold Coast forest zone were gold and kola nuts (widely used as a stimulant among Muslims).[40] Fairly extensive records exist on the caravans of Dyula, Hausa and Mossi traders who brought silks, cloth, salt, pottery, leather goods and spices in exchange for gold and kola; and on the rigid regulations surrounding the exchange rate and sale of these items.[41] The wealth to be made from the trade encouraged the spread of Muslim middlemen communities even in the Techiman, Gyaman and southern Akan areas. Here, they facilitated the commerce between the traders, the local chief and the indigenous people.

The arrival of the Portuguese along the coast in the 1400s—and their interest in gold—not only linked the coastal societies to the Atlantic economic community, but influenced even the interior societies. By the 1500s, villages of the Atie, Ga, Fetu, and many other populations along the coast were transformed from quiet fishing-farming communities to booming commercial enclaves. Some inland chiefs created coastal satellite villages to facilitate control over the trade and its profits. Surplus commodities from Brong-Ashanti were head-carried down to the coast and sold directly by the producer or agents of the chief. DeMaree remarked about the large number of inland rural women who would be visible at daily and periodic markets in coastal port towns by the late 1500s, selling their vegetable produce and food.[42] Chiefs were astute in taxing these producers and market people in order to maintain administrative functions related to the trade, as well as other public functions.

The growing economic relations between Gold Coast peoples and the Europeans on the coast led not only to increased trade, but also to population movements and some anxiety about the European presence. Along the border of contemporary Ivory Coast and Ghana there occurred a gradual and continuous influx of mixed Mande-speaking peoples such as the Senufo, Nefana and Ligby, moving into villages along the northern Brong trade route. In many cases, the Muslim groups were seeking access to kola supplies.[43] Some of the population shifts were political in nature, the major example of this being the Akan royal disputes which resulted in the eighteenth century Akan exodus and dispersal into the Baule area in Ivory Coast. However, even this migration triggered off economic exchanges which tied the Baule back to the Ashanti of the Gold Coast based on economic relations.[44] Although many of the early population shifts were directly related to the northern trade, after 1700 even more significant movements occurred as both Muslim and indigenous people sought access to land on which to grow crops or collect commodities which would bring profit in the coastal or interior markets.[45]

The expansion of the interior as well as the coastal economy led to new pressures for a sizable agricultural and skilled craft labor force, thus exacerbating social differences and stratification among the Akan. Since economic relations generally involved either communal or subordinate/dominant relationships rather than private ones, persons of standing could manipulate patron-client and debt ties to artificially enlarge the group of persons upon whom they could depend for labor. Entire rural villages of poor dependent and indebted persons existed, whose lives were controlled by the elite owners of the land. Rights over these dependent persons or *nkoa* could shift if the land was sold to another royal or chief, and owners often exercised their rights to move whole communities of these persons to coastal areas where labor needs were great.

One effect of increased European contact along the coast was the rise of domestic slavery and the development of transatlantic slavery, which was of a different order and magnitude. Slavery was of secondary importance to the Portuguese, the acquisition of gold being primary.[46] From the beginning, they had taken an increasing number of free and captive Africans to Portugal, where the Africans were initially viewed as curiosities, exotic royalty, then finally as domestic servants and agricultural workers. By the 1500s, however, there had grown up a brisk trade in slaves which the Portuguese acquired from Benin or Sao Tome off the coast of present-day Gabon, and which they traded to the Akan for gold from their forts at Elmina, Axim, Samma and Accra.[47] Slaves on the coast often belonged to chiefs who used them as carriers to bring goods from inland to the coast or employed them as royal representatives on the coast to handle commercial activity. In towns such as Cape Coast and Elmina, slaves were often attached to families who owned businesses for trading, and were frequently assimilated into their household.[48] Whole communities of slaves might be employed as gold workers, or be moved inland to work farms raising kola and other vegetables for chiefs—produce destined for coastal markets. The extent to which Fanti, Ga and Ashanti culture and economy was altered by the contact with the Portuguese—the introduction of maize, certain gold-working techniques and pottery designs and techniques—has been the object of speculation.[49] What is certain, however, is that the Portuguese presence and domestic slavery along the coast increased the desire for agricultural land in the interior of the Gold Coast, and was significant in the northward migrations which occurred after 1600.

Slavery had an important impact on inland Akan societies. Slaves were hardly commonplace during the early subsistence economy, but had become valuable as population densities increased in the forest zone and as social relationships changed to production for profit and for the market. Foreign slaves possessed no community of relatives, and therefore as an *odonko* they could be integrated directly into the master's household. Male as well as female slaves were valuable for external economic activities such as trading, but females had more domestic value because of their reproductive potential.[50] A female slave could be married or given as a concubine to a male within the *abusua* and produce slave children (*odonko-ba*) who belonged to the lineage and bore the *ntoro* of the father. On the other hand, the child of a male slave possessed no *ntoro* identification and remained with its mother's lineage. If, however, the male slave was married to a woman of the owner's lineage, the difficulties were somewhat reduced.[51] An Akan man was able to exert greater control over his children born of slave mothers than over his own freeborn children who belonged to their mother's matrilineage.[52] In fact, there is some suggestion that the occurrence of female slave spouses may have seriously affected Akan kinship relations.

Note, for example, that most *nkoa* (persons of servile status) were from within Akan society, and were already members of matrilineal clans in Brong, Fanti, Agni or Ashanti areas. Such slaves could be incorporated into the matrilineage with relatively few disturbances, if the totemic restrictions were observed.[53] Slaves from patrilineal societies posed other problems for assimilation because of conflicting notions of male control of their own offspring, but within a generation or two such men of slave background would begin to merge into the local population. Their status was protected under Ashanti law, and the proverb *"Obi nkyere obi ase"* (one does not disclose the origins of another)[54] was taken quite seriously. Some Muslim captives were treated quite liberally and were either redeemed by their countrymen or became palace servants and minor bureaucrats to the Asantehene. Although the rights of all slaves were guaranteed by chiefs and ultimately by the king, slaves often retained their *odonko* status over time. Entire sub-lineages with slave status were still identifiable in Akan areas well into the 1970s. Despite the fact that free Ashanti sometimes gave the *Donkor* or *Moshi* name along with a day-name to newborn infants to dissuade negative spirits and forces from claiming the vulnerable child, the community was well aware of the distinction between the freeborn and the servile children who bore these labels.[55]

The increasing activities of Dutch, British and French coastal merchants and slave traders after 1642 began to leave an indelible mark on almost all Akan social and political relations. While Portuguese slaving had triggered population shifts along the coast and increased stratification within Gold Coast societies, the later European slave trade resulted in the introduction of massive quantities of arms and facilitated Akan inter-society and intra-regional conflicts. The Ashanti response to the perceived European threat was the growth of a feudal state bureaucracy with absolute loyalties to the royal center. Thus, the creation of a new elite, one which the increasingly more powerful King of Ashanti (the Asantehene) could control, was to have a lasting effect on Akan social structure. This development meant the slow demise of the predominance of clan organization in social life, and would ultimately introduce both greater flexibility and exploitation for different strata in southern Akan communities, as well as in the more northern Akan-controlled areas.

In the seventeenth century, Akan society was characterized by the spread and competition of localized chiefdoms within the southern forest zone. All these populations were related by language, social customs, clanship based on matrilineal descent and a system of political leadership in which ritual authority as well as limited political power rested in the hands of the *ohene* (chief). Wilks has given an excellent description of the rise to power of the Oyoko clan, its situation as the royal clan in Kumasi, and the increasing dominance of its chief (the *Kumasihene*) over the other clan chiefs (the *amantoo*) during the late 1700s.[56] With the improved military skills and weaponry gained from contact with coastal European groups, the Kumasihene began the expansion of his state, and by the early eighteenth century the Ashanti empire was conquering and expanding along eight major roads which stretched from the coast to beyond the Black Volta river in the north.[57] Through well-executed military campaigns. the Asantehene tightened his control over the gold–producing center in the south, established his superior right of control and tribute from conquered lands, and laid down new relationships with the *mantiase* (conquered and incorporated towns). That Europeans wanted to make contact with the northern trade was obvious, and it made the growth of the Ashanti bureaucracy more necessary from the Ashanti perspective.

It is important to note, however, that as the Ashanti expanded and conquered, using European arms, they enlarged their control over the northern trade routes and territories, and received as tribute thousands of northern slaves. The depopulation of immense stretches of land in Mossi, Dagarti, Grunshi and other areas far north of the forest zone took place, and in the area just north and northwest of Ashanti the new communities displayed interesting forms of cultural accommodation between diverse ethnic groups and the Akan conquerors.[58] While the bulk of the later captives of war were destined for the New World in exchange for arms, many of the early slaves were also settled by their Ashanti owners on rural farms, where they produced goods for consumption and sale within the growing Akan towns.

Land, Labor and Inequality

Just as land and labor, rather than capital, were the critical factors of production for the Ashanti empire, so also would they be critical to the later development of the cocoa industry. The Ashanti forest zone had historically required a larger labor force for agricultural production than was generally available, and was therefore a labor importing area.[59] However, the spiraling demand for labor was only one reflection of how economic involvement in the world economy created more competition for control over the factors of production in Akan areas. Resources such as gold and ivory were clearly under elite control and maximum proceeds from them flowed to chiefs and the Kumasihene (subsequently the Asantehene, as of the reign of Osei Tutu from the mid-1600s). Such elite control also involved private ownership of these items, and records indicate that in the period between 1642 and 1800 elite claims to control over rivers and streams and game continually increased.[60]

As people moved to villages along the coast in response to the European presence, there was a change in the pattern of land tenure. Initially, land tenure procedures often involved the appropriation of vacant land by the stool as representative of the community. Now, land which had been sparsely settled by communities of fishermen and gold workers became the object of competition as Portuguese, Dutch, French and British forts were established. Kea has discussed the hierarchy of coastal and more interior settlements which began to appear in the sixteenth century, and early Portuguese accounts provide evidence that these coastal towns were considerably smaller and less wealthy than their populous parent towns of the interior. The populations which inland chiefs settled on the coast served as links in the expanding trade. The gold, gold mining and food production lay much further inland, while coastal villages contained the specialized workers such as "interpreters, boatmen, pilots, officials, fishermen, and slaves of the inhabitants of interior towns."[61] There is also evidence that local household taxation and land rents were well established in the coastal towns by the 1700s, and this exerted severe pressures on coastal commoners.

Coastal pressures resulted in changes in the interior where the raw materials and surplus was located. Aspiring wealthy commoners, or *obirempon*, often purchased whole towns and villages in order to control the rural producer. The rulers of district capitals and chiefs or kings of the expanding states received tributes, taxes and rents in agricultural produce, gold and labor, representing a fixed percentage of the peasant's yearly production. These surpluses were often used, along with slave produce, to feed the growing armed units that were stationed in the towns. According to Kea, seventeenth century tax and revenue systems of different inland polities extracted from one-fourth to one-half of the value of a peasant family household's annual agricultural output; probably one-half to three-fourths of the gold they earned from market sales was drained in taxes.[62] Many Akan peasants from coastal states fled northward to escape the financial exactions and debt, thereby settling many forest areas which were under Ashanti domination by the mid-eighteenth century.

All of these economic changes had a decided effect on the political organization of the Akan, especially the Ashanti, Fante and related Brong people. There was a gradual transformation of the chief from the position of politico-religious guardian of communal welfare[63] to the new position as politico-economic redistributor of local resources within the hierarchy of the empire. Formerly the kin groups as member units of the corporate community had usufruct rights over any land needed to sustain the extended family, with the exception of elite goods such as gold and slaves. Many of these rights to resources shifted to chiefs by the 1700s.

As the Ashanti empire developed and the position of chiefs was superseded by that of the Asantehene, it became the chiefs' obligation to ensure that rents, land tributes and taxes flowed upward towards the state capital. In addition, millions of *dambas* of gold revenue passed from rural towns to the Asantehene in Kumasi, to be used by him in rewarding members of the growing bureaucracy as well as for ceremonial and religious regalia. The Asantehene could also retract from a chief or official the right of control over proceeds from certain villages, and award these rights to another more loyal or diligent competitor.

The greater availability of land in the more northwestern periphery of the Ashanti empire stimulated considerable conflicts about political allegiance of Brong, Gonja and Gyaman peoples. Rich in gold and kola, these areas had been the goal of migrating western non-Akan folk, as well as of migrating southern Akan such as the Kwahu and Akwamu. In the numerous power shifts and alliances with Kumasi, the more peripheral groups were increasingly dispersed northward and the entire southern and central area became more consistently "Akanized." Nevertheless, few of these northwestern shifts attempted to control land and agricultural resources. Although paying road tolls and taxes, peasants in these areas appeared to retain a greater portion of their agricultural surpluses, and were less exposed to the financial exactions of centralization until well into the eighteenth century. Their ties to the kingdoms of Bono Manso and Takyiman were likely to have provided the food supplies which sustained the migrant trading populations. Not until the Ashanti wars with the northwest in the 1720s and 1730s did control over proceeds of Brong, Gonja and Gyaman lands become significant to Ashanti. This conflict was directly related to the growing militarization of Ashanti; and it occurred because of Ashanti desire to retain tribute in gold from these areas—gold which was used to obtain arms at the southern coastal markets.

The disparate northern migrations which peopled the northwestern lands were often led by sections of matrilineages. These moved together as corporate groups, claiming land over which their chief and stool assumed ownership and which the people received based on customary usufruct principles. In the myths of origin and oral traditions of the Abron and Gyaman area, one finds numerous instances of female leaders, *abusua* heads or queen mothers who, as leaders of splinter groups of royals, left their traditional areas (often following stool disputes) accompanied by elders, stools, fetish-priest and magico-religious regalia, to go in search of new lands for village settlement.[64]

In these early splinter population movements and in the appropriation of land which followed, the stool or the *oman* (the political unit or the nation) as well as the *abusua* were the primary social units which were now capable of controlling land.[65] If the chief managed to secure reserve portions of land for future use, these portions were carefully guarded and allotted to citizens or strangers who offered allegiance, as the situation demanded. Land, in and of itself, had little if any value; rather it was people on the land which created its worth. The focus was not so much to tie people to land, as to guarantee political allegiance and to clarify who had rights to claim the resources and produce from specific portions of land. The pattern of land control and inheritance within an *abusua* was to develop a corresponding specificity as political centralization continued.

The expanding political orbit and the numerous resettlements of rich and productive lands provided additional resources over which the originally small royalty and elite could compete. The tribute of gold (and to a lesser extent, game) from such lands was a powerful incentive for political intrigue. Thus, while splinter-migratory movements among the elite offered them flexibility during the early 1700s, direct land transfers and purchases among the elite also took place during the eighteenth and nineteenth centuries.[66]

While the Asantehene was said to "own" all the land, a member of the royal family might buy a parcel of land from another, send "thanks" to the Asantehene, then resettle a conquered or client population on the land, thus increasing its productivity and his or her own wealth. The record abounds in cases in which wives of royalty received villages and inhabitants as presents; royal women purchased land and became even more wealthy controllers of villages. Such cases declined precipitously in the mid-1800s, as women were gradually removed from public activities because of increased ritual prohibitions and the penetration of a western political climate which did not favor such leadership. Nevertheless, in the nineteenth century, what Wilks terms "the market in towns and villages" was a reflection of the transformed political and economic order. As the wealthy or office-holders met with displeasure of the Asantehene and had to vacate land in order to meet the fine or debt imposed, both land and persons changed ownership.[67] This early monetarization of land control, which was evident among the elite, was normally absent among the common folk. Land control at the mass level (below the *Omanhene* and the *Asantehene*) remained a process controlled by communal and *abusua* rights until the late 1800s.

Labor relationships also provide an index of increasing inequality within Akan areas. Because both the society at large and the *mmusua-kese* were becoming stratified in the seventeenth and eighteenth centuries, social differences became quite obvious at the public level. The existence of slaves and the use of slave labor by royalty, office holders (*ofahene*) or wealthy and privileged commoners (*obirempon* or *sikafo*) is quite clear when one examines accounts of early Ashanti. The royal and the wealthy flaunted their status over the servile commoner groups whom some scholars call the *antihumanifo*. Equally significant, however, was the growing impoverishment of the peasants (*nkwasefo* or villagers) who performed manual labor in order to survive, and the *mbrantee* (young men) who made up military units (*nkwankwaa*).[68] Thus, in addition to the lineage labor force (slave, consanguineal and affinal), there was a small occasional, or wage-labor force. To a large extent, the privileged could extract labor from free peasants who used land owned by their overlords, and the privileged overlord could also extract payment of rent or *aseda* for use of land resources.[69]

As the extraction of tribute or surplus from peasants increased, many peasants fled to the towns in search of more lucrative employment. Some common wage occupations in the seventeenth century were those of stevedores, ferrymen, porters, gold miners, woodcutters, water carriers, musicians, market vendors and cooks. However, such urban workers were also subjected to taxes which often became burdensome. The result was frequently dire poverty, and many of these persons joined the ranks of the dispossessed to be maintained by charity. In fact, Kea points out that it became the responsibility of the wealthy to give regularly to town funds for the maintenance of such persons.[70] While seventeenth century European accounts suggest that beggars did not exist, many poor people were only able to subsist by attaching themselves as "pawns" to persons of wealth or note for whom they worked, and who would in return pay their debts.

Rattray[71] has described the changes in land control and allocation which must have occured among ordinary Akan as the development of "feudal relations" took place. Relatively lax control of land by the stool gradually gave way to greater control by the corporate *abusua*, and finally to personal control over land. Many scholars have noted the tendency of communal property to decline as western contact intensified, with the subsequent increase of private property in land and other resources. Implicit in some of these references, and explicit in others, is the identification of the abusua as a male-dominated, capital-generating entity, especially in relationship to resources such as land.[72]

The categories of "male property" and "female property" seem to develop greater clarity in the period after 1764. Male property included guns and gunpowder; chests or leather bags (*fotuo*); slaves, slave wives and slave children; traps for capturing game; axes, cutlasses and hoes; kola, plantain or other tree and annual crops tended by a man's own labor; and the *kra kukuo* in which he "washed his soul."[73] Female private property included *adsoa* (baskets or bundles containing valuables) such as beads, trinkets, gold dust; clothing; household utensils; *fotuo* and gold weights of no higher equivalence than £1 gold dust; slaves; self-planted peanuts and other domestic crops. Private property, male or female, tended over time to be transformed into *abusua* property, and to devolve to the appropriate male or female heir. Yet, there were cases where valuable female-generated objects which were more normally handled by males devolved to male *abusua* heirs following a woman's demise. In such cases, the distinction between male and female property is blurred.

Female inequality in property ownership is implicit among the Akan by the mid-eighteenth century. However, it appears that this tendency might have been accompanied by the increasing identification of males with public representative positions within the Ashanti *oman* and the state as it was developing.[74] Asantehene Osei Kwadwo's creation of male-occupied, patricentric offices which were outside the traditional matrilineal inheritance line appears to have had as a logical correlate a challenge to female economic and political rights within the society at large. The bureaucratization and militarization which enhanced male status in the eighteenth century also brought economic and property rewards to male officeholders, and future positions to their male heirs. Outside of the small royal elite, women were mostly campaign supporters and camp followers.[75] Although female inequality in land ownership and control over capital-generating resources is startlingly clear in twentieth-century Ghana, it has often been argued by past scholars that early political and economic changes did not substantially alter the operation of female-centered social structures which guaranteed corporate rights.[76] Recent data suggests, however, that we may look to the seventeenth and eighteenth centuries for the roots of male-female inequality in Akan social structures, and gain greater clarity about its operation in contemporary rural situations.

In nineteenth century Ashanti, stratification and inequality with respect to the factors of production were also powerfully symbolized in the institution of "pawning,"[77] which continued to play a significant role in Akan society. Families of the pawn might choose this form of servitude as a means of eradicating their debts, and the pawn could be released from servitude upon full payment of the debt and interest. However, many pawns used this experience as one route to upward mobility, and they became further integrated as clients into the families of their masters. On the surface it would appear that females might be least likely to be chosen as pawns in Akan areas because of the structural importance of women to their lineages. However, in the nineteenth century, female pawns were generally desired by men wanting full control over a wife and children. And although the *abusua* of the woman encountered public shame at the alienation of females, the economic relief sometimes offset social stigma. It is likely that the early existence of slave labor influenced other servile forms such as pawning. Certainly the range of conditions within which pawning took place widened during the eighteenth and nineteenth centuries, as contact with western economies led to a transformation from what Rattray calls feudal relations to more capitalist economic relations.[78] Land and other resources then became drawn into the pawning situation.

Stratification in the mid-nineteenth century bore the marks of the multiple and disparate social forces present within Akan society, and those impinging upon the Gold Coast. By the mid-1800s, the push for western missionary penetration had begun, coastal mercantilists were establishing a complex of economic relationships with ordinary people inland, and the core of Ashanti was being torn between traditional and modern economic approaches. Various internal Ashanti war conflicts took place as the *Omanhene* and the other traditional elites opposed central control and the heavy financial burden of the Ashanti state. Young men had been pulled into urban standing armies, or rural military companies, and in their absence other members of the rural *abusua* were forced to increase their labor output in order to compensate for the absence of men from productive activity. Arhin has described the division of Akan society into those of privileged rank (the holders of power and authority) and those who were primarily poor and underprivileged.[79] However, by the latter part of the nineteenth century, elements of both sectors had begun to react to the deep social and economic tensions affecting the society.

The restlessness and economic innovation among the wealthy was to be matched by the disgruntled actions of the common people and the underprivileged, and after 1880 their mutual discontent would find a common outlet in the rubber trade. Both groups wanted greater freedom to control their own economic resources (whether capital or labor); this necessitated new and more flexible relationships with traditional leaders, a process which generally could not occur peacefully. Given all the contradictory influences of the incipient colonial economy, the fight by the Asantehene to maintain feudal control, and the fluctuating economic status of exploited inland peasant communities, it is not surprising that most strata sought their future in some involvement with the export-oriented economy which was not yet under control of the traditional Ashanti state.

In hindsight, the tensions which Gold Coasters were experiencing during the nineteenth century were symptomatic of what could be deemed a difficult "childbirth." Through laborious British conquest of Ashanti and its hinterland, the offspring of western economic penetration and political control was being brought into existence. Nevertheless, the social and structural disequilibrium created in the process of western penetration was enormous. Problems of rural labor and resource exploitation would continue to plague rural-state relations during the later colonial and independence periods.

Notes

1. H.A.R. Gibb, *The Battuta: Travels in Asia and Africa (1325–54)*. London: Routledge and Kegan Paul, 1929, 380.
2. Mauny, 1965; Walter Rodney, *How Europe Underdeveloped Africa*, Washington, DC: Howard University Press, 1970, 6–15, 41, 56, 64; James Duddy, *Portugese Africa*, Cambridge, MA: Harvard University Press, 1959, 135.
3. Peter Gutkind and Immanuel Wallerstein, *The Political Economy of Contemporary Africa*, Beverly Hills, CA: Sage, 1976, 32–34.

4. Eva Meyerowitz, *The Sacred State of the Akan*, London: Faber & Faber, 1951 and 1957; J.B. Danquah, 1929.
5. Meyerowitz, 1958. For critical appraisal, see J. Goody, "Ethnohistory and the Akan of Ghana," *Africa*, vol. 29, 1959, 67–81; A. Adu Boahen, "The Origins of the Akan," *Ghana Notes and Queries*, #9, 1966, 3–10.
6. Nehemiah Levtzion, 1973, 1–73.
7. Ibid., 117–119.
8. B. Davidson, *A History of West Africa to the Nineteenth Century*, New York: Doubleday, 1966, 56–60; W. Rodney, op. cit., 1970, 26–38.
9. Gibbs, op. cit., 321.
10. Levtzion, 1973, 64.
11. Ta'rikh al-Fattash, 1665, 94–100. See also Basil Davidson, *A History of West Africa to the Nineteenth Century*, 65-69.
12. Levtzion, 115.
13. Davidson, 1966, 72-73.
14. The investigation into cultural and linguistic characteristics of the aboriginal non-Akan peoples has been continuing. The aboriginal peoples would not have included Kur and Mande speakers, who were later arrivals to the area. However, over time, these diverse groups around the bend of the Volta have taken on many Akan characteristics, and have been generally characterized as Brong–Ashanti, because of growing cultural, political and linguistic commonalities. See K. Arhin, *Brong Kyempim: Essays on the History and Politics of the Brong People*, Accra: New Times Corporation, 1979, Introduction; and Posnansky, "Archaeological Aspects of the Brong Ahafo Region," in Arhin (ed.), op. cit., 22–36. See also Rattray, 1929, 64–65.
15. Gibb, op. cit., 322. See also Rodney, 1970, 20–22
16. K.B. Dickson, *A Historical Geography of Ghana*. Cambridge University Press, 1969. Most scholars agree that agriculture is unlikely to have been invented independently in Ghana or in west Africa. Archaeological work on the Dhar Tichitt-Walata area has demonstrated the gradual increase in the role of proto-agriculture during the period from 1100-900 B.C. Both the archaeological accounts and the Arab accounts document the importance of agriculture to the Ghana empire. There is also reason to believe that along with agricultural techniques introduced either from the Arab north or the Nile Valley in the East, there was increasing sophistication in the process of food production in the southern and northern fringes of the expanding Sahara region (Levtzion, 1970). Thus, in addition to early wheat and barley which resulted from outside influences, scholars can point to indigenous crops such as millet, sorghum and fonio, which developed during the neolithic period in west Africa. Around the empires, there is evidence that by A.D. 300 agricultural continuity was shattered by internal warfare between growing states in the area. These disturbances are likely to have pushed Negroid agriculturalists further south, where the savannah and fringe forest areas made foraging extremely productive, and agriculture less necessary.
17. Dickson, op. cit., 34–35.
18. Christopher Wrigley, "Speculation on the Economic Prehistory of Africa," in E.P. Skinner (ed.), *Peoples and Cultures of Africa*, 1973, 93.
19. Shaw, Igbo Ukwu: An Account of Archaeological Discoveries in Eastern Nigeria,

Northwestern University, vol. 1, 1970; see also Calcorovessi, 1975, 205.

20. Ivor Wilks, "Land, Labor and Capital in the Forest Kingdom of Asante," in Friedman and Rowland (ed.), *The Evolution of Social Systems*, London: Duckworth, 1977, 487.
21. Mauny, R. (ed.), 1956, 65–67 (often cited as Pacheco Pereira); Levtzion, 1973, 153.
22. Thurstan Shaw, op. cit., 1970, 262; Mauny, 1965; Merrick Posnansky, "Ghana and the Origins of West African Trade," *African Quarterly*, New Delhi, XI, 1971, 5
23. Basil Davidson, op. cit., 1966, 76.
24. Eva Meyerowitz, *Akan Traditions of Origin*. London; 1952, 29–33.
25. Colin Flight, "The Chronology of the Kings and Queenmothers of Bono-Manso: A Revaluation of the Evidence," *Journal of African History*, XI, 2, 1970: 259–68. For a somewhat different perspective, see Levtzion, *Muslims and Chiefs in West Africa*, Oxford University Press, 1968, 6–7, 194–95.
26. Merrick Posnansky, 1971: 8–11; also 1976, 38.
27. M. Posnansky, 1976, 43.
28. Ibid.; See also E. Meyerowitz, 1958, and "Akan Oral Historical Traditions," *Universitas*, vol. 2, 44–49, 1962.
29. Ivor Wilks, op. cit, 1977, 515–519; Braimah, *The Ashanti and the Gonja at War*. Accra: 170, 32.
30. K. Arhin, 1979, 9–11; R. Bravmann, 1974; Freeman, 1868.
31. Kea, 1982, 92–93. This explanation represents a departure from Rattray's earlier (1923) explanation for the *abusua* system.
32. N.A. Ollenu, 1967, 140–41.
33. N.A. Ollenu, op. cit., 142–43 and R.S. Rattray, 1923. These descriptions refer to the Akan of central and southern Ghana, rather than to coastal or eastern groups such as the Ga or Ewe, or to more northern peoples who were patrilineal or had dual-descent organization. Note that the existence of a conjugal mode of production in the nineteenth century is still an issue for scholars (Arhin, 1984; Wilks, 1977; Eades, 1984, 476).
34. I. Wilks, 1977.
35. K.A. Busia, 1951; R.S. Rattray, 1929; N.A. Ollenu, 1967, 5, 9–11.
36. M. Fortes, 1945 and 1969; also, P. Woodford-Berger, 1977.
37. M. Fortes, 1969.
38. Some of the descriptive terms used for the labor unit and labor relations in nineteenth century Ashanti have been the "lineage mode of production" (E. Terray, 1975), the "tribo-patriarchal mode" of production (R. Howard, 1983), and the "conjugal mode" of production (K. Arhin, 1984).
39. R.S. Rattray, 1929. Many of these occupations were still represented among rural male farmers of the Brong region in 1973.
40. Robert Lystad, 1958, 13–16; I. Wilks, *The Northern Factor in Ashanti History*, Legon, 1961.
41. K.B. Dickson, 1969, 103; Wilks, 1961. Reports indicate that some of the highest quality kola nuts came from the maximum kola production region in Brong–Ashanti areas.
42. DeMarees, Pieter, *Beschryvinghe ende Historische Verhael van het Gout*

Koninckrijck van Gunea anders de Gout-Custe de Mina genaemt liggende in het deel van Africa (ed.), S. P. L'Honore. The Hague: 1912.
43. Rene Bravmann, 1974; I. Wilks, 1961.
44. Chauveau, Jean-Pierre. "Note sur les echanges dans le baule precolonial," *Cahiers d'Etudes Africaines*, 63–64, 18, 1977: 567–602. Also, T.C. Weiskel, "L'histoire socio-economique des peoples baule: problems et perspectives de recherche," *Cahiers* 61–2, 16, (1–2), 1976, 357–95.
45. I. Wilks, 1961; K. Arhin, 1979, 9.
46. Mouezy, 1956, 42–50; Duffy, 1956, 133.
47. Duffy, 1956, 134–36.
48. A similar phenomenon of domestic slavery for business purposes existed among the Akan involved in the northern trade, as well as among.the *signares* (important female traders) of Senegambia. See Brooks, 1976: 20–23.
49. Calcorovessi, 1975.
50. Rattray, 1923, 95.
51. Note that Rattray (1927: 95), Fortes (1969: 196–97) and Miers and Kopytoff (1977: 29–37) differ in their estimation of the stigma involved in marrying slave males to freeborn females in matrilineal societies. Whereas Rattray and Fortes refer to the possible illegitimate status among the Akan of the resulting slave children without freeborn progenitors, Miers and Kopytoff refer to the matrilineal Kongo and Inbangala examples to demonstrate that the male slave's status does not affect that of his children. Indeed, Miers and Kopytoff imply that the male slave may reduce his own "effective marginality" by producing freeborn children for the matrilineage.
52. Kopytoff, 1980.
53. R.S. Rattray, 1923; Agnes Aidoo, 1975, 94–95.
54. R.S. Rattray, 1929; K.A. Busia, 1951; M. Fortes, 1969.
55. R.S. Rattray, 1927, 65. See also K. Poku, 1966: 55–56.
56. I. Wilks, 1968.
57. I. Wilks, 1975. Raymond Dumett (1971, 84) has commented on the early existence of a ninth great road, based on data in colonial reports (A&P 1893 [C. 7225], vol. 60, 7–8).
58. K. Arhin, 1979.
59. I. Wilks, op. cit., 1977.
60. R.S. Rattray, 1929; N.A. Ollenu, 1962, 47.
61. Kea, 1982: DeMarees, 1912, 80.
62. Kea, 1982.
63. K.A. Busia, 1956.
64. I. Wilks, 1977.
65. R.S. Rattray, 1929.
66. I. Wilks, 1975, 106–109; and T.C. McCaskie, 1981, 2.
67. I. Wilks, 1975, 106.
68. See Kea, 1982 on the group called "antihumanifo" On the significance of the "nkwankwaa," see I. Wilks, 1975, xii, 535, 728, 705.
69. T.C. McCaskie, "Office, Land and Subjects in the History of the Manwere Fekuo of

Kumasi: An essay in the Political Economy of the Asante State," *Journal of African History*, 21, no. 2, 1980.

70. Kea, 1982.
71. R.S. Rattray, 1929.
72. G. Mikell, 1984, 195–218.
73. R.S. Rattray, 1929.
74. Wilks has described the increasing representation of the male stools or "mmamma-dwaa" (1968, 1975, 452–55). See also Mikell, 1982, for inquiry into the reflection of this tendency in art and funerary statuary.
75. Arhin, 1983b.
76. I. Wilks, 1968, 214.
77. T.C. McCaskie, op. cit., 1980.
78. Cruickshank, 1856.
79. K. Arhin, 1983, 2–22.

2

Stratification and Wealth Accumulation

The growing influence which Ashanti and the interior had on the economy of the Gold Coast during the seventeenth and eighteenth centuries was to be transformed by capitalist and colonial penetration during the nineteenth century, to culminate in the growth of an Ashanti-based cocoa industry after 1900. This early period is significant for the intensity with which most strata in the interior—royalty, elite and commoners—were jolted by the economic transformations which accompanied increased European contact. While the presence of the Europeans on the Gold Coast littoral did indirectly affect the cohesiveness of the Ashanti empire, there was also a direct and profound effect on the totality of social life and social structures throughout the area. Local leaders faced important decisions about how to deal with the changes flowing from the British, Danish, Dutch, French and American presence along the coast. Perhaps more importantly, they were searching for new ways of integrating an evolving indigenous population while controlling the pace of economic change.

This early period is significant for three reasons: (a) the reformulation of relationships of the coastal chiefs and aristocrats to the new commoner elites and people of wealth, both on the coast and in the interior; (b) the increasing bureaucratization of the interior as Ashanti responded to the economic and political challenges of western penetration; and (c) the growing recognition by rural folk of new economic and political possibilities, especially after 1851, as a result of these earlier socio-economic changes. Certainly, by the mid-nineteenth century, people on the coast could feel the results of the quickening conflicts within the Ashanti forest zone. Under the impact of western economic penetration, the Asantehene's centralized political and religious authority (symbolized by the Golden Stool) and his ultimate ownership and control over wealth accumulation (symbolized by the Golden Elephant's Tail) was under irreversible assault.[1]

Nevertheless, few have concentrated on the impact of all this change on lives of ordinary people, both coastal and in the interior.[2] These people were the mainstay of rural production and colonial trade linking the Gold Coast to Britain and to the United States.[3] Ashanti dealings with the coast had gradually expanded during the seventeenth and eighteenth centuries as Euro-African trade escalated. From the Ashanti perspective, the presumptions of insignificant Cape Coast and Accra merchants made them a thorny inducement to disloyalty for Ashanti state traders. However, by the 1870s, the well-being of the Ashanti state was so affected by the trade and political relations on the coast that a new policy was needed for relations between the Asantehene, coastal and interior chiefs.[4] This policy permitted a more regional political autonomy and resource control than had formerly existed in the sphere of Ashanti. By 1874, Ashanti's economic control was marginal on the coast, but on the interior Ashanti restraints on large traders, state merchants and entrepreneurs was producing internal chaos and war. It was clear by the 1890s that Ashanti attempts to prevent the emergence of both an autonomous rural merchant class and peasantry were futile.

Merchants, Traders and Creoles

The lucrative gold trade which initially drew the Portuguese, Danes, Dutch, French, British and German ships to the Gold Coast was not overshadowed by the trade in palm oil, ivory, kolanuts and slaves until the late 1700s. During that more than three-century-long interval, European and American advancing cultural influences (largely predicated upon the proceeds of the African trade) were matched by a progressive mutation of traditional African culture to include monetarization of resources and commodities as well as social relationships. This development of the economic aspects of traditional African culture proceeded most rapidly in the coastal Fante, Ga and Akwapim areas which were in extensive contact with European traders. By the 1700s, however, the impact of these new relationships was being felt not only on the coast, but also in the Assin, Aowin, Krobo, Ashanti, Brong and Gyaman communities of the interior. The trade in gold which dominated Euro-African commercial relations until the late 1700s initially reinforced traditional concepts of wealth and gave them an enlarged European "yardstick" against which to be measured. Later, the changing economic relations led to greater rural and urban stratification and economic conflicts within Akan society. The conflicts between rural producers and urban elites were particularly exacerbated in the period after the demise of the gold trade.[5]

Much has been written about the royal control over the gold trade, both on the coast and in the interior. Despite the stress on local traditions with respect to this gold trade, it was not simply an African phenomenon. The African tradition was matched by a similar European monopoly, with Portugal as an excellent example.[6] The construction of the Portuguese post of Sao Jorge da Mina in 1482 on land belonging to the African chief Caramansa was the first step which ensured the Portuguese Crown a control leading to a steady revenue until 1540. Commanders of the fortress normally came from the ranks of the lower Portuguese nobility, and at Sao Jorge they exercised virtual sovereignty over the fort.[7] Despite the fact that they had a staff of approximately fifty-five, composed of soldiers, clergy, craftsmen, artisans and cooks, their well-being was for a long time dependent upon the favorable predisposition of coastal chiefs such as Caramansa. Occasionally, the conversion of a chief and his entire people to Catholicism increased trade and the work force of Sao Jorge da Mina. Much more often, however, it was individual Africans who converted, and while this brought them cultural and social advantages, it also meant separation from traditional beliefs and practices. Of great notoriety was the experience of a freed slave woman, Grace, after her conversion to Christianity in 1540. She reverted to worship of traditional gods and ancestral statues despite conversion to Catholicism and was extradited to Portugal, where she stood trial for heresy, and was condemned to perpetual incarceration.[8]

Nevertheless, Portugal's long-term interest lay more in trade than in conversion. The extreme profitability of the Gold Coast trade was widely recognized in Portugal,[9] and provided the economic basis for Portugal's trade with the East and for the expansion of Portugal's army and navy. Naturally, Portugal's trading success also attracted much European competition.[10] Worthy of note, however, was Portugal's limited relationships with peoples of the interior. By 1515, interior Africans had begun to send merchants to the coast to obtain the imported slaves, cloth, clothing, metal hardware, *manilhas* or brass bracelets, shells, cowry, beads and wine in exchange for Akan gold. During the 155 years of Portugal's presence and trade in the Gold Coast, the Portuguese were only moderately successful in extending their influence more than fifty miles inland from the coast. The Gold Coast experience stood in sharp contrast to Portugal's actions on the Upper Guinea Coast, where *lancados* were in intimate contact with Africans in inland villages.[11]

The Danes and Dutch, who replaced the Portuguese in trading influence between 1658 and 1850, had a more decisive influence on the expansion of wealth and stratification among the coastal Fanti, the Accra (Ga) and the Akwapims,[12] than on peoples of the forest zone. The weak Portuguese presence after 1553 gave way to a more permanent Dutch coastal supremacy, and Portugal withdrew, turning its attention to Brazil. Under Dutch control, permanent settlements were created on the coast, and Scandinavians penetrated further inland. They, to a larger extent than the Portuguese, created small communities within which religious conversions, slave trading, and Euro-African amalgamations of life predominated. In addition, the Danes acquired landholdings and experimented unsuccessfully with plantation agriculture between 1780 and 1800.[13] It was the fiercely competitive trading of the Danes, the Dutch and later the English, which fueled the development of indigenous African traders and royal trading representatives, and gave structural support to the growing Creole community.

Initially, only the coastal forts came under direct control of the European merchants. It was, in fact, merchant concern with social and economic factors which gave rise to the early schools among the Creoles at the coast. The offspring of European fathers and African mothers could not fit comfortably into the African community, and schools were established to prepare this Creole group (of primarily Fanti and Ga background) for involvement in trading, the professions and mission work.[14] With the focus on biblical instruction, mathematics, bookkeeping and literacy, they were ultimately to become a cohesive class among which the family names of European traders were often retained. Phillip Quaque was one Creole who, having been educated in England by the Company of Merchants in 1754, returned to be "missionary, schoolmaster, and catechist to the Negroes" at the school at Cape Coast in 1754.[15] Although initially marginal to African life in general, this Creole group ultimately played an important role in Western economic and cultural penetration.

From their base in the coastal forts, the Europeans all used similar techniques to obtain gold in exchange for imported commodities with the small states within the Gold Coast region. With the exception of the area around Mina (which was much less stratified than the larger towns were becoming), the Europeans had to deal with the chief's or the King's adviser, the person whom the Portuguese had referred to as the *xarife*.[16] Rarely did African royalty participate directly in the trading relationship, although they kept watch over the proceedings, demanding an accounting from their representatives. Note the following description of this relationship:

> The trade in these expensive commodities (gold, ivory, slaves, kola and monkey furs and kente cloth, and the imported goods from the north) was in the hands of men (i.e., in contrast to the later dominance of trade by women). To prevent the power of wealth from disrupting the kinship, political and military systems of power, trade was strictly controlled by the state. No one could trade without the permission of the king, or as we might say, a royal patent.[17]

Such state mercantilist relationships led to intense competition between the various small states in the seventeenth century, and a desire on the part of each to exercise some influence on the coast as the site of trade. Thus, the *xarifes* and royal representatives had encouraged the Portuguese *lancados* and other European merchants to grant innumerable gifts in order to facilitate the trading relationship and to obtain concessions from the kings.

The result of such activities was an increase in size of the African trading elite group on the coast. For example, the African merchants around the forts, referred to by the Danes as *klaploppere*,[18] had the advantage of knowing the trade jargon and pidgin used by the various Europeans, and became invaluable interpreters and middlemen. When competition was high, the merchants policed the inland paths to the coast to attract potential buyers; when business was slow or uneven, they encouraged trade by giving the local people small presents and drinks (later known as "dash").[19] Occasionally, they sent slave women to the inland royal representatives or to the king as wives or concubines to encourage further trade. Such gifts and trinkets or finery undoubtedly stimulated trade and increased profits of coastal merchants and Europeans.

While the nature of the northern trans-Saharan trade had permitted almost absolute royal control over trade and limited the penetration of undue foreign influences into the country, the coastal Euro-African trade was less restrictive, both bureaucratically and culturally. While both types of trade initially involved the barter of commodities, coastal traders soon began to use Portuguese, Danish, Dutch or English currency convertible to gold as the standard of value.[20] True, local people and small merchants used gold dust as currency, but given royal control over the bureaucracy as well as over larger nuggets of gold, the royal factor in local and export trade was decisive. Akan kings not only gave their merchants license to trade, but usually also the initial capital with which to trade. The ability of these merchants to create wealth from trade was therefore highly dependent upon the king's favor. The association of the royal trade official and large trade merchants with wealth, while traceable to the Afro-Portuguese activities, underwent further development with the presence of Danish, Dutch and British merchants who competed on the Gold Coast after 1700.

The coastal *caboceers* (the major administrative officials, or the principal lineage elders of a town—the *mpanyimfo*) became important persons in the Afro-European relationship during the Portuguese period.[21] Having received a title and administrative rights from the superior chief or the king[22] he, or in a few cases she,[23] had the responsibility of guaranteeing the prosperity of trade. They often dispensed justice in the coastal Fanti towns around the forts, and protected the king's authority over the area. Usually a shrewd businessperson and politician, the *caboceer* stood to become quite wealthy. The number of dependents, pawns and slaves controlled by this official was certainly one index of his or her economic importance.

Normally, the *caboceer's* presence in an area was also an index of the restriction of European influence to the forts, not extending to the surrounding land or people. Again, the governors of the fort were usually given only rental or purchase rights to land upon which the forts stood. They had no legal rights to press for service or labor from nearby villagers and townspersons. The governors could obtain no African work force without paying wages or buying slaves to work within the forts.[24] However, the European need and willingness to pay for labor attracted those persons to the coast who desired goods and money.

Although some *caboceers* were lenient in their interpretation of the nature of European control, they were generally vigilant in requiring the payment of tribute, custom, or notes, a portion of which was sent to their superior chiefs or king. Of course, Portuguese, Danish company merchants or British governors also predictably gave gifts to the *caboceers* or chiefs, and were often lax in demanding street cleaning and path clearing—duties over which *caboceers* had official as well as unofficial responsibilities, derived from the stipends they received. European trade thus brought with it corruption, and increased local conflicts, which added to the competition for coastal influence, slave dealing and the general drive for social advancement. Anxious to grow wealthy from the trade, chiefs repeatedly requested European traders to establish forts on their land. In some cases, they offered to vacate that land rather than rent it. This alienation of land by chiefs was not a problem in the eighteenth and early nineteenth centuries, but would become so with the resource extraction which occurred in the colonial period after 1880. In the 1700s and early 1800s, however, the desire of chiefs to obtain wealth from trade was a powerful inducement to their cooperation with European traders.

The slave trade, which naturally guaranteed the greatest profit and wealth, came to dominate European intercourse with the Gold Coast states in the 1700s. While the Portuguese initially had imported slaves into the Gold Coast from Benin to exchange them for gold, the later Dutch, Danish and American arrivals stocked their ships with large quantities of inland slaves supplied to the coastal forts by the Fanti, Akwamu and Ashanti. The Ashanti were particularly interested in bartering slaves for European goods rather than using gold to obtain commodities, as they had previously done with the northern Muslim traders.[25] The trade competition between the Danish, British and American "factors" for slaves and gold permitted African merchants to play each factor off against the other.

Trading possibilities likewise encouraged inland states to approach the coast, in order to conquer their neighbors and secure captives (*nnomum*) as slaves.[26] The ethnic identity of the slaves changed as more powerful inland states (which produced many of the desired foodstuffs and gold) conquered coastal areas and sold the people as slaves. Many of the foreign slaves (*nnonkofo*) were absorbed into inland wealthy Akan households or resettled in rural villages to perform agricultural labor for the elite. Given heightened consumption and production needs, the need for more labor remained. Likewise since the coastal and inland middlemen were the persons who arranged both the sale and transportation of slaves, their interest in profit encouraged them simply to shift their allegiances and payment of tributes to the new overlord as the political situation demanded.

The slave trade and the introduction of firearms transformed coastal commerce and dominated Gold Coast life. Slaves had increased in importance because Ashanti wars of conquest against its intransigent neighbors (such as the western and more ethnically mixed Brong, Gyaman, Assini and Nkoranza states) which, although producing slaves, frequently prevented gold and ivory from reaching the coast.[27] Ironically, developments in other parts of the global system were undermining the basis of eighteenth century Gold Coast trade. The problem for the Gold Coast was that by 1800, the cotton and sugar plantations of the Americas had already reached their peak, and both slavery and the slave trade were becoming marginal to Western economic development. The British voted to end the slave trade in 1807, and British merchants were forbidden to stock or ship slaves from their forts. Of course, some pro-slavery British merchants connived with non-British slavers to continue the export of human cargo. Moreover, they were joined by Ashanti chiefs and royals who also bitterly resented the ban on slavery because they saw slavery as a source of profit and of much needed internal labor.[28] The British prohibition became a source of great conflict between Ashanti and coastal merchants and administrators. While the latter were obliged to enforce British law, the Ashanti simply directed slaves towards Assini, Dahomey and other coastal markets not under British control. The British merchants were caught in a bind: internal Gold Coast wars disrupted legitimate trade, American slavers were determined to acquire additional slaves, and the price of goods for legitimate traders had risen inordinately.[29]

The fortunes of African middlemen fluctuated widely during the nineteenth century. As the pattern of trade changed, their ability to make sizable profits became problematic. Most of these African middlemen had little capital, since many of them were not coastal Creoles, but migrant commoners who had come to the coast in search of lucrative employment. Those from the coast often started as canoe men, negotiating with arriving trade ships and using their own canoes to transport goods ashore. While initially many serviced the larger European or Fanti mulatto merchants, by the nineteenth century some attempted to go into business for themselves. Using small canoes which were able to skirt around the forts, they were able to break the attempted monopolies of the European forts.[30] The result was a complex economic gradation of middlemen, ranging from independent entrepreneurs to those who simply worked for others.[31] Certainly the links of African middlemen with interior purchasers was more varied than the links of the European traders. These men were able to remain in business even after steamships increased the amount of West African trade in 1853.

By arrangement with British trading houses, a number of Africans were given goods on credit, and were thereby able to compete for a limited time with the larger companies which had formerly held a virtual monopoly.[32] The problem was that in any economic downswing, the African middlemen were usually short of capital, and suffered because they could not make good their credit. This stratum usually could not afford such innovations as packaging techniques which make distribution easier. Therefore, by the 1870s British houses had ceased loans to many African middlemen. Unable to compete with the larger merchants, these men who had provided one of the main trading ties to the interior began to go out of business.[33] Nevertheless, during their heyday, they had a significant impact on rural folk whose aspirations for individual mobility and for new goods had been stimulated.

Wars, Royalty and Wealth

The force which fueled the engine of societal development after 1800 was the need of the middle stratum to recapture rural labor and resources which during the 1700s had increasingly come under autonomous control by peasants, family groups and local leaders. The rural *abusua* rather than the clan or the urban elite was the important reference group for rural people in the nineteenth century. However, a renewed emphasis in Ashanti on rural production was occurring as the transatlantic slave trade declined and as gold was being depleted. This encouraged the royalty and the traditional elite to attempt to tighten both economic and social control over producers who worked their land, and to make attempts to bring more land and people under their control.[34] At the same time, the privileged stratum of *nouveau riche* had grown—they were beneficiaries of bureaucratic offices created after the 1650s as the Ashanti state was centralized, or wealthy traders whose status was dependent upon clientage to the Asantehene. These new positions, which lay outside of control by matrilineal and kin-based systems, permitted greater political manipulation by the Asantehene who was now more fully in charge of individual rewards. It was political loyalties and offices rather than actual resources on the land which Ashanti chiefs and relatively efficient bureaucrats now controlled.[35] Despite changes in bureaucratic structures, ordinary people continued to give their primary loyalties to the familiar chiefs of their own communities.

The new appointive offices, the *mmammadwa* (or son's stools) coexisted with the traditional stools of the *ohene* (village chief), the *Omanhene* (divisional chief), the *ofahene* (traditional aristocrat or noble) and the titled military official who often became a trading aristocrat or entrepreneur, the *obirempon* (plural: *abirempon*). Some of these newer ranks were wealthy and all of them held trading licenses granted by the king.[36] The king could give them money to begin trading, and they in turn had to render yearly accounts of their wealth. It was this middle stratum of chiefs, nobles, administrators, trading officials and the *abirempon*, rather than the Asantehene who held immediate authority over rural land, people and wealth. Nevertheless, the Asantehene generally delegated authority to these persons, and could reclaim it. This stratum held office or pursued their livelihoods at the pleasure of the king, who could, at the slightest indiscretion, take away their stools, titles, trappings of office, or their gold, wives and slaves. This contradiction between political authority and resource control was to create great havoc within the Ashanti state after 1830.

The state was much too large for the Asantehene to have ruled individually from the center. Delegated civil power rested with the *amanhene* (the divisional chiefs), who had control over their people and affiliated lands on behalf of the king. These men had to ensure that tribute from all important resources such as gold, ivory and game came to them, and that some of it passed upward to the Asantehene. They also had the obligation to marshal communal labor for road clearing, and to conscript specified numbers of soldiers from various villages and towns for warfare. Chiefs and officials often made important military decisions within the regions granted them by the Asantehene. They might also instigate and finance battles in the hopes of making financial gain in slaves and other booty. Here, the status of chiefs and the new elite of bureaucrats and entrepreneurs might merge, because some *abirempon* also financed military actions and became so important that they were granted chieftaincies based on their influence with the Asantehene.

Peasants who had traditional usufruct rights to land within the division not only provided communal labor and/or some form of taxes to the chief (and therefore the *oman* or political unit), but males were also recruited for mandatory military service within their divisions. Ashanti men belonged to a military organization known as an *asafo* company,[37] with headquarters in the nearest town, and they went into battle in these formations. Offices within the *asafo* unit were inherited by heads of clan or lineage groups within the town, and the resulting group of titled elders symbolized the political link between kinship groups and the *oman*. In this way, military service, political allegiance and economic opportunities for the ordinary male were part of a whole. However, because *asafo* units were disbanded after a battle, military structures could not serve as the basis for peacetime organization for males, except for the elders. It was clear that for each stratum in Ashanti, from the *Omanhene* down the smallest *odikro* (village headman) or peasant, politics and economics were inseparable.

To understand social stratification in the nineteenth century it is essential to understand the nature of control over and disposition of rural wealth. Since the 1600s, the urban poor had developed due to the growth of trade, labor specialization to support elite tastes, indebtedness, rural exploitation and militarization. By the 1800s, the political economy of the Ashanti state was changing due to the shift in Islamic-Ashanti relations and the altered nature of the Euro-African relationship.[38] The Ashanti economy became more dependent upon agrarian production to generate surplus and capital, and with this development there was a more intense involvement of the common people with the land. While the urban elite and intermediate groups profited from the labor of dependent pawns and slaves on rural land, the peasants themselves had fairly limited but slowly increasing incomes. They could still wash for gold, but as in the past, any nuggets they found belonged to the *ohene* and to the overlord. Gold dust was generally in short supply and peasants generally had to exchange agricultural products for it in order to purchase cloth and other essentials, or to pay taxes.[39] The common people owned few or no slaves; therefore their way to generate wealth was by natural reproduction and production within the lineage—more hands to work the land for more products in exchange. Urban folk, on the other hand, had access to some wage labor, lineage slave labor, and often the labor and children of female pawns.[40] However, urban dependents were usually a liability if they were not craftspersons, while rural dependents and slaves created even more resources. In the mid-1800s, the thrust of the Ashanti middle stratum was to maximize the uses to which it could put the proceeds of rural production. By funneling goods into the coastal or northern trade, they transformed labor into wealth.

The major opportunities for the Ashanti to enhance their wealth usually came when small states resisted central control by the Asantehene. The resulting wars of conquest generally brought war captives, which were distributed among the higher military ranks. The southern states which the Ashanti had conquered in the 1700s often chafed at the exorbitant tribute and economic control in the 1800s, with the result that the Ashanti fought them again and exacted even more tribute. A case in point was the repeated tribute-demanding wars against the coastal Fanti, who were believed to be unduly profiting from the European trade. Since most arms came from the coast, the Ashanti could exploit inland peoples more effectively by attempting to block their access to the coast, if not satisfied with the tribute received.[41] The Ashanti especially sought women as tribute to be distributed to Ashanti lineages as domestic slaves. Sometimes conquered people, or *nkoa*, were sent as a group to more central areas ruled by chiefs loyal to the king or, barring that, officials were quartered in their territory and outposts were created to assure their allegiance.[42] The only problem here was that the Asantehene viewed the actions of the *sikafo* (the wealthy) or the *abirempon*, who enriched themselves by wars, conquest and plunder as much as by trade, as detrimental to the interests of the Asante state. After the 1860s, the personal ambitions of many *sikafo* and *abirempon* caused major conflicts between them and the state, and curbed Ashanti expansionary wars.

The Decline of the Golden Elephant's Tail

The capacity to accumulate wealth in Ashanti was symbolized by the king's golden elephant tail, and the powers of political and ritual control were symbolized by the golden stool of the Asantehene.[43] The symbols of office and status for other officials (such as the horse-tail whisk) were insignificant in comparison to the honor of the elephant's tail. The Asantehene himself bestowed an ordinary elephant's tale whisk on selected *abirempon*, but it was not a golden one. The strength of the golden elephant's tail, while symbolic of wealth in Ashanti, was dependent upon the effectiveness of the flow of resources between the common folk (the producers) and the elite. Under the impact of capitalist penetration, a break was occurring in the links between these strata, and there was increased assertion of autonomy by peasants and middle-strata from control by the Asantehene and the state.

What threatened the strength of the Ashanti state's resource control in the early 1800s was the additional pressure of taxation and exactions which Ashanti bureaucrats placed on rural producers in order to satisfy needs of the coastal trade. Many rural towns were continually being requested to contribute labor for maintenance of roads around trade routes, but received little compensation for this. In other cases, chiefs of exploited communities tried to relocate their people out of areas of Ashanti control. Personnel in the British forts were frequently inundated with peasants presenting themselves, asking for protection and being resettled on land around the forts. Several significant cases exist, most notably that of the Assin people, who relocated in 1823 to avoid abuses by the Asantehene. The entire community and chiefs simply moved across the River Pra into Fanti-controlled territory, thus being closer to the British Colony where the protection of the forts was available. The Ashanti still had to pass through these Assin communities in order to trade in Cape Coast, but could no longer demand tribute of produce and gold from the Assin people. Needless to say, this was the source of much dialogue and conflict between the Asantehene and the British Governor between 1823 and 1844,[44] particularly since it culminated in "The Bond" between Assin and Fanti chiefs which was temporarily deleterious to Ashanti interests.[45] Sometimes, however, this raised problems, since there was also a tendency for the British to incorporate fleeing people as domestic slaves into the households of European personnel, which was contrary to official British policy after 1807.[46]

The wealthy, nobility and *abirempon* intuitively understood that between

1830 and the 1880, rural folk had become accustomed to and wanted many of the advantages of the increased trade which the Gold Coast experienced.[47] After all, it was these interior folk who harvested the palm oil, palm kernels, kola nuts and animal skins which figured so highly in the Gold Coast trade prior to the 1880s. The surplus of rural production naturally found its way to the urban centers and coastal middlemen—or was funneled upward to the *ahenfo* or the wealthy who owned them as slaves.[48] The yams, plantain, tomatoes and other food from the forest zone fed the urban populations of the interior as well as the coast. Commoners and slaves head-carried the *odikro's* or the *ohene's* produce to town and coastal markets bringing back imported items. European travelers who moved through Ashanti after 1800 often commented on the amount of imported goods displayed for sale in the inland towns, especially in Kumasi, the Ashanti capital.[49]

There was considerable response by peasants to the escalation of the Euro-African trade. Much relocation by rural people also took place as they attempted to move to areas where efficient gathering of natural produce would increase their profits from the trade. In Gyaman and Ahafo, for example, oral traditions establish that early elephant hunting camps had become the basis of future village settlements such as near Akomadan and Manso Nkwanta, with outposts of chiefs and other overlords being added on as Ashanti control developed. As ivory increased in importance in the coastal trade, so did Ashanti pressures on such communities. The increasing importance of the kola nut to Islamic traders after 1807 also encouraged Brong–Ashanti and Gyaman farmers to shift toward greater collecting areas, and they increased their profits from the burgeoning kola trade in the Gyaman and Banda markets. Nevertheless, Ashanti royal control over the kola trade and suspicion of allowing direct contacts between Islamic traders and producers encouraged the Asantehene to keep Islamic traders out of Kumasi. By restricting Islamic traders to the Salaga market, the Asantehene placed limits on their contact with producers.[50]

Palm oil producers were also experiencing many such pressures, but because they were situated closer to the coast, the Europeans played a greater role in controlling peasant movement. The Krobo and Akwapim areas, for example, were the major locations of palm oil production, and they were influenced by the presence of the Danes and Dutch on the eastern coast. As conflicts with Ashanti increased in this eastern area, it was notable that some Krobo oil producers and local merchants resettled with European approval in the Akwapim Hills area where access to the trade was greater. Nevertheless, some of the earliest Gold Coast producer strikes concerned palm oil prices and European-imposed fines in oil for their actions.[51]

European influence on producers may partially account for why rental, purchase and land tenure arrangements on the Akwapim Hills appears more monetized at an earlier point than relationships in other parts of the Gold Coast.[52] European land purchase and plantations were sporadically present in Akwapim from the 1700s, but not in other parts of Ashanti and would only have made a significant impact on Gold Coast relationships in the 1890s. From very early, it was clear that peasants were understanding the importance of shifting to better production and transportation locations to obtain more profit from their production. Perhaps this occurred with greatest frequency in areas where political conflicts arising from relocation were not so likely and where much forest land was available, i.e., in the peripheral areas of Ashanti. This trend toward the relocation of peasant households and even communities was continued and expanded with the later rubber and cocoa industries after 1880, with obvious implications for the ability of producers to effect global economic ties.

The restraint which the village community and its chiefs and officials had formerly been able to exercise over lineage groups containing rural producers had placed limitations upon direct producer involvement in the global economy. On the other hand, the desires of the newer rural and urban elites to ensure greater profitability from production and trade tended to encourage more private and less corporate or communal approaches to production than before. One way in which the changing peasant response could be seen was in the increasing establishment of the conjugal household, within which husbands and male household heads could exercise control over the labor of wives and children. Traditionally, the husband and wife may not have relocated after marriage. Their continued residence in the village would have allowed for continued interest on the part of women and children in the economic welfare of their matrilineages. Thus, dual residence for married women (in both husband's as well as their own natal compound) or movement back and forth between two compounds was and is still quite common for many Brong–Ashanti and Ahafo village women. This dual residence pattern would have been less present in the newer villages where peasant populations were established through recent migration.[53] To an extent perhaps unprecedented before the mid-1800s, migrant rural men were becoming effectively able to control the labor of people not of their own lineage without the necessity of compensating the other matrilineage for this labor.

Arhin, for example,[54] has noted the existence of a patriarchal conjugal household and labor group in the nineteenth century. Although there is still some question as to when this would have arisen, its development would have been stimulated by the heightened economic activity and need for a sizable labor force as the export economy increased in the later half of the 1800s. Ashanti had historically required massive inputs of foreign labor (generally slave) to satisfy Ashanti and southern food requirements.[55] The changing economy would therefore have contributed to the persistence of Akan social structures which generated free and unfree (pawn) wives for males, and this may have continually reproduced the conjugal household. The decline in the size of the unfree and slave labor force under British legal influence is likely to have heightened the desire of males for the conjugal household under the control of the husband. This patriarchal response to economic change, although moderated during the later period of rubber production, would again become significant in the twentieth century.

It is unlikely that Akan conjugal units were a source of wealth accumulation prior to the mid-1880s, except in those communities where matrilineal organization was being altered (such as in Cape Coast and other Fanti areas). There, early contact with western social structures and the capitalist economy allowed African wives and children to work in and enhance business enterprises of coastal middlemen and traders. For rural males, however, this conjugal unit, ofttimes established out of necessity, was to provide a work force which was sufficient for economic maintenance from the 1870s until well into the colonial period, in most parts of southern Ghana. Both husband and wife seem to have participated to some extent in the transporting of skins, palm kernels and palm oil to coastal agents prior to the 1880s. The existence of the conjugal work unit made it possible for many Akwapim men, for example, to leave farming to wives, and to travel for the palm oil trade.[56] Nevertheless, access to the land of both husbands' and wives' communities would have been important to the economic well-being of the conjugal family, particularly in later productive phases of the economy.

The attempts at more autonomous peasant involvement in the expanding economy naturally met with some resistance from the traditional elite and from rulers who stood to lose from this process. One of the most efficient means of quelling peasant mobility and autonomy was to increase the level of exactions and the prices of items which peasants generally wanted but could not produce. Thus, through overpricing, a host of middlemen from chiefs down to local hawkers extracted profits from goods which European and American merchants brought to the Gold Coast, but it was the merchants themselves who obtained the greatest profits.[57] Peasants were constantly encouraged toward greater rural production to acquire the gold necessary to purchase nonessential items.

Despite increased rural access to money, there were also social structural means of reducing peasant mobility. It involved the constant imposition of fines for oaths which were broken and behavior which was considered disrespectful to the elite and the *ahenfo*. For ill-founded rumors and accusations, or for adultery and jealousy, or oversight of allegiance and tribute, peasants were often taken to court and fined.[58] The net effect of this was constant debt and impoverishment in order to pay the imposed fines. Other legitimate responsibilities might impoverish rural folk, such as escalating taxation imposed by chiefs and *abirempon*, or funeral customs requiring use of imported or expensive items. In such cases, a person might have to mortgage lineage property and the successor to the deceased might inherit the debt. The exorbitant interest rates on loans virtually assured that pawned items were seldom reclaimed; and if they were necessary to production, impoverishment was the natural result.

Throughout the nineteenth century, rural indebtedness increased as peasants became more integrated into the syncretic and emerging capitalist economy of the southern Gold Coast. Despite British laws, the incidence of pawning women in lieu of debts persisted. If the owner of the pawn encountered difficulty, they might instruct the pawn to sell himself or herself as a slave to secure additional money; the unfree person had little recourse. As mentioned earlier, the ultimate recourse was flight to distant towns or to the colony where such exactions and debts could not be claimed.[59] However, for most rural cultivators, the increasingly tense conflict generated by economic change, social mobility and political allegiance which was gripping Ashanti society was something which they could not easily escape.

Other factors, such as the penetration of missionaries and the churches, affected peasant autonomy and involvement in the new economic change. From 1827 onward, the Basel and Wesleyan missions had penetrated more southern and eastern rural areas. Here, the church not only spread the gospel, but provided the commoners with new opportunities for petty trading through literacy and mathematics ability.[60] True, the churches did complain that rural young men ran off to the colony as soon as they were educated, and soon lost their moral training as they entered the lower ranks of the "despicable" traders. Some of the educated men returned as *adwadi fo* (retail agents) who were in business for themselves; others became hawkers going from village to village. While this tendency was abhorred by missionaries, it was applauded by the *sikafo*, native middlemen and traders, some of whom contributed to the support of the mission schools.[61] The recruitment of rural commoners certainly served to increase penetration of middlemen and traders into peasant communities where agricultural surplus and labor was available.

The traders and the *abirempon* were compounding their wealth by utilizing the skills and labor of the peasants, as well as by appropriating peasant resources; however, the fortunes of the Ashanti state experienced a decline. In essence, there was an increasing contradiction between the *obirempon's* status and wealth, and his fealty to the Asantehene which might be symbolized by the possession of the ordinary elephant-tail whisk.[62] The wealthy, although generally involved in trade, had to recognize their political obligations to the state and its subordinate representatives in order to remain in business. Both *sikafo* and *abirempon* were additionally bound by a system of "death duties" (*awunnyade*), which made their wealth, upon death, the property of the state. The king might give back to the heir the title if appropriate and a portion of the deceased's wealth, but this was at his own discretion. Death duties were even levied against ordinary citizens who, through diligence, became wealthy. This tax vividly reinforced the fact that the state dominated all aspects of the Ashanti life. In fact, the state would have enriched itself by the good fortunes of its trading strata, had it not been so extortionate after 1831.

By the mid-1800s, the *obirempon*, the *sikafo*, as well as the diligent citizen had begun to weigh his or her desire for public recognition (and therefore declaration of wealth) against the duty of preserving and passing on wealth to lineage members and offspring. The *awunnyade*, when applied to state offices and titles controlled by the Asantehene,[63] was intended to prevent bureaucrats from transforming themselves into a class whose interests were inimical to those of the state. It also served to prevent the dispersion of wealth among the citizenry, and especially to prevent its concentration in certain lineages. However, the evasion of *awunnyade* eventually became commonplace. In many cases, wealthy evaders tried to hide their property and pass it on to their heirs. Women's movable property such as jewelry, beads or slaves were often dispersed prior to death, or hidden to avoid taxation. Even royalty were prone to such avoidance in order to maintain some independence.[64] British accounts of the mid-1800s are sprinkled with references to the recalcitrant *sikafo* and *abirempon* who evaded death duties.[65]

The Ashanti state's desire for wealth even affected the lives of peasants and ordinary people. The prospering peasants hid their wealth. British records cite the case of a woman who, under duress, revealed that while washing for gold her husband found and hid a nugget which should have been turned over to the authorities.[66] Both the elite and the common folk tried to obtain gold so that they could buy British and American goods. Thus, American ships which brought pipes, along with Kentucky or Missouri leaf tobacco, to the Gold Coast between 1846 and 1885 absorbed much of the capital generated by peasants. Naturally, such products found their way into the houses of the elite. Increasingly, though, ordinary folk began to judge their well-being by the extent to which they could afford some of the less expensive imported items. Importation of cloth, for example, was increasing as Manchester prints made inroads into the domestic cloth industry. The net effect of these developing tastes for imported consumer products was the decline of the gold stocks in Ashanti by the mid-1800s. Then as the gold declined, the state attempted to protect its revenue by increased exactions from wealthy and poor alike.

Table 2–1 gives the value of Gold Coast exports to the United States from 1846 to 1885. Table 2–2 gives the value of Gold Coast imports from the U.S. within that period.

TABLE 2–1

Value of Gold Coast Exports to the United States, 1846–1885*
(In Sterling)

Date	Total Exports	Total	Palm Oil	Gold Dust	Gum Copal	Ivory	Palm Kernels
1846	120,000	7,400	3,000	0	0	4,400	0
1847	148,030	9,000	3,600	0	0	5,400	0
1848	167,174	.....	......	.....	.....	.....	.....
1849	167,174	.....	......	.....	.....	.....	.....
1850	168,156	21,295	12,275	3,000	0	6,020	0
1851	219,050	48,500	11,500	36,000	0	1,000	0
1852	159,250	40,890	10,000	26,928	0	800	0
1853	115,000	46,200	29,000	11,000	1,200	5,000	0
1854	200,000	55,500	26,000	28,000	500	1,000	0
1855	140,696	25,900	20,000	200	5,000	300	0
1856	120,999	11,333	9,308	350	0	1,003	0
1857	124,394	16,684	14,736	136	948	320	0
1858	154,136	20,421	19,287	450	285	399	0
1859	118,563	19,718	16,822	0	991	1,884	0
1860	110,457	16,661	11,629	0	739	1,380	0
1861	145,819	30,279	27,069	419	2,080	0	0
1862—6†							
1867	160,745	......	......	.....	.....	.....	.....
1868	148,910	22,513	19,694	360	215	0	1,291
1869	281,913	49,604	47,433	0	0	0	641
1870	378,239	85,794	102,979	0	0	0	4,426
1871	295,208	155,423	50,502	16,084	830	0	1,002
1872	385,281	115,684	110,091	1,649	3,123	53	0
1873	330,624	82,915	81,104	0	1,446	0	0
1874	....	......	......	.....	.....	.....	.....
1875	327,012	48,814	45,449	0	2,682	0	649
1876	465,268	59,169	53,218	0	3,728	0	1,994
1877	387,003	57,773	55,203	0	1,580	0	976
1878	393,457	66,934	66,544	0	0	0	250
1879	751,850	79,243	72,953	4,252	530	100	1,313
1880		85,533	83,527	0	1,606	0	20
1881	337,297	57,507	52,482	0	3,047	0	0
1882	340,019	57,681	57,093	0	4,354	0	2,225
1883	363,868	59,480	55,860	132	235	0	0
1884	1,139,642	62,874	62,450	0	0	0	0
1885	1,110,499	69,258	62,816	130	0	0	3,612

* From G.E. Brooks, Jr., *African Traders, Old Coasters and African Middlemen: A History of American Legitimate Trade with West Africa in The Nineteenth Century*, Boston University Press, 1970, Appendix H, p. 310.

† *Note*: Dots indicate inadequately grouped figures; blanks indicate that figures are not available.

TABLE 2-2

Value of Gold Coast Imports from the United States, 1846-1885 (In Sterling)

Date	Total Imports	Total	Tobacco	Rum	Lumber & Shingles	Flour	Cotton Goods	Kerosene
1846	55,306	8,550	1,600	5,400	0	1,000	0	
1847	79,800	12,000	2,400	6,000	0	2,000	0	
1848	82,950	10,900	2,400	6,000	0	2,000	0	
1849	110,600	12,752	360	550	0	500	0	
1850	88,656	14,125	2,380	4,850	0	1,576	0	
1851	84,880	16,325	2,210	8,600	0	1,120	0	
1852	71,635	17,020	3,800	10,000	0	1,900	0	
1853	60,000	18,000	3,000	12,000	0	850	0	
1854	107,200	25,000	3,600	14,500	0	2,000	0	
1855	149,587	7,496	2,246	2,000	0	500	600	
1856	105,634	24,950	5,956	12,452	373	1,816	1,225	
1857	118,270	28,684	6,115	15,916	301	1,953	609	
1858	122,457	31,123	3,111	21,959	237	1,856	379	
1859	114,596	36,632	6,772	25,719	359	1,317	290	
1860	112,454	45,951	9,120	27,433		1,553	0	
1861	162,971	38,259	5,667	27,803	90	1,427	0	
1862-6**								
1867	206,920	......	......	......	....	.....	....	
1868	140,226	43,447	28,806	11,803	221	158		
1869	213,491	34,828	7,606	22,296	196	124		0
1870	253,398	86,583	2,660	47,469	194	124		245
1871	250,672	63,122	6,274	51,195	302	748		0
1872	260,102	69,588	12,654	50,391	1,675	785		82
1873	225,525	54,378	9,962	40,413	799			60
1874	....	......	.....	......	...	.....		.....
1875	364,672	48,529	3,005	32,595	1,951	1,494		472***
1876	446,088	58,424	10,283	38,699	2,039	1,494		466***
1877	326,914	62,242	10,759	47,141	1,133	532		608
1878	394,253	66,002	9,735	42,490	3,684	907		1,227
1879	323,039	62,237	8,156	44,782	822	917		614
1880	....	......	.....	......	...	.....		.....
1881	398,124	84,180	12,820	62,072	1,539	1,497		1,216
1882	392,975	69,536	12,196	49,993	679	784		1,729
1883	382,582	65,626	8,569	49,122	1,210	757		1,821
1884	1,065,560	110,224	17,060	65,533	1,170	622		865
1885	1,008,988	96,315	12,378	64,734	1,285	1,450		1,161

* From G.E. Brooks, Jr., *African Traders, Old Coasters and African Middlemen: A History of American Legitimate Trade with West Africa in the Nineteenth Century,* Boston University Press, 1970, Appendix G, p. 309.

** Note: dots indicate inadequately grouped figures; blanks indicate that figures are not available.

*** Accra and Cape Coast totals only.

Against this dynamic economic background, the internal restrictions placed on Ashanti residents were glaring. The Asantehene's growing suspicion of the disloyalty of his wealthy subjects was economically well founded. While his victorious army provided additional territory from whose inhabitants the royalty and elite could exact tribute, these persons involved in trade looked askance at the state's activities. The politico-economic gains which the wealthy derived from conquest were ofttimes offset by the trade restrictions imposed on many areas because of continuing warfare. Sometimes, as when Brong and Gyaman rebelled, the Ashanti army was strong enough to prevent the flow of foodstuffs and gold from these areas into the hands of merchants. Increasingly common after 1874, however, was the Asantehene's complaint that the merchants and traders disregarded trade boycotts, thereby permitting guns and other weapons to flow into the rebel areas.[67] Thus, when the Asantehene's political concerns interfered with the elite's inclination to enhance their wealth, problems occurred.

Problems which the Ashanti had faced on the periphery of the empire were soon occurring within the core as well. When exactions increased in the late 1800s, civil war broke out as the Amanhene of various small states sought to secede or, more specifically, to gain economic autonomy. The middle strata, which had developed as a result of the coastal trade, now backed their regional overlords in an attempt to dismantle control by the Asantehene.[68] This internal conflict, perhaps even more than the rebellion in peripheral states, created new economic pressures in Ashanti.

It became increasingly difficult for the Ashanti state to maintain control of internal wealth as well as the movement of external trade when the coastal area posed such an economic challenge. Ashanti merchants and the middle classes saw clearly that in the British coastal society, African traders, Fanti chiefs and the wealthy had much greater flexibility than they did—coastal society offered a "better model of a political economy."[69] In Cape Coast, for example, wealthy local trading families were now the persons with whom Ashanti merchants had to deal in order to conduct business. As internal Ashanti conflict increased, it was not surprising that some *akonkofo* (entrepreneurs) and even some *abirem-pon* and commoner notables—*abirempomma*—fled to the colony. This was particularly true as they sought to prevent state demands for an audit or if they sought to avoid taxation and *awunnyade*. These groups thereby served notice that they wanted new socio-political relationships which contained capitalist initiatives, and that they were open to new methods of capital investment.[70] Their activities naturally strengthened British opposition to Ashanti and brought to a head the opposition of the middle strata, which finally culminated in new Ashanti policies towards the merchant and wealthy strata. From the 1870s onward, a weakened Asantehene could make fewer claims to absolute control over wealth and political power in Ashanti. He ruled over an emergent class-stratified society in which rural transformations related to the penetrating capitalist economy brought endless questioning of the traditional royal and aristocratic privileges.

Notes

1. I. Wilks, 1975, 415, 429–30; 1979, 1–37.
2. The outstanding exception is K. Onwuka Daaku, *Trade and Politics in the Niger Delta, 1830–1885*. Oxford: Clarendon Press, 1956.
3. K. Arhin, 1984.
4. T.C. McCaskie, 1983, 23–43.
5. K. Arhin, 1983, 471–5.
6. Although independent Portuguese merchant ships had plied the Moroccan coast for centuries, and had ventured as far as the Ivory Coast, the discovery of the village of Mina ("the Mine") in 1470 encouraged King Alfonso V of Portugal to reassert royal control over the gold trade (Azurara, 1896; Vogt, 1979, 8–9). The Portuguese were discovering that much gold formerly found in such places as the Gambia had come from the Gold Coast (Rodney, 1970, 77).
7. Vogt, 1979, 43–44.
8. Vogt, 1979, 55–56.
9. Pereira, 121.
10. By the 1580s, British, Dutch and Danish interlopers, as well as Spanish claims to the Portuguese throne, were causing a decline in Portuguese control on the Gold Coast.
11. W. Rodney, 1970, 77.
12. Norregard, 1966, xi.
13. Ibid., p. 3–5, 73, 166-68.
14. Vogt, 1979, 43–44.
15. Phillip Foster, *Education and Social Change in Ghana*, University of Chicago Press, 1965, 43–45. On financial support from merchants for these schools see Accounts & Papers (20), vol. 31, 1851, 207.
16. Vogt, 1979, 87.
17. Daniel McCall, 1956.
18. Rask, 1754, 138–39.
19. Norregard, 162–63.
20. Ibid., 161; W. Rodney, 1970, 85; C. Reindorf, 1895, 47, 86, 275–76.
21. K. Arhin, 1983, 14. See also Cruickshank, 1853, vol. 1.
22. Bowdich (1819) 1966, 250–51.
23. Ibid., 45, 99.
24. Cruickshank, 30–35.
25. I. Wilks, 1971, 130.
26. G. Brooks, 1970, 19, 257.
27. Claridge, vol. 1, 1964, 209; Brooks, 1970, 68. After Ashanti put down the revolt of the more coastal states, it invaded Dagomba, Gonja and the Brong states. According

to Claridge, these states had no hope of success because of their lack of firearms and the destruction of their trade during the hostilities. Soon afterwards, Gyaman, Inta and Tekyiman (Techiman) were subdued and forced to acknowledge tribute to Ashanti.

28. Accounts & Papers (12), 1874, vol. 40 (C. 1007), 1105.
29. Cruickshank, vol. 2, 38–40. See also Brooks, 1970, 19.
30. G. Brooks, 69.
31. K. 0. Dike, 1956, 103.
32. Ibid., 114.
33. Ibid., 114; see also Kimble, 1963, 11–14.
34. K. Arhin, 1976–77, 454-55. See also I. Wilks, 1977, 487–534.
35. I. Wilks, 1968. 214; and 1975, 452–54.
36. T.C. McCaskie, 1983, 23–43. Some differences exist in the analysis of the *obirem - pon* as a group. Arhin assumes a more traditional interpretation of the *obirempon* as simply wealthy traders, not officials (personal communication May 1985). See also K. Arhin, 1983, 1–22.
37. I. Wilks, 1975, 73. R. Kea, 1982, 127–28, 131–32 also discusses the origins of the *akofokum/asafo* (soldier/company) organization in the towns during the late 1600s, but recruits were.of course, drawn from rural areas. This recruitment into company service continued, despite eventual resistance from commoners, until 1901. The *asafo* appear to have then become transformed into local political pressure groups within Asante areas (G. Mikell, 1975, 38–39).
38. I. Wallerstein, "The Three Stages of African Involvement in the World Capitalist Economic System," in P. Gutkind and I. Wallerstein (ed.), *The Political Economy of Contemporary Africa*, 1976.
39. K. Arhin, 1976–77, 454–55.
40. Cruickshank, 1966, 300–310, 321–23. See also McCaskie, 1980, 191–92.
41. G. Brooks, 1970, 270; I. Wilks, 1975, 224, 613–14.
42. K. Arhin, 1979, 56–67.
43. K. Arhin, 1979, 56–67.
44. G. E. Metcalfe, 1964, #62 of 1823, 87; #98 of 1831, 133; and #146 of 2 April 1944, 196.
45. Accounts & Papers, vol. 31, op. cit., 207.
46. Cruickshank, 1966, 343–45. See also Accounts & Papers (5), 1856, vol. 42 (2111), document #433, p. 461, enclosure 2 in #14; also, the Madden Report, H.C. 551, plus C.O. 267/170 of 1842.
47. I. Wilks, 1979, 1–37.
48. Accounts & Papers, vol. 48, 1873 (C.709) nos. 455, 474, pp. 460–61. The British defense of domestic slavery in Africa ran along the following lines:

    ...African slavery as a home industry exists; and it must be admitted that to slave labor we owe our flourishing commerce with Africa... Of the 17,882 oz. of gold dust sent to England, probably not one ounce was obtained by free labor. The European produce is carried from the coast into the interior by slaves. It is not unlikely that for some time to come the growth of our commerce with Africa will strengthen domestic slavery instead of diminishing it; just as the material progress of Russia under Peter the Great intensified the serfdom of eastern Europe in the beginning of the eighteenth century.

49. Cruickshank, vol. 2, 33.
50. I. Wilks, 1971, 124–41. See also E.P. Skinner (1964, 93) for other examples of restricted contact between producers and traders.
51. Reynolds, 1974, 129–30, 135, 139–40.
52. This is a matter of some question. As early as 1787, Isert (a Danish doctor) had purchased land for a plantation and colony, but there is no evidence that the Akwapimhene Obuobi Atiemo considered it other than the cessation of rights to use the land for an unspecified period. See Kwamenapow, 1973, 96–101. Early land purchases among Ashanti royals has already been discussed, but note that the royal land purchases were more related to transference of allegiance than to outright monetary gain (Wilks, 1975, 106–9).
53. M. Fortes has discussed the position of Ashanti women in relationship to their matrilineage, and the importance of jural rights over persons which the lineage can exercise. He has also discussed the tendency of Ashanti women to shift residence and positions of authority based on their assets and responsibilities at various points in their lives. However, what had always been unclear for the pre-European penetration period is the degree of economic control which husbands exercised over wives while wives were co-resident with husbands. More recent work by Woodford-Berger suggests that the dual residence of Brong women involves much economic responsibility to natal (matrilineal) as well as conjugal households. See Fortes, 1970; Fortes, 1969, 154–218; and Woodford-Berger, 1981.
54. K. Arhin, 1984.
55. I. Wilks, 1977, discusses the early necessity of importing agricultural labor. On the suppression of "panyarring" and pawning as well as British complicity in the illegal acts see Accounts and Papers (5) vol. 42, 1856. On African resistance to the suppression of this unfree labor, see passing reference in Accounts & Papers (20), vol. 31, 1852, no. 25.
56. D. Brokensha, 1970; P. Hill, 1963, and Hill, 1970, 24.
57. Accounts & Papers (20), 1852, op. cit.; Accounts & Papers (8), 1865, vol. 37 (3423) Part II and No. 170. The items listed for peasants were supplemented by others which were essentially purchased by elites (guns, gunpowder, provisions, etc.).
58. See T.C. McCaskie, 1981, 477–94. He touches upon an often overlooked element—the extent to which polygyny among the elite sometimes left commoner men without wives, and therefore encouraged adultery conspiracies by husbands to entangle and fine commoner men.
59. Accounts & Papers (5), 1856, vol. 42 (2111), No. 433.
60. Cruickshank, vol. 2, pp. 81–83; also Accounts & Papers (20), 1852, vol. 31, 1851, no. 25, p. 205.
61. Accounts & Papers, vol. 31, 1851, no. 25, p. 207.
62. I. Wilks, 1977, 20–21.
63. Ibid., 30.
64. T.C. McCaskie, 1983, 23–43.

65. McCaskie, 1983, 23–43.
66. Accounts and Papers, 1864, vol. 41, no. 385, pp. 133 and 137–38. Notable in this case was that the wife was in pawn to the husband; this may have been grounds for some of the antagonism between them.
67. A. Aidoo, 1975. See also (C.O. 96/126) 24 July 1879. Usher to Hicks-Beach.
68. I. Wilks, 1975, 702–4.
69. K. Arhin, 1983, 19.
70. K. Arhin, 1983; T.C. McCaskie, 1983.

3

Laying the Basis for Cocoa: Colonialism and Changing Rural Forces

After 1876, western capitalist economic penetration into Gold Coast life intensified, laying the basis for the growth of the cocoa industry. By 1880, even casual observers could note the changing economic relationships of rural inhabitants and the new ways in which they were beginning to relate to the factors of production such as land and labor.[1] Much of the former economic and political pressure exerted by Ashanti bureaucrats against peasant communities had been halted by the British conquest: the burning of Kumasi in 1874, and the dire economic straits of Kumasi nobility after this.[2] The British pushed to establish more direct relationships with such northern production areas as Nkoranza, Salaga, Bonduku and Gyaman, in order to give attention to other areas for which they were in competition with the French and Germans. They were able to cite these efforts in Gyaman and the trans-Volta territory to bolster their claims to them in negotiations at the Berlin Conference which divided Africa.[3] With the center of the Ashanti state in disarray, the divisional chiefs and their people often pursued their own economic interests by establishing treaties with the British. Naturally, they repudiated much of the tribute and death duties formerly levied by the Ashanti state.[4] Members of the elite sometimes fled to the coast to protect their private capital, and rural folk began to migrate, seeking wage labor in the colony.

Despite these significant socio-economic and political changes, the traditional Ashanti political-economy persisted. The second British conquest of Kumasi in 1895 marked the beginning of colonial rule, as well as the removal of the Asantehene from the Gold Coast.[5] This did lead to greater economic penetration, but not to the denial of traditional values by rural people. Rather, colonial control tended to reinforce the increased syncretism between traditional Akan values and institutions and the newer capitalist processes and relationships. Concepts of allegiance and wealth remained, and were imitated and utilized by peasants and new elites alike. The pretensions of these *abirempon* further perpetuated the concepts of "big man" and "small boy" which came to permeate relationships in both rural and urban areas and this replaced notions of "bureaucrat" and "slave" which had belonged to an earlier period.[6] Nevertheless, despite these changes, there was a tendency for the old elite to maintain their positions of leadership in the rural areas.

Pre-Cocoa: Rubber, Mining and Wage Labor

The growth of the rubber industry and wage labor in gold mining introduced features into the Gold Coast that were quite different from those that developed as a result of palm products, coffee and cocoa production. The production of palm oil and palm kernels between the 1830 and 1882 was under indigenous control and generated sizable profits. Even with declining prices in the 1880s, palm oil and kernel exports contributed roughly two-thirds of all Gold Coast exports in 1890.[7] But in contrast to rubber, the palm trade was concentrated in the southern Akwapim area and the northeastern Krobo and Akim areas, and scarcely affected the deeper parts of Ashanti and the northwest.

In the mid-1800s, the British had assumed that given the existence of traditional cotton spinning and cloth production in some interior communities, new cotton production methods would bring as much profit to the Gold Coast as they did to Nigeria. They knew that indigenous cotton production was great enough for some local cloth to be exported to Brazil. The British therefore hoped to transform Gold Coast cotton production by growing and cleaning the fibers locally, then exporting that product to Manchester, with the printed cloth returned for sale in the colony. Their ultimate goal was the mechanization of cotton processing in the Gold Coast with cheap labor and raw materials, with British industry underwriting the initial costs.[8] Nevertheless, except for the eastern and Volta areas where some cotton grew wild and required no cultivation, this plan failed, because the producers did not feel that their labor was amply rewarded by financial returns. Moreover, the chiefs did not encourage cotton production and the transportation system could not yet accommodate this product.

Rubber production elicited quite a different response. It did not initially require a large labor force, special conditions or machinery, and it was possible to transport the latex on the heads of porters to get it to coastal merchants. By the late 1880s a sizable group of rural persons were extracting and transporting raw rubber for personal sale; or alternatively, they worked for the wealthy, transporting rubber to Kumasi from where it was transshipped and sold to coastal agents. Dumett documents the pressure which coastal merchants placed on chiefs and rural entrepreneurs to obtain rubber from the peasants.[9] By 1890, the Gold Coast had become the largest exporter of rubber in the British Empire, largely owing to the activities of rural entrepreneurs and individual producers.

As British timber merchants cut roads and moved into the interior of the country following colonial control in the 1890s, the rubber trade appeared to follow. By 1890, most interior peasant communities had begun to master the art of tapping, without the assistance of agents of the mercantile firms. They simply "felled trees, slashed the bark along the trunk with a cutlass until the latex ceased to run."[10] Nor were they using sophisticated or expensive coagulation techniques, but simply allowing the latex to harden through a natural cooling process which took three to four weeks. Alternatively, coagulants were added to speed up the process, but this drew negative reactions from coastal merchants and European brokers who complained about the quality of the raw product.[11] The development of more sophisticated techniques for climbing and tapping trees, and for removing excess moisture from the rubber, came later, and marked a phase of rubber production which required more capital investment on the part of peasant entrepreneurs.

The rubber trade, therefore, provides a classic example of a situation in which ordinary peasants began to diversify their incomes by becoming linkage figures, thus eliminating the need for extensive penetration of European personnel into inland communities in search of natural products for export. This industry further intensified developing trends in peasant behavior which were noted earlier. There was a rush to spread out to acquire access to more forest land, and to retain autonomous control over production with as little interference from chiefs as possible. Thus, the volume of European demands for rubber began to change the traditional usufruct claims to land rights as people tried to acquire as much land as possible. Migration and resettlement was common as strangers tried to become involved in the industry. Then, local people began to demand tribute from strangers for use of the land in much the same way as royalty and *ahenfo* had formerly done. For example, in Dormaa in the 1880s, local people could tap rubber freely while strangers paid approximately £2 before commencing operations for three or four months.[12] Around Sunyani, women as well as men could be hired to head-transport rubber to the coast, or they worked on behalf of their families.[13] More than any previous product, rubber was having an important impact on the interior.[14]

The increased demands for higher quality rubber encouraged people to seek higher quality trees, and to take better care with processing. Attempts were made to introduce more sophisticated production techniques, and as the costs of transportation climbed, capital availability acted as a weeding-out factor. Those peasants who could utilize the labor of family members, servants, slaves, pawns and paid transporters became quite wealthy rubber brokers. There is some evidence that the farmers and middlemen of the Akwapim Hills became quite astute participants in rubber trading. In contrast, poor peasants who had only their labor to sell could not make as large profits in the rubber production. They could, however, work in rubber processing, and by the 1880s, a German establishment in Accra was already employing 120 women to purify and prepare rubber for shipment.[15] We will see that some of these earnings from rubber would be invested in the emerging cocoa industry.

Inevitably, some chiefs attempted to treat rubber as an "elite good" and to control its collection and sale to coastal merchants.[16] Some chiefs did organize communal labor parties for tapping, allegedly putting proceeds into communal treasuries. Other chiefs sometimes paid local peasants to tap rubber trees on uninhabited land. Nevertheless, all indications were that chiefs and *ahenfo* were largely unsuccessful in exerting control over a trade whose influence penetrated more deeply into the structure of Akan society than had any other export activity except gold mining. While the trans-Saharan gold trade based on barter had been under control of the chiefs until the 1800s, and the palm oil trade had drawn mostly coastal peasants into the money economy, the rubber trade with its emphasis on cash altered the conception of peasant production and linked its participants to the international commercial market economy. Rubber production, more than any previous commodity production, was to initiate the infusion of twentieth century economic relations into the rural areas and to prepare the way for the capitalist cash-crop economy.

While the rubber trade and the export of palm products had become important in the Gold Coast, the parallel increase of gold mining also had comparable impact on the local political economy—especially land relations in the south. For several centuries, Europeans (with the exception of the Danes) had tended to rent and lease land from the Africans rather than try to own it outright.[17] This was probably all to the good because, outside of royal transfers of land, few interior chiefs seemed to have had the right to alienate through sale land which belonged to their stools. Sale of land was generally unnecessary since those persons who had traditional rights over land from the chief could mine gold on their allotments. This would change after 1879 when the European gold-mining industry necessitated long-term unbreakable contracts for land. The desired changes were not always easy, given the close relationship between land and other ancestral and religious aspects of Akan life. This problem not only substantially prevented earlier European gold mining but, as late as 1868, one Cape Coast businessman, Hughes, had his mine closed and his machinery smashed by

Africans angry because the concession violated such sacred social relationships.[18] It is noteworthy that concessions granted to Africans[19] by insolvent chiefs also paved the way for European entrepreneurs.

Table 3–1 gives quantity and value comparisons of palm oil, palm kernels, timber and rubber in Gold Coast trade in the 1890s.

TABLE 3–1

GOLD COAST TRADE IN THE 1890s*

Year	Palm Oil		Palm Kernels		Timber		Rubber	
	Gallons	Value	Tons	Value	Feet	Value	Pounds	Value
1897	2,021,716	107,737	10,836	69,818	15,236,216	90,569	4,957,016	419,913
1898	2,145,138	114,288	9,732	66,378	13,620,965	110,331	5,984,984	551,667
1899	3,323,919	183,204	12,664	106,156	11,990,832	87,076	5,572,554	555,731

* Based on Accounts & Papers (8) 1900, vol. XIV, no. 306, p. 3. Report on the Gold Coast for 1899. Value in sterling.

Many chiefs were so attracted by the competitive offers from Europeans that by 1879 they had granted mine concessions to Europeans at Awudua and Tarkwa.[20] Ashanti was generally an exception, since royal control over the more lucrative gold-mining sites (such as Manso Nkwanta)[21] was effective in limiting European penetration. The Obuasi mine in Ashanti was opened much later. However, the rapid pace of land alienation by southern chiefs even worried colonial administrators, who debated the advisability of assuming government control of unused land to protect it from exploitative speculation. Naturally, these land issues caused some conflicts between chiefs, the government and the educated coastal African elite. Operating through the Aborigines Rights Protection Society (ARPS), the coastal elite pressured for legislation which allowed unused land to remain under the jurisdiction of traditional authorities. However, legal challenges to chiefs based on claims that they had no right to reap individual profits from the collective property of their people also forced chiefs to hire African lawyers to draw up contracts that protected the indigenous interests in land.

Assertions that modern gold mining represented "the first serious impact of western economic forces upon the traditional forms of social organization"[22] have ignored the slave trade's impact upon kinship, gender roles and other aspects of social structure. The impact of mining on the Gold Coast social, political and other socio-cultural systems after 1880 cannot be denied. Of special significance to this study, however, is the impact of gold mining on the availability of rural labor with the resulting implications for technological and social development in the country. The mining industry was certainly not the first process that utilized rural labor for the colonial political economy. It should be noted parenthetically that when the British could not get sufficient military manpower in Cape Coast, they imported personnel from Britain, from the West Indies, and even from Hausaland to assault Kumasi.[23] Then, when they became more involved in extensive interior operations as formal colonialism developed,[24] the British met the occasional labor shortages by encouraging migration to Cape Coast and Accra from Ashanti, Kwahu, and Akwapim.

Table 3–2 gives numbers employed in mining in the Gold Coast and Ashanti in the years from 1907 to 1916.

TABLE 3–2

AVERAGE NUMBER EMPLOYED IN MINING AND DREDGING IN THE GOLD COAST AND ASHANTI, 1907–1916*

Year	Number Employed
1907	15,277
1908	15,796
1910	19,138
1911	19,153
1912	17,633
1913	15,650
1914	15,741
1915	15,300
1916	15,296

*Based on Annual Reports on the Gold Coast, Blue Books 11909–1918, as follows: 1909, lvii, 425; 1912–13, lvii, 485; 1914, lvii, 49 and 539; 1914–16, xliii, 629; 1916, xix, 293; 1917–18, xxii, 249.

The problem for the British was that the need for a large work force on the coast coincided with the need for additional militia to keep the peace and to stimulate development within Ashanti. New roads and communication networks were also needed to facilitate industry and economic growth. This troubled the British, who had always complained about the unwillingness of Gold Coast inhabitants to work seriously at agriculture, much less at other tasks. Then, after 1880, with the general profitability of the gold-mining industry, the need for migrant labor was overwhelming. There is very little evidence of any incentive for free Akan men to move from the forest and southern areas to work for wages in mining towns like Tarkwa. Most of the southern labor migrants were people from the coast, foreigners, or were *nnonkofo* (Muslim slaves) who were despised in Ashanti, and fled to the coast seeking protection and work.[25] The British increasingly turned to northern labor, which they disliked because of the heavy transportation and lodging expenses and its seasonality, and therefore unreliability. The British tried to minimize costs, often at the expense of the quality of life for migrants, but the logistics and cost remained prohibitive.

Table 3–3 provides information on labor employed in Ashanti gold mines and dredging companies in the years 1905–1914.

TABLE 3–3

LABOR EMPLOYED IN GOLD MINES AND DREDGING COMPANIES IN ASHANTI, 1905–1914

Report Year	Actual Year	Population	Surface	Mine	Total	Cumulative Total
1906	1905	European	----	----	250	
		Native	----	----	3,000	3,200
1907	1906	European			157	
		Native			3,356	3,513
1908	1907	European	108	46	154	
		Native	2,056	1,058	3,114	3,268
1909	1908	European	117	25	142	
		Native	1,911	1,341	3,252	3,394
1910	1909	European	99	24	123	
		Native	2,768	989	3,757	3,830
1911	1910	European	122	30	152	
		Native	3,594	1,281	4,875	5,027
1912–13	1911	European	114	38	152	
		Native	3,337	1,518	4,855	5,007
1914	1912	European	106	44	150	
		Native	2,904	1,354	4,268	4,418
1914–16	1913	European	74	47	121	
		Native	2,660	1,262	3,922	4,043
1914–16	1914	European	80	44	124	
		Native	2,393	1,281	3,674	3,798

* Based on Annual Reports of the Commissioners of the Gold Coast, 1906–1916. See endnote [28].

Complicating the use of northern labor was that the Mossi, Lobi, Dagarti, and Grunshi men brought down to the mines were often recruited through questionable "forced labor" procedures. Men were often unwilling to come on their own, and colonial officers set a precedent in assisting industry by "encouraging" traditional authorities to send them out. As the coastal labor shortage became clear by 1905, and again by 1909, more direct demands were made on northern chiefs, and they were paid five shillings head money per man enlisted from their areas. Those recruited underwent a strenuous trek south, were then housed in *zongos*, and experienced rigid European control over their wages and social lives.[26] Desertions were frequent and the mine owners were left bereft of skilled labor for the dangerous underground work. Wala, Dagarti, Isalla and Kassena recruitees from the northwest who reportedly were better treated, returned more frequently for mine work, or they branched out into the newer mines in Ashanti as they opened. Nevertheless, the Gold Coast governor still complained that no reliable labor could be obtained from Ashanti, since the people were "adverse to any form of systematic work."[27] Although mining in Ashanti developed quickly between 1905 and 1914, northerners still accounted for the majority of mining labor.

It was not the unwillingness to work systematically that kept the Akan away from the gold mines, but their satisfaction with their own economic activities, which had earlier been based on slave or dependent labor. Land was still generally plentiful for farming. Moreover, the general economic development from 1880 onward which drew northern laborers to the mines also provided the expanding Ashanti village and town economies with an expanding labor force. Thus, despite traditional Ashanti reticence towards Muslims, the *zongos* (strangers in residence) in Kumasi grew at a phenomenal rate[29] due to the influx of northern migrants who had deserted the forced labor gangs. Other regional towns in the forest zone, such as Sunyani, grew consistently but more slowly. The new laborers competed for jobs as rubber carriers and transporters, and by 1890, had gradually pushed the Akan out of these occupations.

Rural Akan communities along the main roads linking the north with the south developed rapidly as a result of increased trade, infrastructural growth, and the arrival of large numbers of strangers. Population statistics from government stations in or near Ashanti and the Colony show the large growth in southern rural areas.[30] The modernization of Ashanti life which had started with the British conquest of Kumasi in 1874 soon faltered due to British uncertainty about the extent of their political authority, about the direction of economic development, and then about the nature of colonial policies. However, this modernization resumed and dramatically increased as the nineteenth century drew to an end.[31] European competition over African territory and resources, as well as the growth of the rubber industry and gold mining, had removed these constraints and forced the British to be more decisive. Inevitably, their actions resulted in more ethnic diversity, economic stratification and political change in southern Gold Coast areas than ever before. The presence of northern migrants in the mines and in the southern villages and towns had a decisive impact on the economy of rural Ashanti. This development exacerbated the new tensions that had developed between administrative personnel and rural communities with the onset of colonialism.

Conquest and Rural Flux

The traditional Akan social structures in the towns, especially in rural areas, changed dramatically after the 1890s. The rural areas not only felt the exploitation of Kumasi, but to this was added the aggressiveness of the new coastal semi-educated, "up-and-coming" commoner stratum. These communities had succumbed to Ashanti control during the 1700s and the early 1800s, but now faced pressure on several levels. Just prior to British conquest of Ashanti, the *akonkofo* (entrepreneurs and traders) and the *abirempon* had found it no longer profitable or advisable to lend money to the Asantehene to finance battles; they preferred to invest in rubber and gold mining.[32] The Asantehene, for his part, attempted to prevent his underlings from investing in coasting financial ventures by creating a company of state traders.[33] Those traders who sent unapproved funds to the coast were often executed. Also sanctioned by the Asantehene were those chiefs whose people resented continual military conscription for war and who threatened revolt. For example, both the Krachis and the Juabins were so angry with Ashanti in 1874 that British intervention was necessary to prevent them from taking revenge upon an already defeated Ashantehene.[34] Such dissention led the Asantehene to make an unsuccessful request for a British resident in Kumasi to keep the peace. The Asantehene also wanted the British to demand the return of rebel chiefs and people who were "leaving him to starve" by denying allegiance.[35]

This was indeed a development, since the military complex of the Ashanti imperial state had been deep and pervasive. Chiefs, captains and even young men did not usually resist military duty, because they received honor and a share of military booty, especially slaves, when campaigns were successful. With Ashanti's defeat by the British, the "youngmen" and commoners (*nkwankwaa*) who no longer had military duties and therefore no role in politics, became noticeably disgruntled. During the late 1870s a few of these persons had attempted to stimulate conflict against neighboring state, and by the 1880s they had turned to rebelling against their own chiefs and the Asantehene.[36] Since nothing was now gained from external wars, these youngmen wanted to farm for a living and, lacking the labor of slaves, needed as much *abusua* or conjugal labor as they could get. They therefore resented the increased attempts of chiefs to conscript them for labor or to tax them excessively.[37] Moreover, they became furious when village and town chiefs accused them of numerous misdeeds in an effort to get revenues in court fines to send to the Asantehene and Kumasi chiefs. To complicate matters, the subordinate chiefs had to raise local taxation and incur stool debts to send money to their superiors; and the burden ultimately fell on their fellow citizens and the *nkwankwaa*. As local taxation grew, rural people often left their homes, fleeing to the coastal protectorate to ensure their livelihoods.[38]

A few British officials wanted to station a resident in Kumasi to maintain order, but others preferred a roving district officer and the stationing of military forces in the smaller towns. The British actually had plans for a native administration in 1878 and 1883,[39] but hesitated to intervene directly in Ashanti's internal disputes. This was ironic given their intervention in the Adanse stool dispute in favor of Nkansa in 1876, following the defeat of Kumasi.[40] Although the British were hesitant to act in such cases, they were impelled by the fact that trade had noticeably declined in the late 1870s following the upheavals in Ashanti, and they wished to restore a more conducive commercial climate. They were also not above hoping that the old rebellious subordinates of Ashanti (such as Gyaman and Sefwi) would successfully challenge their overlord. In any case, the British were certain that few arms would reach the Kumasi rebels, either through Gyaman or the protectorate, and there would then be a war of attrition. Their optimism was based on the success of the Kwahu *akonkofo* (entrepreneurs) in breaking away from Ashanti and gaining control of the eastern kola trade from Akim Abuakwa to Salaga and Yendi in the north.[41] By the 1880s, however, an increasingly powerful Britain felt that "the only road to improvement is to bring the [coastal] natives into immediate contact with natives of the interior."[42] They were certain that only the larger chiefs and the Akwapim traders would object to British penetration, for fear of having to stop their exploitations, and because "many [of their] convenient little practices will have to be discarded."[43]

The reign of Mensa Bonsu (1874–1883) was racked by revolt, and the chaos which followed caused further tensions between the urban areas and the extremely exploited Ashanti hinterland. While most groups north of the Pra River were in revolt, royal factions battled over support for rival candidates for the kingship.[44] During the rather stressful interregnum of 1883–1884, one could note an interesting trend in populist dissidence and disorder developing. Captain Barrow's report on disturbances in Adansi, for example, stated:

> I have been confirmed in the opinion formed at the moment, that these robberies which produced stoppage of the [trade] roads, were the acts of "youngmen"; possessing a little education, absentees from the towns on the coast-line, who had settled themselves in the villages round about, levying blackmail upon the more inoffensive and innocent dwellers in the villages, by representing themselves as armed with some sort of authority from our government, which these simple and unsuspecting villagers believed, and thereupon admitted them to their private meetings, placed implicit confidence in all that they told them, supplying them with food and money in return, and paying the greatest respect to their evil and corrupt counsels. Thus, these villagers were

> often led astray and often into rebellion and hostility with their lawful or properly constituted kings and chiefs..."[45]

Despite the fact that Captain Barrow may have underestimated the deliberateness of the rural population, what was immediately apparent is that coastal commoner elites were using their education and position in order to foment Ashanti rebellion. Less known is that coastal elites made common cause with the peasants who wanted freedom from excessive exploitation. They also supported rural young Ashanti who wanted more political voice in Ashanti affairs, and the *akonkofo* who sought political autonomy so as to invest more freely in their southern rubber and gold mining enterprises. Thus, southern peasants were also tied into social and political developments in the coastal protectorate, while primarily interested in local autonomy.

The changing roles of the *nkwankwaa* had important implications for the period after 1880. Although this group had historically existed, and their leader or chief had the right to represent public opinion in the councils, their traditional power did not include rights to nominate candidates for the stool, nor could they participate directly in affairs of state. The *nkwankwaa*'s attempts to perform such functions after the mid-1800s were often frustrated, because the Asantehene took advantage of his customary right to disband the military companies in order to weaken the organizations to which these "youngmen" belonged. The outcome was that the *nkwankwaa* could not perpetuate and utilize strong *asafo* companies, such as existed in coastal Fanti areas.[46] Nevertheless, the *nkwankwaa* protested the enstoolment of Agyeman Prempeh as Asantehene in 1888, not so much because they hoped to be successful, but as an indication of their continued dissatisfaction.[47] It is clear then, that in the 1870s and 1880s, the rural *nkwankwaa* and the *akonkofo* joined hands in opposition to Ashanti oppression and economic obsoletism. This concerted action waxed and waned, and was especially quiescent during the reign of Kofi Kakari. However, the partnership would not survive the economic onslaught of the twentieth century.

With Prempeh's enstoolment as Asantehene in 1888, the political situation calmed slightly, and the British increased their interest in Ashanti's internal economy. The Ashanti political-economy was still in shambles, but the *akonkofo* still had resources to invest in gold mining and rubber. Having no need for their formal titles, this group spread themselves out across the southern forest zone as entrepreneurs and middlemen. Their presence was decisive for the Gold Coast economy, and the British (cognizant of this fact) saw in the activities of these African entrepreneurs the model for economic penetration and resource procurement. The British merchants had been convinced that economic progress would never really be made until Britain took control of all the territory from the coast to the river Niger.[48] In a secret memorandum to Griffeth, Ferguson stated that the aim of Great Britain should be:

> to interfere with barbarous practices and native customs which put restrictions on interior trade; to render the roads safe for caravans and traders...to civilize the barbarous tribes....to occupy Ashanti; and to confine the French and Germans west of the Comoe and east of the Oti respectively.[49]

Agriculture and Conquest

With conquest, agriculture, which had declined between the 1860s and the 1880s, began to recover. British interest in the rural area was not so much to control land (although mine concessions were now a significant issue and Crown Colony control would come later), but to encourage "forward thinking" Africans to increase agricultural productivity. The British were convinced that, given the fertility of the soil, it was simply lack of incentive which prevented most farmers from producing a salable surplus. According to colonial estimates, no more than five percent of the soil was brought under cultivation in any one year. An agricultural report for 1889 listed plantains, yams and Indian corn as the basis for *fufu* or *kenkey*, which was the main African food. This was supplemented by a plentiful supply of oranges, limes, bananas, pawpaw (introduced by the Portuguese) and pineapples. Nevertheless, the report listed many indigenous plants commonly used by Gold Coasters and those of the interior for herbs, salads and medicines.[50] British disdain for traditional diets and what they considered inefficient cultivation techniques came through quite clearly as they outlined production processes in Ashanti and the Colony.[51]

Pre-conquest Akan agriculture was undertaken by a family group on land (approximately one or two acres) utilizing usufruct rights, usually held in common. Despite a small incidence of private land ownership, most private rights generally involved ownership of trees which a person or his or her forebears had individually planted, and from which the descendant was entitled to claim the fruit. In general, members of a family would select parcels of the land to be utilized for their own needs, limited only by the requirement that they not alienate the land. Use of the land by outsiders, as earlier mentioned, had to be recognized by receiving public *aseda* (a fee of thanks) or tribute in some form.[52]

Shifting cultivation, using slash-and-burn techniques, was the usual way of using land, and in the 1880s the implements used were metal machetes and wooden hoes with imported iron blades. In Fanti areas, fallow periods of three to five years were allowed once a plot had been utilized, with yam requiring the longest fallow. The occupant simply shifted to another field during the interim, relying heavily on the plantains until the new yam crop was harvested. Intercropping of garden vegetables with the main crop (which even the British recognized as ingenious) resulted in considerable productivity of the land. Moreover, these ancillary crops provided shade or support for the young yam vines. Next to plantain, maize was the crop most extensively cultivated, with cassava, peanuts and rice also being used.

Table 3–4 gives quantities and values of Gold Coast rice imports for the years 1880 to 1888.

TABLE 3–4

GOLD COAST RICE IMPORTATION, 1880–1888*
(valued at)

Year	weight	£.	Shilling	Pence
1880	774 cwts**	373	5	11
1881	2,977 cwts	1,423	5	9
1882	2,287 cwts	1,193	15	3
1883	742 cwts	372	3	0
1884	488 cwts	2,801	1	6
1885	9,450 cwts	5,058	15	6
1886	6,767 cwts	3,192	11	9
1887	4,863 cwts	2,387	12	4
1888	8,992 cwts	4,050	11	11

*Ashanti secession conflicts interfered with trade between 1880 and 1883.[54]
**1 cwt (one hundredweight) = 112 pounds gross or 100 pounds net.
Source: Economic Agriculture on the Gold Coast, *Gold Coast Accounts and Papers* #8, 1890–1891, v. 55.

Indigenous rice and *acha* or "hungry rice" were grown in northern Ghana, but its quantity was inadequate. Because of the limitations of the rice-growing zones within Ghana, southern rice was grown principally in the Ho area of the Volta District.[53] Because of its quality and quantity, it captured colonial attention in the 1880s as a possible subsistence crop. While earlier much of Gold Coast rice had been imported from the Senegal and Sierra Leone area, it was hoped that locally grown rice would begin to obviate the importation of grain.

There were several economic reasons as to why the British wished to diversify agriculture in the Gold Coast, but it is doubtful that they understood the effect of this decision on the lives and social organization of the people. The British complained that the practice of permitting oil palm fruit to fall and rot so as to cut the cost of transportation to the coast resulted in the loss of revenue. They noted that Liberian coffee had been introduced into Nzima and Akwapim, and hoped that it would catch on among the people. As earlier mentioned, colonial officials had introduced cotton a number of times, but southern peasants still resisted it. Any hope that they had for processing commercial products such as palm oil, coconut oil, castor oil and pineapple fibers so as to increase exports had to wait for the future.[55] Meanwhile, they concentrated on rubber, timber, and cocoa products which did, in fact, bring major revenues into the Gold Coast between 1890 and 1920. The Economic Report of 1889 refuted some of the earlier arguments that if Gold Coast agriculture was to prosper, external (metropolitan) investment was necessary. Governor Griffeth, for example, was concerned to demonstrate that Gold Coast agriculture could generate its own revenue without reliance on metropolitan stipends and investors. In any case, it was clear that between 1881 and 1889, Gold Coast agricultural exports of such products as wood, gum copal, palm kernels and palm oil brought in considerable revenue. Table 3–5 gives values of agricultural exports from the Gold coast for the years 1882–1889.

TABLE 3-5

VALUE OF AGRICULTURAL EXPORTS FROM THE GOLD COAST COLONY, 1882–1889*

Articles	1882 £ s. d. **	1883 £ s. d.	1884 £ s. d.	1885 £ s. d.	1886 £ s. d.	1887 £ s. d.	1888 £ s. d.
Camwood	1,651.18.8	1,680.15.11	354.7.3	283.19.3	590.13.3	576.2.6	193.3.10
Coprah	292.4.0	1,277.13.11	1,604.7.0	730.0.0	696.11.2	1,366.14.4	1,087.5.6
Guinea grains	5,655.13.3	1,645.0.8	1,466.19.4	1,092.14.6	1,429.17.11	670.0.0	1,108.17.7
Kola nuts	123.16.6	15.0.0	632.2.0	429.8.4	758.0.6	1,009.16.6	1,549.5.2
Gum copal	7,860.15.6	539.15.3	902.18.3	1,472.14.7	918.5.6	1,109.0.4	1,310.9.10
Palm kernels	50,316.15.5	61,542.19.3	76,530.0.0	52,823.13.9	47,829.15.11	41,613.2.8	68,525.0.2
Palm oil	178,508.9.2	208,721.4.8	282,398.0.0	284,391.6.4	115,978.15.3	143,395.4.8	150,361.3.11
Rubber	0.12.6	2,371.12.0	13,619.17.7	30,234.15.1	69,911.2.8	62,430.1.8	38,048.8.9

**Source*: Economic Agriculture on the Gold Coast, 1889, *Accounts & Papers* (8), 1890–91, vol. 55, No. 110, Schedule A, pp. 40–41.
** pound, shilling, pence.

What put a brake on agricultural development and trade after 1889 was conflict between the British and the Ashanti. The British were deeply concerned over the safety of travelers and traders on the roads, and this increased their hostility towards Ashanti. King Prempeh was, of course, attempting to regain control over northern areas and markets,[56] and thus preyed on traders and travelers. To halt these depredations and to protect the colony, the British moved quickly to disarm Ashanti, exile Prempeh and other close royals, to demand the golden stool and to station a resident at Kumasi. While these actions prevented further hostilities between northwest chiefs and Kumasi, prevented the French and the Germans from infringing on Gold Coast and Ashanti territory, and made travel safe, agricultural development stood still or even declined. Little trade made its way down to the coast.

Much of the agricultural decline between 1896 and 1901 was caused by the intensity of rural upheaval due to the complex tripartite relationship of the British, the Ashanti loyalists, and the *nkwankwaa* and their chiefs. Many Banda, Wenchi and Gaman chiefs and *nkwankwaa* hoped that the British victory would stop the Ashanti from controlling and exploiting them. They were disappointed that, despite their 1889 treaties with the British, Ashanti had pooled its resources to fight them as well as the British during the Yaa Asantewaa War of 1900. These peripheral areas of Ashanti were often deeply divided. In some cases significant groups of rebels disagreed with the anti-Ashanti faction and fought against the British themselves. As the battle for control of the interior moved northwestward into Brong-Ashanti near Berekum and the French territories, the British struck deals with rebel chiefs. These chiefs and their people could escape punishment if they encouraged rebel young men to surrender, and if they helped track down military refugees in the Ahafo forest.[57] Many young men cooperated, but never returned to their natal villages because of fear of reprisals. Instead, they settled down and became citizens in other parts of the Brong and Ahafo districts.

The impact of the "Ashanti Rising of 1900-1901" (as the British called it) and other related hostilities on agriculture and trade in Brong-Ashanti and Ahafo areas was catastrophic. These had been major food-, timber-, rubber- and fiber-producing areas. Yet, the depopulation related to war, and the neglected agricultural tasks took their toll on local welfare, social interaction/and even on exports of the Gold Coast. Many families had lost significant male labor needed for farming. Some areas had experienced whole population shifts to avoid the hostilities. As late as the 1930s and 1940s some of the surviving refugees (particularly elderly women) were still trickling back into their home towns from more southern areas.[58]

In northwest Ashanti, the economic difficulties were compounded by Samory's battles against the French in the Ivory Coast border area. There was looting and burning all the way from Dormaa to Nkoranza, and local markets declined because of insecure roads and the absence of produce. Criticizing the war-indemnity tax levied against Gyaman in 1901, Captain Soden stated:

> A tax of £950 per annum is out of proportion to the wealth of British Jaman as it stands at present...The majority of the natives being merely farmers who grow little more than feeds and clothes them; there being no gold, rubber, kola or paying produce in the country, except a little down about Bedunkra and a small amount of gold dust found toward the French frontier...and the greater

> part of the country is only beginning to recover from the depredations of Samory, who depleted the farming part of the country of even seed.[59]

The British sought to revive the economy of the interior after the Yaa Asantewaa war in 1901 by giving them their first local administrative machinery. These areas were also now incorporated into the Gold Coast with a colonial administration as well. However, many of the northwest districts did not easily accept the control of district commissioners over such things as agriculture and marketing. When Sunyani was declared an administrative center

> ...the D.C. set in motion a system under which each large town supplied the Sunyani market with produce on a particular day. The system never worked well and resulted in higher foodstuff prices in Sunyani than in outlying villages. When any town failed to fulfill its duty for the assigned day, the D.C. warned its chief directly, and if his negligence continued, the D.C. would notify Berekum of an impending fine for improper administration of towns under its control.[60]

By 1904–1906, the local economy was reviving somewhat, and this was reflected in the statistics on trade and caravan tolls along the old northern routes. Throughout Ashanti and Brong kola-producing areas, traders had no problem selling their products. In fact, demand appeared to have exceeded the supply. Nearly every village had a small farm for cultivating tobacco, and some of this also was traded towards the north. However, insufficiency of supply and tastes for European tobacco kept imports high, even in these areas.[61] The caravan tolls on the monthly trade through the northwest Odumasi/Sunyani route, for example, were substantial during peak seasons, as shown in Table 3–6.

The construction of a new road through Sunyani, Tanoso and Abesim in 1907 sparked competition between local chiefs for control of revenue and increased trade for their villages. Chiefs were instructed by the district commissioner to provide labor gangs for construction of major roads, but fears that head chiefs would gain more from revenues collected led lesser chiefs to cut competing roads. In one case, the town of Fiapre moved to a new location so that it could be along the main road.[62]

By 1906 interior districts such as Nkoranza, Wenchi, Techiman and Sunyani were swiftly being incorporated into the larger Gold Coast economy. Rubber processing was flourishing here, while it was declining in the areas more to the south. Moreover, some collectors were now using the newer techniques of processing rubber (similar to those used at Bonduku in the Ivory Coast) which yielded a purer product and brought three to four francs per pound.[63] The reports of the district commissioner indicate that most of this product was being collected and sold in Kumasi, but some collectors around Sekwa in the east sent their rubber to the trans-Volta German territory.[64]

TABLE 3–6

CARAVAN TOLLS FOR 1907
(Sunyani District)

Month	£	Shilling	Pence
Jan	341.	10.	0
Feb	475.	4.	9
Mar	241.	11.	6
Apr	82.	8.	6
May	68.	4.	6

*District Administration Records, Sunyani 1907–1915, #228/07.

The British increased their concern for agricultural diversification. In 1904, the district commissioners advised chiefs to introduce cotton and cocoa, but some chiefs were skeptical about the viability of these crops, saying that it would take six to ten days to transport the product to Kumasi. They preferred to collect rubber, since sixty pounds could be gathered with little labor in twenty-five days, and for that weight they would receive £4.15.0 compensation. The district commissioner in Sunyani noted that the low price of cotton induced few people to grow it.

It is quite clear that the major considerations of the Gold Coast producers were to secure the *maximum profit in agricultural production while maintaining the same basic organization of labor and resources*. Slave labor was now no longer available for exploitation, and the farmers had to adapt to this fact. But there is very little evidence that the administrators understood the importance of the labor factor in the indigenous response to the crops they pushed. This would later also be true of the cocoa industry. Initial labor needs for cocoa facilitated peasant cultivation, and this crop was thriving in Akwapim and the central region while beginning to penetrate into Ahafo. Large-scale planting of cocoa in Brong areas, however, could not begin until after the introduction of lorry transportation after World War I.

The Emerging Social Order

The rigid social status and authority systems of the Ashanti state collapsed between 1874 and 1918. The new emphasis on the rural economy (particularly the land and its resources) as the source of state stability had started to raise the status of the rural population from that of unfree, dependent or servile persons. This social dynamic was primarily occurring in the villages and small towns, rather than in the capital Kumasi. Certainly Britain's decapitation of the Ashanti

Empire facilitated these developments. British exile of Asantehene Prempeh and a number of Kumasi royals to the Seychelles in 1896[65] not only broke the hold of the empire over politics and economics, but also stimulated innovation among rural chiefs and people. However, other major factors, such as the pervasiveness of cash and economic flexibility, also increased the confidence of rural folk.

One major factor was that personal mobility was greater than before. Former slaves could now become full-fledged members of rural communities. In the past, their foreign origin and their lack of membership in an Akan *abusua* prevented Muslim male slaves from making claims to resources such as land.[66] Now that the traditional state had been superseded by the colonial one, even local chiefs (for reasons which shall be later elaborated) were disposed to be more liberal in determining who were "citizens" and thus capable of making claims on the polity. Throughout Ashanti, former male slaves often moved to large towns such as Kumasi and became members of growing Muslim trading populations. Those few who remained in central Ashanti area villages remained somewhat marginal until considerably later. Although political Ashanti traditions prohibit revealing the background of citizens, it was nevertheless easy to hear whispered references to *donkor* status of rural Muslim cultivators. They were still prohibited from holding traditional appointed or inherited offices, and until the new local government ordinances in the 1950s, seldom held public positions of authority. This pattern was more true for central Ashanti than for northwest Brong-Ashanti, Gyaman and Gonja. In the northwestern areas where trading populations such as Muslim Wangaras and Ligbys from the neighboring Ivory Coast had penetrated into local communities, a cultural synthesis took place, and there was greater ethnic and social flexibility.[67]

Ordinary Akan who had been *nkoa* (subjects) of a chief, royal, or person of note, also profited from the greater freedom and economic mobility after 1896. Wilks (1975) and Arhin (1983) have argued that every Akan owed allegiance to a higher authority, and were therefore subjects of some stool or person. Rural producers, especially, had been constantly reminded that they owed labor, taxation, military conscription, tribute or gold to their superiors in return for access to the land and protection. Attempts to resist economic subordination prior to conquest often consisted of such things as washing for gold, fishing or snail catching in streams and forests without sending a portion in tribute to any chief or overlord.

With economic recovery and the cessation of hostilities, farmers took a new attitude toward the land as well as work in general. They made shrewd judgments about the profitability of growing one crop as opposed to another, given their available labor force. They also found other opportunities to earn cash. Whereas craftspersons and farmers might before have been distinct categories of individuals, these activities now began to be merged in the same individuals within rural areas. Weaving, brewing drinks, sewing and tailoring, baking and marketing were some of the rural occupations which brought additional incomes and facilitated a more modern life-style. Other farmers also worked as part-time laborers in the emerging administrative towns, on the construction of roads and post offices. Nevertheless, most farmers were still not affluent, and constantly attempted to resist excessive taxation by their chiefs.

The relationship of chiefs to their people was in full transition. Having resented the exactions of some chiefs during the late 1800s, many persons remained wary of economic claims by chiefs and elders. Chiefs who incurred stool debts during the war period of 1889–1901 often had difficulty raising taxes to pay them, since people were now sensitive to the issue of exploitation. People also resented paying for the personal debts of chiefs (funeral costs, education for children), which were often presented as stool debts. According to the Asantehene:

> In the olden days [when] stool subjects were asked to pay levy to help their stools, they did pay the old levy heartily and without questioning as to why they should pay the levy and as to what purpose it was being put; but today the subjects have become enlightened and as a result they wish to know how a stool debt arose, and if [sic] satisfied with the explanation before they would agree to levy being imposed for the purpose of liquidating such debt.[68]

Interestingly enough, the issue of stool debts appeared not in the Kumasi or Mampong districts, but in the more outlying districts. The reason was that the chiefs competed for the land which was unclaimed so as to secure it for future grants to their people.[69] Some chiefs and elders conspired to snare prosperous incumbents to take the stool, while planning future intrigues to remove these persons from office, leaving the stool in possession of the property of the deposed. Since the selection of chiefs was now often based on wealth or influence rather than as formerly on lineage, the status of chiefs declined considerably in rural communities.

Stratification based on modern education (and often religion) as well as cash, became important variables in achieving status for both chiefs and rural producers. Missionary schools had initially been resisted by Ashanti royalty because they saw missionaries and administrators as purveyors of new and alien ideas which challenged respect for ancestral and political authority and brought conflict into the community.[70] One chief's view on the divisiveness of Christians in the 1870s still remained relevant:

> Christians teach that slaves should be freed. Slaves become stubborn and do not obey their masters. Then everything changes. Slaves rob and kill traders.

> No one works the farms. The chiefs have no servants...The Asante chiefs and people say no to the Christians and to whites.[71]

Despite Ashanti resistance, following conquest the Basel missionaries were able to establish sixteen schools in Ashanti, and the Wesleyans established seven schools.[72] Sometimes conversion and literacy divided traditional communities,[73] but this tension tended to lessen over time. As the Wesleyan and Presbyterian schools penetrated into larger inland towns in the post-World War I period, chiefs as well as farmers of respectable means could afford to send their children to school. While still suspicious of missionaries, chiefs now used privately owned cash to pay for schooling of children. They also sought to ensure that their nephews who might succeed them should also be literate. This was important because the increasingly influential district commissioners favored literate stool candidates, believing that these were more amenable to the colonial approach.

Between 1900 and 1918, educated members of an *abusua* were sometimes resented by their own families, but there is much evidence that many of these persons found work in administrative or business positions in their villages and nearby towns.[75] From oral accounts in the Nkoranza/Sunyani areas, it appears that chiefs who could best afford to do without the labor of their children were most adamant about education. Farmers were faced with a critical choice of education for one child over another, since all could not go to school. In 1973, an 84-year-old elder recalls:

> in 1913 a European came around to gather up all the people who wanted to go to school...so I went. I was a man at that time about 24 years old. I was living with the schoolmaster at Sunyani. I used to visit the family at Fiapre but couldn't get on well. Once when I came home, my mother sat me down to eat fufu, but I couldn't and she became annoyed and slapped me saying that because of education I no longer eat their food. They were against my going to school...but when I became ill they sent me to my father near Kumasi. I continued my schooling at the Methodist school, and when finished I took a clerical job with what has now become UAC. Later, I came back to Fiapre and married.[76]

Education was important for mobility among commoners and royalty alike. It was educated males and females who were usually chosen as elders and queen mothers, or even chiefs. Nevertheless, and despite the lack of clear-cut data, it appears that not very many women in the Ashanti region were educated until considerably later. The early girls's high schools established by the missionaries aimed to turn out "ladies."[77] There is, however, much evidence that some urban coastal females took advantage of the new opportunities for education, business and even marriage into upwardly mobile families. Women in fishing and rural marketing communities along the coast were reportedly not as fortunate. They experienced more difficulties as the economy changed and greater financial responsibilities were placed upon them.[78]

Table 3–7 gives the denominational (and nondenominational) breakdown of education in Ashanti for the years 1905–1914.

TABLE 3–7

EDUCATION IN ASHANTI, 1905–1914

Year		Wesleyan	Basel	R.Catholic	Gov't	Ch.Eng.	Zion Mission	Total	Gold Coast
1905	# Schools	10	--	--	--	--	--	17	139
	Attendance	220	210	--	--	--	--		
1906	# sch.	6	12	--	--	--	--	18	146
	att.	235	215	--	--	--	--		
1907	# sch.	7	13	--	--	--	--	20	148
	att.	326	252	--	--	--	--		
1908	# sch.	8	22	--	--	--	--	30	152
	att.	499	513	--	--	--	--		
1909	# sch.	8	26	1	1			36	162
	att.	441	547	20	287				
1910	# sch.	10	26	2–3	1			39?	163
	att.	--	--	?	203–266				
1911	# sch.	10	28	?	1			39	161
	att.	503*	683	110	224–221				
1912	# sch.	18	26	3	1			48	159
	att.	740	850/658	180	235				
1913	# sch.	8**	24	2**	2			36	155
	att.	526	730	186*	384*				
1914	# sch.	11**	26	2	3†	1	1††	44	160
	att.	585	760	222	465	100	76	2,208	

Most of these schools were "non-assisted" by government funds because of low enrollments. Source: Annual Commissioners Reports for Ashanti. See endnote [74].

*figures given indicate number on the roll, not average attendance.

**refers to day schools, excluding Sunday schools.

†New Girls' schools.

††Sunday school.

Akan women did not appear to be making significant gains in this transitional period. Admittedly, the question of the general status of females in Ashanti was and still is unclear. From pieces of information about rural Ashanti and Brong women based on colonial accounts, native authority records and oral accounts of the period between 1900 and 1948, it appears that since the mid-1600s Akan women had been losing their traditional political/public status. Except for the queen mother or *obaa-panin* (matriarch of the family), women now occupied fewer public positions. While the prohibition on domestic slavery and pawning after Ashanti's defeat did much to release many Akan women from involuntary domestic and marital obligations, this did not improve women's overall status.

The form of marriage was one of the more significant relationships that was changed. While traditionally Akan women and their lineages had the right of control over any children produced (with or without marriage), these women were often given in marriage without their consent or knowledge. The putative husband might give gifts during a woman's early years, and these would be used to offset the expenses of her upbringing. Abrogation of the marriage contract meant returning many of the presents—something that most peasant families found difficult to do. Therefore, most women accepted arranged marriages. Those who were not well disposed towards their husbands opted for separate residences or divorce following the birth of one or two children if economic obligations to the husband were not prohibitive. They then felt free to marry again according to individual desires. In any case, the children belonged to a women's matrilineage, although they bore the *ntoro* or spirit identification of the father's group.[79] One of the things which marriage did was to subordinate the father's spiritual claims over his daughter to the spiritual claims exerted by her husband based on marriage. Marriage also meant that a woman was obligated to contribute subsistence labor to her husband in order to help maintain any children they begot. While remaining a member of her matrilineage, a woman was also a valuable resource to her husband because of the labor she performed.

What became an even more significant index of the worth of all women, both free and servile in the late 1800s, was their ability to reproduce. With increased British vigilance against slavery, male polygyny and enhanced reproductive potential became the means of creating a sufficient labor force. The Akan forest area had historically been one in which low population/land ratios made labor an important economic desideratum.[80] By 1900, the search for wives to bear children was intensified. As usual, elderly or high status men were able to appropriate most women, thereby forcing younger men to remain unmarried well into their forties. One elderly man in the Sunyani/Techiman area explaining why he married late, recalled:

> I had been serving my father. And in addition, women were scarce. Sometimes three men would meet to try and get one woman, and the woman has to decide. Sometimes, even if a woman is already pregnant, a man will go to her and ask that if it is a baby girl, would she please give it to him. And when the girl grows up, even if she doesn't like the man she will be forced to marry him.[81]

The records show that the search for reproductive females which brought polygyny both repelled and infuriated the British. They considered polygyny equivalent to domestic slavery, and therefore a brake to economic development. They would be proven wrong in their view that polygyny hindered economic progress,[82] since it would later be shown that cocoa farmers benefited from multiple spouses.[83] But in the early 1900s, men used all sorts of methods to acquire wives. Recourse was made to concubinage and pawning, although such unions were not as prestigious as unions with free women.[84] On the other hand, many men preferred low-status unions such as the pawn wife, because they had complete control over their wives and offspring—except in the unlikely event that the woman's family could redeem her and their children.

In the early stages of cocoa production, the sizable family labor force under male control would prove instrumental to agricultural success. Individual peasant (as opposed to lineage) control of farms was on the increase between 1890 and 1910, but women were seldom a part of the ownership and controlling group. Men earlier employed as palm oil or rubber transporters and processors now started to acquire land in their own names as opposed to that of their lineages. Lineages would only control such property upon their deaths. Women, on the other hand, maintained traditional control of subsistence plots on lineage or husbands' land, but had not yet begun to own cocoa farms. Naturally some rural women did accumulate wealth in the form of jewelry, gold, cloth or slaves, which they traditionally passed on to their female offspring.[85] However, on the whole, men rather than women appeared to have been breaking free of lineage economic control and, using their resources and labor, they managed to acquire more personal property. In Brong-Ashanti and Ahafo, many of these men started to grow maize, while in the Volta areas, rice farming was on the increase. It was not until the post-1920s period that rural women's economic status was appreciably enhanced by their ability to own farms and cultivate cash crops on their own behalf.[86]

The emerging social order in the early 1900s was that of a colonially controlled and male-focused society in which power and authority were more diffused rather than in the hands of the traditional royalty, bureaucrats and economic elites as in the past. Yet, Akan society still retained the core of its social hierarchy and traditional values. British conquest and rural transformation had shaken the system, but had not destroyed it. Upwardly mobile peasants, *nkwankwaa* ("youngmen"), former *nnonkofo* and *nkramo* (slaves and Muslims), still recognized and valued the status hierarchy. True, the conquest and eclipse of the Ashanti state and bureaucracy ended the status of the *batafo* and the *obirempon*, but the concept survived in that even royalty and commoners granted respect to the *okonkofo* (entrepreneurs). Importantly, Ashanti traditions sometimes refer to the period around 1900 as when "money made the chief."[87] Economic success and wealth earned status in the eyes of the rural community;

and people began to jokingly call the strivers "chief" or *obirempomma*, and often selected such nouveau-riche men as real chiefs. The convergence of economic accumulation and public recognition was also seen in the high esteem in which the *sikafo* (wealthy) were held by the colonial administration. Given the new social mobility, chiefs were divided on whether there were social or political advantages to be gained from the return of Asantehene Prempeh. Many rural Gold Coasters still revered the exiled Asantehene and respected the office of chief, but they were increasingly drawn to recognize those who had achieved modern status with its acoutrements. Persons with money and/or education became the "big-men," even in rural villages. Now even chiefs and royalty attempted to secure their traditional positions by adding modern attributes.

Cocoa, Cash and Migration Patterns

Starting around 1896, the cocoa industry provided the majority of Gold Coast farmers with the first opportunity to gain significant cash incomes. The cocoa industry would also stimulate massive migrations, alter male-female relations, complicate property relationships, and modify deeply entrenched patterns of social stratification. But in the 1890s and the early 1900s, cocoa was only viewed by the British as the ideal Gold Coast export crop when the peasants adopted its cultivation. The cocoa beans had allegedly been brought in by a Ghanaian, Tetteh Quashie, when he returned from working in Fernando Po in 1878. A district officer sent a note to the governor in 1890 stating that Quashie had a successful cocoa plantation of about 300 trees in Mampong, Akwapim. Surrounding farmers were so impressed that they purchased seeds from him, until the Aburi Botanical Gardens took over production of cocoa seedlings in 1890.[88] The economic report of 1889 stated:

> Cocoa is worthy of every attention. Attempts on a small scale have been made to introduce it into the country, but no information is obtainable as to the results. The culture is cheap, and the preparation simple, so that it should receive the attention of the small cultivators. Its only disadvantage is the length of time (five years) before a crop is obtainable, but with so much unoccupied land the growers of cocoa can fill in the time by the cultivation of other crops in the intervals between the necessary handlings of the young trees.[89]

By 1905, the difficulty of road transport caused the British to modify their initial optimism concerning cocoa. Interestingly enough, the transportation problem would be easily solved. The problem of land and labor availability would become critical variables in the Gold Coast's experience with cocoa. In

1895 cocoa cultivation had caught on throughout southern Ghana, with Krobo, Shai and Akwapim farmers in particular seeking larger areas for cultivation. The limited amount of available land in the Akwapim area near where cocoa had first been introduced stimulated the macro-movements of farmers from here into central Ashanti and the eastern areas. Polly Hill's study of the southern migrant cocoa farmers describes the speed of this process and its impact on traditional labor categories and land relations. Those farmers who were patrilineal formed companies to purchase land in large blocs and to divide it into individual farms, whose component plots would be worked by individual wives of the farmer. On the other hand, Akwapim farmers with matrilineal kinship systems often migrated into Akan areas as individuals or as *abusua* units, paid tribute to the chief for the land and settled wives or a wife to manage and work it. Both types of farmers attempted to acquire second or additional farms if labor and resources allowed.[90] In the southern areas, new migrant towns sprang up with the inhabitants having allegiances to their original chiefs, but more importantly, paying tribute to the local chief. Thus, by the 1900s, land in the southern area had become a far more valuable commodity because of cocoa than it had been through gold-mining prospects. Coastal Fanti males took on cocoa farming and migrated north into Ahafo seeking land. By 1903, eastern and southern farmers had spread to Kumasi, and by 1906 cocoa, but not migrants, had reached Sunyani in Brong-Ahafo.

Very early, cocoa began to have an important impact on its cultivators, the areas in which they lived, and the social and political economy of the Gold Coast. First, it caused ethnic diversity through cocoa-induced migrations. Second, cocoa cultivation increased the contact of rural farmers with coastal areas, and government agencies which distributed seedlings, fertilizers and sprays. Third, it increased the need for farmers to control a sizable work force (familial), and it encouraged wage-labor migration into the forest zone. Fourth, it contributed to the growth and dispersal of new villages and towns within rural areas. Hill's earlier work provides an interesting and important view of migrant cocoa-farming areas; nevertheless, the picture may be radically different for those districts and communities in which land had been plentiful, and from which *farmers did not have to migrate as strangers in order to engage in cocoa farming*. In non-migrant farming areas, where only micro-movements for cocoa production were typical, pre-existing social dynamics and local orientations or regionalism could become intensified. As we will see, the way in which cocoa was adopted and became important in many areas of Ghana provides clues to the *ultimate clash between local and broader interests within the Gold Coast*, and will help us understand the chaos which ultimately developed in the cocoa industry.

Prior to cocoa cultivation in Brong-Ashanti areas, land was used primarily for food crops for family consumption, with some occasional production for local markets (kola, yams, etc.). Without any need for larger plots of land, many villages did not know exactly where the land of their stool ended. If, for example, citizens approached chiefs for more land, the chiefs often indicated the starting point and the direction the farm should go, with little regard for where it should end. The extent of cultivation was dictated by individual needs, and the land of a stool technically ended at the furthermost extent of the farms or hunting territory which its people used. Since there were no significant numbers of strangers settled in many Nkoranza, Techiman, Dormaa, Odumasi and Nsuatre towns prior to 1900, the problem of how strangers were to pay tribute for land did not arise as a significant issue until after cocoa cultivation.

Chiefs and elders in the Sunyani District had already begun to grow cocoa by 1906.[91] As commoners entered the industry, this seemed to generate new spatial and ecological relationships. Cocoa as a cash crop required large tracts of forest land; since it was a "heavy feeding crop" (quickly using up the fertility of the soil), food could only be intercropped on cocoa land for approximately five years, or until the cocoa trees matured. The fresh tracts of land were needed for subsistence farming. Since small villages were traditionally three to six miles apart, there was ample space for the requirements of subsistence farming, but insufficient for the larger cocoa farms. Thus, during the early 1900s, small satellite villages would appeal to the parent village for cocoa land, and these requests were generally honored without demands for tribute.

As the cash economy penetrated into the countryside, even the lower political officials interpreted their positions in terms of the economic advantages to be gained from the land which they controlled. Prospective cocoa farmers found that though they paid allegiance to the same *Odikro* or *Ohene*, if they sought land outside of their own villages, they had to pay cocoa tribute to the subchief who controlled the land. Naturally, protests arose, and litigation over cocoa land filled the district commissioners' and the native authority courts. Records from 1938 onwards show that people in Fiapre, a small town outside Sunyani, had complained to the district commissioner of having to pay both communal debts and tribute:

> 1. That we see no reason why a person of Fiapre who tills Sunyani stool land should have to pay a tribute.
> 2. That we know that though we live at Fiapre, but we [and Sunyani] have one head who is Nana Awua of Odumasi since old and up to the present we have one court and treasury.
> 3. That we remember definitely that some time past, when there arose Sunyani stool land case with Nana Appraku of Odumasi #1, the predecessor of Nana Awua led the case and we subjects of Fiapre backed him, and the debts thereabout we paid to secure land for our benefit of our common use of the land.

> Sir, that if we were foreigners or should pay tributes after the land is secured, we would not have backed the said predecessor of Nana Awua and incur debts of about £300 for Fiapre only.
> Sir, on the strength of the above explanations, we see that Fiapre, Odumasi and Sunyani are one and a person from Fiapre should be free from paying any tribute to Sunyani stool.[92]

Tribute from cocoa land was a source of much conflict from 1910 through the 1940s. In the above-cited case, and in many others, the district ruled that tributes should be paid, but they also attempted to clarify the relationship between payment for the use of cocoa land and of village/town debts. One district commissioner ruled that:

> Any person who pays cocoa tribute to the land owner does not contribute towards the payment of any debt incurred by the stool on while land he farms. Some stools treat strangers farming on their land as subjects, and make them enjoy the same privileges as the stool subjects enjoy, and share equally with the stool subjects any debt incurred by the stool on whose land they farm.[93]

There were few true strangers (those from another region or country) in this western Brong area. Most newcomers were in some way related to the local people in the area in which they farmed.[94] A complicating factor was that some of these local people had been Ashanti migrants from other Brong-Ashanti areas between 1700 and the mid-1800s, but they were now almost indistinguishable from the majority. This situation appeared to differ considerably from the Ahafo area, where stranger farmers from Kumasi were settling and purchasing or renting land by 1902, and where by 1906 a few cocoa farms were flourishing.[95] In fact, cocoa land became such a hot commodity in Ahafo, the distinctions between land-rentals and tributes were blurring, as chiefs tried to establish the most lucrative returns from stranger farmers.[96] Nevertheless, the economic importance of cocoa land encouraged even the Brong chiefs to begin to make subtle distinctions between stranger and citizen. With the rush into cocoa farming in the 1920s in the Sunyani district, many of the accessible lands along the main roads had been taken, so that in the 1930s and 1940s, many of those considered strangers were simply Brongs who obtained land from chiefs outside their natal villages.

By the 1930s, small farming communities consisting of migrant populations complete with their own chiefs and elders began to appear in the deeper, more inaccessible cocoa areas of the Sunyani district. Often, each so-called stranger farmer made contracts with the landowners separately, negotiating the amount of tribute to be paid. In border areas, some stranger communities had contracts with several chiefs, but the tributes were seldom substantial. However, as more local people expanded their cocoa farms and used up accessible land, the stranger-farming communities were squeezed for higher tribute payments. By 1940, the district commissioner's court was filled with complaints from stranger farmers against landowners who violated their original contracts. Especially noteworthy was the case of a group of southern strangers who paid £22.10 as *aseda* (fee of thanks) to the *Chiraahene* for a cocoa farm in the 1930s, and signed an agreement to pay £39.5.6d yearly "sheep" tribute; for the maize farm they agreed to pay tribute of 30 shillings per year. But in 1947, the *Chiraahene* demanded £100.17.6d for the cocoa farm, and for the maize farm he insisted on a one-third *abusa* share rather than the originally agreed amount.[97] While one could argue that such rates were still lower than tributes in Ahafo, they represented a hardship for the Sunyani stranger farming community.

As cocoa farms expanded, so also did the need for labor that could not be provided by the extended family or the lineage. The occasional wage labor from the north often limited to mining and trade activities before 1920 now proved insufficient. With increasing demand, people such as Dagarti, Grunshi, Mossi and other northerners, driven by the need to pay colonial taxes,[98] flocked into the forest zone. This meant that the coastal zone experienced a labor shortage, and increasingly relied upon imported labor. This development served as an index of the prosperity of the cocoa and of the manner in which both the forest and the northern zones were incorporated into the world economy.

Meanwhile, in "cocoa country," the traditional *abusa* labor category was increasingly being utilized for cocoa labor relationships. The migrant workers took major responsibility for the cocoa farm, tending it while the trees were young, and receiving one-third of the cocoa crop when it was harvested. Housed on the farm, the *abusa* workers were relatively privileged in that they were supplied with land upon which to raise their own subsistence crops, and often sold their produce in local markets. Later, as the farms matured, farmers employed *nkotokuano* laborers for harvest (or transformed *abusa* workers into this category). These people were paid a set sum for each load of cocoa harvested.[99] Daily workers were also employed seasonally, to weed or pluck the cocoa, or wives and children provided seasonal labor. What is worth noting, however, is that although cocoa farmers farther south were using paid labor in the early 1900s, it was not until about the 1920s that paid labor in cocoa became the norm in Sunyani, Techiman, Odumasi, Nkoransa, Nsuatre and Dormaa.

Rural developments in northwest Ashanti both gave rise to and were spurred by the growth of large towns. Sunyani, for example, was transformed from a small colonial administrative center in 1906 to a commercial center and the hub of a cocoa-transport system. The influx of Europeans and other merchants greatly increased the economic potential of the area, and with it came an increased demand for northern labor. Garrison soldiers were also needed, and these northerners who had previous experience in the colonial militia were recruited.[100] The establishment of a police force and a court system attracted local males. Laborers of all types were needed for transporting and stocking goods, working for small timber concerns, driving trucks for transporting cocoa, and working as night watchmen. Educated men found employment as clerks for European buying firms. All of these persons needed food, causing an increase in the numbers of persons supplying the Sunyani market, and Sunyani came to compete with other market centers such as Techiman and Nkoranza.

Between 1911 and World War II, the population of villages and associated towns in this northwest Brong-Ashanti and cocoa belt rose. Northerners who formerly passed through Sunyani bound for jobs in Kumasi now often settled down to work. The demographic data indicate that a phenomenal growth took place in Sunyani and Berekum. This reflected the towns' normal growth compounded by the increase of administrative and commercial staffs related to cocoa production.

The Sunyani *zongo*, a community which housed most of these northern immigrants and migrants, also grew significantly between 1920 and 1950. Problems often arose between the *zongo* and local people. Faced with this situation, the Sunyani chief and elders in 1927 suggested to the district commissioner that:

> They be allowed to try small and family cases and receive a small fee, as they have no tribunal and there are many strangers and workmen in town who bring their complaints.[101]

Besides the concern for secure town institutions which would preserve law and order, this was also a subtle attempt to assume greater control over the migrant populations in their midst. A tribunal was granted and functioned for a period of time, but native versus stranger conflicts persisted and increased.

Some of those with whom northern laborers had problems were relatively powerful royals or big cocoa farmers. Common cases involved the cocoa farm owner's refusal to pay *abusa* laborers the one-third share if harvests were not good; or landowners who cheated contract workers out of the original sum agreed upon. There was also an interesting case of a Brong farmer who, after pledging indebted cocoa farms to a wealthy northerner to obtain a loan, tried to forcefully reclaim the farms without repaying the loan.[102] A diverse and expanding northern community found itself locked into a situation where their leaders and *zongo* chiefs tried to control them, while southerners attempted the same. Thus, it was not surprising that by the 1940s, there was a backlash. Northern migrants took more complaints over jobs and money to the district commissioner rather than to their own headmen and chiefs, even when only fellow northerners were involved. Finally, the Labor Department, which was established in

Sunyani in the 1940s, took many of these complaints related to cocoa production out of the hands of the district commissioners and the traditional courts.

Table 3–8 gives the 1928 district populations and density for the districts of Western Province Ashanti. Table 3–9 gives populations for the years of 1931, 1948, 1960 and 1970.

TABLE 3–8

DISTRICT POPULATIONS OF WESTERN PROVINCE ASHANTI—1928

District	Area (square miles)	Population	Density
Kintampo	5,020	28,782	5.73
Wenchi	2,140	39,030	18.24
Sunyani	2,030	36,672	18.06
Goaso, Ah	1,900	9,256	4.87
	24,560	406,193	16.53

*Based on Gold Coast Handbook, 1928.

TABLE 3–9

POPULATION WESTERN PROVINCE ASHANTI AND BRONG-ASHANTI TOWNS*

Town	1931	1948	1960	1970
Berekum	1,797	5,386	11,148	14,420
Chiraa	1,725	2,399	5,672	7,374
Dormaa/Ahen	----	----	7,107	9,017
Nkoranza	737	608	6,250	7,094
Nsuatre	----	----	----	4,096
Odumasi	----	----	----	4,071
Sunyani	2,912	4,558	15,810	23,872
Techiman	2,254	2,581	8,755	12,509
Wenchi	5,309	3,812	10,672	13,727

*Figures compiled from Gold Coast and Ghana Census Reports: 1931, 1948, 1960 and 1970.

By the 1930s, the settlement patterns in the Brong-Ashanti area were clearly established. There were regional nuclei with large towns ringed by newer, small cocoa villages. The towns were seats of administration related to cocoa farming. Successful farmers from the region often lived now in these towns rather than their home villages, and rode by truck to their farms when necessary. The "absentee owner" pattern[103] did not develop here as early or to the extent that it did in Ashanti and the Ahafo cocoa areas. This was partly due to the relative insularity of Brong-Ashanti areas from coastal developments. Nevertheless, it was quite clear that by the 1920s, local people were preferring to live in town rather than in villages where large numbers of northerners were employed. There was emerging a rural cocoa "big-man" stratum which was profiting most from the influx of cash into the rural economy. This stratum was not completely new, since it was composed of persons who had entered the cocoa industry with an economic and political advantage.

The rural areas had become quite different in the 1930s and 1940s than they had been at the point of conquest. While mining had not been particularly profitable in the early 1900s because of the challenge provided by the cocoa economy, the vulnerable labor supply and the costs of machinery necessary for mining, the recession of the 1930s pushed Ashanti as well as other Gold Coasters more firmly into the wage-labor market. Indebted southern rural men now took laboring jobs in mining related areas, if not in actual mining because of the stigma associated with it. In the space of four years from 1931 to 1935 the numbers of Africans employed in mining tripled.

Table 3–10 gives mining employment for the years 1931–1935.

TABLE 3–10

EMPLOYMENT IN MINING, 1931–1935

YEAR	AVERAGE NUMBER PER DAY	
	Europeans	Africans
1931	237	11,889
1932	244	11,940
1933	323	14,939
1934	532	23,642
1935	810	32,505

Source: Legislative Council Debates, 1936, pp. 1–23. Sir Arnold Hodson, 20 Feb. 1936.

To a greater extent than before, many former rural families maintained village and town residences and worked in the mining industries which had revived by 1935. Alternatively, they grew food to supply markets in mining towns, or provided imported food and household services in mining areas. The educational backgrounds of the younger group made it more likely that they could be employed as clerks in stores which serviced the growing migrant wage-labor populations. Townspeople who could afford to build houses now could rent out spaces to migrant workers and families. Archival reports indicate that colonial administrators were very much aware of the extent to which dual residence and urban relationships helped to reduce labor costs in the mining areas.

The aspiring chiefs and *ahenfo* not only increased their demands on the resources of their people with large private incomes, but they modified the relationships between local areas and larger political units. Between Prempeh's exile in 1895 and his return in 1924, the rural areas had become the mainstay of the colonial regime. Overlords of these areas had experienced an autonomy they had never enjoyed before.[104] Chiefs and elders were now preoccupied with consolidating the economic and political control they had gained over rural citizens as a result of colonial control and transforming this into political influence. Prempeh's return from exile as Kumasihene with limited political powers in 1924 was generally treated with applause both by Kumasi chiefs and people as well as citizens of outlying Akan areas. For many local people, Prempeh represented cultural legitimacy; the political machinations of the colonial bureaucracy were of less concern than the new cash-cropping, jobs, education and other social changes that had become a part of rural lifestyles. The British, however, saw it in their interests to encourage the development of a unified political and economic structure which had "semi-traditional" support,[105] and which centered around a pliant Kumasihene. The Kumasi chiefs were torn between their desire to retain the autonomy they had achieved during Prempeh's absence, and the desire to keep control of the various small villages and towns such as Odumasi and Fiapre which had become wealthier through cocoa. However (as we shall later see), many outlying Brong-Ashanti chiefs approached the re-establishment of the Ashanti Confederacy Council in 1935 with trepidation, for it had the potential of threatening their material well-being.[106]

Notes

1. British Consul Campbell had predicted of the Gold Coast in 1857 that at such time as the slave trade were eradicated and agricultural pursuits firmly established:

   Its great increase, and the beneficial influence exercised upon it, will lead to a value being put on land capable of being cultivated, and that chiefs and others will then assert sovereignty or proprietor rights, and demand fixed rents for land; but many years must elapse ere this improved state of things is reached; certainly not till the slave trade itself shall have become a legend of past times to the African (Accounts and Papers [14], 1857, vol. 38, Session 2 [2257], p. 263).

   Note that prior to the 1880s, labor patterns rather than land relationships demonstrated greatest change. While wage-labor was on the increase in the coastal areas, the purchase and transfer through debt of rural land and dependent people or slaves was the means by which the interior elite acquired a sizable labor force (McCaskie, 1980, 189–208).

2. Arhin, 1976–77, 458; also Wilks, 1977, 30.
3. See Metcalfe, 1964, pp. 429–30, 447–48, 459, and 462 for excerpts from following documents: (C. 5357), Accts. & Papers (1888) vol. 75; C.P. African West, No. 389, p. 96; African West, No. 435, p. 55; and C. 7917 Accounts & Papers, 1896, lviii.
4. Wilks, 1979, 30.
5. C.O. 96/262 1895. Faced with Ashanti intransigence and challenges from France and Germany for territory which Britain had formerly controlled, the British decided to take Kumasi and establish a resident and a Hausa constabulary there. There is evidence that they wanted to obtain the golden stool, although this was not attempted until later.
6. Arhin, 1976–77; Price, 1974, 173–205.
7. Dike, 1956, 50; Brooks, 1970, 254, 261.
8. The British compared the start of this industry with difficulties encountered with slave-produced cotton in the United States, and they erroneously predicted ultimate adjustment of Gold Coasters to it, just as had occurred in the southern U.S. (A&P, 1857, Session 2, vol. 38, 2257, p. 255).
9. Dumett, 1971, 79–102.
10. C. 5897–40 (8), vol. XLVIII, 1890 Session, 11 Feb. to 18 Aug., p. 11.
11. Arhin, 1972, 32; Dumett, 1971.
12. Arhin, 1972.
13. Mikell, field notes 1973, "Life Histories, Sunyani."
14. A&P (8), 1900, vol. XIV, no. 306, p. 3.
15. A&P (31), 1851, no. 25, Report on Annual Blue Book of the Gold Coast 1851, p. 186. Also Szereszewski, 1965, 39–40. On female employment in rubber processing, see C. 5897–40 (8), vol. XLVIII, 1890, p. 355.
16. Mikell, 1983, 38.
17. Dike, 1956, 8; see also H.C. 551 A&P 1842, vol. XI, pp. iii–xxi, Report of the Select Committee on West Africa—and the Madden Report.
18. Note that the Portuguese opened two mines in the 1600s, but succeeded with neither (Vogt, 1979). On Hughes, see Horton, 1868, 265, cited in Kimble, 1963, 15.
19. In one case, the Bekwaihene leased 100 square miles of land to Fanti concessionaires in 1890 without the approval of the Asantehene. This partially formed the basis of the Ashanti Goldfields Corporation in 1897 (Agnes Aidoo, 1975, 587–88).
20. Kimble, 1963, 16. The much reknowned Ashanti Goldfields Corporation, which had extremely broad operating rights, opened its first mine at Obuasi in 1897, p. 24.
21. Wilks, 1975, 529–30. Upon conquest, the British assumed control of the royal gold mines.
22. Ibid., 21.
23. West Indian regiments proved susceptible to local diseases and ineffective in the interior, thus forcing the British to rely more on Hausa troops. See Thomas, 1973, 85.
24. Ibid., 84.
25. Aidoo (1975, 94–111) has referred to the *nnonkofo* as the only genuinely exploited group in Ashanti society. The *nnonkofo*, foreign slaves and war captives, were despised and mistreated because of their religion and the fact that they did not belong to an Akan lineage. The author has noted their dissatisfaction and insolence

towards Ashanti even after freedom, because they were generally prevented from rising up the social scale.

26. Thomas, 1973, 85.
27. Ibid., 84.
28. 1906, vol lxxiii, 241; 1907, liii, 85; 1908, lxviii, 61; 1919, lvii, 61; 1910, lxiv, 55; 1911, li, 1; 1912–13, lvii, 1; 1914, lvii, 103; 1914–16, xliii, 1 and 29.
29. The Ashanti *Nkramo* community had a traditional spiritual and medical role (later transformed into a political one) with respect to the Asantehene. However, the numbers of Muslim traders and ordinary citizens in Kumasi was limited, and the north-south antagonism was one which the British found advantageous in the 1880s. From conquest in the 1890s and onward, there is evidence that the Ashanti *Nkramo* were instrumental in the growth of the Kumasi Muslim community. See Lewin, 1973, 175, 217, 240n.
30. Despite the fact that the combined total population of the colony and Ashanti was three times that of the Northern Territories in 1911, the northern areas of the Gold Coast were supplying a substantial percentage of the southern mining and transportation labor force. Imported labor (Togo, Ivory Coast and Upper Volta, as well as European) eventually predominated in mining, but northern labor increased consistently, whereas Colony/Ashanti labor contributions to these projects declined (Szereszewski, 1965, 55–57.
31. See Accounts & Papers, C. 1139, pp. 6–13, 1874, regarding Colony status and slavery issue; also C.O. 96/120 and 121, p. 388–9 on relationships of British administrators to chiefs, and on relationships of chiefs, people, and the British to land rights. On British reluctance to intervene directly in Ashanti affairs, see A&P, C. 3687, 1883, XLCIII, 12 Dec. 1882.
32. Aidoo, 1975, 95, 354, 489.
33. Wilks, 1975, 437.
34. C.O. 96/113, Strahan to Carnarvon, 3 Sept. 1874.
35. C.O. 96/113, 3 Sept. 1874.
36. Wilks, 1975, 728, 535; also, Aidoo, 454.
37. Aidoo, 606.
38. Ibid.
39. C.O. 96/120, 10 Feb. 1877; also, Native Jurisdiction Ordinance of 15 Jan. 1883, no. 5.
40. Aidoo, 325.
41. Ibid., 330, 350–4.
42. C.O. 96/130, 21 Jan. 1880.
43. C.O. 96/132, 25 Sept. 1880.
44. Metcalfe, 1964, 412.
45. C. 4052, pp. 32–59, 5 July 1883, Barrow Report.
46. Aidoo, 455.
47. Ibid., 458–59; Wilks, 1975, 535.
48. C.P. African (West) no. 448, p. 3., 8 March 1892.
49. African (West) no. 479, pp. 21–6, 1893.
50. C. 5897–40, p. 355, A&P (8), vol. XLVII, Session, 11 February to 18 August 1890.
51. A&P (8), 1890–1, vol. LV, no. 110, p. 553. Economic Agriculture on the Gold Coast, 1889. See also C. 5879–40, p. 355, 1890, op. cit.

52. Rattray, 1929, 350–52; Basejart, 1962, 265–66.
53. Bruce F. Johnston, *The Staple Food Economies of Western Tropical Africa. Stanford,* 1958, 172–73. See also Kwamina B. Dickson, Cambridge, 1969, 79, 122–23.
54. Rattray, 1929: 350–352. Basejart, 1962: 285–6.
55. C. 5897–40, pp. 355, 1890, op. cit. Also A&P (8), 1890–91, op. cit.
56. Aidoo, 1975, 357–8.
57. C.O. 96/377, Cd. 938, A&P (1902) LXVI, Stewart to Nathan, 14 Jan. 1901.
58. Derived from author's field interviews and life histories, Sunyani District, Brong Ahafo, 1973. See also Mikell, 1975, 33.
59. Ghana National Archives (abbreviated GNA), Sunyani, Adm 11/1137, 1901.
60. A number of these towns, such as Nsuatre, resented Berekum's control, and had to be threatened for failure to comply. GNA, Accra, Adm/54/1/1902.
61. Gold Coast District Commissioner's Report for the Year, 1906.
62. District Administrative Record Book, Sunyani (1907–1915), #277/09, 97/07, and 98/07.
63. Ibid., no. 225/07.
64. District Commissioner's Report for the Year 1906.
65. Tordoff, 1965; Austin, 1965.
66. Aidoo, 1975, 94.
67. The Muslim element was evident here in artistic-ceremonial artifacts such as the *Sacrobundi* mask (Freeman, 1898; Bravmann, 1974). In addition, the *Asante Nkramo* were common figures in the villages surrounding Dormaa, Nkoranza, Techiman, Odumasi and Sunyani (Mikell, field interviews; Nkoranza, 1973).
68. Quoted in Arhin, 1976–7, 463.
69. See St. J. Eyre-Smith, Acting Asst. C.C.A., *Stool Debts* file, Enclosure in no. 3570/21/41.
70. Accounts & Papers (7). vol. XI, 1911, Cd. 5467-16, pp. 1–21, Report on Ashanti.
71. Lewin, T.J. *Asante Before the British: The Prempean Years, 1875–1900.* Regents Press of Kansas, 1978, 61.
72. Their fortunes waxed and waned, particularly around the time the "Ashanti Rising" in 1900–1. However, by 1905, the mission schools were again expanding, and by 1911 the Catholic and the Church of England schools were present in Kumasi (Kimble, 1963, 75).
73. A&P, (7), vol. LI, 1911, Cd. 5467–16, pp. 1–21, Report on Ashanti.
74. 1906, lxxiii, 241; 1907, liii, 85; 1908, lxviii, 61; 1909, lvii, 61; 1910; lxiv, 55; 1911, li, l; 1912–13, lvii, l; 1914, lvii, 103; 1914–16, xliii, l & 29.
75. Mikell, Life Histories, Sunyani, 1973.
77. Ibid.
78. Early mission high schools for girls were established at Cape Coast and Accra following the First Education Ordinance in 1882. The curricula included such domestic arts as needlepoint, sewing, cooking, etc. (Bourret, 1949, 137; Ward 1948, 355; and Kay, 1972, 407).
79. On marriage, see Fortes, 1970, 140–146. On the *ntoro* relationship, see Rattray, 1927, 51, 318.
80. On the use of slaves as a labor force, see Aidoo, 1975, 607–8. On population-land

ratios and agriculture in the forest zone, see Dickson, 1969, 210–11 and Wilks, 1977, 517–20.

81. Mikell, Field Interviews, Sunyani, 1973.
82. Dickson, 1969, 206.
83. Mikell, 1984, 195–218.
84. Vallenga, 1975, 52–82.
85. Rattray, 1929, 336–7.
86. Mikell, 1984, op. cit.
87. Arhin, 1976–7.
88. Dickson, 1969, 206.
89. A&P (8) 1890–91, vol. 55, no. 553, Economic Agriculture on the Gold Coast, 1889.
90. Hill, 1963, 179–80.
91. GNA (Sunyani) Adm 54/1/1, no. 284/04. Annual Report for 1904.
92. GNA (Sunyani) DA0/2/C56, 1946.
93. Ibid., no. 11, 25/9/46.
94. GNA (Sunyani) DA0/1/479; see also Mikell, 1975, 45.
95. Arhin, 1979, 56–7. Mikell, 1975, 24–5, 35–6.
96. Robertson, 1973, 44–5.
97. GNA (Sunyani) DA0/1/479, 1948.
98. Skinner, 1963, no. 30, 275–301.
99. Hill, 1963, 188–9, 158–9, 213.
100. C.O. 96/94. H.C. 171 of 1873, Pope Hennessy to Kimberly. Also *The Times*, 13 May 1874, Earl of Carnarvon.
101. GNA (Sunyani) DA0/1/479, 1948.
102. Ibid.
103. Hill, 1970, 27; Beckett, 1944; Robertson, 1973.
104. Austin, 1970.
105. Mikell, 1975, 43.
106. Austin, 1970, 3.

4

Cocoa: The People's Industry

Cocoa was destined to have as great an impact on the lives of the ordinary Gold Coasters (Ghanaians) as did gold on the fortunes of Ashanti. British concern that cocoa production would be limited to the coastal area and hampered by the lack of transportation was not borne out. Cocoa spread like wildfire between 1905 and 1930, causing revolutionary changes throughout the country. It is true that rubber, timber and gold continued to generate significant resources, but by 1911, cocoa was fast becoming the number one export of the Gold Coast. Because of the force of its penetration into the rural economy, and the way in which it linked peasants and ordinary folk to the international economy, cocoa could truly be called the people's industry. Moreover, cocoa was to have implications for almost every facet of the economic, social and political life of the country.

In the first place, while cocoa cultivation brought new material benefits for the people, especially the elite, it dealt a crushing blow to subsistence production. Access to and control of land for cocoa production commercialized and corrupted traditional land relations. Second, many of the conflicts and discontinuities in nineteenth century Ashanti were exacerbated as various social strata competed for cocoa revenue. The growing exploitation of traditional laborers by cocoa farmers making the transition to primarily wage employment altered rural Akan social and political systems in a way previously undreamt of. Third, because colonial Gold Coast relied so heavily upon cocoa revenues, almost to the exclusion of other export commodities, the rural areas began to experience a pattern of extraction and exploitation which increased rather than decreased between 1911 and 1957. Fourth, and most important, the fluctuation of the price of cocoa in the world market placed all the people of the Gold Coast at the mercy of global forces over which they had limited control.

Land and Chieftaincy Disputes

Even before cocoa dominated the colonial economy, control over land was a major issue for both the British and the chiefs. For the British, the issue was how to conserve it so that chiefs could not squander away traditional rights. Initially, the government thought that the solution was the proposed Public Lands Bill of 1900, which would allow the government to have oversight of any unoccupied rural land. However, the agitation of the chiefs and educated elites through the Aborigines' Rights Protection Society succeeded in preventing the passage of this legislation. The problem of land in the twentieth century was primarily that of its availability and control for cocoa production.

Despite the appearance of an abundance of unused land in the forest zone, the amount of land required for cocoa cultivation led to widespread migration and resettlement in cocoa areas. The farmers attempted to stay put as long as possible, but ultimately they had to move. Naturally, the new communities which sprang up tended to locate themselves first along the main transport roads, then later in the more inaccessible areas. People tended to retain ties to their former communities. The boundaries of traditional stool areas expanded naturally to include the new settlements when this was possible. However, the issue of allegiance and access to land began to emerge as people migrated, and conflicts arose.

The growing conflict between cocoa migrants and local stool chiefs exacerbated the strained Ashanti vs. local tensions that already existed in some communities. This expansionary process had begun even before cocoa, as the British pressured chiefs to cut roads and as administrative centers were created. It had occurred between Kukuom and Sefwi over a town from which rubber was extracted in the 1890s.[1] But the development of cocoa sped up the process and made the search for land more widespread. The Brong-Ahafo areas where I worked intensively provides numerous examples. The dispute between Mim and Wam (Dormaa) was a case in point. In 1906 the Wam people first complained to District Commissioner Fuller that the Ahafo communities such as Mim (which contained Ashanti cocoa migrants) were expanding northward and encroaching on their territory without paying tribute.[2] The case dragged on until 1923 with finer and finer boundaries being drawn where none had previously existed. Finally, District Commissioner Hobbs stated that the claim of Wam was sound, and that they were entitled to tribute since they were the first occupants of the land. Other cases involved small cocoa communities which were growing larger and making a grab for land. In a case between the expanding town of Suma and the Omanhene of Drobo in 1924, the court upheld traditional land relations by announcing that the Sumahene "...had no land in Jaman. It all belonged to the Omanhene of Drobo, who had boundaries with Pamu, Berekum, French Wenchi and Banda."[3] Such disputes over valuable cocoa land took place all over southern Ghana.

The Sunyani-Odumasi towns and villages were the scene of particularly intense competition for land in the less settled Brong-Ahafo forest zone. When the British conquered northwest Ashanti in 1896, they concluded a treaty with an area they called Borumfu. The problem was that although the Ashanti had stationed outposts there to guarantee its loyalty in the eighteenth and nineteenth centuries, the Ashanti overlord (the Duayaw-Nkwanta chief) was not a party to the treaty. The Duayaw-Nkwantahene felt that, with the possible exception of Odumasi, which was a traditionally important town, the smaller towns which had signed the treaty were politically insignificant, and should continue to conduct relations with other states through him.[4] The situation remained ambiguous since, in their antagonism towards Ashanti, the British ignored Duayaw-Nkwanta in favor of Odumasi and its lesser developed villages such as Sunyani, Fiapre and Atronie.

The local political indeterminacy of Odumasi became a source of conflict when there was a scramble for cocoa lands. First of all, Odumasi itself was by no means ethnically homogeneous, and was affected by the curious Brong-Ashanti relationship in this area. The town had two chiefs: one Ashanti and one of Brong origin. To complicate matters, each of the two Odumasi chiefs claimed to have been the first settler on the land. Each also had a different interpretation of the town's origin, and the town's name was variously translated to support one or the other's argument. Since no precise records existed from the early period, only the recorded statements from the two stools after British conquest in 1896 provided historical evidence.

British colonial administrative papers from 1928 onward, recording a dispute between the two Odumasi chiefs over land (Kobina Kuma of the Bosumtwi Stool-Ashanti vs. Kwasi Peseo of the Antepim Stool-Brong), appear to give the Brong the ascendancy. One record reads:

> In this case, however, there is a statement by Chief Kwesi Peseo that Kwame Koran [Bosumtwi Stool] is my junior brother. This statement is not only not denied by Kwame Koran, but it is confirmed by his own evidence, viz., I said that he (Peseo) was my senior brother.

Also:

> All parties agreed, some reluctantly, that the Antepim Stool was the first comer to Odumasi.[5]

In all ceremonies concerning town affairs until well into the colonial period, the Antepim Stool (#1 Brong) held an equal position with the Bosumtwi Stool (#2 Ashanti), and the Antepim Stool was always presented first in ceremonies because of its legitimate claim to prior occupation of the land. Nevertheless, the Ashanti felt superior, because of their dispersions into the area after their conquest of the Bono state, then of Gaman, Banda and Wenchi. Moreover, after the Ashanti civil wars in the 1880, many Ashanti had moved into Brong villages, thus increasing their size and importance.

Although there were points at which social and political identities created disharmony, it was the growing conflict over land which called for a resolution. In 1928, District Commissioner Eyre-Smith wrote:

> It is only since the British occupation that the title *Ohene* has assumed an importance which the people think carries special privilege with the government.
>
> The Bantamas and the Brongs were about equally divided in Odumasi and the whole population was tired of war. It was easier to allow the matter to slide and hope for the best. More than 14 years after British occupation the matter is first heard of...The Antepim Stool is only concerned to prove that his ancestors were the original settlers on the land and *gave* part of the land to Bosumtwi and his people.
>
> Had the whole of Odumasi land remained undeveloped, it is unlikely that any serious claim would have been made by the respondents to Kwame Koran's position, and from Chief Peseo's statement in *Apaw vs. Peseo* it is plain that he had no intention of ever claiming these lands whilst he was actively occupying the stool."[6]

It is important to stress that since Brong and some Ahafo political economies, and especially land allocation systems, were not as highly formalized as those near Kumasi, some chiefs now started to claim more prerogatives over land than ever before. In fact, patterns of land tenure in the western border area were neither as formalized as in Ashanti, nor as free as in some coastal areas. Local identity, based on rights of residence rather than lineal rights of birth or origin, reflected the way in which Brong and Ahafo had been integrated into a larger political economic framework.

Communities like Odumasi had difficulty accepting the incoming colonial administrative system because of the desire of chiefs to manipulate former feudal statuses so as to obtain modern benefits. In Odumasi, District Commissioner Eyre-Smith attempted to introduce some fixed rules:

1. Each Ohene would swear allegiance to the other upon enstoolment, with both queen mothers choosing candidates for either stool.

2. State debts and communal labor to be shared equally.
3. One native tribunal with both chiefs, queen mothers and one half the elders from each stool.
4. One third of all revenue and tribute going to each stool and the remaining one third to the Berekum Division.
5. Land boundaries to remain as they were formerly.
6. A native tribunal to meet at the house of the Antepim Stool chief until a tribunal is built.[7]

Obviously, no real conflicts were settled; they were merely postponed. The development of prosperous cocoa farms in new towns added fuel to the fire. Later, the return of the Asantehene from exile in 1924 also stimulated previously quiescent pro-Ashanti forces in the northwest and in Ahafo to assert themselves. If the Asantehene was able to reconstruct the Ashanti Confederacy, as they hoped, they wanted to be able to dominate the indigenous Brong or Ahafo chief and usurp all tributes from cocoa land. In a court case between tiny Adrobaa and Susuansu in 1921, the Adrobaa villagers claimed rights to surrounding land and refused to pay tribute to Nkwanta which had been the overlord of Susuansu land and was therefore entitled to a share of any tribute received from cocoa. The Adrobaa people based their claims on their decendency from Awua Panyin, the first Ashanti royal of Odumasi #2, who conquered Brong land, then placed their ancestors to live there. Such actions often had full support of local people.[8]

As towns and regional centers became more important to the cocoa industry, colonial administrators began to take sincere interest in whether local chiefs favored economic development and new agricultural practices. Their interest in the selection of head-chiefs quickly became apparent. For example, in 1896 the administration selected the Omanhene of Berekum against local opposition, and in 1905 they selected the paramount chief of Gaman under similar conditions. These two areas were difficult to administer because part of them had formerly been under French control, and the local people still recognized some chief living in the Ivory Coast. In the case of the Gaman people, they chose a candidate to replace the recently demised chief of Wirime. Unfortunately, this man was one whom District Commissioner Fell did not favor. Accordingly, the D.C. summoned all the important Gaman chiefs on a particular day so that he could select a successor to the Paramount. His choice, the chief of Drobo, was sustained despite resistance from several quarters in Gaman.[9]

Most of the chiefs appointed by the colonial administration worked closely with British officials, and they often cultivated the friendship of government so as to be able to increase the development of potentially rich cocoa areas. Those chiefs who were uncooperative saw their areas penalized. The British kept a close watch on the Ahafo area affairs, owing to the availability of land and the cocoa production there. Nevertheless, they were not happy with the Omanhene of Ahafo (Bremansu I), and considered him a troublemaker because of the "palaver" he made over the *Boe* fetish, and because he opposed a new administrative center placed at Kukuom.[10] When the Omanhene died in 1913, the district commissioner considered his death "...sad, but politically timely...[since it] synchronizes well with the opening of the new [cocoa] station at Goaso."[11] Kofi Ntin (who became Omanhene Bremansu II) also disappointed the British.

The D.C. was happier with Kojo Daako, who became Omanhene in 1919, stating that he "...was formerly a cocoa instructor in this division and he can read and write English. Appointment approved."[12] Of Kojo Ahin, who took office in 1929, the D.C. wrote, "The Omanhene who had been six years on the stool was a most progressive chief, a loyal and true friend to the government."[13]

Loyalty to and cooperation with the government often meant that chiefs were traditionalists, and accepted "frozen" Ashanti concepts of allegiance and tribute. True, since 1896 the British had appointed the Omanhene for important areas, elevating certain chiefs and demoting others. But their goal was that the content and operation of the traditional political system would remain intact. The problem was that tradition was in the process of change, particularly with respect to control of cocoa land and usufruct rights. While the people and some of their chiefs recognized this, colonial administrators feared any flexibility would wreak havoc with local administration and cause massive land alienation. In areas like Ahafo, where settlement (and therefore tradition) was relatively recent, chiefs had greater flexibility in working with the government without offending popular sentiment or threatening the economic well-being.[14] On the other hand, in central Ashanti and in Brong-Ashanti areas, what the people considered to be "conspiracy" between chiefs and administrators (often demands for modern improvements which required higher local taxation), became a source of conflict.

The cocoa revenue was making it possible for ordinary folk to afford more amenities than they formerly could, and the availability of ready northern labor relieved them of certain onerous tasks. On the other hand, when the demands of chiefs seemed to escalate along with prosperity, the popular perception was that it threatened to obliterate personal economic gain. Chiefs who had the backing of government were sometimes induced to exceed common sense in their demands for taxation or communal labor. The popular response was "destoolment" (the formal removing of a chief from office), and such incidents escalated after 1920. In the colony, destoolments rose from seven chiefs between 1904–1908 to forty-one chiefs between 1918–1925. The situation in northwest Ashante reflected this trend.

Table 4–1 provides statistics on Gold Coast destoolments in the years 1904–1924.

TABLE 4–1

DESTOOLMENTS IN THE GOLD COAST
1904–1924

Years	Number of chiefs
1904–1908	7
1909–1913	23
1914–1918	38
1918–1924	41

*Source: J.H.S. Frimpong, *The Joint Provincial Council of Chiefs and the Politics of Independence in the Gold Coast,* M.A. Thesis, University of Ghana, Legon. 1966, 31.

The so-called "youngmen" of many of these towns generally tried to reason with stool occupants in an attempt to reach an acceptable settlement and avoid difficult destoolments. When this proved impossible, often because of British support for the incumbents, some rather surprising events occurred, both in the colony and in northwest Ashanti. In the 1920s, there a rash of violent destoolments and murders in the Berekum Division. Sometimes the stool occupants were very modern in outlook; at other times, they were conservative and insisted on retaining or abusing traditional rights. At Nkoranza in 1927, for example, "youngmen" attacked, whipped, and intended to kill their chief, whom they claimed that, from at least 1920, had continually exhibited gross misconduct. This man subsequently resigned and was formally destooled.[15] At Techiman in the same year, both "youngmen" and elders waylaid and killed their Omanhene. They had previously demonstrated against him, to no avail. The breaking point came when a dispute arose over the construction of a Techiman-Chiraa road which the district commissioner had advised chiefs to build with communal labor. Apparently, the "youngmen" objected, preferring taxation and the hiring of a contractor. Later, unsuccessfully, they demanded that the chief himself pay one-third of the cost of road construction. In the words of one report:

> The malcontents argued thus: If we merely destool the Omanhene in the usual way, he will appeal to the government and the latter will support him and put him back to rule over us again. We don't want him ever again...I think the Omanhene's principal offense was his readiness to help the government.16

This case clearly demonstrates the government's desire to utilize rural labor for development projects in cocoa areas. However, Governor Slater stated about the case:

> As you are aware from the policy which I initiated in Sierra Leone, I personally dislike the idea of unpaid communal labor, even for public purposes, but the objections thereto have far less weight here where there is no direct taxation. The fact of the "youngmen" being willing to engage a contractor at considerable expense appears to indicate that the financial aspect is of little moment in the rich cocoa area such as Tekiman.[17]

It was clear, however, that the rural people were against forced labor and were prepared to penalize chiefs who did not oppose it. Destoolments occurred in rapid succession. The Nsuatrehene, the Sunyanihene and the chief of Mo were among the casualties. However, Slater's recommendations that the government station additional district dommissioners in the area to deal with the problem did little to address the deep economic and political tensions which had arisen.[18]

Ironically, many of the "youngmen" who were responsible for these tensions had been beneficiaries of an earlier liberalization initiated by *nkwankwaa* and the *okonkofo* of the previous generation. Now, despite increased cash and economic opportunities, this new generation of "youngmen" saw themselves as victims of a money-grabbing anachronistic traditional bureaucracy collaborating with a colonial bureaucracy which was more intent upon demanding money for political control than liberalizing trade. At first, the concerns of the "youngmen" were officially ignored in many Ashanti villages, but their insistence on participating in politics gradually forced the village elders to confer with commoner leaders. D.C. Slater observed in 1927 that:

> An extraordinary fact has come to light...It is to the effect that in the majority of villages, the person who has power today is the *asafuakye*, not the *odikro*. In some villages, the *odikro* is not informed what his youngmen have done or intend to do. This metamorphosis has taken place in the last year or so.[19]

In the town of Techiman, the elders secretly elected Yaw Ankomah as *asafuakye* (or *safohene*) and organized the people to resist the Omanhene's orders. The elders then enlisted the support of the *asafuakye* and "youngmen" to defy the Omanhene. Despite the statement of the D.C., the rise of the office of *asafuakye* was not an entirely new phenomenon. The local people indicated that the title, referring to a military company leader, had always existed, and the office was only invested with authority in the military sphere whenever situations demanded. Only in Fanti areas did the *safohene* have an authoritative role. Thus, the developing role of the *safohene* in Ashanti and the northwest as a challenge to traditional authority was somewhat of an innovation.[20]

The significance of the rise of the *safohene* was that with the wealth generated by cocoa, and the power of the colonial regime, the traditional political system was subverted by the mass of the people who infused an ordinary office with greater traditional power than it had before. The desired changes were thus implemented in such a way as not to threaten the traditional system of social action. This was an extremely important precedent, in view of the deep impetus to change which cocoa inspired, and the verbalized colonial support for development. Not only did increasing participation in a cash economy make people more amenable to taxation rather than to the contribution of communal labor, but the colonial pressure on chiefs to build new roads and administrative structures, to develop the area, and to obey colonial authority, interfered with the individual, rural and economic entrepreneurship that was developing.

Throughout the early decades of this century, land cases between different stools, questions about ownership of cocoa farms and questions of traditional political rank occupied much of the time of district administrative courts in cocoa growing areas. In 1909, there were cases involving cocoa farm ownership near Hwidiem in Kukuom-Ahafo; boundary disputes between Wenchi and Drobo, involving overlordship; land cases between Sansu and Kukuom, and between Sunyani and Nsuatre; the Wam-Mim boundary disputes; and the repeated destoolments of the Sunyanihene and Krontihene of Sunyani.[21] New wealth in cocoa among rural people was at the heart of these varied disputes. However, not until the restoration of the Ashanti Confederacy in 1935 was there any formal recognition of the socio-political and socio-economic changes in the rural divisions that would clearly affect the central colonial administration. Until then, quantitative change was taking place, but social relations were still cloaked in qualitative traditional garb.

Stratification and Rural Middlemen

By 1910, cocoa was so important to the Akan that any male who had a sufficient familial or servile labor force was already producing it. In the northwest Brong and Ahafo areas where more forest land was available to men, the *abusua* played an active role in supplying the labor or cash to purchase paid labor. Given the increased ability of local wives to reside (at least part-time) with husbands, male farmers also relied heavily upon the conjugal labor force. One might expect objections to arise from the husbands' or the wives' *mmusua* concerning the increasing isolation of the nuclear family and complaints about the use of the labor of sons on fathers' farms. However, this reaction was nipped in the bud by a process whereby men often completed the first farm quickly, then turned it over to their own *mmusua*, and proceeded to make new ones for themselves and their conjugal families.[22] Sometimes, a different course of action was followed: the man would secure an extensive tract of land, and with the help of his wife and sons, would clear and plant a large portion. Half of this portion might be divided into shares for the wife and sons; henceforth, this portion was alienated from the man's control, and often the children's uncle assumed control of it along with the wife. The remaining portion of the developed portion might then be worked by members of a man's *abusua*, particularly his sister's sons, and he was free to turn his attention to the remaining undeveloped portion, to which no one would make claims until his death.

The man's manipulation of kin ties was an attempt to convince the extended family that its rights were not violated, while permitting the farmer to obtain the support of both the lineal and the conjugal groups. What this created was a growing tendency towards "patricentricity." Wives appeared to have had the freedom to sell the food crops which came from their husbands' young cocoa farms; therefore, the relatives of males claimed that wives had been repaid for initial labor by having these food-crops and therefore should make no claims to the proceeds from cocoa.[23] What was not often realized was that women had to rely upon their own *mmusua* to replace the labor expended upon husbands' farms. Unable to fulfill domestic chores and work on farms, wives often took female relatives as household servants. Only occasionally were these girls given the opportunity to go to school, but the higher standard of living enjoyed by successful farmers was an inducement for many families to send girls as servants to relatives in the developing cocoa towns. This manipulation of kin ties to promote cocoa production continued unchallenged until after World War II.

As cocoa production increased, prosperous cocoa farmers found it expedient to hire several categories of labor: *abusa*, annual, contract or daily laborers. The critical category was the *abusa* labor, which did not generally include members of the lineage.[24] *Abusa* laborers managed the entire care, weeding, collection of cocoa pods, and processing of cocoa beans from the farm; therefore they received a one-third share of the proceeds from cocoa. As cocoa farmers found themselves better able to afford paid labor, they gradually withdrew nuclear and extended family members from cocoa farm work, although they often left wives to control food production. When cocoa farmers were financially stable, and had *abusa* laborers to work the farms, they often gave wives a supervisory role over these farms, visiting only periodically to assess progress and labor needs. Should the *abusa* laborers prove untrustworthy, women were on hand to note the true yields of cocoa. Thus their wifely functions extended from the household to the farm, and often to business as their husbands advanced up the economic ladder.

Cocoa farms were by no means the sole method for generating private property, but usually served as a take-off point from which money from cocoa was invested in immovable property. A process similar to that described for Akawapim and Ahafo permitted farmers to invest cocoa profits in buildings within towns.[25] Often an earthen building belonging to a man's *abusua* (lineage) might be enlarged using concrete. Naturally, such an act increased a man's prestige within his family. The problem was that the *abusua* lost direct claims on any houses or structures which the farm owner subsequently built, such as a house for his nuclear family, until his death transformed his personal property into lineage property. This lifetime limitation applied even though one or two members of his *abusua* might live in the conjugal house. In this manner, a successful and industrious farmer might develop into a true capitalist using personally acquired property. He might erect two-story buildings with stores on the lower level, with room for several families to reside on the inside compound, and with rooms on the upper story for himself or the conjugal family. Alternatively, a prosperous farmer might encourage a wife or son to lay the foundation for a building, and then he would supply the resources to complete it. These persons then had exclusive rights to rents and profits from the building. Often farmers invested returns from cocoa to buy trucks to transport cocoa and farm produce. These vehicles were rented out during the harvest season, and used as internal transport in town during the rest of year.

This process of upward economic mobility through cocoa was clearly apparent in the Sunyani District. There were several groups of peasant farmers who had managed to overcome the limitations of conflicting economic claims within the family, who had developed reserves of capital and cocoa land, and who had emerged as prosperous entrepreneurs. Yet, this upward mobility was still not limited to single individuals, but also involved the conjugal family and, to a lesser extent, the extended family. Several factors appeared to be important in this type of rural socio-economic mobility in Brong-Ashanti areas.

Early Land Acquisition

Most people in the Brong-Ashanti area were reluctant to accept cocoa production because they were skeptical that the amounts of labor invested and the costs of transporting the produce would yield a profit. The earliest participants were the elite—chiefs and elders—who, with government encouragement, went or sent their nephews and sons to agricultural training courses to learn cocoa-growing techniques. Thus, sons of the traditional elite had a head start in the industry, and their lead increased with the adoption of the motor truck in 1918. These first farms were small, demonstration pieces, but the farmers quickly moved on to establish second farms. Thus, the early wave of cocoa farmers (those farming between 1913 and 1923) were able to select extensive and contiguous tracts of well situated, fertile land. In many cases, the elite acquired tracts of one-half mile or more in size. Being successful entrepreneurs and anticipating trends that would later develop, they claimed more land than they initially needed, intending to develop the rest at their convenience. Having access to servants, dependents and other kinspersons, this elite thus had a head start in capital accumulation necessary for large-scale cocoa farming. By 1923, they were increasing their land holdings while most commoners (male and female) were struggling to get started in the cocoa industry.

Around Sunyani, the traditional matrilineal structures prevented successful fathers from casually turning farms over to their sons. However, *abusua* and conjugal farms were often contiguous, or on adjacent tracts, it was easy for men to help their sons enter the business. They did this by sharing transportation and labor costs, thereby decreasing expenditure, and were thus able to enrich their offspring. Alternatively, a man could ceremonially turn over a cocoa farm to his son, receiving the traditional *aseda* or "thanks" in the presence of and with the consent of his *abusua*. By such means, the traditional elite used cocoa as a mechanism for enhancing their traditional status with modern attributes.

Early Education and Business Opportunities

After cocoa money, modern education was the next most important factor in social mobility in Brong-Ashanti areas. Prior to 1895, there were few schools in the rural and inaccessible parts of the northwest forest zone. As we have seen, most of the educated Africans were along the coastal area, and seldom came to the Kumasi area as civil servants until the 1930s. The earliest Brong to receive modern education were often the children of those elders or *ahenfo* who, benefiting from cocoa, were able to go to mission schools. The resulting educated men were able to manipulate the market for white-collar skills, especially since (as civil servants or clerks) they were not adverse to serving in the "backwoods" of the northwest. Alternatively, many of them set themselves up in business or also invested in cocoa farms, becoming absentee farmers and significant employers of rural labor.[26] Educated men who had farms often turned them over to be managed by conjugal or extended families while engaging in their own professions. Some of the local "youngmen" who did not have much education also took advantage of the cocoa boom to become "big-men," following careers as financiers, landlords, timber contractors, cocoa brokers and middlemen in trade. Using traditional prestige, they slowly gathered a personal following, cultivated patron-client relationships, and acted as creditors for rural people who had only cocoa farms to pledge as security for a needed loan. Even the depression of the 1930s did not significantly harm this group.

Selective Inheritance and Farm Control Patterns

Under the Akan *abusua* land usufruct system present in this area, the number of family members entitled to benefit from the produce of a particular plot of land could continually increase from one generation to the next. However, the farm was seldom parceled off among matrilineal descendants. Thus, there was little fragmentation of cocoa farms which would have lowered revenue from them. Rather, inheritance of cocoa farms was most frequently to a single matrilineal heir. In Brong-Ashanti areas, cocoa farmers who had acquired land between 1913 and 1923 could maintain considerable control of land and capital if they made no gifts of land to the *abusua* or to the conjugal family prior to death. The emerging trend was of selective inheritance of farms after death by a single brother, not the entire *abusua*. Thus a man obviated the need for land division by selecting as heir the brother with the most economic aptitude, or the one nearest himself in age. Consequently, birth order became an important factor in prosperity of male farmers within a family group. Sometimes the nephew (sister's son) might be chosen, but he had the same obligations as the brother would have, to provide for other members of the lineage from the proceeds of the cocoa farm. Thus, by using the resources of the farm, a man could maintain a family compound and perhaps give members of his *abusua* the capital to enter trading or learn a skill.[27]

Note that because of polygyny, the conjugal family of such a farmer might be large. If he desired to provide for these non-lineage members, he had to be careful not to alienate his lineage by giving a major portion of his property as gifts to his wives and children (something which ultimately benefited the wives' lineages). When a single son received a farm from his father (one intended for the conjugal family), he also incurred the obligation to provide for his sisters and brothers with proceeds from the farm. However, there is some evidence that the practice of late marriages for rural Akan males did much to reduce pressure on them to divide land between their polygynous conjugal families.

By the 1930s, stratification in rural areas had resulted in two clearly defined groups: one composed of former and present *ahenfo* and *sikafo* and their families, whose cocoa wealth generated education and capital for further investments; and the other composed of ordinary folk whose small cocoa farms, impeded by inadequate capital and labor, often caused their indebtedness to the first group. While wealthy farmers could become wealthier, an unusually dry season or diseases which devastated a crop ("black pod" or "akate") often wiped out poorer farmers. Wealthy families could easily absorb the funeral expenses of an *abusua* member, while poorer cocoa farmers were driven into debt by this. Larger farmers did not have to pawn dependents to send a bright child to school, or borrow money for a son's marriage or a daughter's divorce, while poorer neighbors were forced to do so.

Debt quickly became the major problem for most farmers. While debts were formerly repaid primarily by pawning jewelry or slaves, now pledging valuable cocoa farms became the ideal means for dealing with loans. The incidences of pledging farms became high by the 1930s, and increased as the standard of living rose. In the 1930s, Beckett found that two-thirds of cocoa farmers in Akokoaso were indebted, and that the higher their incomes, the higher the amount of the pledge. Bray found a similar situation in the Ahafo villages of the Kukuom and Mim area.[28]

Table 4–2 gives 1959 statistics on the pledging of cocoa farms.

TABLE 4–2

PLEDGING OF COCOA FARMS, 1959

Pledger		Money lender		Cooperative Society		Cocoa Company		Total	Total	Total	Total
Recieved	Due	Recieved	Due	Recieved	Due	Recieved	Due	Recieved	Due	Paid	Outstanding
18,013	21,994	1,650	2,725	160	160	1,450	1,615	21,273	26,504	9,968	16,536

*Source: Bray, 1959, 50. According to Bray, one fourth of those who were indebted owed twice or more than annual income.

A pledged farm might be held for several decades without the family getting the resources to redeem it. Therefore, for all practical purposes, such a farm was completely alienated. The following cases from 1973 survey results in the Sunyani District show the pledges of both poor and more prosperous farmers:

1. A farmer fell into debt for C140 (roughly $110 in 1973 dollars). His cocoa farm annually brought in C140–C180, so he pledged it to another farmer for three years.
2. A farmer received approximately C80 from his farm this year. It had been pledged for one year to cover a debt of C60 and was just returned to him.
3. The chief of a sizable town came to the stool over twenty years ago, and incurred debts in the process. He and his *abusua* pledged two farms to a stranger, and received £2000 (roughly $6,000 at that time). He and his brother have since had no control over the farms. Since his *abusua* have suffered with him, his brother will inherit his own two farms after his death.
4. An elderly farmer fell into debt for C120 and pledged one farm to a woman storekeeper for four years. He estimates that the farm brings in C150–200 each year.
5. A farmer had one farm which brought in C50–60 each year. He owed a man C90 and so pledged his farm for three years.

6. A married woman had three farms, one of which came from her *abusua*. But she fell into debt over the years, and they have all been pledged.[29]

It should be noted that the revenue which the creditor derived from pledged farms far exceeded the size of the actual debt. The difference can best be thought of as interest on a loan. In general, most people were embarrassed to admit having pledged cocoa farms, and were hesitant to give information. They usually claimed that they would soon redeem the pledge. But strangers (particularly northerners) were quick to approach anyone in financial difficulty, offering to receive farm pledges. The reason was that non-indigenous Muslims were rarely able to obtain cocoa farms in their own right, either by tribute or purchase.

By the late 1920s and 1930s, a third and important socio-economic stratum, rural middlemen, was added to the wealthy and poor cocoa farmers. This group arose as wealth in cocoa farms was assured and people branched out into more substantial infrastructural ventures. With cocoa firmly established in the colony, British entrepreneurs had made an all-out effort to guarantee a steady supply of cocoa beans for export each season. Other than building roads and rail systems, they seldom bothered to create the lower-level support structures that could produce steady harvests. Matters such as providing local transportation for crops or building depots were not of their concern. It was left to ambitious African entrepreneurs to create the necessary local-level linkages to facilitate cocoa production. The social stratum best able to finance such endeavors was that of the wealthy cocoa "big-men," and, to a more limited extent, the upwardly mobile, literate rural "youngmen." Rather quickly after the introduction of the truck, these persons became middlemen, using this form of transportation to visit the inaccessible farms, buying cocoa from local farmers at questionable "pressure" prices. Soon, some of the middlemen worked exclusively for such purchasing houses as United Africa Company and Leventis Company, as these two firms competed with each other. Other middlemen simply sold to whichever firm made the most attractive offer.[30]

One result of the role of middlemen in the local cocoa trade was that they were able to give perquisites to chiefs for such favors as extending loans to them, and were able to identify farmers and other rural folk who might wish to pledge land. Another development was that although the *ahenfo* were often middlemen, the peasantry started to distrust this group of traditional elite.[31] Nevertheless, despite the often tense relationships between cocoa producers, chiefs and middlemen in the 1930s, the latter were able to mobilize cocoa farmers against the European buyers. The chiefs thereby regained much of the respect and status they had lost during the previous decades.

A major controversy broke out during the depression years of the 1930s between the European buying firms and the rural producers. After receiving escalating prices for their cocoa from the international market over the years, farmers noted a steady decline of cocoa prices from 1920 onward. Data seem to indicate that despite low prices in the early 1920s, the farmers, keeping in mind the former high prices, maintained planting of cocoa trees and therefore production. The result was that the volume of cocoa production continued, while cocoa prices fell and returns to the farmers decreased.[32] This international economic crisis had disastrous ramifications for these rural people, whose standards of living were now inextricably linked to the global economy.

Further compounding the problem was the perception of rural farmers that the European buying firms were collaborating in an effort to purchase cocoa at a substandard price, thereby exploiting the growers. The reality was that, faced with the depression, the European buying firms attempted to limit internal competition by agreeing to buy a fixed percentage of the annual Gold Coast cocoa crop. Anything beyond the allotted quota would have to be sold to firms which had not yet reached their quotas.[33] Some persons have maintained that such an agreement was unnecessary, given the high level of cocoa production and marketing on the Gold Coast. However, the agreements between marketing syndicates (or "pools," as they were popularly known among farmers) came to symbolize for the Gold Coaster the overwhelming power of international capital as characterized by the Association of West African Merchants. In crop year 1930–31, a cocoa hold-up (an organized withholding of cocoa by producers) was attempted, with little success. However, in crop year 1937–38, a major cocoa hold-up and a boycott of the import stores owned by cocoa shippers seriously affected the United Africa Company and newcomers like the Leventis Company, which handled a combined total of approximately 88% of cocoa purchases.[34] The partial explanation given by the British and the later West African Cocoa Commission Report was that:

> The fall in the price of cocoa which preceded the 1937–38 season threatened considerable losses, the argument runs, to those middlemen who had made advance purchases of cocoa from farmers on the basis of the previous season's high prices; the chiefs therefore declared the hold-up in the expectation that the price would be forced up thereby.

It is understandable from the peasant's point of view that they were striking back at the monopolies. Nevertheless, there is some indication that peasants may have also been pressured by chiefs, middlemen and local "big-men," to act. When the chiefs, intellectuals and farmers remained adamant in their opposition to the monopolistic agreements, a Parliamentary committee (the Nowell Commission) met even while the boycott continued. The commission condemned the buyers' monopoly and the unethical actions of inland middlemen and buyers, recommending the creation of a state producers' organization to deal with the buying companies.[35]

It has been suggested that small-holder cocoa producers were unaffected by the depression, boycotts and hold-ups, but the data tend not to support this. True, the larger farmers often had sufficient resources to allow them to ride out the difficulties of 1937–38, but many poorer farmers were forced to pledge farms in order to meet their financial needs.[36] To make matters worse, outbreaks of "swollen shoot" disease penalized farmers who could not afford to cut out the afflicted trees. Their farms were devastated. Colonial reports of the time also cited a decline in food production as cocoa proportionally spread in the inland districts. The availability of food became a problem for coastal and inland towns, resulting in inadequate diets and unsuccessful demands for higher wages to purchase food.[37] Farmers in rural areas without cash incomes and the ability to pay cocoa laborers encouraged their wives to shift back into production of foodstuffs or into small-scale cocoa production. Even without such incentives some women in the 1930s undertook these tasks in their own right.

In summation, the bulk of Gold Coast cocoa farmers controlled only small amounts of resources, and were greatly affected by the fluctuations of 1930s. The Nowell Commission report in 1939 stated that:

> A survey made in Ashanti some years ago by the Department of Agriculture showed the average area per farmer to be two and one half acres. The size of farms varied from a fraction of an acre to 27 acres, and 60 percent were under one acre...In a typical cocoa village...the number of farmers was 174 males and 180 females, giving a production per head of 924 pounds of cocoa, worth at the then average price of 7s.7d per load, about £5.16s...

One of the undeniable impacts of the 1930s on rural stratification was the concentration of wealth in the hands of the resident emerging middle-class and the educated elite. Subsequent economic development was to destroy the role of the middleman, as a shift was made towards the peasant cooperatives and later towards the creation of the marketing board. But while the rural middleman stratum was in decline even before the 1950s, when the government moved against them, the status of chiefs and other *ahenfo* rose in the estimation of rural folk. Although the Joint Provincial Council of Chiefs was created by the colonial regime in 1925, the increased powers given it in the 1930s reflected a recognition by the Gold Coast government of the continued significance of chiefs in the lives of the majority of people.

Another impact of the 1930s on rural areas was the launching of the cocoa cooperative movement. By 1938, the Department of Agriculture had established

407 agricultural producer cooperatives, most of which were made up of cocoa producers. The members of these groups contributed a small sum per load of produce sold (share capital) which was used to buy equipment, build stores, and transport their crops. Some of the societies also offered loans to members. Nevertheless, the time was not propitious for cocoa cooperatives. The impact of the recession, the cocoa hold-ups and the negative incentives for cocoa growing were reflected in the low price premium paid (6d) per load of cocoa, and the low amount of cocoa sold through the cooperatives in 1938.[38]

Table 4–3 presents 1938 statistics pertaining to Gold Coast agricultural cooperatives in cocoa, copra, banana, citrus and coffee.

TABLE 4–3

GOLD COAST AGRICULTURAL COOPERATIVES, 1938*

Type	Numbers	Members	Share Capital
Cocoa producers	371	9,399	28,298
Copra producers	11	541	632
Fruit (banana) producers	20	348	1,022
Citrus producers	4	464	765
Coffee producers	1	72	110

*Source: Bourret, *The Gold Coast*, Stanford: Stanford Univ. 1949, 127.

There is some indication that the mainstay of the pre-war cocoa cooperatives were those prosperous and middle-sized cocoa farmers who remained unharmed by the machinations of the economy, or who had profited by the economic trauma of the 1930s.

These changing patterns of stratification in the cocoa producing areas of the Gold Coast must be seen in relation to stratification in the country as a whole. As we have seen, the educated elite who had existed from the early 1800s, and had grown through recruitment of the entrepreneurial elite from Ashanti after the 1890s, became politically active in the land and gold mining issues of the period. They were becoming consistent and critical observers of government policy. The teachers, clergy, lawyers, doctors and merchants were well represented in Aborigines' Rights Protection Society in 1897 and, by the 1920s, they were vocal in their demands for Civil Service appointments.[39] Until the 1920s, the policy of "indirect rule" only recognized traditional chiefs as spokesmen for the people. The government adamantly continued to resist the appointment of Africans as district and provincial commissioners until the 1940s.[40]

The opening of Achimota College as the first Gold Coast institution of higher learning in 1927 provided a new mechanism for growth and training of the indigenous elite. It provided an atmosphere in which the African and European elite could confer on issues of government policy.[41] The Achimota Discussion Group, which developed there in 1939 in partial response to the nationalism revealed by the cocoa hold-ups and boycotts, represented an attempt on the part of the elite to have a serious and amicable dialogue with the colonial administration regarding the African role in government. This coastal group was counterbalanced by the existence of the Ashanti confederacy, which was reconstructed in Kumasi after 1935. The confederacy, although headed by the Kumasihene and therefore the subject of much controversy, provided the means for lower and middle chiefs to have some say in rural political life between 1935 and 1945. Noticeable, however, was that the emerging middle strata in rural areas still had no say in the ensuing dialogues between the traditional and modern elites and the colonial administration. It was not until the period of the Second World War that modifications to the 1927 Native Administration Ordinance and the movement towards Constitutional self-government[42] permitted the rural "youngmen" and middling groups which had been spawned by the former prosperity of the cocoa economy to become politically involved.

The Emergence of the Female Cocoa Farmer

Rural women, like their male counterparts, had been involved in the cocoa industry from its inception. Indeed, cocoa farming would not have been possible without the labor of wives and children. Nevertheless, colonial records for 1906–1910 show that the administrators limited their attempts to encourage experimentation with cocoa to male family heads, not to females. The notion that women would have welcomed the chance to engage in cocoa on their own account seems to have been alien to the colonial mind.[43] Even later, women were generally not farm owners in the primarily patrilineal migrant "companies" or in the *abusua* farms in southern Gold Coast as described by Hill. There, the farms of brothers on which they worked were often registered in their names. Records of the existence of the earliest female cocoa farm owners (working on their own account) appear for such indigenous, non-migrant towns and villages as Akokoaso, Asafo, and in Akim Abuakwa.[44] These accounts suggest that there were significant social structural and economic factors which influenced the involvement of Akan women in cocoa production.

While Brong-Ashanti women had traditionally played an important role in agricultural activity between 1900 and 1920, these women's agricultural activities on their own account had been in decline. This was due partly to the decline of periodic markets and trade as a result of the earlier Samory invasion, the Yaa

Asantewaa War of 1900 and colonial conquest. The more significant factor was that the local economy had begun the shift toward cash crop production for an external market, and female subsistence producers had not yet secured an autonomous role in this process. True, women had traditional rights to land, including that placed under cocoa, but their obligations to cultivate for husbands and the conjugal family largely inhibited them from moving into cocoa production on their own account. The period of 1920–1940 was a critical one because a conjunction of the depression and other social changes removed many former constraints to women's involvement in the cash crop sector. The economic expansion and growth of the colonial infrastructure in the 1920s, as well as the economic contraction of the 1930s, provided unique and different incentives for women again to earn their own significant incomes.

While many women took advantage of the "Pax Britannica" to return to farming, the revolutionary high cocoa prices in the 1920s stimulated some of them to enter cocoa farming in their own right. By then, much of the better land had been grabbed by elite males, but enough unutilized forest land remained. Women obtained some of this land, and cultivated cocoa after they had fulfilled labor obligations to their families. In Sunyani, some of these women emerged as serious and successful cocoa farmers, controlling viable farms of their own. Using traditional usufruct rights, these women had requested land from the stool and had gone through the payment of *aseda* to the chief. Even in 1973, many elderly women of this group could remember the ceremony, the witnesses, and the amount or kind of *aseda* offered. Their general comments indicate that the sale of foodstuffs from their food farms enabled them to pay the *aseda* and to buy the necessary labor and cutlasses to maintain the cocoa farm.[45] Other women in the district succeeded in obtaining small plots of one or two acres from their husbands as rewards for their efforts on their husbands' cocoa farms. Income from these farms was, however, quite small, due to the limited acreage. In 1939, Beckett noted that a large percentage of women cocoa farmers in Akokoaso had small plots of approximately 2.7 acres, in contrast to larger male-owned farms.[46]

When one examines the characteristics of these groups of early female cocoa farmers, a number of factors become quite clear. Contrary to popular conceptions, many women were not prevented by early marriages from engaging in cocoa farming. Fortes, for example, had described the domestic cycle of Ashanti women—their tendency to reside virilocally (with husbands) during the early childbearing years, and to be pulled out of virilocal households and back into their *abusua* as they became elderly.[47] The assumption was that as these elderly women became family heads and exercised control over extended family affairs, they (often with the help of their sons) also established cocoa farms of their own, something they could not have done at an earlier point because they were busily working on their husbands' farms. Moreover, it was held that because women moved from their natal areas to reside with husbands, they had no usufruct claims to land. My survey data from Sunyani District cocoa farmers in 1973 shows conclusively that in many indigenous Brong-Ashanti and Ahafo communities, women did not necessarily relocate upon marriage. They could, and did in fact pursue their own economic activities while working on their husbands' farms. Thus, by the 1920s, relatively young women in their maximum childbearing years had started to acquire cocoa farms.

In contrast to the more southern cocoa areas like Akim Abuakwa, women in interior areas like the Sunyani District formed approximately one-eighth of any random sample of cocoa farmers. In Nsuatre, where most of the 232 farmers surveyed lived, many of the female farmers were married and had children. Only twenty-nine of the female cocoa farmers in the sample were widowed or divorced. Of farms owned by women and acquired between 1920 and 1940, some forty-two percent of these units were obtained by the women themselves. Most of the female farmers surveyed tended to be mothers with an average of five children, who possessed an average of 1.94 farms. The adjusted median farm holdings per woman was 7.43 acres—quite small in comparison to median farm holdings per male of over 160 acres. One should note, however, that in an administrative center like Sunyani, both male and female farm sizes were far above normal for this district, and quite high in comparison to earlier data from Ashanti and Brong Ahafo with migrant farming communities. Female farmers of the towns and villages of the interior may well have had greater flexibility than female farmers in the southern and coastal areas.[48]

An unusually high number of female cocoa farmers in the Sunyani District owned more than 200 acres. These women appeared to be the wives of successful male farmers. Twenty-five percent of female farm owners had obtained farms from husbands as payment for their help, but the vast majority of women had made their own farms. Occasionally, husbands assisted them by allowing their paid laborers to weed the wife's farm as well. While many of these women had enlisted their children's aid in starting the farms, they usually preferred to limit the participation of the *mmusua* in their cocoa farm activities. They prided themselves on their own efforts in reaping the benefits for themselves and their dependents, and in their ability to reinvest cocoa proceeds in other financial endeavors.

Significantly, the majority of female cocoa farmers in the sample indicated that the farms they had created with the assistance of their children were destined for their own offspring, those of their daughters and their *mmusua*. They were firm in wanting such farm ownership to give their daughters some independence from economic control by husbands. They had realized that their own economic viability depended greatly on the success and size of their yearly crop. Indeed, in times of low farm yield, their incomes and independence suffered. Sometimes, inadequate cocoa yields or family crises simply made them add their cocoa to that of a brother or husband, and they received minimal rewards for their work.

Table 4–4 gives percentages of the various means by which women acquired cocoa farms.

TABLE 4–4

METHODS BY WHICH WOMEN ACQUIRED COCOA FARMS*

By Herself	42%
From Husband	25%
From Brother	10%
From Mother	10%
From Father	4%
Miscellaneous (Uncle, Sister, Husband, Son)	9%
TOTAL	100%

*Source: Mikell Survey, 1973, Sunyani District.

The factors which encouraged the development of the female cocoa farmer were: available land, general economic prosperity and the high cocoa prices in the 1920s. When these factors changed, women were discouraged from remaining in cocoa farming, and were pushed to enter other activities. One of the results of the decline in cocoa prices during the 1930s was that poor male farmers were pushed to the economic edge. Some young rural men could work on the larger farms of their uncles to make ends meet, although they faced exploitation in the process. Others sold palm oil, sold bush meat or pledged farms. Alternatively, they migrated to urban areas in search of manual jobs, and competed with northerners such as the Mossi, or with more educated men whose job prospects were dim because of the depression and cocoa boycotts. However, for women, there were practically no modern jobs or educational opportunities; therefore, women had a more difficult time.

Those enterprising young females who had acquired cocoa farms as a means of supporting themselves and their children[49] found that their economic activity was essential for family welfare. Vallenga (1977) has shown that in the Tanoso and Abesim areas, women struggled hard to use profits derived from food farming to provide the capital for acquiring or maintaining the potentially more profitable cocoa farms. That few of them succeeded in doing so explains why female cocoa farming blossomed briefly and then declined. The fact was that in the Sunyani area, female cash crop production occurred at the high point of the early 1920s cocoa boom, and it contracted somewhat during the 1930s when the crisis in the operation of capitalist forces made male agricultural enterprises unprofitable. Although many men became indebted and lost control of cocoa farms in the 1930s, females generally could operate with much less profit, since their farms were smaller. Those females who entered the cocoa industry at this point, when there was less competition from males for land, and less pressure from males to use female labor, only began to experience major difficulties with cocoa in the post-war period.

The new female economic roles had interesting repercussions. During the disastrous 1930s, male cocoa farmers were sharply pulled back into the *abusua* socio-economic complex out of necessity. Ironically, the conjugal family and the *abusua* were now more dependent than ever on the new proceeds of female-owned cocoa farms in order to maintain the livelihood of the rural family. The result was a drastic restructuring of male–female economic roles. Despite the fact that the fortunes of female cocoa producers would decline in the post-war years, both *abusua* and conjugal families were developing an interest in female-generated cocoa property. This was, however, only one indication of a much broader shift in kinship relations and in political dynamics which were occurring in the forest zone as a result of cocoa production.

Notes

1. Accra, Adm 54/4/5, 15 Sept 1923, Wam-Mim Boundary Dispute.
2. Syi, DA0/2/C16, 1923.
3. Land Cases, Sunyani District, 1918–1925, Case against the Sumahene, 10 Jan. 1924.
4. Report of Cpt. C. H. Armitage, Traveling Commissioner, 2 Aug. 1901; also MFA/4/1, West African Treaties.
5. Syi, DA0/2/C16, 1928.
6. Ibid.
7. ADM 54/4/5, Land Cases, Sunyani, 1918–1925.
8. Accra, ADM 54/4/5.
9. ADM 11/1309, no. 87, 1913, Ross, 8 Sept. 1913.
10. Ibid.
11. ADM 11/1309, Conf. 9603, no. 3, H.B., 23 Dec. 1913.
12. ADM 11/1309, T1/19, Wheatley, 4 Feb. 1919.
13. ADM 11/1309, no. 2378/Case 252, 1929, Maxwell, 24 Dec. 1929.
14. Dunn and Robertson, 1973.
15. ADM 11/1332 MPS, NA Case 13/21, Slater to Avery, 30 Sept. 1927.
16. Ibid.
17. ADM 11/1332, SS Conf. 2, Slater to Avery, 7 Nov. 1927.
18. Ibid. Also MPS, NA, Case 13/21, 1927.

19. Ibid.
20. Tordoff, 1965, 373.
21. Mikell, 1975, 65–8.
22. Hill, 1970.
23. ADM.
24. The derivation of this term is unclear. This category of agricultural labor which received one-third of the profits appears to predate the cocoa industry. See Hill, 1970.
25. Brokensha, 1966; Adomako-Sarfo, 1971.
26. Mikell, 1975, 60–61. Life Histories, Sunyani area.
27. Asante, 1975; Ollenu, 1960.
28. Beckett, 1947, 46. Bray, 1959, 50.
29. Mikell, social survey of 233 cooperative society cocoa farmers in the Sunyani District, 1973.
30. Dunn and Robertson, 1973.
31. Nyanteng, 1978; Gunnarson, 1978, 94–96, 138.
32. ADM 54/1/3, p. 54, 14 March 1931.
33. Rhodie, 1968, no. 9, 105–18.
34. Bauer, 1967, 256; Kofi, 1976.
35. Bouret, 1960, 66–67. See also Cmd. 5845, Report on the Commission on the Marketing of West African Cocoa, 1938.
36. Gunnarson supports the interpretation that the depression and cocoa hold-ups would have adversely affected rural stratification by making small farmers indebted to middlemen and financiers (Gunnarson, 1978, 141–2). For an analysis of the impact that price would have had on cocoa plantings, see Nyanteng, 1978 and Gunnarson, 1978, 100–103.
37. Cmd. 2744, 1926, Report of W.G.A. Ormsby-Gore.
38. Bourret, 1960, 122.
39. Bourret, 1960, 49–50; see also Leg. Council Debates 1926–7, pp. 10–36, Guggisberg speech 22 Feb. 1926.
40. Lucy Mair, *Native Policies in Africa*. London, 1936, pp. 12–18, 157–68, 264–9.
41. For colonial discussions see G.C.S.P.3 of 1924–5, Governor's address to Legislative Council, 6 March 1924; also Bourret, 1960, 72–3.
42. Bourret, 1960: 180–1.
43. ADM 54/1/1, no. 284/04, 1904.
44. Hill, 1958: also, 1963, 11, 42, 116.
45. Mikell, social survey of 233 Sunyani Areas Cooperative Society cocoa farmers, 1973.
46. Beckett, 1944, 61.
47. Fortes, 1949.
48. Compare these statistics with those of Okali and Kotey, 1971, 15, 32.
49. The work of Beckett (1944), Hill (1958), and Okali & Kotey (1975), show that this female involvement in cocoa was much more widespread than just in the Sunyani area.

5

Cocoa Alters Kinship

Cocoa, as the people's industry, not only brought changes in the social structure of Gold Coast society, but altered the kinship system and domestic organization as well. One reason for this impact was that family and marital relations were at the heart of Gold Coast cocoa production. One of the things that made cocoa the largest export industry in the Gold Coast by 1910, and the Gold Coast the number one cocoa-producing country by 1911, was the role of families and smallholders.[1] Paradoxically, it was these very factors that concerned early colonial administrators and would prove problematic in economic relations of the cocoa industry. True, there were some plantations, and some cocoa-producing lands were privately owned, especially in the southwest Ahafo region. However, by and large, land tenure for cocoa farming in most of the central Akan forest belt was initially lineage- and usufruct-based, rather than based on private property ownership. Labor was drawn from within the *abusua*, rather than from paid workers. Therefore, the productive forces and relations for cocoa remained primarily familial rather than private or commercial until well into the 1930s.[2] Cocoa production thereby transformed family relations and was transformed by them.

One of the main reasons why the early European monopolistic firms made such fantastic profits from cocoa was that they had no expensive overheads such as interior land acquisitions, inordinately expensive developmental infrastructure, high agricultural wages or supportive services for cocoa producers. The underlying social and human costs, largely invisible to European export agents, were absorbed by, and later transformed, the traditional domestic structures. Not until after the depression of the 1930s did the accumulating economic pressure on domestic organization explode to fuel opposition to capitalist exploitation of cocoa producers.[3] It was only at that point that it was possible to see the outlines of the subtle alterations that were taking place in the dynamics of family units and in matrilineal kinship and jural relations as a result of cocoa production.

By World War II, the direction of changing kinship dynamics in Akan cocoa areas was clearly visible.[4] Patrilineal vs. matrilineal identities were in conflict; lineage solidarity was in flux, and cognatic/affinal relations (over-utilized to secure economic benefit) were sorely tested. Again, because cocoa production had been detrimental to the lineage-based subsistence economy, those lineage members without cocoa farms were discovering that they were at risk. Whereas traditional law clearly recognized matrilineal *abusua* property, and the obligation to transfer these to matrilineal relatives, some persons (primarily men) were now beginning to own private cocoa farms to which the economic claims of lineage members might be precluded. After World War II, the problem for traditional courts, local authorities and urban courts was whether to uphold the principle of *abusua* inheritance of cocoa farms in cases where spouses had participated in making farms owned by husbands. Here, the interests of wives and children on the one hand, and lineage members of both male and female farm owners on the other hand, often came into conflict.

By the 1950s, international, national, rural, ethnic and domestic stratification conflicts were converging to such an extent that there were deep divisions of interests within co-residential family units, between kin groups and between the lineages, many of which traditionally provided the chiefs and elders for rural communities. Thus, while cocoa production permitted Gold Coast males to become more autonomous economic actors (as contrasted to females), it speeded up the jural fragmentation of rural communities and eroded the traditional lineage base of local representation. These changes conspired against the economic interests of rural women, sisters as well as wives, thereby making matrilineal families more vulnerable under contemporary economic conditions.

Early Pressures Toward Change

Cocoa farming, while responsible for major changes in Gold Coast matrilineage and family structures, was not the first development to do so. Caseley Hayford, Rattray, Fortes, Wilks, Arhin and others[5] have delineated the structural changes that affected the role of women in the jural and political evolution of Akan society. However, there has been fluctuation in the centrality of these structures to processes of Akan life. Particularly during the process of state development in the seventeenth and eighteenth centuries, matrilineal principles continued to operate in the domestic sphere, and even within the aristocracy. However, new patrifilial tendencies began to influence access to achieved rather than ascribed political offices and public statuses.[6] Changing economic and political factors marginalized ordinary women and decreased the role of even elite women as leaders and political representatives. Women were always involved as supporters in political endeavors, but decreasingly involved as leaders and political representatives. In myths and oral traditions, many female members of royal families appeared as chiefs and led splinter groups to found new states on the peripheries. They were said to marry and then turn over the stools and political regalia to sons; but even these traditions began to change. Menstrual blood began to be judged polluting, making women virtually unfit for many public positions. Some myths now charged that if females performed some of their previous ritual duties, they would suffer a penalty of barrenness.[7] There are hints of this new relationship in material culture. For example, in some areas male representations of political status figures increased in funerary pottery and other artifacts, while more encompassing lineage and female representations declined. It is noteworthy that this changing ritual status, while extreme in Ashanti, was less so in the peripheral Akan areas of Aowin and Krinjambo, where women retained some important public positions.[8] Changing family form with heavy emphasis on the conjugal and patricentric household, also became evident during this period of political change. Increasing wars of conquest permitted Ashanti males to acquire slave wives and thereby rear the children of these women as members of their own *mmusua* (something that should have been the prerogative of the wife's lineage).[9]

By the nineteenth century, warfare and political conquest had transformed the role of Ashanti males into that of warriors, for whom the *asafo*[10] (military) company was a very significant social unit. Correspondingly, for the majority of Akan women of that period, primary status was defined by their traditional roles as mothers and reproducers for the lineage as well as for the conjugal household. For both males and females, the traditional importance of the role of the matrilineage and its representation in the local community was significantly changed. Both male and female roles and relations were to be further altered by the interacting factors of colonialism, Christianity and the dynamics of cocoa production during the twentieth century.

Akan Kinship and Marriage

By affecting the already changing roles of males and females, cocoa production modified Akan patterns of marriage and divorce. During the late nineteenth and early twentieth centuries, the dynamics of the export-based colonial economy caused men to predominate in production of export crops, leaving women to play ancillary economic roles. While husband and wife or brother and sister often worked jointly on economic enterprises, it was males who appeared as the owners of goods produced, as well as of businesses owned. By the mid-1900s, the traditional division of labor and the relations to cocoa production had so transformed Akan domestic life that tensions within Akan households had become inevitable.

Traditionally, Akan matrilineal structures made women central to life, since descent passed through them. It has been said that brothers and sisters were bound together in mutual interest through the sister's children, who were the future heirs of the lineage. The sister's tie to her lineage was therefore an extremely strong one. Perhaps the paramount expression of this fact is that rural Akan women often do not give up residence in their natal compounds or villages after marriage, but remain structurally and emotionally part of their matrilineage. In a typical traditional marriage, the husband and wife had a regular visiting relationship, while each continued to reside in the home compound with mothers and/or sisters. Post-marital residence was somewhat different in the larger towns, or areas where there was significant migration, but there was still general recognition of the structural importance of women to their lineage groups over the entire course of their lives. Nevertheless, while women were the vessels for transmitting access to resources and authority within the matri-group (the "blood-group" or *mogya-group*), they were not themselves the loci of power and authority. Brothers and uncles were the major actors in matrilineal groups, even though the lineage segments or *yamfunu* groups were structured around sisters and their offspring, and could thus become the focal point of segmentation.[11] We shall see that these relations changed. A Twi proverb symbolizes this family unity despite structural divisions: "*Abusua* te se mfwiren; egugu akuw-akuw (A family is like flowers; it throws off in clusters)."

Despite the traditional structural centrality of women, male control over females was demonstrated first in the father's ritual relationship to the daughter; second and mainly, in the control which the mother's brother exercised over his niece; and third in the rights *in uxorem* which husbands exercised over wives. In the case of the father-daughter relationship, one notes that while a man had no jural authority over his children since they belonged to another lineage, it was necessary that his paternity be recognized to ensure their legitimacy. Moreover, he had a moral obligation for the welfare of his children by virtue of them sharing his *ntoro* or *ntron* (spiritual identification).[12] This obligation continued longest for the son, whom the father would normally train, and who would then pass on the spiritual connection (but not the *mogya* connection) to his children.[13] With respect to the daughter, the father had a ritual responsibility to approve his daughter's choice of marriage mate, as was clearly shown in the girl's puberty and marriage ceremonies. In the nubility rites, the father or a member of his lineage gave a gift of money or valuables to the daughter, emphasizing her social and economic autonomy, but relinquishing any responsibility for her.[14] Henceforth, the daughter assumed responsibility for herself, and upon marriage her husband had partial responsibility for her support and that of the children. Upon the payment of the bridewealth and the headwine (*tiri nsa*—the ritual symbol of marital legitimacy) the rights to exclusive sexual control and conjugal services could be exercised by the husband. A couple's children might reside within a different compound from their father, but they visited regularly, often carrying a father's meals from their mother's compound. In addition to the *ntoro* food taboos and ritual obligations, children had the responsibility to pay for their father's casket, thereby indicating their grief at his death and their affective ties to him and his lineage.[15] On the other hand, should the man die, his widow could be inherited by his heir, who would have responsibility to maintain her and the children as the husband would have.

Traditionally, a woman's brother's authority over niece and nephew lasted throughout their lives. For the nephew, this authority was offset by his right to inherit lineage and other property from the uncle upon death. But for the niece, this authority was demonstrated by the uncle's right to choose a marriage partner for her (as contrasted with the need for a father's approval). The man chosen should be from a different *abusua* as well as *ntoro* group, and should be morally upstanding and self-supporting. It was not unusual for an uncle to marry his niece to his own son in order to satisfy both affective and lineage responsibilities. An uncle thereby consolidated his jural as well as moral responsibilities to niece and son, and assured his own continued participation (through the new couple) in property which jurally belonged to his *abusua*. Cross-cousin marriage was frequent in traditional Akan society, and scarcely met with the kind of opposition that it encountered later, as Christianization and modernization increased.[16]

Instead of marrying a niece to his son, an uncle might arrange a marriage between her and a more wealthy patron who, by paying a debt, helped offset family expenses. An uncle could also pawn a niece outright to defray a debt. The ability of males to pawn even their married nieces (who often dwelled within the lineage compound) increased men's ability to muster financial support in the late nineteenth century, even from in-laws. These kinds of revenue accumulating techniques, although resented by the pawned subjects, male or female, were frequently used by indebted rural folk to extract themselves from debt or to keep their heads above water. Pawning of women in traditional society was a serious affair since it meant possibly alienating the reproductive collateral of the lineage, which could be realized from conjugal and affinal support networks. However, females were a resource of great value expression, readily acceptable as valuables in economic matters.[17] The pregnancy of such a pawn did not entitle a man to damages, such as he could claim for another wife, should she engage in sexual relations with another man—since neither he nor his lineage had given any bridewealth or *tiri nsa* (headwine) for her. Nevertheless, one should not conclude that a man could pawn his female dependents with impunity. Such acts could reflect upon his own status within the local community and upon the character of his matrilineage; it was likely to elicit disapproval from fathers who would not accept with equanimity the pawning of their daughters.

Many of the tensions that were inherent in African matrilineal societies were exacerbated when cocoa production was added to the attack on Akan systems of kinship and marriage by the other forces of western Christendom.

Falling Between Two Lineages

A major problem for the Akan matrilineage was conflict between maternal and paternal matrilineal groups on the one hand, and cyclical assertions of patricentricity on the other hand. In addition. the cocoa economy spawned increased divergences of interest *within* the matrilineage—especially between a man and the children of his matrilineage, for example. Many early cocoa farmers had been assisted by uncles to enter the cocoa business, especially in the Sunyani area, where this was true of approximately fifty percent of male cocoa farmers who were surveyed. However, the new social climate and economic needs were changing this pattern. Instead, the new conflicts of interest resulted in the solidification of lineage interests around brothers to an unprecedented extent. In many cases, wives and children were pawns in this process of socio-economic transformation and emerging patricentricity. Individuals were often uncertain as to whether their interests were best served by their lineages of birth (the family of orientation), or by the kin group to which they belonged by marriage (the family of procreation). This conflict reflected a weakening of corporate lineage solidarity and decreased recognition of lineage responsibilities and obligations, primarily with respect to economic resources and property.

The notion that the Akan matrilineage is in full demise has long been asserted, even though the issue is still controversial. K.A. Busia, an early Ghanaian scholar, sociologist and former head of state, quoted a farmer when he said that "Cocoa destroys kinship, and divides blood relations." Busia wrote in 1951:

> There is a tension in the social structure which is a counterpart to the economic tension about property and inheritance. In the matrilineal system of Ashanti one result of the laws of succession was to emphasize and maintain a closer bond between brother and sister than between husband and wife. The solidarity of the lineage derived considerable strength from the solidarity of siblings. The

> desire to pass on some of a man's property to his sons instead of siblings has resulted in a weakening of the bond between siblings, which shows itself in strained relationships and frequent quarrels, especially between a man's wives and his sisters who are the mothers or potential mothers of his sons and heirs, respectively.[18]

The persisting role in southern Ghana of the matrilineage in maintaining Akan cocoa farms as late as the 1970s has made us question the conclusion that the cocoa industry was destroying matrilineal kinship. It is clear that the Gold Coast could scarcely have achieved such economic development without the social base which familial relations of production provided. Nevertheless, the tensions Busia identified were real and did alter family dynamics. Moreover, it was not simple greed which brought this about. Subtle changes in traditional and legal treatment of private property as well as lineage property (primarily cocoa farms) were major factors that resulted in the tensions noted above. Whereas, prior to cocoa penetration there was relatively little private property in land and farms except among the traditional elite (who owned whole villages), Brong-Ashanti male farmers who were "forward thinking" attempted to create private cocoa farms. Over the thirty to forty year production life of cocoa farms, these men would have to rely heavily on both family and paid labor. Hence, there was the question of how to compensate family members who had invested labor or capital on "own account" or on the private farms of male relatives. Wives, sons and daughters constituted the bulk of this labor-contributing group. By helping the father acquire some financial autonomy, the conjugal family promoted his future ability to satisfy his moral obligations to his own children (in contrast to those of his sister), placing their lives on a more solid footing. For example, in the Sunyani District, most farmers depended upon this conjugal labor force to cultivate cocoa farms. Nevertheless, in the 1970s, more than sixty percent of District farmers who were surveyed employed additional, non-family labor at some point, even if only an annual laborer, or occasional daily laborers.[19]

By choosing to reside and work with the father on his farm, children often neglected identification and residence with their own lineage. The contradiction here was that the labor of the children was supposed to benefit their own *mmusua* and not that of the father. This was clearly changing. Doubtlessly, the joint efforts of a man's family of procreation increased his recognition of his moral obligations to his progeny—especially in education and training. In traditional times, this obligation posed few financial problems. However, given the escalation of desires for formal education in rural areas during the colonial period, fathers now faced escalating costs. True, the children (primarily sons) earned their way by assisting their fathers, and often the children's lineage might even encourage them to do so, especially if it was not a prosperous group. This, however, was not in accordance with tradition, and was engendered by cocoa production.

Table 5–1 gives percentages of family labor and paid labor on cocoa farms.

TABLE 5–1

FAMILY VS. PAID LABOR ON COCOA FARMS*

			paid labor					
	self	**wife & child**	**one**	**2–3**	**4–6**	**7–10**	**11–12**	***Abusa***
relative	19.3%	13.7	14.2	23.6	10.3	2.1	11.5	5.2
cumulative	19.3%	33.0	47.2	70.8	81.1	83.3	94.8	100%

*Includes both *abusua* and private cocoa farms of 233 sample farmers in the Sunyani District, 1973.

Although traditionally a man's matrilineage expected him to train his sons, many men objected to the increasing costs of educating them, considering such expenses as detrimental to the interest of the corporate lineage. Many fathers, aware of the contributions of their domestic family to their own-account farms, took care to deed a defined portion of their property to their sons or daughters through the traditional ceremonies, thus receiving *aseda* or public recognition of this act. Of course, poor men did not succeed in acquiring own-account farms, and therefore had little inducement or lineage support in dividing property which they controlled prior to their death. In the 1973 Sunyani study, only twenty-five percent of the sample had already divided their cocoa-farm holdings and, significantly, these were exclusively men with own-account farms.

When men did divide farm holdings, they tended to transfer property in their private (own-account) farms to children rather than to wives. The problem here was that wills were seldom made, and cocoa farms were sometimes transferred without legal papers or ceremonies. Even when a farmer stated publically that after his death a part of the farm was intended for the "wife and children," it often simply passed through the caretakership of the wife, and was ultimately destined for the children when they came of age. Since daughters generally married before fathers died, fathers usually made ceremonial gifts of money to them—or, if they were prosperous, buildings—rather than leaving them part of their farms. Women who received such gifts used them, or rents from inherited buildings, to trade for themselves. Sons generally remained with prosperous fathers in the hopes of inheriting. Nevertheless, sons who labored on their fathers' farms well into advanced adulthood without receiving anything were often considered foolish. The assumption was that unless the father turned over some property to the son by the time the latter was thirty-five years old, the likelihood of the son receiving anything after his death was not great.

The following data from Sunyani District farmers, given in Table 5–2, shows that the lineage was still the major inheritor of men's property; but there was also a growing tendency for non-*abusua* heirs to receive something.

TABLE 5–2

WHO WILL INHERIT FROM YOU?

Responses of Male Farmers: Heirs	Sunyani/Fiapre		Nsuatre		Odumasi	
	#	%	#	%	#	%
Brother	49	42	59	46	19	68
Nephew	8	7	21	16.5	5	18
Children	29	25	23	18	2	7
Wives	19	16	11	8.5	1	3.5
Abusua	7	6	5	4	1	3.5
Sister	2	2	5	4	0	0
Mother	2	2	4	3	0	0
	116	100%	128	100%	28	100%

What one observes, both from the data and from farmers' comments, is the development of patrifocal tendencies in how male cocoa farmers wanted to treat property. While these responses reflected ideal culture rather than real life, the inheritance of cocoa farms by sons had started to challenge that of the matrilineal corporate group.[20]

Until the end of World War I, colonial legal structures tended to support this patrifilial development.[21] The 1898 "Ordinance Marriage" statute's inheritance provisions, established by the colonial administration, permitted wives and children to inherit two-thirds of a man's property. However, these laws were often supported by Christian church converts, but resisted by the mass of Gold Coast people. The assertion of traditional inheritance and land tenure patterns in the late 1920s further arrested the brief flowering of these patrilineal tendencies. Nevertheless, the impact of these practices varied. In Sunyani, inheritance by sons was fairly significant, while in the more traditional villages such as Odumasi, it was held to a minimum. In some traditional areas, such as Akokoaso in the eastern region, matrilineal inheritance predominated, making brothers and nephews the major heirs, with sons the next group of inheritors. In response to pressures from elite women for guarantees for wives and children, the Ghana government proposed a "Marriage, Divorce and Inheritance Bill" in 1963, but it was subsequently withdrawn.[22] However, by 1971 in many areas, such as Akokoaso where the Presbyterian church was well established, new local by-laws existed which required the division of a man's estate into three parts, giving one-third to the *abusua* and two-thirds to the widow and the children.[23] Nevertheless, these were local rather than national laws.

Although colonial administrators initially tended to focus on defining and guaranteeing the rights of ordinance-married wives in monogamous unions,[24] they were also concerned with "native slaves and pawns." The early missionaries had little success in westernizing African marriage practices,[25] but Christianity and education did succeed in the assault against the pawning of females. Pawning continued at a contained level well into the 1940s in inland areas such as the Sunyani District. It had artificially escalated in response to the scarcity of women and social upheaval around the turn of the twentieth century, then declined with economic prosperity which resulted from cocoa farming. However, this declining practice was again temporarily bolstered during the economic upheavals of the 1930s, and a rash of cases were brought by female pawns as they became aware that colonial administrators and courts were somewhat sympathetic to their position. It is noteworthy that while the colonial attitude aimed at freeing them from marital and family oppression (polygyny, forced marriage and pawning), it gave them few rights in other than domestic areas. The colonial courts hesitated to consider the rights of women with respect to economic/property issues, preferring to see such cases handled by the native tribunals. Therefore, many women's cases in the administrative courts were presented in terms of kinship rather than in terms of revenue/property.

Whereas prior to 1940 the majority of cases involving women were instigated by men seeking adultery fees and seduction damages from guilty males, after 1940 these cases were matched by a substantial number of cases presented by women seeking redress for their own grievances. In coastal areas such as Akwapim, there was evidence that as a result of "westernization" as well as affluence flowing from the cocoa economy, many of these women's cases were suits for divorce, maintenance or breach of marriage contracts. However, in archival files from the Sunyani District Court (1940s) where western influences were less marked, it became apparent that the cases of women were more varied and complex. These complaints generally fell into several categories: (a) complaints against members of their own *abusua* or against their husband's *abusua*; (b) intricate cases dealing with traditional law and new economic environment; (c) claims for divorce, because of the failure of the *abusua* to support women attempting to dissolve marriages. The following cases are typical:

1. A woman complains that she was given in marriage by her uncle to a man who paid a debt belonging to the uncle. When her own father died, she incurred funeral debts, so she has referred the creditor to the uncle, whom

she thought would pay it for her. The uncle has refused and the creditor is still worrying her. She claims that by rights, the uncle should have paid her subsequent funeral debts, since her marriage occurred as a means of securing money to pay his original debt.

2. A married woman has several children, but her husband has mistreated her and refused to give food and clothing. She asked for divorce; but her uncle refused to perform the customary necessities so that the divorce could take place (repayment of the marriage *aseda*). She requests that the D.C. persuade the uncle to do so.
3. A woman complains that she has consistently been mistreated by her husband, so she has requested a divorce. He has refused and she seeks legal judgment.
4. The granddaughter of a late chief has been attending school in Ashanti and wanted to finish. The present chief, her uncle, arranged for her to marry another big chief. She objected and made herself pregnant by a man she likes, but he still insists that she marry the other chief, and the other chief still wants her. She requests that the D.C. prevent this forced marriage.[26]

In all of these cases, the women were not acting independently of their orbit, despite having brought their cases to the District court. They seemed to feel that vindication of their rights was dependent upon the actions taken by other kinspersons. Fearing that strict adherence to traditional norms would not now result in the traditionally desired results, they resorted to laws and to the new colonial courts to reinforce the norms. In some cases, no traditional "wrong" had been committed against the female complainants; however, relying upon recent economic changes and the principles of conjugal and nuclear family structure, they were making a new order of claims.

The adamant stance taken by the above complainants would have been unthinkable in the early 1900s in this area of Ashanti, because of the lack of colonial, legal, administrative or social supports for their position. Their ability to pursue these cases was also based on their increased social and economic independence during the cocoa boom period. Many of these women recognized their own labor contributions to their husbands' cocoa farms, and felt that they could maintain themselves on their own cocoa farms. The possibility of independent incomes appears to have made them less tolerant of what they considered repressive conditions.

These cases must also be seen against the backdrop of changing social conditions in rural areas. Social stability (despite colonial occupation) following British conquest, a low migration rate for Akan males,[27] as well as heightened natural increase as a result of better medical facilities and the need for a sizable family workforce for cocoa, helped to bring about changes in the rural demography. This, in turn, brought about new patterns of marriage and divorce. Wives were now more available than they had been at the turn of century, and more necessary to manage cocoa farms; therefore polygyny was likely to have increased after 1920. Fertility has traditionally been quite high in Ghana, but this would have taken a leap in the period prior to World War 1I, in response to cocoa production and prosperity. The recorded average number of children in Ghana was 5.8 in 1931 and it rose to 6.6 in 1948.[28] In 1960, the fertility rate was 7.1, although women in rural Brong-Ashanti areas produced many more children than did most Ghanaian women.[29] Paradoxically, in the maximum cocoa production areas around Sunyani, the average number of children of female cocoa farmers who were surveyed in 1972 was five.[30]

Many of the early male cocoa farmers in this area who married before or during the 1930s had more than one wife. Data from a survey of 233 Sunyani area cocoa farmers in 1973 showed that the mean number of wives for male farmers was 1.6, and suggested that the sizes of these men's families were much larger than they would have been before cocoa. It is significant that in this survey, 86 percent of the 233 farmers (male and female) were married, with only 7 percent widowed or divorced. Most of the male interviewees with two or more wives were concentrated in the over-60 age group which constituted 37 percent of the sample. Thus, although the trend toward monogamy and the nuclear family was found among the younger farmers (67 percent of the sample), it is clear that among the older group, polygyny and large family size were assets in early cocoa farm production. The conjugal family in Brong-Ashanti cocoa areas was seldom an independent unit; rather, it was bound into the relationships of the component lineages to which the partners belonged. In terms of residence, as was already mentioned, they might also live with their own lineage members, rather than together.[31] In 1960 approximately 40 percent of married females in the Sunyani District were residing "in houses other than those in which their husbands were staying."[32] These facts, combined with the high Akan divorce rate, has led many to consider the Akan marital unit as inherently unstable. Traditionally, the most important grounds for divorce were: (a) adultery or misconduct, (b) infertility, and (c) failure to maintain the wife and children economically or to educate the children. While both partners possessed a right to request a divorce, women now requested it more often than men, generally citing economic reasons.

Data from a survey on marriage and divorce in Berekum illustrates some of the problems that were occurring in Brong-Ashanti cocoa areas. Sixty percent of married respondents had undergone customary rites, 25 percent had Ordinance marriages, and 15 percent had the low-status *Mpena awadie* (common law) marriage.[33] It was not unusual for a spouse to have been married two or three times: approximately 33 percent of males and 37.5 percent of females had been divorced at some point. Unlike many rural southern areas, where migrant cocoa farming may have temporarily increased the incidence of cohabitation of spouses,[34] in Berekum the traditionally separate residences also permitted polygyny or infidelity which threatened these marriages. Thus, despite the fact that cocoa farming increased the cash that a man had at his disposal, many women complained that it was spent on another woman. Men complained that wives divorced them because they disapproved of polygyny; so if these men married again, they chose *mpena awadie* unions, which gave women no recourse to actions based on polygyny. Some women also complained that ex-husbands had been unwilling to give sufficient "chop money" or to pay school-fees for the children. Since the children belonged to the women's lineage anyway, men often underestimated their responsibility for maintenance. Matrilineality plus cocoa, wives implied, had made Brong-Ashanti men irresponsible. This simple explanation must also be supplemented by the realization that the pace of change encouraged more individual choice and less lineage participation in marriage relationships—thus more frequent divorces. However, it is clear that cocoa production had influenced both the dynamics and the rate of divorce.

Married women who had devoted their efforts to their husbands' cocoa farms resented their ambiguous position when divorce resulted, as may be noted in the cases below:

1. An older woman has been married for years, but produced no issue. She assisted her husband in making and cultivating a large farm, but he has now divorced her with no means of subsistence.
2. A woman's husband died, and his nephew (as heir) inherited his cocoa farms plus responsibility for maintaining the widow and the children. Instead, he has proceeded to divorce her, thus negating his responsibility to care for her and the children. She requests intervention.
3. An older woman has several children and has worked for years on her husband's farms. He has now divorced her, depriving her of an income and refusing to support or educate the children. She seeks one of the cocoa farms to support them.

Some women were far luckier than those in the above cases. Often generous husbands divided profits from the farm, giving the wife a small sum with which to go into business for herself. She then began petty trading, reinvesting profits and expanding until she was self-sufficient and could not realistically expect further support for herself and the children. Should divorce occur, the husband owed nothing to them; rather his *abusua* might demand that she return the marriage *aseda* and the initial capital given her for trading.

Economic expansion and contraction as well as rural dependence upon a familial labor force and familial investments in cocoa farming were, however, together to alter reciprocal understandings between husbands and wives, and between farmers and their lineages. Especially after World War II, many wives began to weigh the relative benefits of marriage, as against divorce, if husbands did not compensate them for their labor after a specific period of time. It was better to cut losses by divorcing, and try to find a more secure way of providing support for the children. The heightened incidence of divorce and lineage fragmentation in the post-World War II period may therefore be partially traced to the increased social pressures stemming from the economic dynamics of the cocoa industry.

Wives of cocoa farmers appear to have been in a somewhat ambiguous position. Both traditional and popular folklore derided the wife who remained poor because of dependence upon a husband, but such cases were nevertheless becoming more common. Often wives had neglected their own lineage affairs in order to participate in the advancement of their husband's economic position, and faced complex legal problems if divorce or marital estrangement resulted. Even when men made gifts of cocoa farms to wives and this had been acknowledged by the wife's *abusua*, the questions sometimes arose as to whether the gift was intended for a man's children or for the wife herself. In many cases, husbands delayed turning over farms to the wife in order to assure her loyalty and labor participation. A man's *abusua* might allow him to give a farm to his children in recognition of his "moral" obligations as well as their labor input. And while this, too, was an alienation of his *abusua's* property, it was not judged the same way as a gift to a wife. After all, given the fragility of marriage among the Akan, a wife might go off on her own. In one such case (Addy v. Armah & Others),[35] an aggrieved wife attempted to claim ownership of a cocoa farm which the husband insisted he had given to the daughter. This case was decided in favor of the daughter. The judge stated that the mother had only the traditional ritual obligation to represent the child on behalf of its *abusua*.

The family issue concerning offspring's labor participation in cocoa farms and their subsequent rights to inherit that property was especially acute in the matrilineal Ashanti region where the traditional heirs were usually brothers and nephews. True, there was pressure on the traditional system to recognize the growing importance of the conjugal family and patrifiliation. Busia had pointed out how these factors had encouraged the Asantehene and the Confederacy Council to alter customary inheritance law in 1941, so that personal or self-acquired property could be given away, according to the wishes of the individual.[36]

Besides the issue of alienating cocoa farms, one emerging issue was whether the conjugal family had developed an "interest" in the husband's cocoa-derived property, and a right to continued maintenance from it even following his death. Traditionally, the husband owned the economic product of any joint labor between the spouses. A woman's responsibility as wife obliged her to engage in "conjugal labor" which, while it might increase the husband's economic mobility, was primarily designed to help support children of the union. If, for example, a widow had helped her husband on the farms and had lived with him in a house which he had built from cocoa funds, she and her children were entitled under customary law to be allowed by the husband's heir to continue residing there. Since the heir would assume ownership of the house as well as other cocoa farms, and would profit from them, he was expected also to shoulder the responsibility for feeding and educating the children, as the father would have done. However, heirs often interpreted their responsibilities loosely, and refused to house the widow or pay school fees. The argument was that the widow had only made those contributions to the cocoa farms which which could be normally expected from a wife; and that this did not give an economic interest in the property. Although legal challenges to these notions did occasionally occur in the 1960s, it was not until much later that the courts offered redress to those widows who could *prove* that their economic contributions went above and beyond the call of duty.[37]

The trend toward the patrifilial family in rural matrilineal areas was not independent of its earlier occurrence in some coastal Akan areas, notably in Fanti towns such as Cape Coast. Along the coast, Christianity had played a major role in speeding up the process. Among the Fanti, the emergence of mulatto trading families which bore the names of their European fathers and family heads was a quite early development. Nevertheless, even in these town populations, core matrilineal kinship patterns remained, despite the shift towards greater male control over family relations. Inland, some patrifilial developments had resulted from early Ashanti state growth, but most changes there had been generated by the economic dynamics of cocoa farming.

It would be erroneous to assume that the majority of conflict surrounding cocoa property pitted the conjugal family against the lineage. Notably, there were significant and increasing divergences between brothers and nephews on the issue of inheritance of cocoa farms. According to Ashanti traditions, brothers stand first in line of inheritance for *abusua* property, and they incur a responsibility to look after the welfare of their sisters' children with proceeds from this property. Thus, their nephews and nieces as members may stand to gain more from a man's industriousness than his own children, according to traditional customs. Nephews often worked on *abusua* farms controlled by uncles, and sometimes have been jokingly described as waiting around for the uncle to die so that they could inherit.

If we refer back to Table 5–2 we see that between 42 percent and 68 percent of the responses of male cocoa farmers indicate that brothers were the intended heirs. This is certainly appropriate if, as traditional custom required, *abusua* property was being passed on to junior brothers. Moreover, in the Sunyani data, there is some indication that a large percentage of personally acquired property was passing to brothers as well. Although approximately 17 percent of males' farms originally came from their *mmusua*, a considerably larger percentage of farms was intended for brothers.

Brothers were evidently being drawn together in economic, social and ritual relationships perhaps more tightly than other members of the *abusua*. Male members of the matrilineage hold a high social status in everyday life relative to females, corresponding to their economic and political responsibilities. This is qualified only by age, which brings authority and status to women past the childbearing phase, and allows them the possibility of assuming roles as household head and some non-family leadership positions. Thus, brothers tend to act as mutual economic supporters as they age, and have the possibility of achieving socio-economic autonomy from the lineage over their lifetimes. Should a financial crisis occur, brothers are the likely persons to provide loans to each other, or to redeem a pledged farm, whether *abusua* or personal property. This is understandable in light of the greater economic resources which males are able to accumulate.

What is also clear from the Sunyani data is that brothers are inheriting from each other generally to the exclusion of nephews, while at the same time passing property from father to son. Certainly there is evidence of a restriction of matrilineal inheritance so that property is concentrated in fewer hands, rather than being allowed to spread across generations in the *abusua*. This allowed men to reinforce the patrifilial tendencies which had emerged, while continuing to accumulate *abusua* resources. Thus, lineage farms are concentrated among those who pass on the *ntoro* connection, rather than among those who share the broader matricentric relationship.

Traditionally, there were reasonable chances that *abusua* property would devolve upon the nephew; however, this began to change as male-owned private property in cocoa farms increased. The main reason was that men now invested less energy in *abusua* endeavors than before, and more into their own-account farms which they ran as carefully and efficiently as possible. Second, in the post-World War II period, nephews were now likely to have some education or job/career aspirations, thus tending to migrate rather than wait for an uncle's inheritance. They were, therefore, not around as frequently to be employed by uncles on cocoa farms as they formerly would have been. Third, as already mentioned, traditional cross-cousin marriage, which tied uncles and nephews/nieces into a closer relationship, had been slowly disappearing; therefore, expectations of economic and social support from uncles had declined. Previously, cross-cousin marriage allowed an uncle to protect interests of both his children and his nephews/nieces. It was particularly advantageous for uncles who belonged to an *abusua* more prosperous than that of their wives, since they compounded uncle status with that of father-in-law within their own lineage. This also meant that the *ntoro* group to which the new couple's children belonged would be identical to that of the uncle and his sister, thus compounding the ritual dimension already present within the lineage. Although it requires further documentation, it seems that the decline in cross-cousin marriage may have contributed to the shallow depth in *ntoro* relationships, which was already visible by the 1920s and 1930s. It is possible to conclude, however, that the relationship between brothers (also a variation of the *ntoro* relationship) emerged as the more economically significant lineage relationship in the post-1948 period in various parts of Ashanti while the relationship between uncles and nephews diminished in importance.

All this began to change under the impact of education, westernization, Christianization and migration. By the 1920s it was becoming clear that children were more inclined to choose their own mates than marry cross-cousins. Oft-times, propinquity was a factor, with men choosing wives in villages near their cocoa farms or jobs. By the late 1940s, men were beginning to prefer wives who were semi-literate or literate.

There were additional socio-economic reasons for the weakening uncle/nephew relationship in cocoa farm ownership. Men only passed farms to nephews in the absence of appropriate older male heirs. In some cases, men held onto farms until these were no longer self-supporting or had incurred debts, by which time nephews had moved on to other endeavors. In numerous villages, there were cases where nephews had come into possession of farms which had been neglected and indebted or pledged. This was particularly true in Akwapim or in older cocoa areas of the Eastern Region. The cost of recovery and maintenance for these farms might be higher than anticipated benefits, in which case farms would be abandoned. Nephews sometimes reasoned that it was better to pluck a few cocoa pods occasionally from the farms, making enough to pay for books and school fees, or to patch up roofs on dwellings, etc., rather than make any further investment in them.[38]

Perhaps a combination of pre-colonial political patrifiliation and kinship restructuring in response to economic penetration explains the dominance of male relatives (as fathers, husbands or uncles) in economic affairs after the beginning of cocoa production. This contemporarily enhanced, traditional tendency effectively placed women at the economic margins of lineage relationships in cocoa farming areas; it was a significant counterpoint to the symbolic importance of Akan women in the kinship structures themselves.

Sister/Brother, Lineage Property and Stratification

In the post-war period, many of the social and economic dynamics in Brong-Ashanti cocoa areas were calling into question the traditional social roles of males and females within the lineage. One consequential issue was the relationship of women to lineage property in their multiple roles as sisters, wives and mothers. The growth of female cocoa farmers in the 1920s through the 1940s provided proof that women as a group were capable of participating in the benefits of cocoa development, but the question remained as to what extent. A close inspection of the more recent relationships of Brong-Ashanti women to cocoa farms and to the *abusua* seems to provide confirmation of the economic marginalization of sisters and mothers, despite their earlier benefits from cocoa. While this marginalization indicated subtle development and distortion in the operations of the matrilineal systems with respect to property control and inheritance, it might best be seen as an indication of the economic pressures to which Akan cocoa farmers and their families have been subjected.

During the early cocoa phase (1910–1930), it appeared that where contradictions or ambiguities appeared in traditional norms respecting male and female economic roles, these were often decided in favor of males whom the colonial regime emphasized as family and lineage heads. One major ambiguity centered on the treatment of male property vs. female property. Traditional customs had been quite clear in delineating distinctions between the two groups of items, and their appropriate heirs. Male property (including hunting equipment, weapons, *kutuo* for storing gold) generally devolved to a man's male heirs following his death. Gold and slaves might be either male or female property, but jewelry and household utensils were clearly female property, and were transmitted to daughters or the next female heir following a woman's death.

Land had little capital-generating value prior to the late nineteenth century; rather, it was economic activity of people on land which was economically significant. Land had previously been handled in terms of corporate rights, which were not specific as to male or female ownership. Hence, land holdings were seldom inherited, except for entire towns and villages being transferred from control of one royal to another. Instead, the stool was the custodian of the land, and confirmed the rights of families and even title-holders, to the usufruct of land within its jurisdiction. When land did begin to generate produce and raw materials intended for commodity sale (such as palm oil and rubber) in international markets, and thereby generating capital, males tended to acquire it (often on behalf of lineages) and pass it on to males.

We can date part of the ambiguity about female relationships to property in cocoa farms from this early period. While ordinary women had traditionally had garden plots or small vegetable farms from which they generated items for local and regional trade, only royal women had significant access to land for producing important resources. And while by the 1920s there was evidence of female land ownership, lineage principles regarding female property in land remained unclear, as was evidenced in the later treatment of female cocoa farms.[39]

Notably, early women who possessed cocoa farms intended that these be transmitted as female property, often to sisters and then daughters. But few women had resources to generate cocoa farms larger than about five acres. In one outstanding recorded case,[40] by 1913, three sisters of the stool family of New Juaben, together with the assistance of their husbands and children, had created a total of twenty eight cocoa farms. Significantly, although two of the three sisters later became queen mothers, these farms were kept quite distinct from stool property, and were passed down to the female descendants of the three original founders. Not until 1959 was a case brought by a later stool occupant in New Juaben, claiming that the cocoa farm had become merged into the property of the stool. It is noteworthy that the case was decided in favor of the successors and families of the three founders, but there was no reference to the validity of female property in cocoa land and farms. Thus, the court was silent on the issue of whether female generated property belongs to the lineage and therefore to *abusua*-controlled positions, or to individual female heirs. In general, however, a subtle challenge to the existence of female property in cocoa farms and land was characteristic of the post-1940s period.

The issue of the merger of female generated property into *abusua*-property may have been more widespread than generally recognized. Part of the problem may lie in the fact that women treated their own possessions as female property, and intended them to be utilized by specific members of the lineage (their own children) rather than by all lineage members. The problem was that after the death of a female owner, her property often became transformed into lineage property. In this context, it becomes important to listen to what women cocoa farmers in the Sunyani District had to say about their property. In responses given by a sample of 38 women farmers in 1973, all of whom had acquired their farms prior to 1940, it was quite clear (as shown in Table 5–3) what they wanted to happen to their farms. Proud of what they had been able to accomplish, these farmers were equally quite clear about whom they wanted to inherit their property.

TABLE 5–3

"WHO WILL INHERIT FROM YOU?"*

Responses of female cocoa farmers:		**#**	**%**
Children		21	54
	Daughters	7	19
	Sons	2	5
Sisters		8	22
		38	100%

*Drawn from author's sample of 233 cocoa farmers in the Sunyani District, 1973.

Most women desired to transmit their property to their children, to daughters, or to sisters. It is worth noting that while a woman's brother is most often the *abusua* head and normal successor (as distinct from the woman's heir), he was not mentioned by any of the women as the intended heir. Even sons were seldom listed. The paradox was that while most elderly cocoa farmers said that their wives owned cocoa farms, there were virtually no younger female cocoa farmers represented in the Sunyani sample, and very few present in the district. Either early generations of women did not have the same views of inheritance, a possibility that appears quite unlikely, or women appear not to be inheriting farms from mothers as one might expect. Plausible explanations must include the possibility that given the small size of women's farms, they were often transformed into food farms rather than remaining as cocoa farms. Apropos of this, while many women in the town indicated that they acquired their food farms from mothers, they seldom reported that they acquired cocoa farms from them (refer again to Table 5–2).

The general failure of women to transmit their cocoa farms to female descendants may be partially explained by several other factors characteristic of differential male/female behavior as well as by lineage processes. Women view their property as important to their own maintenance, and as a means of guaranteeing autonomy from their husbands. Wives appear to be quite aware that husbands have dual obligations to the conjugal family as well as to the lineage, and that husbands have divided loyalties regarding the distribution of cocoa land and revenues despite the fact that their wives and children have assisted in making the farms. Because of these facts, women hold on to their property as long as possible, seeking to derive maximum benefit from it for themselves and their children. Women, in contrast to men, therefore tend not to divide property prior to their death. Consequently, they do not pass on cocoa farms to their verbalized intended heirs. The end result of failing to give land to children prior to death is that women's cocoa farms often become transformed into *abusua* property, and are consequently controlled by male heirs.

Since elite women succeeded in transferring to female heirs their property in gold, slaves, and even cocoa land prior to the 1940s, there is a need to understand why this inheritance pattern should be disappearing. Even men seldom comment about the merger of female-owned cocoa farms into *abusua* property, despite the fact that 17 percent of the men surveyed claim to own farms derived from their *mmusua*. Men apparently make the assumption that women have a greater interest in the continuity of the matrilineage than they do.

These trends raise questions about who continues to provide for the economic security of sisters, wives and children, if female ownership of cocoa farms tends to move toward brothers within the *abusua* and towards husbands' lineages within the conjugal family. If the lineage is the refuge for sister and brother, as traditional idiom stresses, how can this continue to be so, given evidence that males are moving outside the lineage orbit in most of their economic relationships? There is no question about the widening gulf between brothers and sisters, as a function of differential perceptions of the relationship of men's personally acquired property to that of the lineage. Busia's 1951 comments[41] about the frequent arguments between a man's sisters and his wives over cocoa farms and resources must be re-examined. Is it possible that in the final analysis women, as the basis of families, were being sensitized to an economic reality largely characterized by cyclical boom and recession of the earlier cocoa economy? This reality began to fade given the diverging interests of sister and brother in the period which followed.

Characteristic of the booming cocoa economy of the 1950s was that male farmers increasingly paid school fees to educate their own children, who did not belong to their matrilineages. In many cases, prosperous farmers relocated to towns, and their sons migrated to even larger cities in search of more modern jobs or a college education. During the post-war economic boom the massive rural labor needs were often met through the use of migrant northern wage labor (Mossi, Grunshi, Dagarti, Lobi)[42] on a daily or contract basis, thus allowing a decreased dependence upon nephews and other lineage laborers. Women also often took the proceeds from cocoa farms to help pay school fees for their children; when they were traders, they used profits to put children through college. In such ways, women continued their interest and investments in their lineages.

Male dependence upon the lineage was decreased still further as large numbers of successful Sunyani District male farmers built their own houses in town, and no longer resided in matrilineal compounds in which mothers and sisters were symbolically important. With their absence, their contributions of money to sisters' compounds also began to decline. The issue was compounded by the increase in divorces, with few women continuing to receive support from former husbands. In some more distant towns such as Dormaa, there was an increase in female-headed households from which women occasionally visited their husbands' compounds.[43] One should note that the declining everyday role of lineage males was accompanied by the increasing strength of the conjugal family and household.

The brother-sister relationship was further weakened by geographical mobility due to cocoa farming. By the 1950s, many men acquired fresh cocoa farms farther south, and as the local price of cocoa fell relative to food crops, they began to acquire land for maize farms in the south through purchase or tribute. Sunyani District men who could afford it purchased land in the Ahafo area, often locating a second wife on the farm and spending a good portion of time in residence there. When this absentee cocoa farmer pattern began to increase in Sunyani, it was accompanied by the lessening involvement of either sisters or lineage members in the migrants' households. Data from Okali and others[44] also confirm that migrants do not readily employ lineage members on these new Ahafo and Western Region farms. Thus, one observes increasing distance between brother and sister during economic booms. We will later see that both distance and economic vulnerability were conditions affecting sisters at subsequent difficult economic phases.

A correlate of the increased divergence of interests within the lineage was a corresponding clearer distinction between the offspring of grandmothers who, though belonging to different *yamfunu* groups, were nevertheless members of the lineage. Although this distinction was not new, the process of lineage fragmentation had an increasing effect on later generations. Men who have been educated by fathers or by mothers hesitate to use their personally acquired resources outside their families of orientation. Parallel cousins who in the past called each other "brother" and "sister" and were often treated as such, now have few expectations of sharing in resources generated by their mothers' sisters or other maternal relatives.

The social and economic factors which undergirded the increasing divergence between individuals and segments within the lineage became more complex. Cocoa was not totally responsible for all the kinship changes. Rather, cash crop production under the constraints of an extractive, colonial/capitalist economy led to social patterns which exploited and then altered kinship relations. These were often buttressed by the other forces of western Christendom. That the lineage continued to play an important role in rural rather than in urban areas is due more to the economic needs of cocoa, rather than to the inherent cohesiveness of lineage relations.

Ethnic Diversity and the Impact of Cocoa on Kinship

Ashanti and Brong cocoa areas have tolerated considerable familial, religious and sub-cultural diversity, while remaining quite "Akan." It is well known that in the eastern and central regions, the arrival and settlement of Kwahu, Ewe and Shai migrant cocoa farmers resulted in considerable intermarriage between the newcomers and the Akan. Even in the Brong-Ashanti areas, the label "*donkor*" referred to descendants of outsiders who, while having formerly been slaves, had become Akanized.[45] One of the less recognized results of the cocoa economy was increasing inter-ethnic contact between Akan farm owners and northern migrant workers. There was a subtle process of intermarriage which satisfied both the labor and economic needs of cocoa farms. Although the importance of Akan-northern relations were ignored at the public level, they began to have significant impact on the operation of the matrilineal household, and on cultural flexibility at the village and community level. The reasons for this kinship dynamic was twofold: Akan men sought to utilize relations through their females to create dependent affinal relationships with northern migrant cocoa laborers; and conjunctively, Akan women made efforts to create viable conjugal units with northerners so that they could maintain cocoa farms. Both of these factors were obvious in Brong-Ashanti villages of the Sunyani District during the 1950s, 1960s and 1970s.

The pattern of inter-ethnic relations during the cocoa period was radically different from the pre-colonial period, when captured northerners [*nnonkofo*] were integrated into the lineages of their Akan captors as unfree or slave dependents.[46] After the conquest, for a variety of historical and cultural reasons, the classic northern groups targeted for intermarriage with Akan women were the Mossi. The Mossi fit more neatly into the patterns of accommodation between the Ashanti/Akan and northerners, most of whom (unlike the Mossi) were Muslim.[47] For political as well as commercial reasons, during the eighteenth and nineteenth centuries, the Ashanti had restricted Muslim traders to residence in urban *zongos* (stranger quarters).[48] In time, the Muslim identity appears to have become the only non-Akan identity to which the Ashanti granted relative respect. In Kumasi and other large towns, for example, the Muslim community (which included some Mossized Muslim Yarse) provided spiritual and talismanic protections for war, as well as facilitated links with traders and slavers along the trade routes. The Muslim label was applied to all Mossi traders, as well as to later Mossi migrants into the Gold Coast.

Whereas Muslims in Asante *zongo* communities were initially insulated from relations with the wider Akan communities, the northern migrants who later came to rural cocoa villages had daily contact with the Akan. Many of the first migrants (1900–1948) from northern Gold Coast and southern Upper Volta, had fled colonial forced labor conditions in their home communities. They prolonged their stay in the south, learned Twi, and even married Akan wives. For many a Mossi migrant, getting a wife was a distinct advantage, because traditional Mossi fathers often postponed marriage for sons until relatively late in life, and some men never married until their fathers died, leaving wives for the sons to inherit.[49] Because of these factors, there was considerable intermarriage between Mossi migrants (especially those who did not plan to return home) and Gold Coast women in the northern territories of Ghana, and in the south among the Akan.

By the 1940s, there was a large group of Mossi migrants in the Sunyani area where they worked as *abusa* laborers (earning one-third share of the cocoa crop), as *nkotokuano* laborers (paid by the load of cocoa picked). or as contract laborers who "bought a field" (earned a set wage for a job). The majority were, however, *abusa* laborers, and these had ongoing relationships with farm owners.

They often lived on these farms, where they relied upon their employers to supply land for their own food farming, or they rented space in nearby rural villages which increasingly had *zongos* with *zongo* chiefs. Those Mossi *abusa* men who resided on the farms developed strong patron-client ties with the Brong-Ashanti. They actualized their plans to remain by marrying Akan women, often encountered hostility and scorn from other Mossi who claimed that they engaged in "slave marriage." However, their detractors ignored the economic factors in marriages which gave the Mossi access to cocoa land; the situation was much more complex than they realized.

For both economic and political reasons, Mossi migrants had left home and by chance found themselves living and working within matrilineal areas where divorce rates for Akan women were relatively high. Many of the divorced or widowed women still had responsibilities to maintain cocoa farms which they had made or which were given to them by former husbands, and needed male farm labor, which most of them could scarcely afford. The Mossi men who worked for these women sometimes found that marriage to an Ashanti woman farmer offered them economic security. In some cases, Akan men encouraged divorced or widowed sisters to marry such men, since it made these women more economically stable and gave brothers matrilineal heirs that were more under their control.[50]

The Mossi men faced a dilemma. They were patrilineal, had no wives, had little expectation of getting one from home, but retained the traditional anxiety over getting a wife. Marrying an Akan woman had the advantage of getting possible access to land, but not the children produced by Brong-Ashanti women, since these belonged to their mother's matrilineage, and were Akan. They could now own farms and rental property—which would have been impossible in their own hometown—but they could not count on owning their own children. There were cases where Mossi migrants tried to bargain for half of the children produced by their Ashanti wives.[51] Sometimes, Mossi men attempted to steal "their" children and return home. In still other cases, when Mossi men died, their relatives came down to the Gold Coast and tried to claim the children. They were rarely successful, since these children were also Akan, legally citizens of the Gold Coast, and preferred the easier life there.

Despite the significant amount of intermarriage, Brong-Ashanti farmers in the 1940s and 1950s did not generally approve of northerners (Mossi or others) who stepped across ethnic boundaries into new social and economic roles. An increasingly common stereotype of northerners was of country bumpkins, ignorant and irresponsible, and Akan cocoa farmers could become hostile to those who did not fit the pattern. In one recorded case, a man from the Northern Territories who accepted an indebted farm that was pledged to him by a local Brong-Ashanti man, met exceptional obstacles. His problems arose when he had to return to his hometown to settle domestic affairs after a death in his family occurred, and he appointed a man of mixed Mossi extraction to act as *abusa* caretaker. The Mossi caretaker was authorized to pluck the cocoa for three years, using the proceeds to pay back the original debt plus interest. However, after the "pledgee" took his departure, the Brong-Ashanti farm owner seized the farm, forcibly removed the caretaker, and refused to surrender the cocoa. When the pledgee returned from the north three years later, the original farm-owner claimed the contract had expired; thus the northern man was forced to take the case to the District Commissioners Court to reclaim his investment.[52] Throughout the 1930s and 1940s, there were numerous cases where Ashanti and Brong cocoa farmers tried to exploit or cheat northern migrants in wages or economic deals, being halted only by the courts.

The growing presence of northerners coincided with other kinship economic and religious changes taking place. First, there was increasing visibility of the Asante *nkramo* (Muslims), as compared to earlier periods. There had always been some *nkramo* scattered through rural villages, particularly those villages along historical trade routes. Moreover, as Akan rather than strangers, the *nkramo* had access to farm land, acquired simply by the payment of an *aseda* (thanks fee), like most citizens of rural towns. However, with the development of cocoa farming and the influx of northern laborers, the intermarriage between these Muslim Akan and the new strangers gave men more control over the nuclear family. Much of the new change in family relations was reflected in the increasing incidence of Muslim marriage in Brong-Ashanti areas. Whereas only 7 percent of marriages in Ashanti were contracted under Muslim law, 10 percent of marriages in Brong Ahafo were contracted in this manner.[53]

This increasing Islamicization brought about new conflicts. Not only did the *nkramo* have new allies in the northern Muslim strangers, but some northerners took advantage of the alliance to change their *donkor* status. Complicating this situation is the fact that the *nkramo* are influenced to move towards a greater expression of patrilineality by the marriages under Muslim law.[54] However, they acquire their cocoa farms through traditional matrilineal land tenure procedures.[55] Relatively few of them had received their farms from fathers. While the local *nkramo* had not yet passed on their farms to heirs, they were divided as to whether they would practice Akan matrilineal inheritance patterns, Islamic ones in which the brother or the son inherited property, or whether they would share equally between the matrilineage and the male heirs. About one-third of the Muslim respondents in the 1973 Sunyani District survey stated that they would follow the Islamic pattern; but the rest indicated a desire for compromise with their own *abusua*, and in many cases the nephew was identified as heir. Despite their Islamic affiliation, the *nkramo* in rural villages were more integrated into the ideology of Akan life than the urban Muslims. In general, it could be stated that Brong-Ashanti communities were becoming culturally more diverse, while nevertheless remaining jurally Akan.

Another significant development was that cocoa farming enhanced the upward mobility of formerly servile and slave lineages among the Akan. Following British conquest and the abolition of domestic slavery in 1896, many Brong-Ashanti with slave ancestry (the *nnonkofor*) were nominally freed, but retained the stigma of a servile past. The penetration of Christianity encouraged slave abandonment of rural areas, but large numbers remained. Although the *donkor* stigma decreased with time, they were prohibited from occupying lineage offices or the chieftaincy, and had to exhibit their status on certain ritual occasions such as funerals. Nevertheless, the prosperity from cocoa money tended to benefit both slave and free Akan, and the former slave segments of lineages were quick to utilize their new resources to acquire respectability within the lineage. In some cases where education, upward mobility and migration from rural villages had taken place for the bulk of their lineage, former slaves were often the only remaining lineage segments available to occupy certain titles. Thus, *donkor* status could be conveniently forgotten while the segment merged into the mainstream of the lineage. By the 1970s, the bulk of those in rural villages whose names ended in *Donkor* or *Moshi* were not of those origins, but were real Akans who, as children, were given the foreign ritual names so as to protect them against death in infancy from local spirits. Their names had nothing to do with northern, Islamic or slave status.

Cocoa and Royalty

Just as the demands of the cocoa industry created diverse pressures which changed dynamics within the matrilineage, so it generated tensions which increased the distance between jural segments within the *oman*, between the various kin groups and the royal or chiefly lineages in local communities. The expectations placed on chiefs changed as a result of cocoa wealth, and it also had implications for the ways in which the royal lineages selected new candidates for chieftaincy. Whereas earlier the royal family would try to achieve unanimity by selecting popular and capable stool occupants,[56] now wealthy persons openly competed for stools, often utilizing bribes to royal electors in order to be selected. Inevitably, this lowered prestige for the chieftaincy itself, and increased stool debts as a result of extravagant electioneering.[57]

At the root of most of this change in the perception and operations of chieftancy was a challenge to the cohesion of Akan communities—to the principle of lineage representation that structured political relations at the local, regional and national levels.[58] While earlier Christianity had challenged the ritual authority of chiefs, economic change was the impetus for a challenge to the stratification system, which sanctioned political leadership within the community. Just as cocoa had stimulated social distance between segments of a lineage and had blurred slave and free distinctions within a lineage, so also it affected the allegiance of lineages to the status hierarchies of their natal villages, towns and leaders.

Cocoa has been a great leveller—giving ordinary commoners access to funds and thereby raising their political visibility in a manner inconceivable before 1900. However, just at the time when chiefs and communities had begun to have potential for considerable wealth because of the export economy, and chiefly control over communal labor and unused forest land, the cocoa industry pulled people out of the grasp of chiefs, and made them autonomous economic entrepreneurs. Commoners—cocoa farmers and their children—then sought new leadership opportunities which had been denied them at an earlier period, and utilized different types of strategies. The miniscule Kumasi-educated elite (operating through the Ashanti-Kotoko Union Society) used its skills during the 1920s and 1930s to argue for the restoration of unitary political control to the Asantehene within the Ashanti Confederacy.[59] In contrast, during the 1920s, the influential coastal elite had utilized their strength based on education and enlightenment to challenge the legitimacy of chiefs, and to become more involved in colonial decision making. They proposed a limitation of chiefly authority to the local, ritual and customary realm, a suggestion which would have limited chiefly representation on colonial political committees and councils. However, the assertiveness of educated chiefs such as Nana Ofori-Atta kept the colonial administration aware that chiefs were increasingly seeing their challenge as that of becoming more educated, thereby staving off the challenge to their leadership in local and national level affairs in the Gold Coast.[60]

At the local levels the early battle between emergent and aristocratic elites had been complicated by the involvement of the colonial administration in choosing chiefs who were favorable to cocoa development. By the 1930s this struggle was further complicated by the growth of that segment of "cocoa chiefs" whose ties to exploitative middlemen and European buying firms marked them as enemies of the people. On the other hand, those chiefs who desired to retain their respected position within local communities hastened to become leaders in the mass struggle against the cocoa monopolies, thereby salvaging much of their traditional status.[61] The problem was that the cocoa economy was rapidly changing the communities of which they were a part. Social mobility as a result of cocoa farming often meant the migration of large segments of a lineage from one town to a larger one, with those who remained often wanting more representation than that which could be obtained through lineage elders or lineage offices.[62] Cocoa income had created wealthy and knowledgeable citizens who were demanding greater participation in local administrative and political decisions. By the 1950s chiefs were faced with the necessity of an elective or appointive ward system which would allow for these local leaders to come to the foreground in town politics. All such trends went against the traditional jural pattern, in which lineage membership structured political participation.

Perhaps most indicative of change was the shifting loci of jural cases within Ashanti and Brong areas. Instead of appealing to the Asantehene, factions of the royal lineage often battled each other within district courts. There was also a decline in the extent to which citizens brought their jural/legal cases to chief's courts for resolution. Domestic cases regarding divorce or settlement of claims for cocoa property were more frequently being brought to district or other courts for decisions. This was particularly true of claims between family or lineage members, because traditional courts were judged more likely rigidly to uphold traditional rather than modern social principles. By the 1950s a feeling had emerged that modern problems called for the intervention of those with power and money: landlords, local "big-men" or formal courts. People were often actively resisting the attempts of chiefs to oversee all local developments. In cases involving traditional land tenure rights, people took them to the chiefs' courts, which had the appropriate adjudicatory institutions; in many other cases, chiefly judgment was being avoided rather than sought.

Although Ghanaian cocoa farming derived its initial impetus from its reliance upon a familial labor force, and a corporate-usufruct approach to land ownership and political relations, further developments in the cocoa industry systematically altered and in many cases challenged these traditional elements. Family loyalties were divided, as private property ownership separated the interests of members of the *abusua*; people sought to protect their new property rights from assault by chiefs and representatives of the traditional jural order. Throughout the post-war period, it was clear that the operational principles of the matrilineal system, although not destroyed, were seriously attenuated by the dynamics of cocoa. As a result of this kinship change, there would be a number of serious social problems which would confront Ghanaian leaders in Akan urban as well as rural communities—problems which could not have been imagined prior to cocoa.

Notes

1. Kay, G.B. *The Political Economy of Colonialism in Ghana*, Cambridge: Cambridge University Press, 1972, 238, 242.
2. Except in the more crowded southern areas around Akwapim and the central region

where cocoa farming was oldest, families were not immediately disrupted by the necessity of migration to acquire cocoa land. Although there was some migration of farmers from Akwapim as well as more southeastern areas, cocoa farming could be (and generally was) incorporated into the totality of family relations until the depression of the 1930s. See Polly Hill, *Migrant Cocoa Farmers of Southern Ghana*, Cambridge University Press, 1963, 75–108.

3. Sam Rhodie, "Gold Coast Cocoa Hold-Ups of 1930–31," *Transactions of the Historical Society of Ghana*, vol. 9, 1969, pp. 104–118; see also Nowell Commission Report, 1938.
4. Busia, K.A. *The Position of the Chief in the Modern Political System of Ashanti*, 1951, 127.
5. See Rattray, Ashanti. Oxford, 1923; Caseley-Hayford, *Gold Coast Native Institutions*, Sweet and Maxwell, 1903; M. Fortes, "Time and Social Structure: An Ashanti Case Study," in Fortes (ed.), 1970, 1–35; Fortes, *Kinship and the Social Order*, 1969, 138–190; Arhin, K. "The Political and Military Roles of Akan Women," in C. Oppong (ed.), *Male and Female in West Africa*, Allen & Unwin, 1983, 91–98.
6. Wilks, 1975, 453; see also Fortes, 1970, 191–218 for a review of the traditional patrilateral and male-focused roles within Ashanti.
7. Rattray, R.S., *Religion and Art in Ashanti*, London: Oxford University Press, 1927, 301.
8. Mikell, G., *Akan Funerary Terracottas and Ethnohistorical Change*. Research report, Smithsonian Institution, Museum of African Art, 1982. See Patricia Coronel for the Aowin ("Aowin Terracotta Sculpture," in *African Arts*, 13, #1, 1979, 28–35, 97–8). A remaining research exercise is to compare the changing social roles within Gold Coast societies (which were at the center of centralization) with the historical roles of males and females in groups such as the Baule and Anyi, which were more heavily impacted by Ashanti statehood.
9. Wilks, 1975, 177, 674–5, 705–6.
10. There are diverging views on the structural role of the *asafo* companies in Ashanti life. Some argue that they were primarily derived from the militarization of Ashanti, usually composed of unfree rather than free men, and thus declined as state fear of rebellion caused it to restrict them in the late 1800s (Wilks, 1975, 676–7). Others argue that they are patrifilial social institutions, and therefore complementary to the matrilineage (Rattray, 1927; Fortes, 1970). For this last perspective, see I. Chukwukere, "Perspectives on the *Asafo* Institution in Southern Ghana," *Journal of African Studies*, 7, 1, Spring 1980, 39–47.
11. The absorption of a considerable number of slaves into these *mmusua*, especially in the mid-nineteenth century, provided an additional basis of differentiation between descendants of free and unfree segments of the *abusua*. In many cases, these "lower classes of the free" became recognized as the *ahiafo* (Wilks, 1975, 708–9).
12. Meyer Fortes, "The Submerged Descent Line Among the Akan," in I. Schapera (ed.), *Studies in Kinship and Marriage*, London: RAIGE, 1963.
13. After 1900, fathers tried to shoulder this responsibility by paying school fees for sons, thus giving them modern training for upward mobility.

14. Bishop Peter Sarpong, *Girls' Nubility Rites in Ashanti*, Accra: Ghana Publishing Co., 1976. See also M. Fortes, *Kinship and the Social Order*, 1969.
15. Ollenu, *Customary Land Law in Ghana*, London: Sweet and Maxwell, 1962, 161; R.S. Rattray, *Religion and Art in Ashanti*, 156–60.
16. Western Christian influence was a major factor in opposition to cross-cousin marriage. Despite this fact, data from Akwapim (where Basel missionaries had settled from 1836) indicate that women's challenges to traditional marriage arrangements were not statistically significant until the 1940s. See also D.D. Vallenga, "Arenas of Judgment," in C. Oppong (ed.), *Domestic Rights and Duties in Southern Ghana*, Legon Family Research Papers No. 1, IAS, University of Ghana, Legon. 1974, 77–101.
17. McCaskie, John. "State and Society, Marriage and Adultery: Some Considerations Towards a Social History of Pre-Colonial Asante," in *Journal of African History*, XXII, IV, 1981, 474–491.
18. K.A. Busia, *The Position of the Chief in the Modern Political System of Ashanti*, 1951, 209–210.
19. Daily wages were approximately .80 peswahs to Cl.00 in 1973 wages.
20. Perhaps not surprisingly, 53% of the current sample of cocoa farmers were first- through third-born children in birth-order within their conjugal families, indicating one of several possibilities: (a) older children tended to have entered farming earlier, when land and incentives towards agricultural production were most available (at a later point, education and other job possibilities were opening up for successive siblings); or (b) first through third children were usually chosen to inherit cocoa farms and property within the *abusua*, or from parents, indicating the expansion of conjugal inheritance patterns.
21. Birmingham, Neustadt, and Omaboe (ed). *Some Aspects of Social Structure in Ghana*, Allen & Unwin. 1967, 206. See also Tekyiwaah Manuh, "Law and the Status of Women in Ghana," United Nations Economic Commission for Africa, Research Series, Addis Ababa, 1984.
22. Walter Birmingham, I. Neustadt and E.N. Omaboe, *Some Aspects of Social Structure in Ghana*, vol. 2, 1967, 68. See also Dorothy Dee Vallenga, "Attempts to Change the Marriage Laws in Ghana and the Ivory Coast," in A.R. Zolberg and P. Foster (eds.), *Ghana and Ivory Coast: Perspectives on Modernization*, Chicago, University of Chicago, 1970.
23. This is based on the division of property which occurs intestate succession among ordinance-married couples in Ghana. The Ordinance Inheritance Provisions are themselves modeled upon intestate laws in effect in England on 19 November, 1844.
24. Dorothy Dee Vallenga's Ph.D. thesis, Columbia University, Department of Sociology, 1974.
25. The missionary complaint against Akan marriage practice was that they saw the "headwine" as fetishistic, while among the Akan, this *nsa* was the supernatural glue of the marriage bond.
26. Ghana National Archives, Sunyani (DA0/1/479), Complaints, Chiraa-Abesim Area, 1948–1852.

27. Birmingham, Neustadt, and Omaboe, op. cit., p. 97.
28. S.K. Gasie and K.T. de Graft-Johnson, *The Population of Ghana*, University of Ghana-Legon, CICRED 1976: 10.
29. Ibid., p. 96.
30. Mikell's 1973 survey of cooperative society cocoa farmers in the Sunyani District of Brong Ahafo. There is a question as to whether in some areas the existence of autonomous women cocoa farm owners may have acted as a *disincentive* towards the normally high rural female fertility rate. See G. Mikell, "Filiation, Economic Crisis, and the Status of Women in Rural Ghana, " *Canadian Journal African of Studies*, vol. 18, #1, Jan. 1984, 195-218.
31. Even when the conjugal family resided together with their children as a unit, the residence usually contained members from the lineages of one or both spouses. The most likely probability was that members of the husband's lineage resided with them.
32. Birmingham, Neustadt and Omaboe, op. cit., p. 213.
33. Kwabena Kusi-Appiah, A Sociological Study on Marriage Among the Inhabitants of Berekum, B.A. Honors Dissertation, Department of Sociology, University of Ghana-Legon.
34. M. Fortes. "Time and Social Structure: An Ashanti Case-Study," in *Social Structure: Studies Presented to Radcliffe-Brown*, Cambridge: The University Press, 1949.
35. N.A. Ollenu, 1962, 240–245.
36. K.A. Busia, *The Position of the Chief in the Modern Political System of Ashanti.* 1951, 127.
37. Tekyiwaah Manuh, 1984, 21–26. Reference is made especially to the cases of *Takyiwaah v. Adu*, GLR 1971, as well as to *Abebreseh v. Krah*, *Clerk v. Clerk*, *Quartey v. Armah*, and *Yeboah v. Yeboah*, GLR 1968.
38. Okali and Kotey, 1971, "Akokoaso: A Resurvey," Institute for Social, Statistical, and Economic Research, University of Ghana-Legon.
39. Mikell, 1984, 195–218.
40. Case of *Serwah v. Kesse*, cited in N.A. Ollenu, 1962, 201–7.
41. Op. cit.
42. Elliott P. Skinner, "Labor Migration and its Relation to Socio-Cultural Change in Mossi Society," *Africa*, 30, 1960, 275–301.
43. Woodford-Berger, "Women in Houses: The Organization of Residence and Work in Ghana," in *Anthropologiska Studies*, no. 30–31, pp. 3–35.
44. Christine Okali, *Cocoa and Kinship*, London: Allen & Unwin, 1982.
45. K. Poku, "Traditional Roles and People of Slave Origins in Modern Ashanti—A Few Impressions," in *Ghana Journal of Sociology*, vol. 5, #1, Feb. 1969. On the assimilation of indigenous, Akan, and Muslim culture in Brong areas, see Rene Bravmann, *Islam and Tribal Art in West Africa*, 1974.
46. Ivor Wilks, "Land, Labor and Capital in the Forest Kingdom of Asante," in Friedman and Rowland (eds.), *The Evolution of Social Systems*, London: Ducksworth Publishing, 1977, 487. Agnes Aidoo, *Political Crisis and Social*

Change in the Asante Kingdom, 1867–1901, Ph.D. thesis, University of California-L.A., 1975, 94, 607.

47. Ivor Wilks, "The Northern Factor in Asante History," University of Ghana-Legon, Institute of African Studies, 1961. Nehemiah Levtzion argues, somewhat differently, that the Muslim impact on Ghana was peripheral (*Muslims and Chiefs in West Africa*, 1968, 87). See also Enid Schildkrout, *People of the Zongo: Changing Ethnic Identities in Kumasi, Ghana*, Cambridge, 1978.
48. Schildkrout, op. cit., 1978, 67–97.
49. E.P. Skinner, "Intergenerational Tensions Between Mossi Fathers and Sons," in Skinner (ed.), Peoples and Cultures of Africa, New York: Doubleday, 1973.
50. Schildkrout, 1978, 51.
51. Elliott P. Skinner, Mossi Field Notes, 1955–1956, "Interviews with Returning Migrants."
52. DA0/1/479, Complaints, Chiraa-Abesim Area, Case #52, 1948.
53. Birmingham, Neustadt, and Omaboe, 1967, vol. 2, p. 207.
54. Wives of these farmers were generally not secluded, but neither did they own cocoa farms or work on the farms of their husbands.
55. Mikell, 1973 survey, Sunyani District.
56. Rattray, *Ashanti Law and Constitution*, 1929.
57. Busia, *The Position or the Chief in the Modern Political System of Ashanti*, 1951, 209–10.
58. Fortes, "The Ashanti: State and Citizenship," in Fortes (ed.), *Kinship and the Social Order*, 1969, 138–152; also, Rattray, *Ashanti Law and Constitution*, 1927.
59. William Tordoff, *Asante Under the Prempehs*, 196, 175–6.
60. Legislative Council Debates, 1926–27, Proceedings in Council, 18 March, 1926.
61. Busia, 1951, 33; also C. Gunnarson, *The Gold Coast Cocoa Industry 1900–1939*, 1978, 139–47; also, *Report of the Nowell Commission*, 1938.
62. K.A. Busia, *The Position of the Chief in the Modern Political System of Ashanti*, 1951.

△ *Drying of cocoa in Ghana, 1958. (UPI / Bettman Newsphotos.)*

▽ *Convention of People's Party Rally, 1960. (UPI / Bettman Newsphotos.)*

△ ***Ghanaian workers rally for more pay, 1960. President Kwame Nkrumah pictured in foreground. (UPI / Bettman Newsphotos.)***

Kofi A. Busia, 1968. (deKun Photos.) ▷

△ *Ignatius Acheampong, in center, 1973. (Information Services Department, Accra, Ghana.)*

◁ ▽ ***Soldiers during Acheampong government, handing out bonuses to officials of Cocoa Marketing Organizations, Sunyani, 1973***

◁ *The Chief of Sunyani and his family, 1973.*

▽ *The Dosoos: A "dual civil servant" family, employees of the Cocoa Marketing Board, 1976.*

◁ *President Limann in the Presidential chair at Parliament House, shortly after taking power. (Information Services Department, Accra, Ghana)*

▽ *Jerry Rawlings exhorts his people, 1981. (UPI / Bettman Newsphotos)*

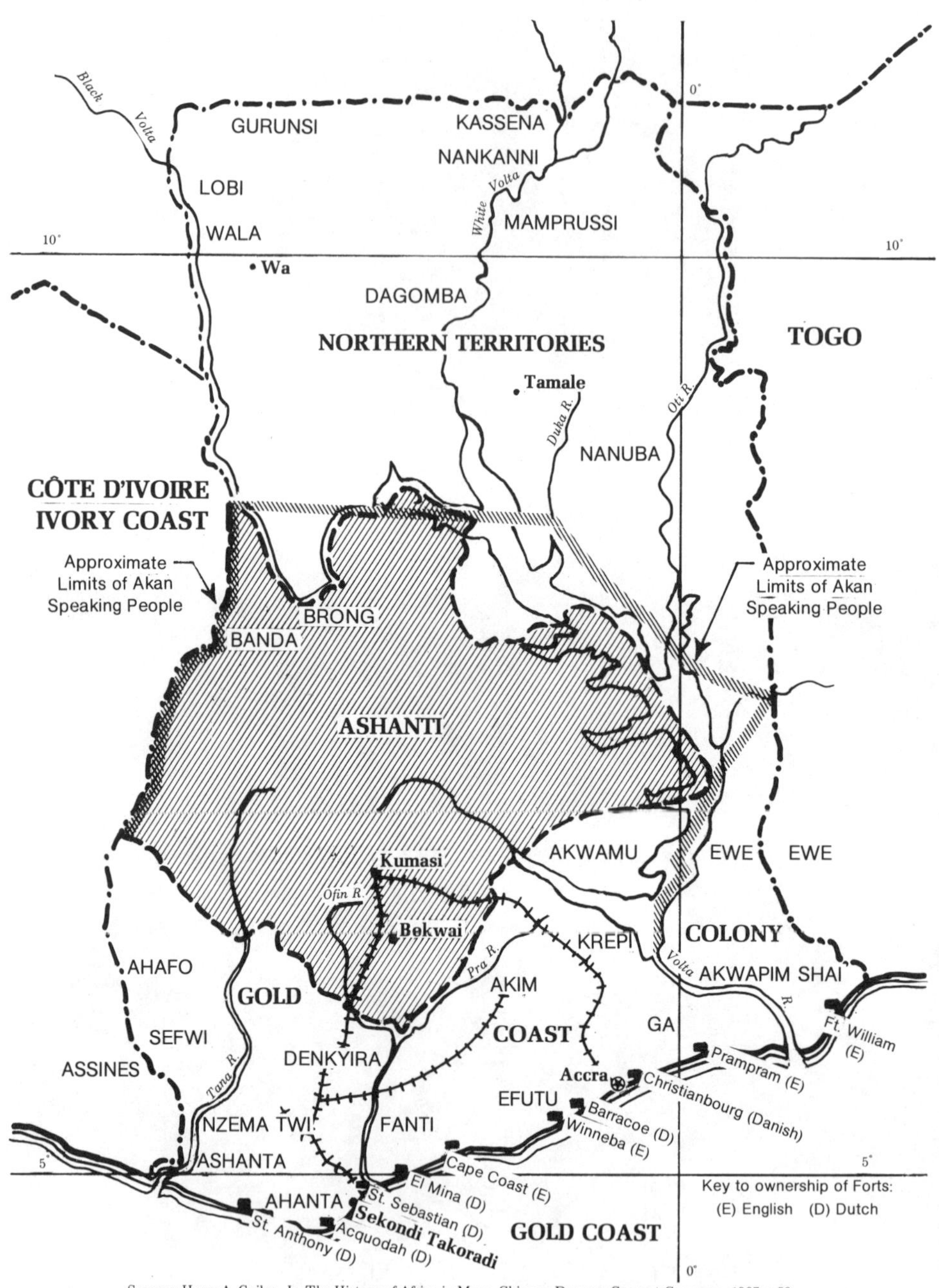

Sources: Harry A. Gailey, Jr. The History of Africa in Maps, Chicago: Denoyer-Geppert Company, 1967, p.59.
Meyer Fortes, "The Ashanti Social Survey: A Preliminary Report", Journal of the Rhodes-Livingstone Institute, 1945.

Ghana with 19th Century Forts and Tribes

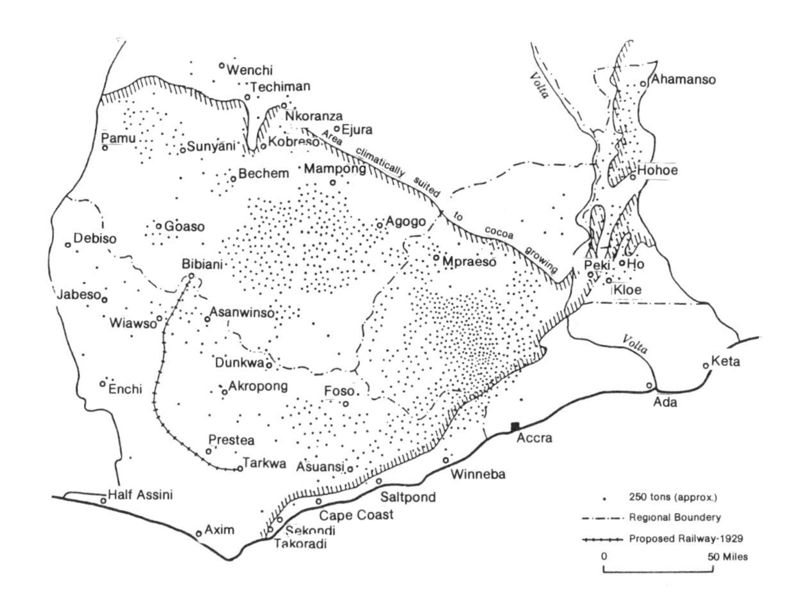

Source: K.B. Dickson, A Historical Geography of Ghana, Cambridge at the University, 1969, p.169

Cocoa purchases, 1936-7

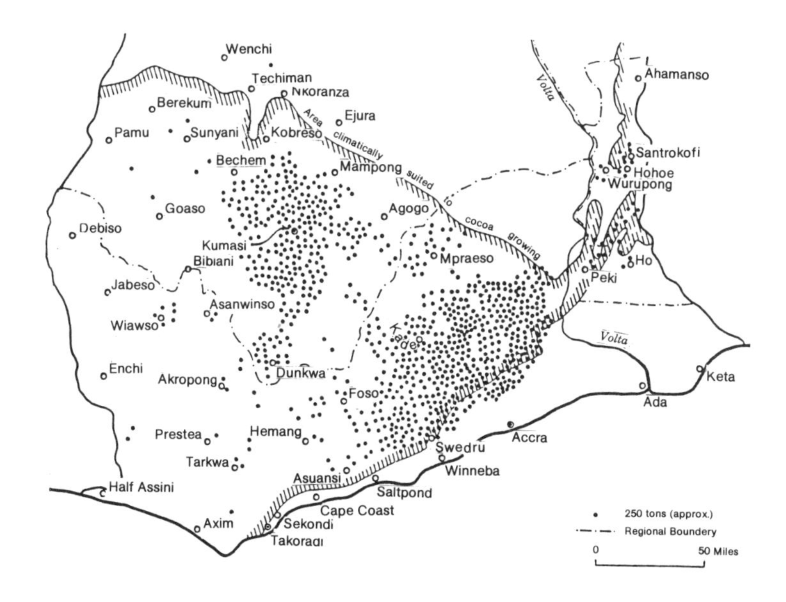

Source: K.B. Dickson, A Historical Geography of Ghana, Cambridge at the University, 1969, p.168

Cocoa Purchases, 1927

6

Vote for Cocoa

The politics of cocoa was to create upheaval and transformation in rural areas where people demanded recognition of their rights to participation in, if not the creation of, a national political agenda. As a result of the cocoa economy, the rural Gold Coast on the eve of World War II was ripe for drastic economic and political change. Although Ashanti had trailed behind the colony in social developments from 1884 through the 1920s, developments during World War I and during the Guggisberg administration were altering this.[1] Through changes in educational access, occupational mobility, and income from cocoa farming, new possibilities appeared which would have seemed fanciful at the turn of the century. The aspirations of the new rural "youngmen" and "big-men" inevitably brought them into a head-on clash with the traditional rulers, into competition among themselves for regional control, and then into clashes with the political leaders of the emerging independent state of Ghana. Cocoa was as much the cause as well as the symbol of these changes.

Recognizing their economic power, the rural people—particularly those in the Akan cocoa belt—became major protagonists in the new politics of nationalism. Their concerns dramatically marked local, regional and national politics before the country's independence in 1957. It would be fair to say that their participation in the colonially derived cocoa industry affected pre-colonial feudal and ethnic domination and produced the dynamic which thrust the Gold Coast to the forefront of the African independence movement. It was tempting to label these early political conflicts as merely local economic squabbles. However, northwest Ashanti provides an outstanding example of the way in which traditional conflicts in the cocoa zone became the basis of regional economic alliances and further energized the nationalist struggle. In the early period, these disputes appeared deceptively local, and therefore parochial, involving only economic interests. For example, around Goaso, Mim and Kukuom, continual shifts in political alignments, and therefore conflict, occurred throughout the 1930s and 1940s as towns manipulated traditional alliances in order to maximize their proceeds from cocoa land and tributes.[2] In towns like Goaso where there were large stranger communities as well as stores and offices like Cadbury or United Africa Company, local chiefs tried to control revenues from leases and ground rents, instead of letting these go into the Asantehene's treasury. Even in Sunyani, Odumasi and Nsuatre, there were disputes about control over cocoa tribute from strangers, and the desired participation of commoners in native court decision-making. Such issues ultimately would link local people into the larger nationalist political issues.

It was the desire of all rural status groups, both aristocratic and commoner, to gain or retain control of cocoa resources which was to confront Nkrumah and other politicians during the 1940s and 1950s. The resulting sectarian politics reflected more than the difficult initiation of the Gold Coast into democratic political institutions. More importantly, the politics reflected the anger of various rural, ethnic and class groups about external manipulations of cocoa resources. Gold Coast politics also reflected the depth to which rural economic stratification, based on monocrop production, could impact on state processes. Naturally, the issues were complicated, but central to them were questions of how the emerging political elite would use rural relationships and resources to fuel urban and national developments. Apter has shown us that those who questioned the necessity of this biased urban and national program were first and foremost the rural chiefs, who tried to hold onto their political autonomy and economic power as much as was possible.[3] The real problems that faced the Gold Coast were: Who should control the emerging state—the traditional chiefs or the new "youngmen," politicians and bureaucrats? To what extent should rural economic resources remain locally controlled, despite their vital importance to national well-being and stability? To what extent could national or socialist organizations (parastatals) be created and superimposed upon existing rural organizations? And what were the appropriate geopolitical units within which peasants, urbanites, chiefs and politicians could be involved in national developments?

As we shall see, the Nkrumah government would have little success in creating a political-economic ethos in which cocoa was seen as a national resource to be utilized legitimately in the interest of national development as well as in the welfare of rural producers. Nkrumah himself, a Nzima, had always striven for nationalist and Pan-African (rather than ethnic) frames of reference, and his education in the United States and London had helped him to achieve this.[4] He was committed to building the kind of anti-colonial political base that he and other leaders in the London-based "circle" had envisioned. However, once in the Gold Coast, myriad local and regional interests complicated this great national design: conflicts between traditional aristocrats and commoners within the cocoa belt; between the aspirations of local and national elites throughout the Gold Coast; and class interests between peasants and rural entrepreneurs. Despite Nkrumah's emphasis on elections and full participation of all the people in the 1950s, and on "seeking first the political kingdom,"[5] he failed to understand that democracy and political order would have to overcome the emerging economic and ethnic difficulties. By 1957, it was clear that Nkrumah's political strategy faced its greatest challenge in the ethnic and class disparities which existed within the cocoa belt, and that these would affect the relationship between the cocoa region and the rest of the nation. To complicate matters, this issue was only partially conditioned by internal factors, being equally affected by global economic control over cocoa prices. In the early 1950s, the international and national control over the marketing of cocoa was only dimly perceived as an issue in the stability of the state, but by 1957 this relationship had become startlingly clear.

Rural and Urban Socio-Structural Relations

The sharp disparity between rural and urban social patterns which existed during the early years of the twentieth century was gradually eroded as education and upward mobility increased in Ashanti as a result of revenue derived from the cocoa industry. By the 1850s, the coastal educated groups were becoming so vocal and significant that colonial officials sarcastically referred to them as "the curse of the West Coast."[6] This group of largely urban lawyers, doctors, missionaries and traders had been active advocates for "local" advancement since the 1870s. Operating through the Aborigines Rights Protection Society (ARPS), they had achieved some especially significant legislation in 1897, including the right of traditional stools to retain control of land at a time when European and indigenous mining concessions, as well as colonial ambitions, had endangered land control.[7] In contrast, Ashanti resisted western education and Christianization, viewed as intimately related to European penetration.[8] Ashanti acceptance of eduction was painfully slow, but as mission schools increased and government schools were begun in Kumasi, change had started. Even in 1909, colonial administrators stated that:

> The Ashanti organization, so powerful in the older days, still maintains many elements of cohesion, but with the spread of western civilization and more liberal ideas, inevitable conflict between youth and authority has already commenced.[9]

Nevertheless, instead of becoming an immediate challenge to traditional authority as the administrators expected, the earliest rural elite, particularly in Ashanti, provided valuable service to traditional rulers and assisted them in dealing with the colonial administration.

Significant political change was also slow. There had been no group comparable to the ARPS in existence within Ashanti and the Brong-Ashanti. The various regional groupings of chiefs in these areas deliberated within separate, often ineffective councils; this colonial-enforced fragmentation prevented both concerted regional politics as well as regional participation in the affairs of the colonial society. Part of the problem was solved when teachers, prosperous educated cocoa traders and clerks formed the Ashanti-Kotoko-Union Society (AKUS) in 1916.[10] Although this group was conservative in its political stance, and was supportive of the powers of traditional chieftaincy, it was a leadership group which provided a counterpoint to other administrative and regional ideas concerning the Gold Coast. The AKUS was important in discussions surrounding the restoration of the Ashanti Confederacy in the 1930s.

As early as 1920, the coastal elite was agitating for the franchise and for elected African participation in the Gold Coast Legislative Council, and they had formed an organization called the National Congress of British West Africa (NCBWA).[11] However, such issues were not significantly addressed within Ashanti and other rural areas until after 1935. The colonial regime was hostile to demands for the franchise made by the NCBWA. The governor implied that the rightful role of the educated elite was to achieve representation through their chiefs and stools, and he accused the NCBWA of

> committing a deadly sin against the Gold Coast...widening day by day, and month by month the gap between the black the white man; they are increasing and creating this racial feeling.[12]

The British were more sympathetic to demands from Akan cocoa areas for the return of King Prempeh, and for regaining some of the local political structures and autonomy which had been lost or delayed as a result of British conquest and disenfranchisement of Ashanti in 1895.

The colonial regime ultimately yielded to coastal pressures for local governance and it gave the elite a few appointed positions. The government permitted Prempeh's return as a private citizen in 1924, and passed ordinances in 1927 which increased the powers of chiefs and their ability to control native courts and treasuries.[13] Then, as chiefs regained control over rural decision making, respect for chieftaincy increased and destoolments decreased. Chiefs became increasingly visible due to permission given them by the government to become involved in legislative councils; because of their strategic roles in the cocoa hold-ups and boycotts of 1937–38; and because of their attempts to acquire education which would keep them in step with the social trends of the times. Between 1933 and 1944 the government did revise legislation to eradicate some of the alleged abusive control of the chiefs over the local-level judicial and representative processes,[14] and there was fear that chiefs might lose out to the increasingly vocal educated group. In response, Nana Ofori Atta became an ardent advocate for the traditional right of chiefs to represent the people of the Gold Coast, as well as for an educated and enlightened chieftaincy.[15]

Meanwhile, the desire of a sizable modern and socially conscious population in the coastal towns to participate in political affairs had increased. Accra-Christianborg, Seconde, and Cape Coast already had local town councils, but there was pressure to extend this right further inland.[16] The feeling grew that the dialogue between chiefs, other appointed officials and the government was not enough, and that local government and town councils were necessary to permit ordinary persons to have political input. The government adamantly resisted these demands, claiming that illiteracy and inexperience made such mass participation difficult even in coastal towns and unthinkable in the interior. However, the issue grew and in the 1940s it was voiced all over inland cocoa communities as well as on the coast. Now it became linked to the issue of "no taxation without representation." Some of the pressure was temporarily released when the government appointed additional members to the legislative council, thus making it possible for the elite to raise issues of both local and national importance. However, such incomplete constitutional measures did not stem the tide of demands.

With the Great Depression of 1929, local and global economic change had stimulated a potent nationalist consciousness among both coastal and rural representatives. The first phase of the depression led to the fall in the price of cocoa in 1931 and induced some, but not all, Gold Coast farmers and chiefs to launch a boycott in an attempt to break the monopolistic agreements of European cocoa buyers in the Gold Coast. Significantly, the Ashanti did not participate in the cocoa hold-ups for fear that this might endanger their goals of restoring the Ashanti Confederacy. This led the British to conclude:

> The Ashanti...took no part [in the 1931 hold-up], and no doubt they benefited accordingly. There need be no fear that they will use the confederacy to cause embarrassment to their government: on the contrary, it will intensify their loyalty.[17]

This inactivity on the part of Ashanti cocoa interests was, however, temporary and deceptive. The farmers needed the revenue because by the 1930s the Ashanti had already made a heavy commitment to education in the interest of upward mobility. The slow acceptance of education had been reversed, and record numbers of children of cocoa farmers were attending primary and secondary schools.

It is possible that Ashanti cocoa farmers could not have afforded the luxury of participating in the 1931 hold-up, since cocoa was their major crop, often to the exclusion of other crops except yam (unlike the more coastal areas which had maize, cassava and palm products as well as cocoa). In addition, they had to balance off economic factors against the desired political goal of re-achieving political unity. These two factors were increasingly juxtaposed. Note, however, that on the eve of the Ashanti Confederacy, some of the Ashanti elite had already begun subtly expressing the economic needs of their farmers over their own political ambitions.

In the absence of appropriate political structures for articulating their grievances, both coastal and Ashanti elite began to create institutions to voice their dissatisfaction with international and local economic measures. In 1931, the Ashanti barrister Isaac Kwadjo Agyeman, Dr. J.B. Danquah and other coastal elites petitioned London for constitutional and representative changes which would improve the economic and political life of the Gold Coast people. They stressed the need for cocoa and agricultural cooperatives, an Agricultural Development Bank to provide development capital for farmers, and a Conference of World Producers of Cocoa to discuss strategy for ameliorating economic problems.[18] The petitioners drew attention to the plight of Gold Coast farmers, many of whom had become deeply indebted since the Depression. Certainly the actions of the Gold Coast elite helped lay the basis for the economic reforms in agriculture of the late 1930s.

Just prior to the outbreak of World War II, the Nowell Commission—which had investigated the marketing of cocoa in the aftermath of the 1937 cocoa hold-up—remarked on the dire conditions facing the majority of Gold Coast cocoa farmers.[19] These conditions were exacerbated by the lack of organizational and institutional mechanisms available to offset economic debt, and create investment potential. Thus, despite their dissatisfaction, cocoa farmers had been relatively helpless in the face of powerful European purchasing companies. There had been legislation in 1931 to create cooperatives,[20] but no real effective action had been taken by the Department of Agriculture until after the 1937 events.[21] To a large extent, the outbreak of World War II prevented action on these plans. However, in 1939, in order to meet its war needs, the British government established a control board and quota system, under which the entire Gold Coast cocoa crop was purchased through specified approved government and African buyers. While the policy guaranteed cocoa farmers the sale of their crop, it was at an artificially low price.[22] Africans were dissatisfied with the continuance of a cocoa price monopoly, but raised little opposition during the war. New legislation created the Gold Coast Marketing Board in 1947.

World War II revived the dismal depression economy of the Gold Coast, despite the limitations imposed by Britain on transport and rail developments, and on imports in an effort to conserve resources. While the cost of living rose astronomically in the coastal areas, the rural areas were not adversely affected because there was less wage employment and less reliance on the import economy. The war effort did, however, have great social implications for rural areas. Military forces such as the Gold Coast Regiment had historically been drawn from northern, predominantly Muslim areas, and this remained true during the Second World War. The Ashanti were not initially welcomed into the British army, but by 1917 they had been allowed to contribute a regiment of soldiers to fight in World War I, and in World War II Ashantis had fought alongside volunteers from the central and eastern regions.[23]

The war provided rural citizens with unexpected room for economic maneuver. Despite the restrictions placed on cocoa prices, demands for food produce, palm oil, peanuts and timber increased, bringing respectable returns to peasants.[24] Men who remained in rural areas took the opportunity to branch out into other economic ventures with profits acquired from agriculture. In addition, uneducated men who could scarcely receive remunerative employment prior to the war used their experience as war recruits to do so. All this extended the economic and political horizons of rural folk.

Social conditions were altered substantially within the Gold Coast during and especially after the war. Africans who felt that they had made valiant contributions to the war effort were anxious to see the country rewarded for this loyalty. The British responded to the increased pressure for economic autonomy and self-government by enacting a rash of legislation between 1943 and 1946. This legislation permitted more African participation in staffing and controlling local government institutions in the Gold Coast, and increased African representation in the Legislative Council.[25] Nevertheless, by 1947, urban as well as rural folk were clearly dissatisfied with the government's pace of liberalization.

Cocoa farmers were especially outspoken about their difficulties. In 1944, the outbreak of the contagious swollen shoot virus disease affected the eastern and western cocoa areas, and an alarmed government had the Agricultural Department implement a forced "cut-out campaign"of diseased cocoa trees. By 1946, the infection had spread into Ashanti, and here the cut-out campaign produced massive resistance from economically vulnerable farmers. So important was the issue that the Ashanti chiefs (using the Confederacy Council) had to reinforce the government's efforts by limiting new plantings of cocoa, and by implementing its own disease control ordinance in 1946. Nevertheless, even these actions were controversial, since they raised suspicions of collaboration between the colonial system and the chiefs. Moreover, Brong chiefs and people in other peripheral areas of Ashanti felt discriminated against, since they had more recently entered the cocoa industry and did not feel that their farms were threatened by the disease.[26] They united in their complaints against the swollen shoot control programs, and although resistance abated somewhat, general dissatisfaction continued into 1948, the year of the Gold Coast riots.

The disturbances in the Gold Coast during 1948 were due to various causes: high expectations among returning soldiers; reactions to the continuance of wartime import controls; the existence of a swollen shoot cut-out program, which cocoa farmers inadequately understood; the centralized control of the Cocoa Marketing Board over cocoa proceeds; and the slow development of education/vocational training and housing availability in the Gold Coast. Nevertheless, even in the face of the critical report from the Commission of Enquiry, the colonial administration voiced its commitment to gradual change, and stressed the moral justification for remaining in the Gold Coast until that country attained the educational and political consciousness which would make "democracy" feasible.[27]

There was little awareness that the dynamic for change in the Gold Coast was coming from the more distant towns and rural villages, rather than only from the coastline as had been the case in the nineteenth century. While the economic basis for the country's wealth had always been due to the gold, rubber and now cocoa located on the interior, the coastal urban areas had always been viewed as the area to provide the "native" input for the colonial system. Now, under the impetus of the cocoa economy, rural peoples were demanding participation in the franchise and in self-government. The reason for the rural dynamic comes through clearly when one notes the educational and occupational change which was occurring in Brong-Ashanti areas between 1911 and 1948. People were combining farming with more modern pursuits as reflected in the following data, shown in Table 6–1, on the occupations of children of early cocoa farmers in distant Sunyani.

Table 6–1

OCCUPATIONS OF CHILDREN OF EARLY COCOA FARMERS*

Relative percentage of farmers who had children in these occupations: (n=233 farmers)	
Farming	39.9%
Crafts & trades	18.0%
Trading and selling	15.4%
Civil service and clerical	22.7%
Advanced professions	2.1%

*Data derived from 1973 survey of Brong/Ashanti cocoa farmers in the Sunyani District. Average was 9 children per farmer, and the occupational data reflected multiple answers per respondent depending on the number of his/her children.

It should be noted that while relatively few children of cocoa farmers attended such elite educational institutions as Achimota along the coast, they had taken advantage of an increasing number of inland schools. By 1948, some of the youngsters were ready to take part in the opportunities provided by the opening of the University College (which became the University of Ghana-Legon).[28] Although the greater portion of rural folk had only lower-level education, they too were applying pressure for the right to participate in local decision-making and to become leaders. Groups of farmers, timber contractors, traders and teachers had begun to mobilize so that their contributions to the rural economy would be reflected in the politics of the Gold Coast and in the future state of Ghana.

Rural "Big-Men" and the Cocoa Cooperatives

The illiterate "big-men" of the cocoa areas had largely ignored the nationalist agitation of the 1940s and the early 1950s, because they perceived these developments as a force threatening their local level economic control. Long before the NCBWA assumed economic importance, and long before cocoa farmers became conscious of playing a role in nationalist politics within the Gold Coast, these rural "big-men" were already involved in economic organizations which represented their local interests and were striving to give the "big-man" national significance. The earliest of these cocoa societies existed even before World War I in the coastal, Akwapim and northwestern areas.[29] Nevertheless, most farmers became sensitive to the links between economics and politics as a result of their 1937–38 hold-up and boycotts, as well as through the Cocoa Marketing Board monopoly during World War II.

Changes in cocoa prices significantly affected the fortunes of the local communities, towns and regional areas within which farmers played out their lives. While conscious of the role that local organizations could play as challenges to European cocoa monopolies, farmers still conceived of these organizations in local terms, rather than as institutions of national importance. Therefore, until the nationalist CPP politics of the 1950s, it was the local and regional, rather than the national arena, upon which the politically or civically aware cocoa farmers focused their attentions.

While generally focusing attention on those cocoa purchasing organizations which were developed by the United Ghana Farmers Council (UGFC) and the Convention Peoples' Party (CPP) after 1948—for example, the Ghana Farmers' Congress and the Cocoa Purchasing Company—scholars have tended to ignore the role of the earlier cocoa organizations and leaders. The role which these persons and organizations played at the grass roots level created some difficulty in the nationalist and independence periods. Early organizations such as the Farmers' Liberation Movement at Nsawam (1924), the Ashanti Farmers' Union and the Gold Coast Farmers' Association (1930s), and the Farmers' Committee of British West Africa (1939), were joined in 1937 by the new local cocoa cooperatives.[30] The degree of militancy varied in these organizations, but they shared the goal of combating the European cocoa monopoly and strove for increased African participation in marketing of cocoa, thereby attempting to increase the price paid to farmers. For these groups, economics would be more important than nationalist politics. Nevertheless, these organizations also aimed at producing local leaders who could represent farmers to the colonial government, as well as take positions on cocoa marketing conditions.

These local leaders were not working in a vacuum. As early as 1906, the colonial government had sought their assistance in speeding the penetration of the cocoa industry, then, in the 1930s, in disseminating information about agricultural techniques and disease control. In 1938, local representation took on new meaning in the aftermath of the commission report. As the government moved to eliminate cocoa purchasing abuses which it perceived as caused by middlemen, officials relied heavily upon the institution of the "chief farmer" or the "head farmer." The idea of such a representative initially appeared consistent with the traditional patterns of commoner leaders who participated in local decision-making, and in the post-World War II period, local farmers in many areas formed groups and elected successful farmers as their representatives. In 1952, as shown in Table 6–2, the government had officially recognized at least seven regional farmers associations, each of which, like the western Ashanti regional one, contained local unions and their representatives:

TABLE 6–2

WESTERN ASHANTI REGIONAL FARMERS' ASSOCIATIONS—1952

Union	# Registered Farmers	# Representatives
Dormaa	over 1,500 farmers	3
Berekum	over 1,500 farmers	3
Techiman	over 1,500 farmers	3
Drobo	1,001–1,500 farmers	2
Nkoranza	300–1000 farmers	1
Sunyani	over 1,500 farmers	3
Kwatwuma	300 farmers	1
Sumah	1,001–1,500 farmers	2
Wenchi	1,001–1,500 farmers	2

Source: Ghana National Archives, DCOS—Sunyani, C.0295. File: Cocoa Farmers' Organizations, p. 10.

There were many cases in which, contrary to tradition, chiefs appointed a representative farmer. In areas where this did not take place, the colonial government often appointed a local farmer as a contact or agricultural enforcement agent. While this development strengthened links between governmental and local levels in agriculture, it also stimulated some local conflicts due to the growing centralization in economics and politics. The chief farmer position opened up new channels for mobility and status for aspiring and successful farmers who often lacked modern educational qualifications. Since the chief farmers had potential political influence, they were often given monetary rewards for their cooperation.

The chief farmers soon found themselves faced with a growing cooperative movement as a competitor for economic and political power in the rural areas. The cooperative movement had waned following the depression and during World War II, but the cooperatives emerged from the war as the strongest local cocoa purchasing organizations. This coincided with the establishment of the Cocoa Marketing Board (CMB) with its controversial price policy designed to accumulate capital for national agricultural development.[31] To facilitate this process, the CMB licensed its major buying agencies in 1947, with the cooperatives as one of these agencies.

The differential affiliation of farmers with the cooperatives, as opposed to other buying agencies or the CMB directly, influenced local economics as well as politics. Okali and Kotey's 1971 study of Akokoaso[32] indicated that although cooperative membership had tripled since 1933, female farmers preferred to sell to the cooperatives rather than the CMB. Robertson's and Hill's studies of Hwidiem[33] in the Ahafo area in the 1950s suggests that it was the more productive members of the community who utilized the cooperatives. Thus, it is quite possible that differential economic statuses may have been a factor in the distinctiveness and success of the cooperatives. While both wealthy and ordinary cocoa farmers in many Brong-Ashanti areas tended to sell their cocoa through the cooperatives, the local leaders of the cooperatives were for the most part persons who had exceptional abilities in financial matters, regardless of their educational achievements.

As the post-war economy improved, the "big-men" of the cocoa cooperatives became distinguished from the educated clerical group which was growing in rural towns such as Koforidua, Swedru, Bekwai, Goaso, Mampong, Sunyani and Dormaa Ahenkro. The war had provided many of the cocoa "big-men" with an opportunity to diversify and invest their profits in transportation, timber, or rental property. Thus, having demonstrated their organizational abilities and businesslike orientation, they were natural candidates for the local cooperative boards. They could be trusted with the resources of the cooperatives, and they also had connections which could be used to the benefit of these organizations.

After all, from the farmers' perspective, "to have money is to be able to get money."

The Sunyani area cooperatives provided examples of this important economic and political development. While many of the cooperative "big-men" had derived land and other benefits from links to traditional royals through lineage or marriage, their status was largely derived from their economic prowess. A few of them had incomes over C4,000, and the wealthiest member had an annual income from cocoa which exceeded C18,000 ($16,000 in 1974). They used polygynous marriage, kinship and other informal patron-client networks to enhance the membership of the cooperative societies. These men were respectful towards traditional political leadership, despite the fact that their existence was sometimes a challenge to chiefs with respect to local economic development. The leadership style of the "big-men" was an effective blend of traditionalism and capitalism. The secretary-receiver of the society was often the only highly literate person in the leadership. However, just as the power of local chiefs was closely guarded and checked by sub-chiefs and elders, the power of the secretary-receiver of the cooperatives was checked by members of the cooperative leadership.

Sunyani's cooperative cocoa farmers gave primarily economic rather than political rationales for joining the cooperatives instead of selling cocoa through the Cocoa Purchasing Company (CPC)—the state-owned buying agency—during the 1950s (See Chapter 6 Appendix). First, the cooperatives paid larger bonuses, since it shared out among its members the bonus which the state normally paid to a licensed buying firm. Second, many farmers preferred to have their shares in the cooperatives function as a savings, rather than receive profits from cocoa. In addition, the cooperatives provided access to loans which were otherwise difficult for many small farmers to obtain. In this way, the cooperatives stimulated the investment of local capital within the local arena.

The cooperatives represented an arena within which the colonial administration had little direct effect, and within which the nationalist politicians could not effectively penetrate. Nevertheless, local chiefs sometimes were able to exercise influence within these organizations. This link between the chiefs and the cooperatives was by no means exceptional either in Ashanti or the colony, but it sometimes led to local problems. In 1943, Secretary of Agriculture Wright had stated to the Confederacy Council:

> Many of you are the most difficult obstacles on the path to progress. In the large percentage of cases where a chief was favorable to cooperatives, we found that the members of the society, in a very natural manner, elected their chief as president of the society. That at first seemed an excellent thing. Unfortunately, experience has taught us that for farmers to elect their chief as president...spells certain failure...Our strong enthusiastic and progressive

> societies are those where the chief is not included in the membership. Now why is this?...You object to having an independent organization in your village, and a cooperative society concerns only the farmers...You resent this and it is this feeling of resentment which constitutes a very real bar to progress.[34]

In summation, the cooperatives provided an arena for local level economic activity, but many other social and political functions were deliberately eliminated from their operations by virtue of their links to the traditional political system. Although the "big-men" of the co-ops might be involved in petty aspects of modern politics in their individual capacities, the two sets of functions seldom overlapped prior to 1952. Nevertheless, nationalist politicization and the growing competition of party politics during the 1950s did spill over into the cooperatives (as will be later seen). Instead of merging smoothly into organizational activities, the politicization came into conflict with the economic *raison d'etre* of the co-ops. The activities of the Cocoa Purchasing Company (CPC) from 1952 and the growing strength of the CPP set in motion political forces which antagonized not only the leadership of the Sunyani area cooperatives, but of most such rural economic organizations in the south.[35] Thus, when CPP politics intensified in the late 1950s and early 1960s, Nkrumah and other politicians had adversaries rather than supporters in the leadership of grass roots economic organizations. The "vote for cocoa" which would emerge from the cooperative leadership, for example, was one which would attempt to preclude state control over cocoa revenues because they feared government interference at the local as well as the regional level.[36]

Chiefs, Land Resources and Local Representation

There were Gold Coast nationalists who, during the late 1940s and the 1950s, wished to take advantage of the unity which had existed between chiefs and local farmers during the cocoa hold-ups and the resistance to the government's swollen shoot cut-out campaign to mobilize the local people. However, most were not fully aware of the divergent views between chiefs and people, and between ethnic groups, about how commoners should be involved in decision-making processes with respect to rural economic and political issues. There were also growing divisions between chiefs and people over allegiances to the emerging national groupings, particularly between 1946 and 1952. The first issue temporarily overshadowed the second because of its immediacy in rural areas. While chiefs had been vocal in defense of cocoa farmers—most being cocoa farmers themselves—they were worried about the sharply increasing demands of ordinary people for inclusion in the political debates being conducted by educated young men and prosperous cocoa farmers. They were aware of the proliferation of youth associations throughout the country,[37] as well as of the formation of the United Gold Coast Convention Party (UGCC) by the educated elite in 1947. The UGFCC was contemporary with the formation of the Ashanti Youth Association in August 1947. To many farmers it appeared that traditional Ashanti chiefs were facing, or were about to face, competition for decision-making control from local citizens' groups as well as with regional and national level organizations.

The challenges to rural chiefs in 1946 and after generally fell into three categories: (a) local authorities, who had increasingly assumed control over the cocoa industry, land and timber tributes, thus depriving chiefs of tribute and sufficient funds for traditional purposes; (b) influential "youngmen" (commoners) who were increasing control of new local government institutions; and (c) the educated elite whose increasing power within new nationalist organizations affected their loyalty to rural chiefs. At the root of all three problems were the projected constitutional and local government reforms which encouraged people to take advantage of the flux to effect a greater liberalization of local economic and political structures.

The concern of the chiefs was that the minimal participation of "youngmen" in political affairs was changing. In the early period, only the coastal areas had elected or appointed municipal councils, and by 1900 Kumasi had been granted non-official African representation.[38] Native authorities and treasuries in the colony as well as Ashanti were only recognized by legislation in 1927, 1936 and 1939. The input of ordinary citizens in local decision-making was minimal, however, until the 1943 legislation authorized elected town councils in cities such as Kumasi. Rural citizens then profited from the passage of the Native Authorities Ordinance in 1944 which distinguished between traditional powers of state councils over such things as marriage and inheritance on the one hand, and the government functions of native authorities on the other hand. Then, in 1949 the Coussey Constitutional Committee, charged with constitutional and local government reform, recognized the widespread demand for "universal adult suffrage."

While the Coussey Constitutional Committee supported an important role for chiefs within the evolving political structures of the Gold Coast,[39] it was forced to note some of the deficiencies of the "native authorities," including their strict membership of only chiefs, their old-fashioned (non-literate) procedures, and large staffs. The committee recommended that local, district and municipal councils be created, with two-thirds of the membership popularly elected. All of this took place against the overwhelming demands for self-government within the Gold Coast, fueled by Nkrumah's actions following his separation from the UGCC on November 12, 1949, and his 1951 election as Minister of Government on the Convention Peoples' Platform.[40]

National politics tended to overshadow the local concerns of rural people.

Following the inauguration of Nkrumah's government, attention shifted to the rural arena. The Local Government Ordinance of 1951 created democratically elected local, district and urban councils, and became the real instrument for local politics. By 1957 in Ashanti, eighty-three local and urban councils and ten district councils were created, with most of them based on the old native authorities, a few of which had populations as large as 10,000 people.[41] The problem was that when the old native authorities formed the basis for the new local governments, great strains arose between chiefs and people over political and economic control.

The main problem, as chiefs saw it, was to retain former control over political decisions, land and resources. Under the traditional political system the local *ohene* or *odikro* passed a percentage of local revenue and tributes upward to the paramount chief, and ultimately to the Asantehene. When the newly enfranchised rural citizenry complained about the inadequate amounts of money being retained for local development, they came into conflict with chiefs loyal to the Asantehene. These local conflicts raised the twin issues of how much change should take place in the traditional, hierarchical system of tribute and governance, and the extent to which people who contributed to the well-being of local areas should determine how revenues were used. In essence, the traditional political system was being challenged by the emerging nation-state.

Among the issues facing rural people was the allocation of revenue from stranger farmers seeking cocoa land, or payments for timber and rubber gathered on public land. During and after World War II, local timber merchants and entrepreneurs (mostly separate, but some through joint ventures), as well as Lebanese, began realizing substantial profits from communal land, and paid tribute or rent to the chief for this privilege. Then, between 1949 and 1952, with the growing responsibilities of native authorities, area councils and local councils to generate funds, many persons felt that the chiefs did not have the right to collect tributes and rents as they had in the past. To complicate matters, some officials from area councils with responsibilities for collecting tributes and passing 65 percent to the Kumasi divisional treasury, often conveniently overlooked some tenants while they leaned on others, or were ignorant of the number of "strangers" from whom tribute was expected. Again, some Kumasi clan chiefs chose to defy the Asantehene's orders to pay into the Kumasi treasury the tributes from Ahafo land which they controlled.[42] While ethnicity played some role in this situation, political allegiance was the major factor in this differential payment of tribute. Whether intentional or by oversight, the decrease in revenue was viewed by chiefs as a political as well as an economic challenge, and they requested the intervention of the district commissioner. The D.C. was obliged to compile lists of tribute payers, which could be verified when necessary.

District administrative and area files for the Goaso, Bechem and Ahafo areas show quite clearly the nature and extent of the conflict over cocoa and timber resources, as well as the amounts of money involved.[43] The re-establishment of the Ashanti Confederacy in 1935 had tied Akan chiefs more closely to Kumasi than they had been since the 1890s. In the Ahafo area in particular, where, because of high migration and settlement rates, some chiefs acquired more revenue, they attempted to deny their allegiance (and therefore tribute) to Kumasi in an effort to retain the funds. On the other hand, chiefs loyal to Kumasi found that some migrants and indigenous people did not wish tribute to go to the Asantehene. Faced with this resistance some Kumasi chiefs, fearing their overlordship in Ahafo areas was threatened by local autonomy, often demanded a higher tribute than ever before. Matters were not helped when the Confederacy Council, in an effort to generate more funds, doubled the rate of cocoa tribute for the 1950–51 cocoa season from one-half farthing to one farthing per tree.

TABLE 6–3

COCOA TRIBUTE—AHAFO AREA*

Kumasi Chiefs	1949/50	arrears	1950/51	arrears	1951/52
Akwabohene	£288. 7s.	183.10s.	259.17s.	265. 7s.	140.10s.
Oyokohene	£490.10s.	----	128.14s.	498.14.6d	----
Hiahene	£158. 6s.	66. 5s.	205.13s.	118.17s.	----
Hiawuhene	£166.10s.	----	----	----	----
TOTAL	£1103.13s.	249.15s.	594.04s.	882.19s.	140.10s
65% Kumasi	£716.19s.	162.06s.3	386.04s.7	573.18s.7	91.06.6
35% local	£386.14s.	87.08s.15	207.19s.5	309. 0s.5	49.03.6

*From File DAO/Goaso 2/280, Cocoa Tribute 1949–58, documents numbered G0016/51, #8 of 1949; #9, #14, #19 and G.106/618 of 1949; No. 29/G.9.47 of 1950; No. 63/G.9/47 of 1950; No. 0367 of 1950, No. 100/G.9/47 of 1950; No. 216/G.0014/50 of 1950; No. 118/G.0014/50 of 1951; No. 81 of 1951; and No. 17/G.0014/50 of 1952.

The data in Table 6–3 show the considerable variation in the responses of Kumasi chiefs to changes in collection of cocoa tribute. For example, beginning in 1949, the Hiawuhene refused to pay tributes into the area treasury. The Akwabohene asked his own collectors to get tributes from Hwediem, Goaso, Nkasaam, Nyumsu, Mim and Mehane, since the local government collectors were unreliable.

Nevertheless, both the Akwabohene and the Hiahene often avoided paying their entire amount into the area treasury, preferring to directly pay the 65 percent allocations to Kumasi. Even the D.C.'s intervention did not guarantee that chiefs would recognize local government authority over tributes. Most chiefs objected fundamentally to commoners controlling cocoa resources. They clearly foresaw the coming political threat behind the economic aggressiveness of rural people.

Tables 6–4 and 6–5 show timber concessions and revenues.

TABLE 6–4

STOOL LAND REVENUE—TIMBER*
Sunyani Areas Local Council

AREA	1955	1956	1957	1958	1959
Nsuatre	£27.10s.	607.14s.6	1,109.15	1,064.13.6	542.10.
Odumasi (A)	£178.10s.	4.10s	41.0.	71.14	55.06.
Odumasi (B)	£----	610.14s.	12.02.	33. 0.	141.07.
Odumasi (other)	£----	137.05s.6	13. 0.	1,277. 0.	1,250. 0.
Susuanso	£----	78.06s.	12.11.6	957.03.8	143.05.
Domasua	£----	2.15s.	7. 0.	----	18. 0.
Forest Reserves	£----	111. 0s.	111. 0.	111. 0.	----
TOTAL	£206. 0.	1,372. 0.16	2,686.16.12	2,291.10.14	2,149.18.

*Derived from Ghana National Archives, File DA0/1/66, Stool Land Revenue, Sunyani Council.

TABLE 6–5

TIMBER CONCESSIONS 1957–58*

Area/ Company	Signatory Chiefs	Surface Rent	Duration	Concession Rent	Area Size
Antronie (Mim Timb)	Atronie Odumasi Sunyani	10/s	20 yrs.	1 sq. mi.	65 sq. mi.
Chiraa (AA. Lang)	Chiraa Dormaa	10/s	15 yrs.	1 sq. mi.	190.4 sq. mi.
Pruhu (Mim Timb)	Wamfie+ Dormaa	10/s	20 yrs.	1 sq. mi.	104 sq. mi.
Kesepa (Mim Timb)	Wamfie+ Dormaa	10/s	20 yrs.	1 sq. mi.	42 sq. mi.
Mpameso (Mim Timb)	Dormaa	10/s	20 yrs.	1 sq. mi.	26 sq. mi.
Tain #1 (AA. Lang)	Dormaa Berekum	10/s	20 yrs.	1 sq. mi.	?

*Data derived from GNA (Accra) files: Timber Concessions, DA0/3/C335; DA0/3/C336; and Stool Lands Revenue File DA0/1/66.

+Concession rights were contested between the two chiefs listed.

The heightened involvement of locals in timber concessions generated additional political problems for chiefs. By the mid-1950s, chiefs in Brong-Ashanti and Ahafo areas gave out a rash of timber concessions, under which contractors paid both rents for the land and royalties per tree to the chiefs involved. There, royalties on 17 different kinds of marketable trees ranged from £l for kyenkyen, ofram and walnut, to £4 for a mahogany tree. The problem was that most of the concessions were in forest reserves on land controlled by both traditional stools and local governments. Sometimes the land given as concession was claimed by two or more chiefs because traditional boundaries had never been clarified, or because lower chiefs challenged the claims of overlords to the now valuable land. To resolve such problems, some local councils approved duplicate timber contracts with the contesting chiefs, but held the proceeds. They thereby permitted timber contractors to start work despite court battles over the land. In this way, commoners whittled away the prerogatives of the chiefs.

By the time that Nkrumah gained political leadership, it was common for those chiefs who had uncontested rights to forest land to hasten the granting of timber concessions in an effort to retain control of the land. Typical of these was the Susuansohene, who owed allegiance to the Asantehene. Under the Susuansohene's agreement with Ramia Ltd. of Obuasi, the contractor paid £1,460 to fell 400 mahogany, kokrodua, sapele, baku, and utile trees within a period of one year, and paid compensation for any cocoa and rubber trees destroyed in the process.[44] Nevertheless, through the local D.C.s, the local authorities kept close tabs on chiefs who had granted timber contracts. In Sunyani, care was taken that when royalties were paid into the area treasury, 55 percent went to the Kumasi traditional council and 45 percent to the Sunyani Area Local Council. It was up to Kumasi to pay out the 35 percent of the revenue it received to local chiefs whose land had been granted as concessions.

Conflicts over revenue and political authority in rural areas were not limited to cocoa farmers, timber merchants, chiefs and local authorities, but extended to persons such as urban wage earners, petty clerks and farmers who paid the escalating town taxes. Strangers and local people who resided in towns often felt that they received little in return for their taxes, and in many cases were subjected to double taxes—local as well as basic urban rates of £l.10/ per male and 15/ per female.[45] Increasingly, the newly established Youth Associations voiced discontent with local taxation because they had no real participation in political decision-making. In 1954, the Sunyani Youth Association even requested that local stool lands be placed under the authority of the Sunyani Urban Council, on which they had gained representation.[46] Shocked by such demands, the two Odumasi *ohene* not only declared that traditionally the Sunyani chief was their subordinate and owned no land, but they resorted to coercive tactics to prevent commoners from controlling local government institutions. Ultimately, none of these efforts by the chiefs had the desired effect.

The discussion of alternative court systems which would allow wider participation in local decision-making made chiefs of many traditional areas fear that the new towns would threaten their traditional importance. Some divisional chiefs even threatened to change their residence to the larger towns, and they had to be restrained by their chiefs, elders and the district commissioner. The sympathies of the D.C. were clearly with the chiefs of these large towns who faced immense administrative responsibilities, but the colonial administration also tried to protect the integrity of the confederacy which had control of many aspects of native administration such as the courts. However, there were other problems. The chiefs were not adverse to using the courts as a source of revenue. Especially greedy chiefs often raised "unlawful levies" and charged those who did not pay; therefore elders and "youngmen" found it necessary to cooperate in preventing such abuses. In one well-known case against Nsuatrehene Yaw Nti, the chief illegally imposed a levy and then charged elders and "youngmen" with "unlawful assembly" when they gathered to oppose it. On the appeal of this case to the Asantehene, it was discovered that the Nsuatrehene had misappropriated stool funds, and used local tributes and rents to purchase a personal car.[47] Nevertheless, because of the Nsuatrehene's traditional importance to the Ashanti hierarchy, the final decision found fault with the queen mother, the "youngmen" and the elders, but not with the Nsuatrehene. What the case demonstrated was that the Asantehene sometimes found it necessary to support errant chiefs against "youngmen" and elders in vain efforts to halt the increased demands of commoners for greater political involvement.

The Native Courts (Ashanti) Ordinances of 1951 and 1952, which were designed to curb abuses, gave impetus to tho political demands of commoners and semi-educated "youngmen." The new courts were to draw both traditional and modern representatives from all the towns in an area, but the balance between the two types of representatives was the subject of controversy. Many divisional chiefs seemed to prefer that subordinate towns send educated elders or commoners, since they feared being eclipsed by one of their lesser chiefs. The chiefs of subordinate towns, for their part, agitated for a balance between commoners and nobility, so as to escape abusive control by the *ahenfo*.[48] Ultimately, it was the educated commoners who would pose the greatest challenge to traditional authority in rural areas.

Because towns such as Sunyani were centers of administration in the economically significant cocoa areas, the traditional chiefs could not overcome the political reality of commoner political representation. Many chiefs ignored the Asantehene's 1943 warning to lower level Ashanti chiefs, that:

> The present system of elections is very bad; some of the electors make their personal choice without the approval of the "youngmen." I must explain that although the "youngmen" have no voice in the administration, since they are the taxpayers, it is always necessary that they be consulted.[49]

Nevertheless, the emergence of local government began to force the hands of the chiefs. In 1953, Sunyani had been declared an urban planning area, and there was discussion of a western Ashanti branch railway and an airstrip.[50] Naturally, chiefs could no longer postpone mass involvement in either local, district or urban councils and courts. Ambitious commoners, many of whom were members of the Youth Association, were adamant that traditional representatives could not speak on behalf of the entire community. Moreover, within the local area councils they were successful in getting four commoner representatives to every one traditional representative. Of the eighteen members from different towns on the Sunyani District Council, nine were commoners while the other nine were traditional chiefs. The presidency of council was filled only by chiefs, each in annual rotation.[51]

Table 6–6 gives the composition in 1954 of the Sunyani District Council.

TABLE 6–6

COMPOSITION OF SUNYANI DISTRICT COUNCIL–1954*

Berekum Urban	**Berekum Local**
C.Y. Agyei (R)	D. Asafo Agyei (R)
J.F. Buabeng (T)	S.K. Nyame (R)
	C.A. Amoah (R)
	I.W. Benneh (T)
W. Dormaa Local	**Sunyani Urban**
N. Anane Agyei (R)	D.T. Nkromah (R)
G. Ben Yeboah (R)	D.K. Amankwaah (T)
S.E. Baa-Bentu (R)	
Nana Kwame Ntow II (T)	
Nkwanta Local	**Sunyani Local**
P.K. Amponsah (R)	J.E. Boama (R)
J.Y. Arful (R)	D.K. Bresah (R)
Edu Gyamfi (R)	Kojo Amoh (R)
J.H. Gambrah (T)	

*Source: Ghana National Archives, DA0/1/460, Sunyani District Council (1952–1959), no. 71 23rd August 1954.

Despite the success of rural "youngmen" who, like their urban counterparts, were gaining political power, the conflict with traditional chiefs continued. The chiefs increasingly resented the popular and generally better educated "youngmen," and tried to compensate by selecting as their representatives the most educated chiefs or persons who were friendly to them. For example, on the Sunyani Urban council was D.T. Nkromah, a wealthy contractor and absentee cocoa farmer, and D. K. Amankwah, the traditional representative for Sunyani, who had been the chief's liaison with the cooperatives in their formative stage.

On the Sunyani Local Council, Moses Adu (an educated man) represented the two Odumasi chiefs in an attempt to prevent Sunyani's growing autonomy from its traditional overlords.

These battles for local political control between cocoa farmers and townspersons against the traditional aristocracy loomed greater as nationalist politicians tried to increase their constituencies. Some of the emerging political parties were trying to break down the automatic traditional allegiance of rural folk to the political choices of their chiefs. The problem, however, was more complicated than these political actors imagined. In the political competition which confirmed Nkrumah's leadership role between 1954 and 1957, commoner vs. elite factionalism in rural areas would often be eclipsed by ethnic, regional and class interests in the struggle over the cocoa and other resources which were of critical importance to the emerging state.

Ashanti vs. Brong: Rural, Urban and Regional Alignments

While between 1951 and 1957, most of the Gold Coast nationalists were struggling to create a unitary state, the cocoa interests within the Brong-Ashanti areas were concerned with the regional balance of power in the future independent state. Rural people were concerned that although urban and nationalist politicians were arguing about how cocoa resources should be used in building a future Ghana, little attention was being paid to their local concerns and realities. Moreover, many rural people felt a sense of immediacy—unless they resolved some pressing political problems before the country became independent, they might lose the opportunity to do so.

For the people in the Brong Ahafo area, ethnic affiliation and sub-group loyalty to the Ashanti Confederacy were an issue about which there was considerable conflict. Views on these issues were influenced by the larger issues of local government, self-government and independence. As we have seen, the upheaval and migration during the Ashanti wars and British conquest, as well as in response to the mobility of the cocoa economy, had resulted in considerable ethnic heterogeneity within rural cocoa areas. The southward migration of northern cocoa laborers only compounded the mix of Akwapim, Shai, Krobo, Fanti, Ga, Ewe, Brong, Gyama and Gonja peoples within towns and villages in the Ashanti region. The problem was that each people had tended to retain allegiances to their hometown and ethnic origin, even while sinking new roots into other communities within the cocoa belt. In some cases, ethnic diversity was discussed in terms of the Islamic *zongos* in large towns such as Kumasi and Accra,[52] but this was quickly eclipsed by the Ashanti vs. Brong conflicts in western Ashanti.

The intricate weave of issues in the Ashanti vs. Brong conflict of 1954 deserves note because it was replicated on a larger or smaller scale throughout the country, often bringing chaos in its train. Central to this conflict were the following factors: (a) it represented a major challenge to historical Ashanti territorial domination as well as to its rights to control proceeds from the cocoa industry; (b) it foreshadowed the larger and still unrecognized issue of whether chieftaincy and traditional aristocracy deserved a dominant place in modern Gold Coast politics, as contrasted to popular and democratic representation in non-traditional units and organizations; and (c) it revealed the depth of conflict concerning national and urban as against ethnic control of resources and capital generated in rural areas.

Ethnic identity in the Brong-Ashanti areas, while relatively flexible, had always been predominantly Akan. As indicated above, to the original inhabitants of the Brong states and the early Islamic settlers[53] had been added the populations in the east and west forest area which, during the seventeenth and nineteenth centuries, had moved north to escape increasing Ashanti hegemony.

Then, as we have seen, the resulting small states of Attebubu, Prang, Krakye and Nkoranza had not only successfully resisted Ashanti domination due to religious belief (the Denteh oracle) as well as military force,[54] but developed a distinct Brong dialect of Akan and a sub-cultural blend of matrilineality, patrifilial tendencies, and flexibility in kin/residential organization.[55] The efforts of the Brong to escape exploitation by Kumasi for gold, land and manpower were aided by British conquest of Ashanti in 1896. This increased their autonomy, and helped them to resist incorporation into the Ashanti Confederacy in 1935.

The Brong in 1954 were quite aware that policies adopted by the British in 1901 to facilitate indirect rule had often exacerbated their relations with Ashanti. For example, the promotion of Berekum (as opposed to Duayaw Nkwanta or Dormaa) as paramount in 1901, had created resentment within the Berekum Division.[56] The chiefs of Suma, Dabone and Damine, who had originally protested that colonial boundaries cut them off from their traditional headchief, who resided in the Ivory Coast, resisted for a long time until given a paramountcy, which the Drobo chief occupied. However, British selection of the Drobo chief as paramount against the wishes of the Gyaman chiefs and elders thus further exacerbated poor relationships within the Gyaman Division.[57]

True, some Brong communities under the impetus of their chiefs or "bigmen," gave allegiance to Ashanti and identified with it after the establishment of the confederacy in 1935, in turn receiving many political and economic privileges.[58] In the Odumasi/Sunyani area these dual identities, expressed in disagreement over chieftaincies within the town, led to the initial destoolment of pro-Brong chiefs, and finally to the destoolment of pro-Ashanti ones.[59] Justifiable or not, such conflicting identities continued to be the source of conflict in the Nkoranza, Techiman and Dormaa areas as the Committee of Privileges discovered in 1935 when it made inquiries into traditional status. In many cases, some of the newer Brong identities represented convenient reinterpretation of history, rather than actual fact.[60]

The restoration of the Ashanti Confederacy and the removal of nine villages from the control of the Techimanhene in 1935, and their return to control of Kumasi chiefs, was the decisive factor in alienating the Brongs. In this act, both political loyalties and economic resources of these villages were taken away from Techiman. Tensions within the nine villages increased when the Techimanhene claimed autochthonous status and, despite government pressure, decided not to recognize the authority of the Kumasihene. The Brong areas were further angered by the attempted restrictions on cocoa planting during the swollen shoot epidemic, because they insisted that there was more pressure upon them than on Ashanti cocoa areas. In 1948 the Techimanhene highlighted Brong opposition to Ashanti control by withdrawal from the Confederacy Council, and by 1951 he had created the Brong Kyempim Federation (BKF) as the first step in uniting the Brong into a separate political unit.[61]

The growing alliance of the Brong states during the 1950s was perhaps more a response to old Ashanti/Brong grievances and fear of new political/economic changes attending the end of colonialism, than it was an expression of ethnic unity and micro-nationalism.[62] The "true Brong" chiefs, such as the Techimanhene and the Dormaahene, claimed that they had never willingly served Ashanti, and were therefore symbols of Brong legitimacy, despite considerable evidence to the contrary. Although the Ashanti tried to lessen the significance of Brong nationalism by claiming that territorial unity was not sufficient basis for disrupting the Ashanti Confederacy, the Brongs were successful in stimulating government investigation of their complaints through the Mate Kole Commission. The BKF complaints also encouraged the Mate Kole Commission to look more critically at the Ashanti Confederacy courts, and the Commission's recommendation to decentralize the courts was well received in the northwest area.[63] Thus, the pressure of the BKF was well timed, coinciding as it did with the general movement towards area, district, and local governing councils and courts. The CPP was correct in its assessment of the Brong movement as a significant political force which might help them break the archaic influences of Ashanti on Gold Coast politics. Nevertheless, F.K. Drah's suggestion that the CPP was ambivalent about the political expediency of supporting the Brong movement is understandable:[64] Brong nationalism did assist the CPP in the movement towards independence, but the ethnic, regional, and economic conflicts it fueled contributed to the CPP's undoing.

While the control over cocoa was the significant factor influencing Brong political attitudes, this was seldom noted at the national level until much later. The local conflict was interpreted as competition between those towns which claimed to be Brong (considered pro-Nkrumah or pro-CPP) and those which claimed to be Ashanti (said to be pro-NLM). In one case the Bechemhene, as president of the Bechem Local Council, tried to destool the Tanoso chief because he decided to join the pro-CPP Sunyani Local Council.[65] What seemed to be a purely political decision was in reality based on the desire of Tanoso elders and "youngmen" to gain economic and political control over cocoa tributes by becoming autonomous from the Sunyani areas' local council. The council, while Brong in sentiment, had not yet joined the BKF.

Brong land claims tended to be based on traditional boundaries, whereas Ashanti claims to land within the Odumasi/Sunyani area were continually increasing because Ashanti migrant farmers expanded cocoa production into these areas. Thus Ashanti economic exactions were based on the political allegiance of their expanding constituency, a concept which was increasingly challenged.[66] In response, Sunyani people continually emphasized that, in addition to resisting Brong political domination by Ashanti, their desire was "to prevent local revenue from rents, cocoa tributes and forest concessions from being controlled by the traditional overlord, as opposed to equal distribution of resources among all towns." Moreover, they wanted to "insure that significant stool lands were under the control of the councils and committees, as opposed to being subject to misuse at the hands of unscrupulous chiefs."[67] By 1955, Sunyani had formally seceded from the Kumasi State Council, joined the BKF, and increased its struggle against Kumasi control of any cocoa camps and villages in the area, as well as rights to tributes or rents from property within the township.

The economic and political bases of this growing ethnic dispute are easy to understand. Between 1952 and 1955, the export price for cocoa rose to an all-time high, but through the actions of the Cocoa Purchasing Company acting as an auxiliary for the Cocoa Marketing Board, the prices paid to farmers were not correspondingly increased.[68] In the cocoa belt, Ashanti chiefs and farmers complained that the new state of Ghana was being built upon the backs of cocoa farmers—that they were being unfairly exploited and taxed to support the CPP, the CMB and unscrupulous loans made by the CPC. To oppose this trend, Ashanti chiefs, wealthy cocoa farmers and Kumasi merchants (excluding the Syrian and Lebanese)[69] supported the creation of an opposition movement called the National Liberation Movement (NLM). The NLM protested against CMB retention and use of cocoa resources, and on a local level supported Ashanti opposition to the fact that tribute and taxes would no longer flow into Kumasi under the proposed unitary state structure. The Brong, on the other hand, were hoping that if they supported the CPP, they might get that political autonomy which would guarantee them greater control over local cocoa tributes, rents, timber and other resources.

Initially, Nkrumah's CPP government, in its anxiety to prevent the claims of small regional autonomy from jeopardizing its drive for independence, tried to contain the Brong-Ashanti conflict. Its decision to intervene was largely due to increasing Ashanti determination not to be dominated by the urban "verandah boys" as the partisans of the CPP were called. Facing this increased opposition, the CPP felt that one way of defeating Ashanti and the NLM opposition was to support the Brong states. Nkrumah was determined to prevent what he perceived as a combination of Ashanti nationalism and the class interests of the large cocoa farmers from threatening national unity and independence. The CPP decided to support the decision of the BKF which had formalized itself into the Brong Kyempim Council under the leadership of Nana Agyeman Badu, the Dormaahene.

One can understand Ashanti's fear of domination by outsiders, given its historical greatness, its defeat by the British, and its struggle to restore its confederation. For the Ashanti, some form of federalism was the best hope of remaining autonomous in a unitary Ghana. The problem which they faced, and this was also true of the Brong, was how to support the political parties. The Ashanti faced the problem of the Cocoa Purchasing Company, which distributed economic favors such as loans, and used its power to induce farmers to affiliate with the CPP.[70] The CPP could also persuade influential rural chiefs to use their informal patron-client relations to encourage local and stranger cocoa farmers to vote for the CPP. This chiefly control over the granting of land use was indeed an important weapon when used for political purposes. Even those long-time migrant workers (such as the Mossi) who understood Twi and who had paid local taxes were being encouraged to vote CPP by *zongo* or village chiefs working in conjunction with important area chiefs.[71]

On the other hand, the Ashanti could use the same tactics to persuade friendly rural chiefs in Brong areas to support the NLM. They used this tactic with considerable effect in the villages immediately around Kumasi. In regional cocoa towns, CPP and NLM support was dispersed and highly dependent upon the town population. In places such as Kumasi, with a majority of Ashanti merchants, building owners, businesspersons, and large *zongo* communities, it was not surprising that the votes were heavily NLM. This phenomenon of support among *zongo* chiefs and migrant workers for the NLM continued for a long period.[72] Noteworthy, however, was that many "youngmen" among *zongo* residents tended to vote CPP, and by doing so created dissention in the *zongo*.[73]

Despite the NLM's blatant appeal to class interests and Ashanti ethnicity in the 1956 elections, as well as its campaign slogan, "Vote Cocoa," it failed to defeat the CPP either in the rural areas or in urban centers. Nevertheless, the cost of CPP dominance over the NLM was a heavy one, since it had supported minority ethnic movements within large traditional polities, both within Ashanti and the north.[74] In many ways, the CPP provided incentive for rural peoples who formerly had little stake in national politics to utilize the political party apparatus to overthrow the former overlords. Many of the poorer cocoa farmers were able to counter the pro-NLM stance of local chiefs. To guarantee an alliance between the CPP and the BKF in the 1955 elections, Nkrumah promised to create a new Brong-Ahafo region in the northeastern and western portions of Ashanti.[75] Although this alliance succeeded in providing Nkrumah with the votes needed for an electoral majority and therefore unitary independence in 1957, promises to the Brongs had created unrealistic ethnic economic as well as political expectations.

The youth associations and women's groups actively supported the claims of minority constituents such as the BKC. These groups felt a sense of power they had not known before. Yet the elections created bitter conflicts even within families. In one remarkable case from Sunyani, a father who felt deep loyalties to his Ashanti roots was offended by his son's involvement with the youth associations and the CPP, and drove him from the household. The son wrote to the district commissioner, asking him to intervene on his behalf to bring harmony back into the family.[76] Youth such as these, by taking an uncompromising stand on Brong autonomy, pushed chiefs and local politicians to make firm demands on Nkrumah and the CPP.

As often happens, promises which politicians make to their constituents during the heat of campaigns have largely unforeseen consequences. The Brong-Ahafo region was indeed created by CPP legislation in 1959, two years after independence, but it represented far more than the fulfillment of a promise to the Brongs. The B/A region was also an example of Nkrumah's retaliation against those who supported the NLM, and his efforts to prevent Ashanti from becoming a political giant within the state of Ghana. Drah's (1978) analysis of how the Brong movement fit into nationalist politics is therefore quite insightful. There was, in 1959, a real danger that Ashanti would continue to dominate Ghanaian politics as they had dominated southern Gold Coast politics prior to 1896—but this time using the politics of cocoa money as the chief instrument. While Ashanti political reaction had been largely based on fear of southern domination such as they had experienced since 1896, they were also quite conscious of the potential power of cocoa. Creation of the B/A region had, however, separated the newer and more productive cocoa-producing areas in Ahafo from Ashanti control, with an administrative capital in Sunyani where the new educated Brong-Ashanti "youngmen" and elite were able to operate more effectively. Ideally, this would have confirmed the marriage of the B/A region to the CPP.

The problem for the people of Sunyani, the CPP and Ghana was that economic realities due to world commodity cocoa prices interfered. Local level politics of communities such as the Sunyani district continued to be focused on regional ethnic, economic and political factors, rather than on national ones. Cocoa farmers in the Sunyani district, for example, were conscious that the acquisition of independence and global economics affected their country's livelihood, but they viewed these matters as belonging to another universe until they affected them directly. By 1959, the effects of the global realities had started to become obvious to many local cocoa farmers. National and global factors heightened political dissention within cocoa areas. Economics would contribute to conflict within the cocoa industry both in Ashanti and the new Brong Ahafo, and it would presage grave difficulties for all Ghanaians.

Appendix to Chapter 6: Cooperative Society Interviews

Excerpts from interviews with elderly members of the Sunyani, Odumasi and Nsuatre Cooperative Produce Buying Societies in 1973, who provided information on the early period of the cooperative's development and its internal relations, follow:

Q: When the society was formed in 1947, did it cover just Sunyani, or was it covering all the areas around Sunyani too?

A: The Union [National Cooperative Union] was formed in 1947 and the Sunyani Society was formed in 1947 too. There were societies in other areas as well...Yes, the farmers liked it...they supported it strongly.

Q: Were there any other organizations which were competing with the cooperative movement?

A: There were no societies competing with them except Cadbury and Frye, United Africa Company and the rest. But the cooperatives were formed by the *farmers* so that they could sell their cocoa abroad!

Q: Who was the secretary-receiver of the Sunyani society from the beginning?

A: One Mr. Moses K. Kyeremeh...the members chose Mr. Kyeremeh to write the names of those who wished to join the society. At first it was in Abesim, Wamfie, Dormaa, Aboabo and Berekum, and they also wanted to have one in Sunyani town...It was Mr. Kyeremeh who walked around in the town to collect the names, so they said that since he had done that work for them, then he should be the secretary.

Q: So from that day, all the farmers had the right to choose the secretary-receiver?

A: Exactly, in fact the [Cooperative] Department was there only as an adviser. And if the farmers should find that he [the secretary-receiver] was not in their interest, they would not accept him.

Q: How was the society set up?

A: When they started forming the society, they asked them to pay £l, then 2 shillings, for buying paper, etc. The £l was share capital, so that at any time you left the society, they would give it back to you. Then from every load of cocoa you brought in, they subtracted 1 shilling as shares here in Sunyani.

Q: What would determine how much they would subtract? Would one are a take 10 shillings and another take 1 shilling?

A: Well, some members were extremely keen on these shares that they were making, so that instead of keeping these savings they contributed the money for more shares.

Q: What was done with the money?

A: We rendered our account during our annual meeting, and whatever surplus we realized, part of it was laid down as reserves, building reserves...for the society. They would use some to send someone abroad; or in case they should get in a very bad debt, they would use some of the reserve. And if they want to put up a building they can use some...And we had statutory reserves...that you can't withdraw without permission of the registrar of the cooperatives.

Q: You are all members of the cooperative committee. What does the committee do within the society?

A: The duty of the committee is to supervise everything...how the cocoa is weighed...and at the end of every month they used to meet and direct the secretary-receiver how to do things. When the bonus is shared [at the end of the year], a small amount goes to the committee members.

Q: What do the ordinary members do?

A: They come to sell their cocoa. At the end of the year they come to the annual meeting and talk about what is to be done [raise problems]. They collect their bonus at meetings. If they want new committee members, then there is voting. If not, then the members stay.

Q: Suppose a farmer has financial trouble. Can he come to the cooperative society and ask for money?

A: Yes, both short-term and long-term loans. When any farmer wants a loan, he writes an application, and then another farmer witnesses so that if he doesn't pay, the other farmer will be asked for it...Every member has a personal ledger recording the amount of cocoa in the last season, and if it was good, he may get the loan.

Q: How is it paid back?

A: When he brings in the first batch, he pays back some of the loan, then a little the next time, until at the end of the year the loan is paid back...Even if he wants to buy more land, he must have enough cocoa to cover the loan. They look at his personal ledger. If he has trouble, they can help him to sell his things and redeem them again. At times a member might fall into debt, and as a result of this his farm would forfeit, they could be sold forever. So when we have the shares, the money is there. We will give it to the farmer. He will be plucking the cocoa and paying back the debt.

Source: Mikell Interviews, Brong-Ahafo Cooperative Produce Buying Association, Sunyani, 1973.

Notes

1. One of the major developments involved road and rail transportation, which facilitated the movement of cocoa to ports. See Gold Coast, Special Papers, #3, 1924–5: Governor's address to Legislative Council, 6 March 1924. On limits to this development, see Metcalfe, 1964, 609–615, Report by the Hon. W.G.A. Ormsby-Gore on his Visit to West Africa during the Year 1926.
2. A.F. Robertson, *Dependence and Opportunity: Political Change in Ahafo*, Cambridge University Press, 1973.
3. David Apter, *Ghana in Transition*, New York: Atheneum, 1968, 18, 80, 160–161.
4. Kwame Nkrumah was born in Nkroful in September 1912 by his mother's calculations (September 21, 1909 according to Catholic Church baptismal records). He attended elementary school in Half Assini, and then went to the Accra Training College in 1926 and later to Achimota college. Nkrumah taught in the Roman Catholic Junior School in Axim for two years, then at the Roman Catholic Seminary at Amissano near Elmina until 1935. Even then, Nkrumah was an admirer of Namdi Azikwe, and deeply interested in nationalist philosophy. Having gained admission to Lincoln University with financial help from a relative in Lagos, Nkrumah went to Liverpool to obtain a U.S. visa. Then he sailed to New York, and entered Lincoln University, where he worked his way through school. Nkrumah received his Bachelor of Arts degree in economics and sociology from Lincoln in 1939, and then received his Master of Arts degree in theology from Lincoln in 1943. Although Nkrumah passed preliminary examinations for the Doctorate of Philosophy degree, financial problems and illness prevented his completion of the degree. He established close ties with black scholars and with C.L.R. James. In addition to teaching, he worked at the Sun Shipbuilding Yard in Chester, Pennsylvania, until he left for London in May 1945. Through his acquaintance with George Padmore, T.R. Makonnen and Peter Abrahams, Nkrumah became involved in organizing for the Fifth Pan-African Congress. He eventually became Vice-President of the West African Students' Union, Secretary of the West African National Secretariat, and finally chairman of a vanguard anti-colonialist group called "the Circle." In 1947, upon the invitation of J.B. Danquah, Nkrumah returned to the Gold Coast to take up the job as general secretary of the Gold Coast Convention. He left London for the Gold Coast aboard the "Accra" in the company of Kojo Botsio. See K. Nkrumah, *Ghana: The Autobiography of Kwame Nkrumah*, Edinburgh: Thomas Nelson & Sons, 1959.
5. Kwame Nkrumah, *Dark Days in Ghana*, Panaf, 1968; also, *Neo-Colonialism: The Last Stage of Imperialism*, London: Heinemann, 1965.
6. David Kimble, *A Political History of Ghana: The Rise of Gold Coast Nationalism, 1850–1928*, Oxford University Press, 1963.
7. Metcalfe, 1964, 471, 539, 542–3.
8. T.J. Lewin, *Asante Before the British: The Prempean Years, 1875–1900*, Regents Press of Kansas, 1968, 71. Also, Accounts & Papers (7). vol. LI, 1911 Cd. 5467–16, pp. 1–21, Report on Ashanti.

9. Accounts & Papers, Colonial Report for Ashanti 1909. This was a trend which the colonial government sought to discourage, as evidenced by its support for the traditional authority of chiefs reflected in the subsequent Colonial Report for 1910. See also K.A. Busia, *The Position of the Chief in the Modern Political System of Ashanti*, Oxford University Press, IAI, 1951, 106–8.
10. William Tordoff, *Ashanti Under the Prempehs*, 1965, 175–6 ; Kimble, 1963, 481–4.
11. G.C., S.P. 7 of 1919–20, Petition of National Congress of British West Africa, 19 Oct. 1920. The NCBWA was composed of 42 Gold Coast delegates along with six Nigerians, three Sierra Leonians, and possibly one Gambian. See Metcalfe, 1964, 583.
12. G.C. S.P. 10 of 1920–21, Governor's Speech to Council, 27 April 1921.
13. The Joint Provincial Council of Chiefs became active in 1925, and the Native Administration Ordinances came into effect in 1927.
14. Legislative Council Debates 1933, Governor Thomas to Council 22 March 1933. See also Native Courts (Colony) Ordinance of 1944, No. 22 of 1944.
15. Leg. Council Debates 1926, Proceedings 18 March 1926. See also Ofori-Atta's Speech to Council, 4 March 1943 (in Leg. Council Debates, 1943).
16. G.C. S.P. 17 of 1922–3, Report by the Town Council Committee 22 May 1922.
17. Papers Relating to the Restoration of the Ashanti Confederacy, Accra 1935.
18. Annual Reports of Commissions for Ashanti: 1906 LXXII, 241; 1907 LIII, 85; 1908 LXVIII, 61; 1910 LXIV, 55; 1911 LI, 1; 1912–13 LVII, 1; 1914–1916 XLII, 1 and 29. Annual Reports on the Gold Coast (Blue Books): 1905 LI, 463; LXXIV, 29; 1908 LXVII, 665; 1909 LVII, 425; 1910 LXIC, 373; 1911 LI, 289; 1912–13 LVII, 485; 1914 LVII, 49 and 539; 1914–16 XLIII, 629.
19. Sessional Paper No. 11 of 1934, "Petition of the Delegates from the Gold Coast and Ashanti, 1934."
20. Cmd. 5845, Report of the Commission on the Marketing of West African Cocoa, 1938.
21. Legislative Council Ordinance, No. 4 of 1931.
22. Gold Coast Annual Report, 1938, p. 28.
23. Bourret, *Ghana:1919–1957*, London: Oxford University Press. 1960, 150–1.
24. Papers Related to the Restoration of the Ashanti Confederacy. Accra, 1935.
25. P.T. Bauer, *West African Trade*. Cambridge University Press, 1954; see also R. Szerenski, *Structural Changes in the Economy of Ghana 1981–1911*. London: Weidenfeld and Nicholson, 1965.
26. Leg. Council Debates, 1943; also Native Courts (Colony) Ordinance, 1944, No. 22.
27. Dennis Austin, *Politics in Ghana: 1946–1960*, London: Oxford University Press. 1965.
28. See Metcalfe, pp. 682–688, for extracts from the Report of the Commission of Enquiry into Disturbances in the Gold Coast, 1948, Colonial No. 231; also, Statement by his Majesty's Government on the Report of the Commission of Enquiry into Disturbances in the Gold Coast, 1948, Colonial No. 232.
29. Phillip Foster, *Education and Social Change in Ghana*, Chicago: Univ. of Chicago, 1965, 197–8, 216n, 263–4; also see Metcalfe, 1964, 584, 599 for discussion of instruments establishing the University College of the Gold Coast.

30. David Kimble, 1963.
31. Bauer, *West African Trade*. London: Routledge & Kegan, 1963, 324–5.
32. Christine Okali and R.A. Kotey, *Akokoaso: A Resurvey*. Technical Publication Series #15; Legon: Institute for Statistical, Social and Economic Research. 1971.
33. A. W. Robertson, *Dependence and Opportunity: Political Change in Ahafo*, Cambridge University, 1973, 64; see also Polly Hill, *The Gold Coast Cocoa Farmer*, 1958.
34. Austin, 1970, 25.
35. Austin, Politics in Ghana: 1946–60, Oxford University Press. 1970, 172–3.
36. *Report of the Committee of Enquiry into the affairs of the Cocoa Purchasing Company*, Accra, 1956.
37. Austin, 1970, 56–7; also Legislative Council Debates, 1947, no. III.
38. Nsarkoh, *Local Government in Ghana*, Accra: 1964, 5.
39. For background, see *Report of the Commission of Enquiry into Disturbances in the Gold Coast, 1948*. See also the Coussey Committee Report *Report by the Committee on Constitutional Reform*, Colonial No. 248, London, 1949.
40. See Metcalfe, 1964, 703–10, *Convention People's Party, General Election Manifesto*, Accra: 1951; also Austin, 1970, 27.
41. Nsarkoh, op. cit., 19.
42. Ghana National Archives, District Administrative Files (Sunyani). File DAO/Goaso/2/280–Cocoa Tributes 1949-58.
43. A.F. Robertson, *Dependence and Opportunity: Political Change in Ahafo*, Cambridge University Press, 1973, 77–84.
44. GNA, DAO/1/66, Stool Lands Revenue File, no. 223S, vol. 9/T3.
45. GNA, Stool Land Revenues, Sunyani Areas Local Council, B. 2009/SF.10/vol. 2/143 of 20 Sept. 1956.
46. GNA, DAO/1/68, Area of Jurisdiction of Sunyani Urban Council, Memo of Sunyani Youth Association to Acting Chief Regional Officer, Sept 17, 1954.
47. GNA, DAO/3/C83, Nsuatre State Council Affairs, 1947–1961, nos. 7–33, 1949–1950.
48. GNA, DAO/1/579, Odumasi Areas Court, Membership 1952-3, nos. 1–29, 1950–1951.
49. Austin, 1970.
50. GNA, Sunyani Town Planning documents, DAO/1/575 (No. 29/SFC/7) of 1952; J5/4 of June 16, 1953, and June 29, 1954.
51. GNA, Sunyani District Council (1952–1959), DAO/1/460, #9 of 1952. See also Instrument establishing District Council, #53–55, #71.
52. A. Addo-Aryee Brown, "Historical Account of Mohammedanism in the Gold Coast," *Gold Coast Review*, July–Dec. 1927; Bruce Grindal, "Islamic Affiliations and Urban Adaptation: The Sisala Migrant in Accra, Ghana," *Africa*, xliii, 1973, 4: 333–46; and Enid Schildkrout, *People of the Zongo: Changing Ethnic Identities in Kumasi, Ghana*, Cambridge, 1978.
53. R. S. Rattray, *Tribes of the Ashanti Hinterland, 1931*; see also K. Arhin, *Traders in Nineteenth Century Ashanti*, 1978.
54. K.Y. Daaku, "Politics Among the Eastern Brong, 1700–1960," in *Brong Kyempim:*

Essays on the Society, History and Politics of the Brong People. Ed. Kwame Arhin. New Times Corporation, Accra, 1979, 80–87. See also Ivor Wilks, *Asante in the Nineteenth Century*, Cambridge 1975.

55. Florence A. Dolphyne, "The Brong (Bono) Dialect of Akan," in Arhin (ed.) op. cit., 1979, 88–118. On Brong social structure, see R.S. Rattray's earlier account, in *Ashanti*, Cambridge, 1929, 64.
56. GNA ADM 54/1/1, District Administrative records, Sunyani 1903–1906. 62/05.
57. GNA Accra ADM 54/1/3, Sunyani District Records, 1907–1915. No. 166/07.
58. In some cases, this identification was based on lineage and cultural connections with Ashanti, many of which had been created as Ashanti established 'outposts' in the northwest during the 1700s to ensure loyalty of distant political units to Kumasi. Odumasi was a classic case in which these Brong/Ashanti disputes concerned seniority of indigenous vs. Ashanti chiefs within a single traditional area. See also Arhin on outposts.
59. GNA DAO/2/C16 Odumasi Native Affairs, 1928–1939. See also GNA DAO/2/81 Sunyani Native Affairs, 1926–1936, documents nos. 4, 10, 12, 20, 22, 31 (1927–35).
60. W. Tordoff, "The Brong Ahafo Region," in *Economic Bulletin*, May 1959.
61. D. Austin, 1970, 293–5.
62. F.K. Drah, "The Brong Political Movement," in Arhin (ed.), op. cit., 1979, 119–162.
63. Ibid., pp. 128–129.
64. F.K. Drah, "The Brong Political Movement," in K. Arhin (ed.), *Brong Kyempim*, op. cit., pp. 119–162.
65. GNA Accra, ADM 54/1/18, #97, Sunyani Areas Local Council, 1951–1952.
66. GNA, Sunyani DAO/l/C, #135. Odumasi Area Affairs, 1947–1958.
67. GNA Accra ADM 54/1/18, and Sunyani DAO/1/460.
68. Nyanteng, V.K., *The Declining Cocoa Industry: An Analysis of Some Fundamental Problems*, Legon: ISSER. Technical Publication #40. 1978. See also Fitch and Oppenheimer, 1966, 41.
69. The NLM was matched, however, by the Trans-Volta Congress which advocated higher prices for Togo cocoa crops and the reunification of Gold Coast and Togoland Ewe people by the secession of the Trans-Volta region from Ghana. See Gold Coast, *Legislative Assembly Debates*, August 12, 1955; also B. Fitch and M. Oppenheimer, *Ghana: End of An Illusion*, New York: Monthly Review Press, 1966, 56–57.
70. Austin, 1970, 172–3.
71. G. Mikell, "Changing Islamic/Akan Relations in Southern Rural Ghana," paper presented at the African Studies Association Meetings, New Orleans, Nov. 23. 1985. I am indebted to Dr. Elliott P. Skinner for use of his field notes and with Mossi migrant laborers who were returning from work in the Gold Coast, 1955–1956. This allowed comparison with my own data on migrant workers in Ashanti and in the Sunyani areas, 1971 and 1972–3.
72. E.P. Skinner, *Field Notes on Mossi Migrants*, 1955–56. See also Enid Schildkrout, *People of the Zongo: The Transformation of Ethnic Identities in Ghana*. Cambridge, 1978, 206–9.
73. Enid Schildkrout, op. cit., pp. 206–9.

74. *The Lions of Dagbone*. See also David Apter, *Ghana in Transition*, New York: Atheneum Press, 1965; Austin, 1970.
75. The Achimota Conference (at which the NLM declined representation) was held in February 1956 to reach decisions regarding the new regions proposed by the Bourne Report of 1955. However, the BKC led by Nana Agyeman Badu was present and played an influential role. See the Drah article op. cit., (1978), in K. Arhin (ed.), *Brong Kyempim*.
76. Ghana National Archives, DAO/l/C9, "Brong Federation Dispute between Certain Brong Chiefs and the Asanteman Council, 1951–1956."

7

Cocoa Is Not Enough

Although cocoa was not a major factor in Nkrumah's founding of the CPP in 1949 or in his election as head of government in 1951, cocoa had become a central feature in the politics of the CPP by 1955, and the country's dependence upon cocoa was dramatically underscored in Ghanaian politics from 1957 onwards. Nkrumah's shrewd exploitation of the cocoa factor made it possible for the CPP to remain in power, but cocoa politics was also responsible for his fall in 1966. Cocoa resources were simply not enough to satisfy the conflicting ambitions of local, regional and national factions in Ghana; nor could these resources permit that state to extricate itself from continual capital exploitation, or to emancipate all the European colonies in Africa.

The early elites involved in the formation of the CPP were primarily intellectuals and civil servants whose nationalism took precedence over their economic interests. There was undoubtedly the feeling of many members of the CPP elite as well as the literate "youngmen" that Nkrumah and the party had a historic mission to fulfill, namely the creation of the first post-colonial independent African state. That they saw their primary task as building a strong national unity rather than federation comes through clearly in Nkrumah's rhetoric and in CPP documents of the period.[1] The task as stated was to give the people a chance to participate in national politics without restraints imposed by regionalism and parochial economic interests.

Nevertheless, the manipulation of cocoa interests became an important part of the strategy used by the CPP to create the Republic of Ghana. By 1952, Nkrumah had already seen how the Ashanti could use stranger groups in cocoa areas to enhance their economic and political strength within the country, and he sought to counter this. For example, in an attempt to gain control over the Kumasi Muslim community which supported the NLM, the CPP installed one of its Hausa supporters as *Serikin Zongo* and proceeded to banish or exile many of the more critical Hausa, Mossi and Yoruba leaders who opposed the CPP.[2] Using a Nationality Act and the Deportation Acts, the CPP effectively demonstrated that it would neither permit the Ashanti region to exploit client relations with strangers, nor allow non-Ghanaians to interfere in the country's domestic politics.

The assault against strangers was also accompanied by an assault against domestic opposition. The CPP-sponsored State Councils (Ashanti) Amendment of 1955 gave chiefs in cocoa areas (especially Brongs) who had been destooled by Kumasi primarily for "rebelliousness" and other political reasons, the right to appeal their destoolment.[3] As intended, this amendment had the effect of immediately strengthening the CPP within the northwest Ashanti cocoa belt, and of diluting the economic and political power of the NLM. In addition, the "Avoidance of Discrimination Act" of 1957, which forbade any political competition based on ethnic, religious or regional interests, prevented direct campaigning for Ashanti interests. Cocoa interests had been effectively restrained from interfering with the transition to independence although, as we shall see, they reemerged with a vengeance following independence.[4]

The problem of state control over cocoa resources which had emerged even before independence in the controversy over the activities of the Cocoa Purchasing Company (CPC) was significant and perhaps prophetic of several recurring, unresolved issues which faced Nkrumah. In brief, these issues were: (a) the degree of separation which should exist between cocoa purchasing organizations and state political structures; (b) the advisability of multiple independent purchasing organizations vs. parastatals; (c) the extent to which decision making within agricultural purchasing organizations should be under local control as opposed to central control; and (d) whether cocoa revenue could *or should* justifiably be used to stimulate developments in other sectors of the economy.

Nkrumah's early Pan-African vision was of an independent state in which economic resources, however derived, were to be used to create an industrial base which would serve to promote development within Ghana as well as in surrounding African countries. In order to use the CPP to further these objectives, he placed the party's officials in well-paid positions within CPC, where they could build relations with farmers by giving out loans, thereby using cocoa for political benefit.[5] Foreign multinational cocoa purchasing organizations such as Cadbury and Frye as well as United Africa Company were judged inimical to the CPP's political and development goals. The CPP saw the strengthening of cocoa purchasing organizations such as the CPC and the UGFCC as the structural means for accomplishing this grand task.[6] Overlooked were the complicated, actual day-to-day operations of these companies, which would involve farmers in competitive and conflictual relationships with officials of the CPP and other subsidiaries of the Cocoa Marketing Board (CMB). Thus, the stage was set for a struggle between Nkrumah's vision and the local, national and global dynamics of the cocoa economy.

The continuing problem for Ghana was that it had only a limited number of resources which could feed the export sector and bring in foreign exchange for the state. Furthermore, these resources—cocoa, gold, diamonds, manganese, bauxite and timber—were located in the southern forest and coastal zone, rather than well distributed across the country. The result was that these wealthy zones claimed economic as well as political preeminence. Moreover, they were not prepared to yield their local interests to Nkrumah's national, Pan-African or global aspirations.

Table 7–1 gives the value of Gold coast exports, by commodity, for the years 1952–53.

TABLE 7–1

VALUE OF GOLD COAST EXPORTS, 1952–53

	1952		**1953**	
goods	**quantity**	**value f.o.b. £**	**quantity**	**value f.o.b. £**
Cocoa	212,005 tns.	52,533,085	236,634 tns.	56,143,022
Gold	705,815 fine oz. troy.	9,255,704	730,156 fine oz. troy.	9,390,581
Diamonds	2,133,873 carat	5,399,885	2,164,262 carat	3,924,755
Manganese ore	794,192 tns.	8,332,847	745,990 tns.	8,722,222
Bauxite	74,368 tns.	137,581	115,075 tns.	201,383
Timber*	10,556,268 cu.ft.	4,157,402	15,088,860 cu.ft.	5,880,117

*Unmanufactured timber: includes logs, sawn timber and veneers.
Source: W.A. Lewis, "Report on Industrialisation In the Gold Coast," in Metcalfe, 1964, 712.

Implicit in Ghana's first development plan was an assumption that the country's economic development would be based on a combination of local resources and the use of foreign capital. Little thought was given to what this would mean for the differential exploitation of the country's zonal resources. Since this meant a greater exploitation of the resources of the south and trans-Volta Togoland, it is not surprising that the most intense political conflicts took place there. Trans-Volta Togoland representatives argued that Nkrumah's economic approaches placed "the burden of our development almost entirely on the shoulders of our cocoa farmers."[7]

Ghana's political problems were exacerbated by the fact that cocoa revenue, which had supplied almost two-thirds of export earnings in 1953, fluctuated wildly in response to cocoa diseases, western stockpiling of cocoa supplies, and corresponding fluctuations in the international price of cocoa.[8] The deterioration in the material lives of Ghana's rural producers provided verification of Nkrumah's new realization that the "economic kingdom" was indeed of paramount importance in stabilizing the political kingdom. By 1961, he clearly recognized that the cocoa economy was not enough. He was now convinced that the monocrop nature of Ghana's economy had to be changed by industrialization using hydroelectric power—a development which he felt implied the building of socialist state structures. The movement into a planned economy, without successful diversification of the economic base would, however, trigger rural crisis, urban upheaval, and the 1966 coup which overthrew him.

UGFCC: The Clash of Elites and Peasants

In order to harness the rural peasants to his development schemes, Nkrumah created the United Ghana Farmers' Council. The relationship of this body to the rural producers was by no means a steady or tranquil one, since many cocoa farmers supported opposition parties which had combined into the United Party that still challenged Nkrumah and the CPP for leadership. Then, when he won the 1960 plebiscite which validated his new constitution, solidified his control, and placed increased power in his hands, he began to reshape cocoa organizations and bureaucracies to fit into the new design.[9] The former United Ghana Farmers' Council (UGFC)[10] became the only officially recognized farmers' organization in the country. With the UP silenced and the opposition divided, Nkrumah now had the first real opportunity to build the kind of economic and political structures which would fulfill his increasingly socialist vision of Ghana's future.

With the expulsion of such foreign buying firms as United Africa Company in 1959, the UGFC assumed central control of the cocoa industry. It took advantage of this position to deduct, on behalf of the CPP, 12 shillings per load of cocoa (or 17 percent of the producer price) as the farmers' "voluntary contribution" to the Ghana Second Development Plan.[11] The UGFC also provided services, loans and development assistance to rural producers. The political goals and economic means became deeply intertwined, even at the grass roots level. UGFC was further transformed in 1961 into the United Ghana Farmers' Council Cooperatives (UGFCC), a state agency which would be under the direct control of the Cocoa Marketing Board, and whose roots would then sink deeply into the rural area. Nevertheless, it was far from being a cooperative in the old sense of the term, and the question of how the bulk of local farmers were to be involved in this organization was a source of much conflict.

In giving the United Ghana Farmers Council Cooperatives a monopoly on cocoa purchasing, Nkrumah's government eliminated the older cocoa cooperatives from the purchasing scene, but not without difficulty. Members of the old cooperatives as well as individual CPP members who were also cocoa traders and middlemen, disagreed with Nkrumah's policies because they destroyed private capitalist initiatives and local economic interests which profited from cocoa purchasing. It is noteworthy that this opposition had the backing of the Ministry of Labor and Cooperatives and the Department of Cooperatives, which objected to what was seen as threatening the independence of the cooperative movement. Nevertheless, Nkrumah pushed forward his state monopoly plan, slowing fragmenting the national cooperative movement, and making UGFCC the only recognized cocoa purchasing cooperative.[12] The old cooperative societies in Ashanti, Brong, Ahafo and Sefwi were particularly disgruntled with the CPP's actions. They amalgamated their separate units into an organization called ABASCO, and sought to give it a separate identity under UGFCC leadership.[13] Recognizing the difficulties this would introduce in party control over UGFCC, Nkrumah rejected this proposal. In reaction to the CPP's highhandedness, farmers in Ashanti and Brong Ahafo engaged in widespread rioting.

Despite the protests of cooperative supporters, the UGFCC did emerge as a cocoa-monopoly; the cocoa cooperatives were officially liquidated and their property and assets were absorbed into UGFCC. Dissention within the CPP over the explosive cooperative issue was muted because opponents to the cocoa trading monopoly were compensated by being given leadership positions in UGFCC. They were therefore able to reorient their business activities to fit into the CPP's new plans. Most of these men neither understood nor cared to understand Nkrumah's new emphasis on socialism, as long as they were able to profit from lower-level economic activities, which still allowed for the accumulation of profit. Local level feelings tended to remain cool towards the CPP, in contrast to the reaction of national elites who eventually accepted the UGFCC's relationship to the CPP in the interest of party loyalty. The emergence of the UGFCC monopoly did mean a real financial loss to local farmer-entrepreneurs, and this disrupted the balance of power that had been painfully developed between the cooperative farmer-entrepreneurs and the chiefs. The new prominence of the UGFCC permitted the national elite to extend control to the local level in ways which had formerly been impossible.

The old cooperative members who now belonged to the UGFCC retained considerable bitterness toward Nkrumah. Nkrumah's vaunted charismatic recognition in the nation and in the world meant little to them, since their local economic and political leadership had been jeopardized. During an interview in 1973 with former members of the old Sunyani Cooperative Produce Buying Association in 1973, one leader asserted that:

> The first announcement made by [Nkrumah's] ministers was that the entire buying power was to be given to the UGFCC. This was a very big blow. All the cooperative representatives went to Accra and stayed there three days, trying to persuade the government, but all efforts were fruitless. So there was a merger between Union and Union, society and society, of both Cooperatives and Farmers' Union. Here, UGFCC had no building, no society...so they moved into the cooperative buildings and sheds...the farmers now had no voice. All our money had been taken over. They chose people from Appiah Danquah's group. The committee of the cooperatives always had a seven-man committee. But after the merger they had nine. Since UGFCC was supposed to be the mouthpiece of the government, UGFCC had five representatives and the cooperatives had four. Any time there was any voting, we lost. And the president always came from the Ghana Farmers' Council.

> They took most of the CPP activists [as secretary-receivers]...If you were a secretary-receiver and you were not CPP they would sack you...UGFCC people were made presidents and committee members because of their role in the party, [but] some people who have got no farms at all were made members because they could talk to convince people of the CPP...When the UGFCC came, they took the committee kind of like a chieftaincy. When any case came up they would sit down and decide [it] as someone before a chief...For having a case decided against you, you had to be fined. Sometimes someone would have a dispute with a friend or a brother, and he would come to lodge a complaint...they should only have dealt with the farmers in connection with their dignity in producing cocoa. The district farmer, or the regional marketing officer could overrule decisions...So [there was] any amount of trouble when they are choosing a chief farmer! It was not a small thing...people with money. A very strong man.[14]

This view was not unique to Sunyani area cooperative members, but was also expressed by members of cocoa cooperative societies in the Goaso-Ahafo area of varying political persuasions. It was not so much that the Brong-Ashanti held political opinions which conflicted with CPP leaders, but rather that they resented the national organization's presumed right to preempt local level control of land and resources.

The conflict between the former cooperative membership and the UGFCC at the local level indicated clearly that while these largely capitalist entrepreneurs had emphasized African economic interests in opposition to European cocoa purchasers, with independence and the need for national development, their purely local concern had been transformed into a nationalistic and socialistic one. In retaining their local "capitalist" orientation, the cooperative "big-men" saw state deductions for development as a drain on their overall income, and therefore repressive. They would have preferred that the local councils be the sole initiators of local taxation.

The former isolation from nationalist politics which the cooperative "big-men" had tried to maintain during the 1950s was being ruthlessly destroyed between 1961 and 1966. As the CPP used UGFCC to broaden its political base and increase its membership, local farmers were learning to develop a position on national issues. At the same time, they became quite cynical about national politics. Political factions which had previously ignored each other were brought into intimate contact because of UGFCC local politics. Older conflicts were resuscitated, as former United Party constituents were now punished by CPP members and deprived of influence or local positions.[15] Ironically, the earlier development of Brong nationalism in this area due to conflicting cocoa and land interests helped feed opposition to the CPP's political design. In some areas of Brong Ahafo, the UGFCC was anti-CPP because of the former United Party constituency within the area. Some places like Sunyani openly protested against displaying the CPP flag in front of the UGFCC building.[16]

Local concerns were obviously at the heart of the conflict between the cooperative "big-men" and the UGFCC's political tacticians. UGFCC officials often perceived Sunyani leaders as "country bumpkins," thus ignorant of modern political realities. Therefore, in seeking to replace traditional political structures and to function in "grass roots" ways, they often misjudged situations. Cooperative "big-men" had already made clear distinctions between modern and traditional social styles, and within the cocoa cooperatives modern capitalist behavior was stressed. It was not surprising, then, that UGFCC behavior was often viewed as behind the times by disgruntled cooperative members. Nevertheless, despite the tensions which existed between former cooperative and CPP members within local UGFCC units, the government did have some success in moving large numbers of rural farmers into greater contact with national elites and national politics. This made them conscious of, if not cynical about, national priorities. As a national organization for marketing cocoa, UGFCC's structures were undoubtedly far more efficient than pre-existing ones, since its determined penetration allowed thorough extraction of cocoa profits. In the short run, UGFCC was also an effective tool for combating the economic nationalism which accompanied the emergent regionalism of the late 1950s and early 1960s; however, the backlash response was greater ethnic and regional consciousness in the cocoa areas.

Regionalism, Resources and Politics

Adding fuel to the controversy about national control over local cocoa resources was the CPP's strategy of redrawing regional boundaries and reordering intra-regional relationships between dominant and subordinate chiefs in such a way as to reduce opposition to the CPP. The problem for Nkrumah was how to weaken the potential political and economic strength which the Ashanti region could array against him.[17] The issue of the politics of regionalism had surfaced earliest with the agitation of the Brong Kyempim Federation for autonomy from Ashanti, and was heightened with the irredentist politics of the NLM and the Trans-Volta Togoland Association. Despite legislation which increasingly curbed Ashanti and NLM opposition, Nkrumah still had not fulfilled his promise to the Brongs to give them regional administrative autonomy in return for their 1956 electoral support.[18] As we have seen, while most Brong-Ashanti people welcomed this change, selected Brong chiefs such as the Berekumhene, Drobohene, Bechemhene, Tanosohene and Awua Odumasihene bitterly opposed it.[19] It is noteworthy that although Nkrumah delayed the payoff until 1959, the immediate political return was the support which the region gave Nkrumah in his push towards presidential and constitutional consolidation in 1960.

The creation of the Brong Ahafo Region in 1959 more than fulfilled Nkrumah's promise, since it also brought the prosperous and mainly pro-Ashanti Ahafo area into the administrative unit. Nevertheless, the act and the legislation which flowed from it contained a mass of contradictions. For example, the act created a new region with its own House of Chiefs and its own Paramount Chiefs, yet section 63 of Act 370 read:

> Nothing in this act shall be deemed to prejudice any right of allegiance to which a chief of one region is entitled from a chief in another region, or any right of a stool in one region to any property movable or immovable, situate or existing in another region.

Nevertheless, CPP actions permitted the destoolment of pro-Ashanti chiefs in the area, and the continued recognition of those chiefs who had been promoted by government before and after the restoration of the confederacy in 1936. Control over cocoa land and tribute became a major regional issue, as pro-CPP chiefs challenged the flow of any resources to Kumasi because of historical allegiance. The result was that these conflicts prevented the newly created Brong House of Chiefs from actually conducting regional business. Pro-Ashanti and Brong chiefs not only disputed villages and revenues, but jeopardized the regional autonomy of Ahafo as far as conflicting timber revenue, as well as cocoa revenue, was involved.[20]

In the Ahafo area, the CPP/BKC challenge to Ashanti chiefs affiliated to the NLM, had earlier induced violent confrontations in large towns such as Goaso, Hwidiem, Kukuom and Mim. For Ahafo chiefs like the Kukuomhene, Brong nationalism provided an opportunity to reclaim pre-1935 autonomy while gaining national political importance through CPP connections. In 1956 and 1957, much to the concern of many chiefs, a great deal of the local cocoa surtax which was being collected from stranger and native farmers in the area had been spent by the Kukuomhene on enhancing CPP organizational strength rather than on local development.[21] Then in 1958, despite the considerable support in Ahafo for Ashanti, the pro-CPP Kukuomhene (who had long argued his independence from Kumasi) was named as paramount chief of Ahafo, and the next year many other lesser chiefs were replaced with CPP backers. The new chiefs often took office without receiving the stool paraphernalia from their predecessors, and continued to face opposition within their constituencies. The composition of Ahafo also made it a difficult area for the CPP to penetrate and control. There were large numbers of stranger cocoa farmers and laborers whose loyalties were elsewhere. As non-Ghanaians, these strangers could usually play no role in the political process; however, their economic interests were carefully bound up with those of chiefs from whom they had acquired land. True, the presence of the CPP provided new access for the young educated group to national politics, but this by no means resolved the local Ashanti/CPP conflicts. Ahafo remained deeply divided. The issue as many Ahafo chiefs saw it, was that local cocoa and timber resources were being involuntarily extracted for national political goals, while they, their people and their region, received no benefits from it.[22]

The CPP government's 1961 Local Government Act allowed local Brong and Ahafo authorities to begin to collect all stool land revenues including those from cocoa and timber, and to pay it into the government treasury. Upon receipt of approved local authority estimates, the stool's share of the revenue as well as any other development money could then be returned to the stool. But other laws deprived the Native Authority police from collecting fines for local infringements, and gave this responsibility to national revenue collectors. The result was that local chiefs were no longer able to generate revenue for certain local development projects, and central revenue collectors were ill-suited for the task. These measures resulted in an administrative structure which placed the chiefs and the locality in a dependent relationship to the central government with respect to getting funds to maintain their administrative functions.

Despite the control which the central government increasingly exercised over regional resources and political decisions, the issue of allegiances between superior and subordinate chiefs possessed a dynamic of its own. Implicitly, chiefs understood that any break in national political control would revive the problem of the economic factors and local traditional autonomy would re-emerge as an issue. Therefore, chiefs such as the Odumasihene (in the Sunyani District) and the Kukuomhene continued to insist upon their traditional autonomy.

Crisis: The Politics of Agriculture and Development

The CPP's drive to gain control of local level politics was enhanced by the penetration of the Brong and Ahafo cocoa areas by the United Ghana Farmers' Council Cooperatives. In these non-Ashanti areas, the power of the regional House of Chiefs was also diminished in direct proportion to CPP penetration.

Had the Ghanaian economy remained stable, regional economic nationalism would have been greatly reduced by the success of national political structures and economic relations. However, by 1961, Nkrumah was conscious of the declining export earnings from cocoa, and was attempting to devise political and budgetary approaches for developing economic potential while limiting political competition. The Winneba Ideological Institute, which was in operation by 1962, was used for educating the bureaucratic elites about the new socialist strategies which Nkrumah hoped would produce a viable pan-Africanist state.[23] However, there is little evidence that the new socialist directions were really understood by Ghana's elite,[24] or were of any importance to the ordinary rural producers. Of greater significance to rural producers at that time was the price paid for agricultural products including cocoa, and the uses to which agricultural export earnings were being put within the Ghanaian economy.

The Ghanaian economy in the early 1960s was still as heavily dominated by agricultural and cocoa production as it had been in 1953. Capital generated by cocoa production had contributed to a high standard of living relative to most other African countries;[25] it contributed also to a lively market trade and to a dynamic construction industry, as producers built houses and other commercial properties. This capital availability attracted considerable migrant labor from surrounding countries to work in agriculture and urban construction. However, the economic potential which was evident was stymied by the fact that the economy was not well integrated. Sales to producers were low, and value added was greatest in services rather than in productive sectors. In addition, capital was not invested in sectors which generated more goods and services but in those which simply consumed resources. Savings were not invested in production areas, since even farmers within cocoa areas were heavily involved in the market economy and depended upon it for foodstuffs, clothing and health items. The increasing dependence upon cocoa to generate capital earnings made the Ghanaian economy potentially quite vulnerable, although the consequences were not evident until 1961.

Whereas low imports in the 1950s resulted in a balance of payments surplus, the situation had changed by the time of Ghanaian independence. There were basically two reasons: First, it appeared that Nkrumah wanted the acquisition of "the political kingdom" to be enjoyed by everyone. The developing tastes of the Ghanaian public resulted in increased imports, which more rapidly depleted the foreign exchange reserves. The CPP's socialist stance emphasized provision of social and welfare services, and the largely free education and health services were much better than those available in neighboring Ivory Coast. Therefore, government expenditure doubled between 1954 and 1961, amounting to £G113.7 million;[26] and after 1961 government expenditure was generally paid out of current export earnings since reserves were depleted. The second reason for the declining balance of payments was that the CPP had adopted a development strategy which relied upon export earnings to pay for imported machinery, spare parts and tools used in diversifying the agricultural sector and in developing the industrial sector. This new economic situation meant that export tax on cocoa, and voluntary contributions by cocoa producers to Ghana's Second Development Plan were necessary to any internal development which would take place.

Table 7–2 lists the sectors of the Ghanian economy, giving totals for output, sales to producers, and value added for the year 1960.

TABLE 7–2

SECTORS OF THE GHANAIAN ECONOMY, 1960

Sector	Output		Sales to producers		Gross Value Added	
	G million	%	G million	%	G million	%
Agriculture	87.9	16.6	4.0	9.9	87.6	20.8
Forestry	21.1	4.0	5.7	14.0	20.3	4.8
Cocoa	46.2	8.7	2.1	5.2	45.9	10.9
Mining/Quarrying	27.2	5.1	0.6	1.5	22.4	5.3
Manufacturing	26.4	5.0	6.6	16.3	8.2	2.0
Electricity	2.4	0.5	1.1	2.7	1.1	0.3
Construction	65.9	12.4	---	---	42.6	10.1
Fuel	14.6	2.8	11.1	27.3	3.5	0.8
Public Utilities	11.1	2.1	1.9	4.7	7.8	1.9
Services	182.0	34.3	7.5	18.5	157.2	37.4
Public Consumption	46.1	8.7	---	---	23.9	5.7
Total	530.9	100.0	40.6	100.0	420.5	100.0

Source: Birmingham, et al., *The Study of Contemporary Ghana*. Vol. 1, The Economy of Ghana. Northwestern University Press, Evanston. 1966, p. 68.

By the 1960s Ghana's economy had not substantially changed from a classic colonial one; agricultural and raw materials were being extracted, but they were not yet generating a return from internal industrialization or development. Massive urbanization was under way as educated Ghanaian youth left rural areas for opportunities in the city. Naturally this shift created new tensions between government and urban unions, as the incoming workers agitated for more work and better working conditions. In order to increase its hold over the rambunctious unions,[27] the CPP kept urban wages reasonably high, and this helped defuse urban economic dissatisfaction.

Nkrumah was quite aware of Ghana's "urban bias" (the concentration of resources in urban employment and development rather than in rural production) inherited from the colonial period, and he intended to alter it. However, since private enterprise had apparently not succeeded in generating sufficient investment capital, CPP plans called for a new strategy—building a mixed economy in which private agricultural enterprises existed alongside joint state-private ventures and other fully owned state corporations. The cocoa industry especially attracted the attention of government. Despite its experiences with cocoa cooperatives (or perhaps because of it), the CPP was basically skeptical whether capitalist farmers could be relied upon to raise rural production to the needed levels. There was a desire to check the development of capitalist tendencies which, it was believed, was responsible for much of the rural resistance to the CPP. Many CPP officials believed that the state had to take the lead in the planned agricultural development.

Nevertheless, the CPP was willing to give farmers a chance to participate in socialist agricultural production. The UGFCC was expanded to include real cooperative farms for crops other than cocoa. Using mechanization, the UGFCC helped a small number of farmers with plots too small for cocoa farming (or alternatively, northern migrant laborers who could not easily obtain land for cocoa farming) to produce other crops. Such marginal farmers welcomed government help, and established cooperative maize, peanut, tomato and cassava farms. The problem was, however, that despite the considerable resources that the government put into mechanization, which decreased the cost of labor, production returns on such sizable investments were pitifully low. Moreover, enthusiasm for these cooperative ventures did not increase. For example, in Brong areas which lay outside the maximum cocoa production zone (Japekrom, Dormaa, Ahenkro, Sampa) less land was used for cultivating food crops than was actually available. Data from 1965 from the Sunyani area, where some of these collective farms were established is given in Table 7-3 on page 185.

The poor performance of the UGFCC food cooperatives was not unique. The State Farms Corporation (SFC), which was developed in 1963 from the consolidated of earlier unsuccessful colonial economic ventures, was heavily funded for mechanized agriculture, but its performance was also low. In 1965, SFC's 105 farms had planted only 104,000 acres of their available one million acres, and had already lost $19.8 million.[28] Although assisted by trained government agricultural officers, State Farm workers produced only about one-fourth as much as ordinary peasant farmers.[29] Nevertheless, private farmers who wanted to produce commercialized crops often found that land which they acquired and prepared was subsequently requisitioned for the state, or they were unable to obtain permits to initiate agricultural enterprises. This preferential treatment which the state gave its own agricultural corporations angered most small farmers, especially those entrepreneurs who had earlier been a quite dynamic force in cocoa brokering and transportation. This resentment smoldered quietly (for now) within the UGFCC branches, but would have grave consequences.

TABLE 7–3

UGFCC NON-COCOA COOPERATIVES, DECEMBER 1965
Sunyani District

Block	Society	Members	# Farms	Land Available	Cultivated* previous month	total	Crop	Acres
Sunyani	Odumasi 1	24	1	798.	3.3	3.2	yams, plantain	0.2
	Odumasi 2	11	1	600.	--	--	cassava	1.0
	Nsoatre 1	24	1	447.5	25.6	25.6	cassava,	20.0
							cocoyam,	
							citrus	2.5
							pineapple	3.0
	Nsoatre 2	23	1	200.0	--	--	-------	---
	TOTAL	**82**	**4**	**2,045.5**	**28.9**	**28.8**		**26.7**
Berekum	Berekum	10	1	50.0	--	--	-------	---
	Nsapor	11	1	500.0	--	--	-------	---
	Dukukrom	10	3	500.0	6.5	6.5	plantain	6.5
	Fatentaa	10	1	500.0	--	--	-------	---
	Senase	--	1	---	1.0	1.0	cassava	---
	Numesua	10	1	500.0	--	--	-------	---
	Nyamekrom	10	1	50.0	5.0	5.0	cassava	5.0
	TOTAL	**61**	**9**	**2,100.0**	**12.5**	**12.5**		**11.5**
Japekrom	Japekrom	46	1	250.0	24.0	24.0	maize	20.0
							cassava	2.0
	Nyame	19	1	350.0	12.0	12.0	plantain	2.0
	Npuasu	20	1	150.0	--	--	maize	10.0
	TOTAL	**75**	**3**	**750.0**	**36.0**	**36.0**		**34.0**
Dormaa Ahenkro	Atasikrom	26	1	182.9	3.0	3.0	cassava	3.0
	Kyeremasu	10	1	50.0	--	--	-------	---
	TOTAL	**36**	**2**	**232.9**	**3.0**	**3.0**		**3.0**
Sampa	Sampa 1	17	1	350.0	7.0	7.0	maize	7.0
	Sampa 2	10	1	450.0	33.5	33.5	cassava	14.5
							maize	14.0
	Sampa Town						vegetable	5.0
	committee	12	1	300.0	11.0	11.0	cassava	11.0
	Morle	10	1	100.0	--	--	-------	---
	TOTAL	**49**	**4**	**1,200.0**	**51.5**	**51.5**		**51.5**

*No land was cultivated during the month of December 1965, when this data was assembled.
Source: Ghana Archives, Sunyani. [RA0/305] UGFCC Agric. Forms, December 1965.

Ideally, what the CPP aimed to do was reduce the country's dependence upon the monocrop economy by generating sufficient revenue to launch its basic industrialization program. The state acquired plants for construction materials, pharmaceuticals, boat building, furniture making, stone quarrying, food processing and cocoa processing, but these were never efficiently run. The strategy of decreasing food and other imports, while at the same time increasing metal processing, hydroelectric and other energy sources, ran into difficulty. Since local investment capital was lacking, the CPP needed international loans for such development. However, the terms for many such loans were usurious, largely insufficient for productive returns, and their repayment threatened to place heavy strains upon the Ghanaian economy. For example, the visionary Volta Dam project proposed in 1952[30] was intended both to smelt bauxite located in the eastern, western, and Ashanti regions, and as a source of cheap hydroelectric power for Ghana and surrounding countries. However, profitable commercial terms proved difficult to secure. In the end Ghana was obliged to accept a deal involving twenty-five- to thirty-year loans from the US, Kaiser Aluminum and UK development agencies just for the hydroelectric portion (Volta River Authority), with enormous debt-servicing costs. Even prior to the completion of the dam, much of the hydroelectric supply was already committed to Kaiser's aluminum processing plant (VALCO) at low costs, rather than to African producers and entrepreneurs. In addition, Valco relied on imported bauxite, and local ore deposits were never developed.[31] Thus, while Ghana dipped heavily into its cocoa revenues and delayed other development projects to pay for the building of the Volta River Project, it received little in return.

The commitment which Ghana's Seven-Year Plan of 1962 made to the Volta River Project, to state cooperative farms, and to sixty-eight industries that had been established, ranging from automobile assembly to insecticides and distilleries,[32] continued to distress cocoa farmers. They were alarmed that agriculture ranked second to industry in the government's plans,[33] while these questionable investments not only came directly out of cocoa earnings, but also depressed the standard of living of cocoa farmers. In fact, by 1962 the formerly voluntary contribution of the farmers to the government (6 shillings per load of cocoa sold) was transformed into an income tax. Farmers now saw themselves as being doubly exploited by the very farmers' organization that was supposed to represent them. One CPP opponent, warning of a possible upheaval among cocoa farmers, stated that:

> It is treacherous for the Farmers' Council to impress upon the government that the farmers have agreed to contribute, while in fact they have not. It is surprising to know that secretary/receivers who are paid between £15 and £20 a month ride in cars, while the farmers go on foot.[34]

The CPP's program of "Work and Happiness" received few favorable responses, even from cocoa farmers who were party supporters, because it brought them no obvious benefits. The government's suggestion that the farmers received subsidies in the form of sprays and cutlasses was greeted by the farmers' demands for much more. They admitted that the investment in education and social services, partially funded by cocoa revenue, benefited their own children as much if not more than those of urbanites, but they felt that such benefits were short-lived. What they noted was that the literate children of farmers were migrating to urban areas, attracted either by schools, jobs or the more modern lifestyle. In the growing shortage of family labor, farmers were becoming more dependent upon migrant labor, which became even more costly as the economic situation worsened.[35] Moreover, farmers had difficulty meeting these labor costs as government deductions from cocoa income increased.

By 1964, at a time when the volume of cocoa harvested was exceptionally high, the price of cocoa on the world market plummeted. While the international Cocoa Producers' Alliance unsuccessfully negotiated for higher prices, cocoa sales fell off, and the Ghana government had insufficient capital to meet debts or to continue supporting internal development. Although the government paid farmers the agreed cocoa price for the 1964–65 main season, this depleted reserves and exacerbated inflation. It seemed that the only available option was to decrease the producer price of cocoa in the 1965 buying season, in order to use the differential in paying interest on international loans and to meet government obligations.

The drop in the price of cocoa was tragic for farmers, who could no longer afford to harvest and transport their crop, given the producer price. In its dialogue with farmers, Nkrumah and the CPP stressed Ghana's vulnerability to capitalist marketplace fluctuations, and the need for socialist responses from farmers to conquer this dependence. During the early part of this crisis, there is evidence that farmers were willing to continue making sacrifices in the interest of the country in spite of their individual problems of indebtedness. However, the reduced cocoa price had the effect of reducing farmers' incentives as well as the resources necessary for new cocoa plantings. Much of the northern migrant labor which abandoned Brong-Ashanti cocoa areas during this period for farms in the Ivory Coast never returned. Cocoa production over the next seven years was to be unalterably affected by the price recessions in 1964–65. Ghana's cocoa industry had entered a crisis phase, and it was no longer possible to maintain the illusion of using agriculture to stimulate industrial development. As the CPP struggled to salvage the national economy, it neglected to safeguard the standard of living of rural folk.

In 1965–66, while urban dissatisfaction with the economic and political situation was visible and sometimes violent, rural dissatisfaction had been deep and smoldering. It was only a question of time before both rural and urban reactions demanded some form of change. Despite regional variations in food self-sufficiency, rural areas had produced more than 50 percent of what they consumed, and cocoa income provided the partial means to satisfy clothing, transportation, health and utility needs. On the other hand, populations in the major urban centers scarcely produced over five percent of what they consumed, and local food was generally less than 40 percent of the food, drink and tobacco expenditures of urban people.[36] The heavy urban dependence upon imported food and other necessities meant that city folk were hit rather early by the declining balance of payments which affected imports. In such towns as Accra, Kumasi and Takoradi, there were lines for sugar, flour, milk and other necessities. Nevertheless, there were blatant disparities between classes within Accra, for example. Elites and bureaucrats often managed to secure commodities when ordinary folk could not, leading Nkrumah to declare on April 18, 1965 that officials:

> diverted the goods to the wives and relatives of ministers, regional and district commissioners, civil servants, party officials, parliamentarians, managing directors, and directors of state corporations, factories and state farms. By hoarding and reselling the goods at exorbitant prices and thus enriching themselves and their relatives, these public men proved unworthy of the public cause.[37]

Strikes and marches took place in Accra as workers protested wage cuts, salary freezes and inadequate necessities. This was the vocal urban opposition, but in the rural areas where the crisis was more destructive, production declines were the response. Given the crisis, Nkrumah's step-by-step extraction of cocoa savings and producer taxes from farm areas in order to pursue his national and global ambitions had been crushing that sector which could least afford it.

While many members of Ghana's elite took pride in the praise that Nkrumah's pan-Africanism and foreign policies brought to their country, others questioned whether providing asylum for political exiles, establishing ideological centers, and participating in such anti-colonial organizations as the Casablanca Group, was in their best interests. Perhaps such dangerous adventurism would have them land in communist hands!38 The negative sentiments—that cocoa revenues were badly used in the support of projects such as VALCO—also increased. Then, when the declining balance of payments resulted in a food crisis, and western powers refused to grant loans to Nkrumah to purchase needed food, Nkrumah was blamed. Finally, the precipitous fall of the price of cocoa on the international market led many people to judge the event as an example of the West putting an economic squeeze on Nkrumah and the country. Rumors that foreign countries were displeased by Nkrumah's criticism of the United States' role in Vietnam, and that they were planning to overthrow him, were widely disseminated. Therefore, when the military staged a coup on February 24, 1966, with Nkrumah en route to Beijing to endeavor to bring peace to Vietnam, these actions won wide approval.[39]

Table 7–4 gives cocoa prices and real (indexed) wages for the years 1956–65.

TABLE 7–4

Cocoa Prices and Real Wages 1956–1965*
(Indices of Real Value)

	Cocoa Producer Prices	Minimum wage, Accra	Average earnings, Accra
1956	100	100	100
1957	89	100	106
1958	89	107	109
1959	73	104	110
1960	72	120	130
1961	61	113	129
1962	59	104	123
1963	55	100	121
1964	49	88	106
1965	33	69	86

*Values deflated by average monthly index numbers of retail prices for Accra, (June 1954=100).
Source: Bjorn Beckman, *Organizing the Farmers*. 1976, p. 222. Based on *CMB Annual Reports, Economic Surveys.*

In the immediate aftermath of the 1966 coup, Nkrumah blamed the action on the lack of commitment of elites to a revolutionary process which would transform Africa, and on African bourgeois cooperation with those imperialists who sought to continue neocolonialism.[40] Nkrumah criticized the role that market collaboration among the western powers had played in undermining the strength of the Ghanaian economy, and concluded about Africa, that:

> however much it increases its agricultural output, [it] will not benefit unless it is sufficiently politically and economically united to force the developed world to pay it a fair price for its cash crops...Nevertheless, even if Africa could dictate the price of its cash crops this would not by itself provide the balanced economy which is necessary for development. The answer must be industrialization.[41]

In arguing that problems of economic development in individual African countries would not be solved until unified and coordinated economic planning took place, Nkrumah implicitly revealed that he understood some of the problems posed by the well-intentioned development approach which he had taken.

Nkrumah never explicitly admitted that his policies created any crisis for Ghana, despite the $768 million foreign debt which Ghana had incurred since 1957.[42] Nevertheless, Nkrumah quoted Dudley Seers's observations on the relationship between urbanization, industrialization and food production:

> Materials are needed for growing industries; more importantly, the swelling town labor force needs to be fed, and this implies that a rising surplus of food has to be produced in the countryside...To over-emphasize industry, as some countries have found to their cost, leads paradoxically in the end to a slower rate of industrialization.[43]

It was these rural-urban contradictions which would continue to plague future leaders of Ghana, as they searched for a means of developing the state.

Notes

1. Convention People's Party, General Election Manifesto, Accra, 1951. Excerpts contained in Metcalfe, 1964, 704–707. See also Austin, 1970, 334, or Fitch and Oppenheimer, 1966, 75–6.
2. Niara Sudarkasa, "From Stranger to Alien: The Socio-Political History of the Nigerian Yoruba in Ghana, 1900–1970," in W. Shack and E.P. Skinner (eds.) *Strangers In African Societies*. Berkeley: University of California Press, 1979, 161–163.
3. Nkrumah, 1966, 60.
4. Note Nkrumah's call for a committee to investigate the federal proposals offered by the NLM, the Muslim Association, the Ghana Action Party, the Ghana Congress Party, and Ashanti Youth Association, the Anlo Youth Association and the Togoland Congress. However, the report of the government-appointed constitutional adviser Sir Frederick C. Bourne rejected the federal proposals as untenable, and recommended unitary independence within a regional structure. See Metcalfe, 1964, 723–724.
5. Owusu, 1970, 255–61.
6. The report from the Jibowu Commission investigating the CPC in 1956 clearly showed how the CPC used funds channeled to it by the CPP to offer loans to local farmers in Ashanti, thus encouraging them to become CPP rather than NLM members. According to George Padmore (*The Gold Coast Revolution*, 1953, 204–5), Nkrumah saw the CPC as breaking the European purchasing monopoly, and saw its loan program as providing alternatives so that farmers would not have to lose farms to these firms because of inability to repay advances. However, one also finds reports that the NLM used similar tactics of providing Cadbury and Frye loans to supporters (Austin, 1970, 343).
7. Gold Coast Legislative Assembly *Debates*, August 12, 1955, p. 342.
8. Fitch & Oppenheimer, 1966, 86.
9. Other organizations, such as the Trade Union Congress and the National Cooperative

Council, were also given recognition as affiliates of the CPP, rather than as independent organizations. Austin, 1970, 382.

10. The evidence is unclear as to whether Nkrumah or Albert Baruku and Ashie Nikoi were the initial architects in the founding of the Ghana Farmers' Congress, the parent organization of the UGFC. However, when Nikoi and Nkrumah began to differ over the ideal relationship between the CPP and the organization, Nkrumah and A.R. Dennis became the architects of a new organization which was called the Ghana Farmers' Council (Beckman, 1976, 53–4).
11. Beckman, 1976, 71–77.
12. The Trade Union Congress supported Nkrumah and helped develop a scheme for the structuring of other non-agricultural, union-owned, and state-controlled cooperatives.
13. Beckman, 1975, 91–93.
14. Mikell, 1975, 125–6.
15. Sunyani Archives, File 164, 8/5/64, "Resolution of the Duayaw Nkwanta Branch of the Convention People's Party."
16. Sunyani Archives, United Ghana Farmers' Council Cooperatives, File 164, 5/8/61.
17. Drah, 1979, 146–149.
18. In the 1956 elections, although the NLM won two-thirds of the vote in old Ashanti areas, the CPP winning two-thirds of the vote in Brong areas. The CPP carried 57% of the total votes cast in the election (Austin, 1970, 353–4).
19. Their opposition to the formation of the Brong-Ahafo region is registered by the telegrams of protest which were sent following the Achimota Conference where the regional issue was discussed in March 1956. See GNA, DAO/l/C9, file "Brong Federation Dispute between Certain Brong Chiefs and the Asanteman Council." Document nos.: 200-221.
20. Robertson, 1973.
21. Robertson, 1973, 340.
22. Ibid., 341–2.
23. About the Winneba ideological institute, Nkrumah states that although:

    ...I had hoped [it] might be used to teach some general understanding of what we were attempting, it was clear to me that many in high positions still failed to understand the political and social purposes of the state. On Ghana's external policy, however, depended to a large extent the progressive line which Africa used to follow. I had to weigh against the desire to move fast at home the dangers of concentrating too much upon internal matters and achieving a revolution at home at the cost of temporarily withdrawing from the international field (1968, 73).

24. Nkrumah was gradually moving closer to socialist thinking and rhetoric during the 1950s, but his tendencies were quite distinct from those of the CPP during this period. While George Padmore and other Marxist-Leninists were increasingly being drawn into Nkrumah's circle, the party and its documents represented a number of conflicting tendencies. One could only generalize about the nationalism that was predominant, noting its clash with the emergent socialist philosophy after 1961. See B.D.G. Folson, "The Development of Socialist Ideology in Ghana, 1949–59, Part I," in *Ghana Social Science Journal*, vol. 1, no. 1, May 1971, 1–20.

25. Birmingham, et al., say that Ghana's capital output ratio in 1963 compared favorably with that of the United States in 1955 and of Japan in 1955; but that investment of capital in areas which were not productive meant that Ghana's infrastructure was supporting far less economic activity than it could have (1966, 20).
26. Ibid., 27.
27. As the government instituted compulsory savings among wage-workers in 1961 to meet budget deficits caused by depleted reserves, general strikes broke out in Accra and Sekondi-Takoradi. However, as the CPP increased its control over the unions, the number of strikes decreased from 49 in 1958–59 to 26 in 1960–61. See Birmingham, Neustadt and Omaboe, *A Study of Contemporary Ghana: The Economy of Ghana*, vol. 1, Evanston: Northwestern University Press, 1966, 147; and Bob Fitch and Mary Oppenheimer, *Ghana: End of an Illusion*, New York: Monthly Review Press, 1966, 102–3.
28. Crawford Young, *Ideology and Development in Africa*, New Haven: Yale University Press, 1982, 158.
29. Marvin Miracle and Ann Seidman, *State Farms in Ghana*. Land Tenure Center Paper, no. 43. Madison: University of Wisconsin. 1968, 19. See also Tony Killick, *Development Economics in Action*, London: Heinneman, 1968, 193, and Crawford Young, 1982, op cit., 158–9.
30. Tony Killick, "The Volta River Project," in W. Birmingham, I. Neustadt, and E.N. Omaboe (eds.), *A Study of Contemporary Ghana: The Economy of Ghana*, vol. 1, Evanston: Northwestern University Press, 1966, 390–410.
31. Bob Fitch and Mary Oppenheimer, *Ghana: End of an Illusion*, New York, Monthly Review Press, 1966, 125–6.
32. C. Dorm Adzobu, "The State and Industrial Development in Ghana," *Ghana Social Science Journal*, vol. 1, no. 1, 1971, 108–115.
33. Ibid., 456.
34. Bjorn Beckman, 1976, 213.
35. Ibid., 219–220.
36. Birmingham, Neustadt, and Omaboe, op. cit., 111.
37. Quoted in Peter C. Garlick, *African Traders and Economic Development in Ghana*. Oxford: Clarendon Press, 1971, 24. Taken from *Africa Diary*, London, May 8-14, 1965, 2, 313.
38. Dennis Austin, *Ghana Observed: Essays on the Politics of a West African Republic*, Manchester: Manchester University Press, 1976, 105.
39. Jack Goody, "Consensus and Dissent in Ghana," *Political Science Quarterly*, vol. LXXXIII, no. 3, 1968, 337–352.
40. Kwame Nkrumah, *Dark Days in Ghana*, 1968, 9.
41. Nkrumah, Neo-colonialism: the Last Stage of Imperialism. London: Heinemann Educational Books, 1968, 9,11.
42. Crawford Young, *Ideology and Development in Africa*, Hartford, CT: Yale University Press, 1982, 163.
43. Ibid., 29. Also Dudley Seers, *The Role of Industry in Development: Some Fallacies*.

8

The Collapse of Cocoa

Convinced that Nkrumah had abused the cocoa industry by attempting to use it to accomplish impossible dreams, his successors were generally led to underestimate the dangers to Ghanaian society engendered by reliance upon a single crop. The 1966 crisis in the cocoa industry and consequently in food availability should have dramatically convinced Ghanaians that agriculture for the raising of food as well as for cash crops was vital to further economic development. However, subsequent leaders attempted unsuccessfully to find replacements for cocoa production, rather than deal with the complex issues confronting single crop societies within the global economic arena. The dominant question which preoccupied them after 1966 was what kind of reasonable political path to pursue to national economic recovery. Any existing public sympathy with socialist approaches had either dissipated or remained quiescent in the aftermath of the coup. Therefore the administrative apparatus of the state needed to be restructured. There was a resolve that state corporations should cease to function as formerly, and accordingly the state industries and cooperative farms were immediately abandoned. Many of these were sold off to private entrepreneurs or simply allowed to fall into disrepair while machinery rusted. In this way, many already badly managed state funds were further dissipated, not through corruption, but through neglect during the new liberalization.[1]

The putschists of the National Liberation Council revived political parties, and the highly energized electorate debated the issues. Many of the old political actors, such as K.A. Busia, Joe Appiah, and Gbedemah, were again on the scene.[2] Formerly silenced minority constituencies were again heard from.[3]

When elections were finally held, the Progress Party (PP) under Dr. Kofi Busia came to power in 1969. Economic conditions generally improved and problems abated as rural and urban incomes rose. Producer prices for cocoa had risen to C6.50 in 1967, and were again raised to C8 by Busia's Second Republic in 1969. There was, however, one emerging problem. Busia's supporters were primarily young, middle-class professionals, and most of them were from the Akan areas.[4] His party became one which was stereotyped as favoring the cocoa growers, and it was judged incapable of achieving the consensus necessary to hold the country together. The resulting ethnic tensions and political paralysis prevented a revival of the economy.

Faced with a growing economic crisis, Busia then precipitated an international political incident by attempting to use "strangers" as economic scapegoats. Charging that these foreigners were sabotaging the economy, Busia encouraged the passage of an Aliens' Compliance Act. Its stated intention was to remove foreigners whose intervention in the Ghanaian economy was judged to have negative economic effects.[5] The problem, however, was that many of the aliens had replaced Akan young people who had migrated from cocoa areas. Thus, the impact of the act was to further deprive an already labor-starved rural area of needed manpower. Non-citizen Mossi, Hausa, and other northerners or casual workers generally left Ghana for work in the Ivory Coast or Nigeria. The result was to raise daily wage-rates among resident cocoa laborers, who now controlled the labor market. Another development was that the owners of aging cocoa farms, who were unable to afford paid labor, abandoned cocoa production and shifted to food farming. Some poorer farmers, including women, could only earn a living by becoming wage-laborers on the farms of others, after working their own farms. Finally, the homelands of the migrants complained that Nkrumah's successors had abandoned any Pan-Africanist sentiments by engaging in economic actions judged detrimental to surrounding states.[6]

Busia's failure to establish new national and rural economic policies led to a deeper crisis in which the still fragile rural economy almost disintegrated. His emphasis on "rural development," which mainly meant providing services such as clean water, electricity, roads, etc., was designed to retain a stable rural population and to stem urban migration. Paradoxically, most parts of the country, even the Ashanti region, felt that this policy was primarily designed to help Busia's Brong Ahafo region get development projects such as roads. Moreover, there were complaints that problems of capital investment and labor investment in rural economic enterprises were never adequately addressed. Although under Busia the Agricultural Development Bank granted credit to small farmers for development,[7] the beneficiaries appeared to be established and prosperous male food farmers, rather than poor men and women most in need of assistance.

Busia's Second Republic also failed to improve the cocoa buying institutions.

New private cocoa buying agencies such as Asempaneye and Ghana Federation of Farmers had sprung into existence after the dissolution of the UGFCC in 1966. Nevertheless, each organization had to use creative and competitive techniques to attract more members, and thus collect a higher bonus for their activities. The old cooperative movement was revived, but it lacked the huge reserves and share capital which it had possessed at the time of its liquidation by the CPP in 1961. Equipment for weighing and transporting cocoa beans had to be purchased out of money allotted for buying cocoa, so the cooperative societies found themselves in debt at the end of each year. The farmers did not help matters, because they objected to their individual bonuses being utilized to clear away the debt. In an effort to survive, the cooperatives, like a number of other buying agencies, began to issue "chits" or receipts to its members for future payment for cocoa. This did not help; they sank further into debt amid charges of corruption and financial mismanagement. When the growing debt prevented the cooperatives from buying cocoa, many of its members reluctantly shifted over to the Cocoa Marketing Board's organization, the Produce Buying Agency. Thus, a monolithic structure for cocoa purchasing was again being created in rural areas. This time it was through fierce competition in a declining economic environment, rather than through state "socialist" policies.

Despite a sluggish economy, the rural farmers were slightly better off during the Busia years than they had been in 1965 (particularly if they were engaged in food farming rather than cocoa farming).[8] However, a combination of low cocoa prices and political fragmentation within Busia's power base created problems for Ghana. In December 1971, Busia devalued the Cedi by 43.8 percent, but sought to avoid a crisis by granting producer price and wage increases to farmers and workers.[9] This, however, was not enough. Colonel Ignatius Acheampong and the military seized power in 1972.[10] The soldiers of the new National Redemption Council vowed to take a more active interest in the rural areas, and to increase food production. Even from the beginning, this program was threatened as more young people migrated from rural areas. They had lost confidence in the cocoa production industry.

A study of the socio-economic data on the period between the 1966 coup and the early Acheampong years dramatizes the economic plight of cocoa farmers. Table 8-1, which was constructed with data gathered from the cooperative society in Sunyani, Brong-Ahafo, reflects the fluctuation in farmers' economic well-being, as the country shifted from economic approaches of the NLC to those of the CPP and the NRC.

Cocoa farmers in many older, more southern parts of Ghana were in much more desperate situations than those who lived in towns and villages in the Sunyani area. The Sunyani area cocoa farmers often had larger farms and younger, more productive cocoa trees. Yet the impact of the economic crisis is

TABLE 8-1

INCOMES FOR COCOA FARMERS

	Mean ¢[1]			50th Percentile			75th Percentile			90th Percentile			100th Percentile		
	Total	Male	Female	Total	Male	Female	Total	Male	Female	Total	Male	Female	Total	Male	Female
1967	331	495	205	198	221	130	464	521	242	1,041	1,311	447	10,127	10,127	1,655
1968	458	554	143	135	168	74	343	411	200	748	856	302	8,750	8,750	1,482
1969	463	557	158	182	250	93	431	521	192	937	1,164	369	9,952	9,952	1,591
1970	374	429	219	115	140	64	307	380	150	764	1,041	326	10,000	7,375	10,000
1971	—	—	—	—	—	—	—	—	—	—	—	—	—	—	—
1972	509	662	133	141	202	51	410	575	159	1,093	1,597	340	18,070	18,070	1,850

Source: Records of the Cooperative Produce Marketing Society, Brong-Ahafo, Ghana (Sunyani).

1. Income figures given in Cedis. The value of one Cedi (¢1) in 1973 was approximately US$.80. Figures have been rounded off to the nearest Cedi.

evident. The data clearly shows that cocoa farmers' incomes were improving between 1967 and 1969, rising from a mean income of C331 to C463 in 1969. However, the fluctuation in the national economic and political situation is reflected in the drop of median income to C374 in the 1970 crop year.

It is instructive to note that the economic crisis is exaggerated among female farmers. The income of male farmers temporarily began to increase with the changing economic policies of the Acheampong regime in 1972, with mean incomes rising to C509 during the 1972 crop year. During the same period, median female income appears to be consistently less than male income, and it finally falls to C133 in 1972. Although approximately one-fourth of the members of these cooperatives are women, these women only own about 5.2 percent of the cocoa sold through the cooperatives. Much of this is probably due to the smaller size of female cocoa farms, as compared to those of males. Women thus produced fewer loads of cocoa and also had a more limited family or paid labor force than men. There are geographical differences in female cocoa production: in the older, smaller, and less accessible villages such as in the Odumasi area, the percentage of cocoa crops produced on women's farms dropped drastically. However, in newer towns which grew as a result of the cocoa industry and colonial administrative complex (such as Sunyani and Fiapre), women's production rates were somewhat higher. Despite these differences, it is obvious (as shown in Table 8-2) that female cocoa farmers were especially hard hit by the fluctuations in the Ghanaian economy, and the resulting kin and social obligations which limited cocoa farming success.[11]

TABLE 8-2

1973 PRODUCTION RATES FOR FEMALE COCOA FARMERS

Marketing Society	Total Members	Female Members	Total* loads cocoa	%Female produced	Male average loads	Female average loads
Abronye	60	16	1,432.66	6.5	30.45	5.80
Bofoukrom	69	13	860.16	3.0	14.89	2.02
Adantia	40	9	252.00	6.0	7.63	1.70
Sunyani	43	10	3,674.72	2.0	109.22	7.03
Fiapre	72	15	2,137.61	8.6	27.50	12.50

Source: Records of the Cooperative Produce Marketing Societies, Sunyani District.
*Production rates are given in loads. One load equals 60 pounds of cocoa.
†Abronye, Boufoukrom and Adantia are small villages within the Odumasi area. Available land has become limited, and production figures are lower than for centrally located towns such as Sunyani and Fiapre.

The plight of the Sunyani District female cocoa farmer was paralleled elsewhere in Ghana during this period. In Akokoaso in the eastern region, the number of female farmers was clearly declining. This is intriguing, since roughly one-fifth of those who had inherited farms had obtained them from women.[12] In Akokoaso, as in the Sunyani area, females were seldom able to produce more than ten loads of cocoa from their farms. In Abesim and Tanoso also, one notes that younger women under forty were no longer able to obtain and/or maintain cocoa farms. It was mainly women over sixty years of age who even owned cocoa farms.[13] In the Dormaa area as well, it was the exceptional young women who owned cocoa farms rather than simply working on their husbands' farms.[14]

The rural-oriented economic policy of Acheampong's early years, increased stratification among cocoa farmers as more prosperous male farmers diversified food production (maize) in addition to cocoa production. The results were a rise in the pledging of cocoa farms by poorer males, and the decline of the female cocoa farmer. At the personal level, these were rational responses to a national economic environment which did not adequately compensate cocoa farmers for the labor and time invested in raising export crops. At the national level, it posed severe problems for a state which was primarily dependent upon the monocrop economy for generating operational revenue. While the NRC was sympathetic to the production problems of rural chiefs and farmers, it did not adequately comprehend the problems. The major issues, as the NRC saw them, were not those of rural impoverishment, but a) that cocoa farmers were smuggling cocoa across the borders to Ivory Coast or to Togo in order to take advantage of a producer price which was often five times higher than that paid in Ghana. In response, the military border patrols (particularly in the Trans-Volta and the Brong Ahafo areas) organized to prevent smuggling of cocoa either by Ghanaian nationals or by foreigners. b) Despite the efforts of more prosperous farmers to diversify, the general decline in domestic food production in rural areas increasingly necessitated the increased importation of food, and the expenditure of scarce foreign exchange. Acheampong aimed to change this second problem through Operation Feed Yourself which he launched in 1972.

Operation Feed Yourself and Economic Disintegration

It was tragic for Ghana that this program for increasing food production came at the same time that there were wild fluctuations in the international price of cocoa and sharp declines in the volume of cocoa produced in Ghana.[15] Since returns from cocoa were so uncertain, incentives to plant cocoa were practically nil. Those cocoa farmers who had sufficient fertile land and other capital made logical decisions to shift into more lucrative maize production or, in northern areas, to expand into rice production.

However, only the minority of farmers could make these decisions. In general, as cocoa production fell, rural unemployment rose and urban migration increased because poor farmers did not have the supportive structures for food production and marketing. As a small practical measure, Acheampong's NRC government encouraged back yard gardens, even in urban areas, as a way of limiting reliance upon imported food. However, an overall picture of OFY will show that it did little to contribute to enhanced rural production possibilities.

OFY was essentially a populist strategy which emphasized self-reliance, concerted local effort and better rationalization of local resources. To facilitate this, the NRC created Regional Development Corporations (RDCs) for the supervision of OFY activities. In line with its populist strategy, the government provided loans to stable male farmers through the Agricultural Development Bank to encourage food farming. It distributed subsidized fertilizers, seed and rice, thereby temporarily aiding food development, not only in the traditional cocoa belt but also in more northern areas. The result was agricultural growth from 2.6 percent between 1970 and 1972, and 4.1 percent growth between 1972 and 1975. There was also a great improvement in the urban food supply between 1974 and 1976, and by 1975 it was no longer necessary to import rice.[16] Although this positive development led some to characterize OFY as Ghana's Green Revolution, this agricultural progress was short-lived.[17]

In general, the NRC had not deeply understood the labor and resource constraints on rural production. As men withdrew from cocoa production, they tended also to withdraw their investments in the infrastructure which supported the food production industry. The decreased supply of sheds for storing produce, trucks for transporting it, and stores for selling it, handicapped the local marketing industry. This ultimately had an effect on small farmers, especially women food farmers, since their normally small profits were achieved mainly from the rapid sale of fresh agricultural produce.[18] With the reduction in the marketing infrastructure, market women were prevented from selling goods at a reasonable price, because of the increased transportation costs and uncertainty of supply. Urban food prices naturally rose, but the distribution of rural profits remained small. The point has justifiably been made that food shortages and rising prices were a function of deteriorating rural conditions,[19] that these were having a serious impact on rural producers—primarily women.

The NRC never dealt adequately with the plight of women food producers. Faced with the decline in cocoa production and the growing dependence upon an appropriate local food supply, one would have thought that the government would have provided more assistance to many small women farmers. This was not the case. Rather the NRC relied upon the initiatives of local communities toward food production, by encouraging chiefs to grant land for communal farming plots. There was only limited justification in assuming that local initiatives could address some of the problems. When cooperative cocoa farmers in the Sunyani District were questioned about their attitudes toward OFY in 1973, their responses were positive but not enthusiastic. Well-off male farmers commented that they had already increased the maize and cocoyam portions on their farms; other male farmers said that it was a good thing to do, but they did not expect many results. Female farmers were more unequivocally negative in their responses. They understood that however much they wanted to participate in OFY, they could expect little assistance in the form of Agricultural Development Bank loans—their farms and the capital they controlled were too small for that. One typical female response was "It (OFY) is good...but where can I get the land and get the laborers to produce more food?"[20]

Local chiefs often did make plots available, but the ambiguous local response indicated that the problem was more complicated than the NRC had anticipated. As the women indicated, accessible land was not the only critical variable; labor, coordination and sufficient inputs were often needed to make projects successful. Those communal OFY projects which supplied these things appeared to draw primarily women. In 1973, at one communal food farm near Abesim, the largely women participants were raising tomatoes, okra, eggplants and other small vegetable crops. Much of the coordinated female food-farming initiative may have been provided by the publicity and low-level project funding related to the International Decade of Women, and the development of a number of regional Women-In-Development (WID) projects. The 1976 WID documents show that these groups approached chiefs in many northern and Brong-Ashanti areas asking for additional land for farm projects. Beside producing foodstuffs, these projects aimed at utilizing byproducts of locally grown food in order to manufacture things like soap and cooking fats.

Had OFY lived up to its initial projections, it might have provided the growth capital necessary for Operation Feed Your Industries (OFYI), which was the industrialization portion of Acheampong's Five-Year Development Plan for 1975–1980. However, OFYI was never consummated. Such plans were doomed to failure by the increasing deterioration of the economy, the oil crisis, sustained urban migration, and the subsequent effects on the rural economic climate. Fortunately, international cocoa prices experienced a boom during this period, and cocoa earnings helped bolster incomes of cocoa farmers and the general economy until 1977.[21] Nevertheless, other economic problems ate away at these cocoa earnings. As the price of petrol went up, food and transportation prices increased, and inflation soared.[22] By 1976, inability to pay for needed petrol necessitated reliance upon the gift of petrol from Nigeria in order to keep state vehicles, factories and rural processing equipment in operation. It had become clear that the cash cropping and food production arrangement in Ghana was one which made the state a dependent entity. Moreover, current economic strategies did not allow for sufficient rural investment to encourage sufficient food or cash crop production to stave off a crisis at the state level.

In attempting to deal with its economic problems, the NRC changed its structure. Initially, it was a highly authoritarian, hierarchical coalition between the army, the civil service and the chiefs. It was ethnically diverse and representative, and sought to eliminate the emphasis on politics which had preoccupied the Nkrumah years. Acheampong preferred a regionally based bureaucracy in which decisions and actions necessary for self-reliance and Operation Feed Yourself could take place; and he utilized the rhetoric of "mass participation" to achieve legitimacy.[23] There were some elites (primarily entrepreneurs) who argued that by emphasizing rural production to fuel the "feed your industries" portion of his policy, Acheampong deprived private investors of incentive. Nevertheless, prior to 1975, it was possible for dissent to be expressed through various networks into the NRC. However, the government's legitimacy was increasingly challenged because, although cocoa revenue had begun to increase dramatically and the income from domestic rice produced in northern areas was rising, this was being eaten away by public expenditure and dependence upon non-food imports. In 1975, northerners protested the artificially low rice prices paid through the Marketing Board; then in 1976, when there was no positive government response, they smuggled rice across the borders to be sold, and simply stored paddy rice rather than sell it to the Marketing Board. It took coercive government action to get northern rice farmers to accept the low producer price. One could argue that the Ghana government was doing what other West African governments had done—keeping producer prices as low as possible in order to use the surplus to pay for state expenditures.[24] However, their actions also destroyed the illusion of mass participation in solving internal problems and opposing international forces. Dissent was heightened, even within the NRC.

As the economic problems of inflation and the country's dependence upon cocoa revenues became more intense and public dissatisfaction more vocal, Acheampong's response was to tighten national administrative structures so as to more effectively control the country. Accordingly, in November 1975, Acheampong formed the Supreme Military Council, made up of heads of the various branches of the armed service. Since authority now lay with the SMC II and former civilian members of the NRC were either subordinated or dismissed, the role of the populace had been minimized. By this one action, Acheampong had created a broad-based opposition composed of many alienated former politicians who still possessed significant ethnic or geographical constituencies, and who could become the focal point for dissent.

Acheampong's emphasis upon Ghanaian self-reliance caused him to repudiate past foreign debts totaling $94.4 million, and begin plans for expropriating foreign holdings and nationalizing indigenous enterprises.[25] Naturally, this placed him in an unfavorable position with foreign countries. Continued credit for food and household imports became impossible, but the people still partially blamed foreign countries for attempting to crush the economy. However, Acheampong refused to devalue the Cedi, despite soaring inflation between 1974 and 1977. In 1978, as various ministers of government and private entrepreneurs struggled with the lack of foreign exchange to pay for essential imports, Ghana's docks were loaded with goods which could not be claimed. Rather than addressing the implicit foreign exchange problem, Acheampong's government warned both entrepreneurs and government offices to claim the goods or face high storage charges.[26] Without imported equipment, Ghana was unable to maintain internal transportation and production systems, or even to replace worn parts and machinery on cocoa conveyor belts at Tema Port.

Not all Ghanaians suffered equally. Those who controlled essential imported commodities and those with connections or sufficient capital were now able to push smaller entrepreneurs out of business. The primarily Muslim butchers' association complained that the intervention of "middlewomen" in meat sales caused the price to rise unduly high, and asked the Cattle Development Board to sell meat only to butchers.[27] Members of the Ghanaian Caterers and Bakers Association also competed viciously with large stores as well as non-organized bakers for preferential distribution of scarce imported flour. In this competitive atmosphere, naturally some goods were shifted onto the black market for sale. The government began to publicize several distribution schemes in an effort to convince market women that goods would be available,[28] and that there was no need to hoard and sell goods for more than the control price. Although the government also urged the populace to "form cooperative bodies for easy acquisition of goods,"[29] it was mainly those privileged entrepreneurs who could even consider this option.

For both urban and rural populations, the economic crisis and the SMC's response to it proved disastrous. Corruption was widespread, especially among the military whose functions in controlling contraband gave them the opportunity to confiscate goods for their own use. Thus, in border areas such as Sunyani, military officers were often a major supplier of scarce imported goods. Within government offices and businesses, people watched carefully to see whether employees were diverting resources or funds for personal use, rather than guaranteeing state efficiency which would save money. The government still sought to win support by its public searches for enemies of the people, i.e., those engaged in *kalabule* (selling goods above the control price or black-marketeering). In 1978, for example, Ghanaian newspapers were filled with stories of market women in major towns such as Accra or Koforidua, as well as in rural villages, who were given jail sentences for selling three tins of milk for C1.80

instead of for 66 peswahs; or of traders who sold overpriced straw mats or bolts of cloth.[30] The trading sector literally fell apart, since even the customary small profits were no longer possible. The infrastructure of the state was gradually decaying for lack of funds; in the face of this, there was no public sympathy for those who economically abused their own society.

At the same time, there was a growing skepticism about whether these specific economic measures could really address what was also a political problem. The elite had already organized themselves into an opposition to respond to the government's exclusion of civilians from policy making. Both within the SMC and within the general populace there was a growing realization of need for a more explicit political agenda to demonstrate mass participation in selecting leaders and setting policy. Acheampong's response in 1976 and 1977 was to propose a union government (UNIGOV) which would have representatives from all the significant social groups in the society (military, church, civil service, traditional leaders, etc.). Ironically, UNIGOV was presented as "a purely African system" of politics, meant to replace the alien type of governments of the past. Acheampong refused to allow competition for office between political parties or constituencies. The result was that a broad cross-section of the people remained skeptical of the stated goal of UNIGOV to return the country to civilian rule.[31] Acheampong then attempted to use his control over the press to create an impression of popular support. Government supporters succeeded in organizing rallies of government workers throughout the country (even in places like Sunyani)[32] in favor of UNIGOV and Acheampong, but this was minuscule in proportion to the rampant anti-government sentiment.

It was the student, worker, and professional strikes of 1977 and 1978 which practically brought the country to a standstill, forcing Acheampong to agree that if people supported the referendum for UNIGOV, he would return the country to civilian rule within two years. Acheampong did win the March 1978 referendum with significant Upper and Northern Region support[33] but there was widespread electoral fraud and voter intimidation. In reaction, government repression increased, but this only stimulated more potent protest movements. The civil servants and workers went on strike, and urbanites demonstrated; the cities almost ceased to function.[34] These events surprised the government, since the quality of urban life (if assessed by services and resources) had always been far superior to the quality of rural life. Perhaps because of this, the economic decline was felt most sharply by urbanites whose political disapproval was always disastrous for the Ghana government.[35]

More ominous for the future of the country was the growing chaos in the rural areas. Towns such as Sunyani had been economically integrated for some time. However, Sunyani had only been politically integrated following local-government reforms in the 1950s, was more autonomous than many southern areas, and thus made far fewer demands than the more southern areas. However, it was now experiencing political as well as economic disjuncture. During the Busia period,[36] its population had come to expect political support and economic development. Now they began to demonstrate some degree of cynicism about the government they felt was abandoning them. In 1973, it was quite evident that Sunyani farmers *felt* the need to ask their local council or their regional commissioner to initiate needed developments or make policy changes. Whether officials took action on these needs was unclear,[37] but as insecticides and other inputs for farms declined, the Sunyani people felt increasingly alienated from national politics.[38] Most of this malaise, it should be noted, was felt by farmers within the cocoa zone or along the coast. Those in Sunyani complained that their political and economic payoff was far less than what they had contributed to the national and regional welfare. Roads and public buildings had deteriorated, and public utilities simply no longer operated. As they became conscious of this, many began to complain bitterly about the Acheampong government. They opted out, unwilling to give Acheampong additional legitimacy.

There were several other indices of increasing malaise in southern cocoa communities. Massive out-migration began to take place. First young men, then young women, and finally many older farmers abandoned their dispersed cocoa farms and returned to their home villages where they joined other female members in maintaining family compounds and food farms. For rural young men who would normally have drifted back and forth between Ghanaian towns and rural areas, the usual destination was now Nigeria, where the oil economy was making jobs plentiful and salaries competitive.

Alternatively, they went to find work in Abidjan, and the few who could acquire the means for air passage went to join relatives and friends in the USA or in the UK. Additionally, many rural farmers were unwilling to participate as deeply in the export economy as before. Some cocoa communities curtailed cocoa growing in favor of maize or vegetable growing for self-sufficiency and local sales. Others which had never grown cocoa (such as Hani in Brong Ahafo)[39] simply dug in their heels, and many farmers shifted to more intensive food crop cultivation. People relearned how to make the indigenous cooking oils and soaps from oleaginous plants, since imported soaps were unavailable. They repaired old hoes and knives, and relearned to make the local earthenware which had virtually been replaced by plastic containers in the 1960s. This transition was occasionally to their advantage since they now earned more for their domestic food crops, given the inflated prices and the absence of imported food alternatives. In such communities, it was rather the small middle-class—the teachers and clerks on fixed incomes—whose lack of subsistence production made them the more disadvantaged sector, and therefore the most antagonistic towards the state.

Thus, while one cannot say that the entire rural sector had withdrawn into itself, the historically most significant sectors certainly did. The north, which had historically been economically and politically disadvantaged, had become more integrated into national affairs mainly through the policies of Operation Feed Yourself. However, in the north it was not the indigenous small farmer, but the migrant, capitalist, southern civil servant/part-time farmer who took advantage of abundant supplies of land and labor in the north to grow rice.[40]

As inflation and rural collapse occurred in the cocoa zones, northern labor returned home to become employed on rice farms. While indigenous small farmers grew peanuts, maize, yams and cotton (or experienced famine in the north-east), capitalist migrant farmers from the south grew rice with the assistance of ADB and other bank loans.[41] Although rice farmers were replacing traditional cocoa farmers in importance, they could not generate the foreign exchange that cocoa formerly did. In fact, rice farmers depended upon the foreign exchange from cocoa for many of the subsidies which made rice farming prosper after 1977.

Politically, this shifting of the political-economic focus to the north was good for Acheampong, but bad for Ghana. Prior to the late 1970s, northern constituencies had no economic basis upon which they could make demands upon the state. However, the altered economic picture was changing this. While north-eastern subsistence farmers were migrating to rice areas because of famine, the rice zone was discovering a new ability to gain recognition by giving political support to Acheampong. Whereas previous governments had been willing to sacrifice the interests of the north to the demands of more significant southern areas,[42] this too was changing. Economic change in the north perhaps explains the heavy but cynical support which Acheampong received from the Upper Region and Northern Region for his UNIGOV referendum of 1978. Such specialized political interest perhaps parallels (except for its cynicism) the strong political participation of the Brong cocoa area during the 1954 and 1956 elections that sustained Nkrumah.

By 1978, it was clear that Acheampong had not found a viable replacement for the role that cocoa had formerly played in national life. The cocoa economy, which had historically provided the wherewithal to support state institutions, was still being assaulted by both international and domestic forces. Acheampong's failure to restructure rural relations to generate a more acceptable set of conditions for cocoa farmers, along with his attempt to rely upon the fledgling support of new northern farming areas, scuttled his government. But this decision would have long-term implications for the country. The majority of southern rural areas had lost confidence in the state, while the northern elite farming community had not done so. Therefore, it was mainly the north which would ultimately be in a position to influence the direction of government when Acheampong finally fell.

Personal Tragedies: Community, Kinship and Economic Decline

When one descends from the macro-level to examine the content and quality of social relations within communities as the cocoa-based state fragmented between 1975 and 1980, a different but equally troublesome picture forms. The disequilibrium in political economy which been created by the dialectics of cocoa, but exacerbated under Acheampong, created massive disjunctures within corporate groups, between males and females, and between males and their communities. With the decline of cocoa, young males migrated from many southern rural towns and villages in search of jobs and cash, and it was mainly women, children, and the elderly who still resided there.[43] It was clear that although the country was faced with declines in cocoa and food production, the government was unwilling to assist rural women who still had some incentives toward food production; rather it continued investment in urban areas to forestall political upheavals there.[44] This meant considerable hardship for village folk, as social structures were pushed almost to the breaking point. For many villages such as Hani, there was no choice but for residents to abandon it; young women either found employment as domestics to families in the Ivory Coast,[45] or drifted into quasi-prostitution to earn enough to eat.

Among Akan families in the south, increasing male migration had profound social impact on relations between men and their lineages. Whereas uncles traditionally had more responsibility for the maintenance and welfare of nephews and nieces than their own fathers, uncles were increasingly refusing to shoulder such obligations. This often left youth without the economic or social support system they felt they needed. In New Tafo, a suburb of Kumasi, when one examines the views of Akan men, one finds evidence of differential perceptions (based on age and social status) about the roles of fathers and uncles.[46] Not surprisingly, elders felt that they had been helped by uncles, and hoped that young men would continue to rely on uncles rather than fathers; elders had no desire to see modern behavior challenge traditional role responsibilities and inheritance patterns. Many elite men had been partially educated by uncles and recognized the responsibilities which these men shouldered; however, the elites were concerned about the welfare of their own wives and children, since they could not expect uncles or other lineage members to care for them as well as they would wish. Young men were openly hostile about what they perceived as an abrogation of responsibility on the part of uncles towards the education and mobility of their nephews; they wished that they could make legitimate demands on fathers, but usually they could not. When uncles and fathers migrated, most were unable to send back the needed money to assist these young men.

Women's economic roles and status also changed as a function of deteriorating economic conditions.[47] Urban markets at places like Accra, Kumasi, Bechem and Koforidua became extremely crowded and competitive as women protested the shortage of market stalls, negotiated with local politicians to obtain those available, or hawked their goods along the streets. A significant event took place in Koforidua in 1977, when market women organized a food boycott in response to government/police harassment and restrictions on food prices.[48] Despite such concerted action, there was growing stratification among women traders in such urban areas as Accra. Robertson's study of Ga female traders[49] was to reveal that wholesalers, store owners and market stall holders were the most privileged groups, with the bulk of Ga female traders who sold prepared food at fixed locations, or hawked items on the street, being at the bottom of the ladder.

Most of these women had resorted to urban trading because it offered them the greatest autonomy, given the limitations of other urban employment.[50] The profitability of urban trading declined as the economy declined between 1975 and 1980, but trading permitted many young women to live with husbands while raising children and contributing to the household income.[51] Trading also provided some small economic security for husbands and wives when jobs or businesses failed. Those young women who could not get into or remain in urban marketing were generally destitute if they did not have husbands or brothers to fall back upon. After independence in 1957 more women managed to find paid employment in cities than before.[52] In addition to the limited factory work and trading which was available to them in the 1960s, many women had begun working as domestics, as cleaning women in government offices, or as clerks in stores. But with inflation and the rising cost of living, they were now becoming more dependent upon males than they would have been in rural areas.[53] While female urban migration had been a rational response to the crisis that was occurring in cocoa farming and food farming, women and families were encountering a different kind of crisis in the cities during the late 1970s.

The ways in which urban groups handled the economic pressures depended on their social class and ethnic background. Among the elite Akan, for example, tensions focused around how to expend the two declining pools of money.[54] While both spouses wanted to maintain traditional autonomy and the right to contribute to the support of their own lineages, both husband and wife tried to achieve greater control over a "household" or "conjugal" budget that had not existed before. All of it was now needed to purchase scarce essentials. When they could no longer achieve an acceptable standard of living on what should have been a respectable income, many elites chose to emigrate or seek temporary jobs in other countries, thus adding to the brain-drain from Ghana. Nigeria absorbed a significant percentage of the teachers, professors and clerks. Among those who remained, there was virulent hostility (not without envy) against this elite group, because this group was seen as abandoning the country at its greatest moment of need. Ordinary folk somehow managed, by relying on backyard gardens, occasional items sent into the country by relatives abroad, and by recycling clothing and household items.

Among the urban working class and the poor, people resorted to a more intensified form of trading and other non-formal work modes. Men were willing to work longer hours at sign painting, tailoring, handyman jobs, or the like to earn available cash. In Accra, the majority of women were already employed in the informal market or food sales sector. Nevertheless, when jobs folded or salaries became insufficient, even educated or semi-educated women joined the ranks of this informal trading sector to maintain their contribution to their families' support. They had slightly more capital or contacts, which facilitated their trading. So poor women shifted further down to niches requiring even less capital investment. The numbers of ice-water sellers and orange sellers multiplied, but even this could not guarantee poor women an adequate income. The major problem appeared to be that the fixed prices set by the Acheampong, Rawlings and Limann governments did not take into account the price which market women had to pay to obtain the goods. Enforcement of the control price meant that traders could make no profit. It was a constant struggle for market women to secure capital with which to purchase goods, and sell them to make penny profits. The government's crackdown and confiscation of "overpriced" items (or alternatively, military harassment of market women) pushed female traders over the edge, and into the "unemployed" or "sub-proletarian"[55] category.

As Ghana's economic crisis worsened, a phenomenal rise in prostitution occurred among former market women. In Accra, for example, many women found this necessary to supplement inadequate income from trading. However, a much more significant phenomenon was the movement of market women across Ghana's borders into Ivory Coast for prostitution when their trading collapsed.[56] Many saw the shift as temporary. They endured unsanitary and degrading conditions, disease and the abuse of border guards who knew that they were unprotected, in order to accumulate capital for stockpiling goods. Then they would make arrangements with border guards to smuggle the goods back into Ghana, where the profit would again establish them in trading. If husbands or male members of the family had migrated, this might be the only means of supporting children or other lineage members. However, this usually turned out to be cyclical, rather than temporary; in a few months the women found themselves without goods or profit, and were off to the Ivory Coast again. Some young women found it more advantageous to go to Nigeria and work as a servants or quasi-trader/prostitutes, returning to Ghana occasionally in order to bring support money or goods to relatives.[57] The Ghanaian prostitute was only one symptomatic response to the larger economic crisis.

At the grass roots level, communities could not effectively mediate those tensions within families that were reflected in the community as a result of the political economy. Communities were no longer as capable of self-regulation at intimate levels because many of the local institutional supports were damaged through migration or political fear. People's identification with chiefs remained strong, and perhaps grew stronger as national-level conflicts increased. However, chiefs could no longer effectively mediate most local disputes because the operational factors were beyond their control, and participants in disputes often drifted away or migrated as needs dictated. In addition, the conflictual politics and heightened stratification of the past few years made leaders fearful to exercise uncalled for authority, even over things which had previously been "traditional" responsibilities.

Such things certainly affected the family, because men who traditionally took great pride in the subsistence maintenance of wives and children often no longer had the jobs or wherewithal to do so. Mothers who were former traders and now unemployed were forced into greater economic dependence upon males and husbands in ways they would not have found comfortable during an earlier and more economically hospitable time. On the other hand, polygyny among males meant that the escalating economic demands from multiple conjugal families had to be juggled, often at the expense of children's proper feeding and maintenance. Accra women of many different ethnic groups sometimes found that they could no longer expect traditional leaders to exercise the necessary persuasion to get men to satisfy these economic needs. Even the Akan women, who traditionally had such strong ties to matrilineages, often found that they could not fall back upon lineage members, who were themselves experiencing economic difficulties. Thus, destitute women and children had become a problem which the district and local government was being forced to deal with.

Public sentiment toward legal guarantees for the welfare of women and children had existed for some time, but had become submerged by the political and economic upheavals in the country.[58] In places like Accra, family tribunal administrators found it difficult to decide whether the reason for the precipitous rise in cases concerning divorced or widowed women and the need for support from ex-spouses was the economic crisis in the country, or the crisis in moral behavior of spouses. It seems evident, however, that the two suggested explanations were deeply interrelated. Divorce and conjugal breakup were becoming more common. Without sufficient economic support from men, many women could not understand the necessity to maintain a marriage. Men could not understand the necessity to continue providing maintenance for a woman and her children if she was no longer the wife. Women still hesitated to bring cases to court, but the intensifying economic crisis was breaking their resistance.

The courts in Accra were forced to deal with something that was originally triggered by the dynamics of cocoa, i.e., the extent to which traditional kinship structures will endure the pressures exerted upon them by the economic demands of modernization. Should matrilineal peoples make legal demands upon fathers for support of offspring? Should wives in patrilineal couples seek custody of children while asking husbands to support them? When the dynamics of local economies that are firmly tied to global ones generate spasms which disturb traditional kinship structures, such questions arise. These questions are especially intense for the Akan, because the mechanisms which governments use to encourage fathers to play a stronger financial role in the upkeep of their children are essentially patrifocal, and therefore in conflict with the spirit of matrilineal principles. Even Busia, the sociologist and former head of state, recognized the divisive impact of cocoa on kinship relations among the Akan in the 1940s. The problems have become deeper and more systemic since that time. As the courts enter the arena of family issues, they attempt to tread lightly; they do not claim to be striving to create the patrilineal family. Likewise, neither Ghanaian judges, magistrates, nor the female complainants themselves were willing to challenge the corporate matrilineage principle itself, but it was being subtly altered in a deteriorating economic and political environment. It is noteworthy that, especially in urban areas, female-controlled as well as female-headed households are emerging among the Akan as among other patrilineal peoples, and these households attempt to retain a desperate financial grip on fathers residing elsewhere. The major question is how to restructure the rural and national economies in ways that offer support for female economic autonomy, and thus continue to support traditional kinship, marriage and conjugal relations.

Socio-Political Disintegration and Failed Economic Policies

It was only a matter of time before most people in Ghana began feeling that Acheampong had failed to halt the growing dissolution of the country. The view from the rural area sharpened our perspectives on the scope of the social, economic and political disintegration throughout Ghana. The key question was, of course: Disintegration in relationship to what? What kinds of integration did the various constituencies and communities have with the state prior to Nkrumah and Acheampong? To what extent did this integration lessen in the face of the cocoa crisis? One can make distinctions between the southern and western rural areas which had been closely integrated into colonial and national politics and economics through the cocoa industry since 1900, and the more northern, rural areas whose demographic balance and resource-poor conditions kept them on the margins of Ghanaian political life until well after World War II. The proverbial "revolution of rising expectations" did occur in the Ashanti, Brong-Ashanti, central, eastern and coastal areas as schools, hospitals, roads and other services penetrated rural towns after 1948. Southerners had come to expect from the state the kinds of services which made them increasingly more upwardly mobile, and they were more willing to demand this from politicians.[59] However, this increased access also made the southerners more willing to take on more local-level initiative to get the things they needed. When Acheampong failed to solve the country's problems, his rejection was evidenced in the disengagement of both rural and urban folk, and in the massive flow of young people and the elites out of the country to find jobs. Therefore, the Supreme Military Council demanded that he step down, and in July 1978, Lt. Gen. Akuffo assumed power as head of the SMC II.

With the departure of Acheampong, Akuffo's government attempted to stabilize the economy and prepare the country for civilian rule. Unfortunately, there were no short-term measures that he could take to revive the almost decimated cocoa industry. Much of the remaining cocoa crop continued to be smuggled across the borders, where it fetched higher prices. Instead, Akuffo worked on reducing inflation by cutting back government expenditures and by devaluating the Cedi by 58.2 percent.[60] While this did control inflation, Akuffo's policies could not remove the stranglehold that the west was exerting on an economy which lacked foreign exchange for imports. Corruption again became endemic, even among military officers. The stores were frequently empty, but goods could be obtained provided people had sufficient money or connections. The SMC II made plans for the return of democratic politics, and a new constitution was being drawn up in 1978. Meanwhile, the economy of Ghana did not change fast enough, and continued simply to limp along.

Faced with what they viewed as economic and political chaos, the junior ranks of the military led an abortive coup in May 1979, headed by Flight Lt. Jerry Rawlings. However, the popular response was overwhelming, and Rawlings and the Armed Forces Revolutionary Council (AFRC) were able to assume power in Ghana. An Ewe, born of a Scottish father and a Ghanaian mother, Rawlings was married to an Ashanti woman, and was socially quite sensitive to what was required to achieve reconciliation between groups. Nevertheless, for Rawlings and the AFRC, things were black and white: since the marketplaces were deemed the loci of such corruption, those traders and market women who hoarded and sold items above government prices were persecuted as major transgressors. Their resistance to selling goods at what they perceived to be unfair prices was met with brutal force. Makola Market was burned to the ground, [61] later to be renamed Rawlings Park. For four months, Rawlings conducted a sustained assault on corruption, by jailing or executing corrupt civilians, entrepreneurs and military officers alike. However, the most controversial and condemned events were the executions of three high military officers and previous heads of state (Acheampong, Akuffo, and Afrifa) in June

1979.[62] Many claim that when Nigeria, which had been supplying Ghana with oil, signaled its displeasure by turning its oil tanker around, Rawlings prepared to step down.

Rawlings's drastic approach did temporarily restore public confidence. Nevertheless, none of his actions gave new policy directions that would move Ghana back to economic and fiscal stability or lessen political instability. Implicit in his actions (as indeed in those of the SMC II) was the assumption that it was the political and social environment, and not the economy, which had become distorted. The restoration of good government in a moral sense was judged by the AFRC as the necessary goal. To achieve this, drastic action, including political detentions and executions, had set examples. Then, with the housecleaning well in hand, Rawlings and the AFRC authorized the revival of party politics, and prepared to return to their barracks. National elections brought the Peoples' National Party (PNP) of Hilla Limann to power on September 24, 1979, as the country's third elected government.

The PNP immediately proclaimed its major goal to be the economic and social reconstruction of the country, and chose agricultural reform as its top priority.[63] Perhaps this is not surprising, given that Limann's backing came from many people in the northern areas. He thus had a powerful elite and an agriculture-based constituency, which wanted to ensure the continuation of that northern development which had taken place under Acheampong.

Nevertheless, Limann's Third Republic also emphasized increased mining and mineral exploration as a way of attracting foreign investors and supplementing cocoa income. He also stated his intention to rebuild industry to meet Ghana's material needs. While Limann insisted that it would take an austere budget to accomplish his economic recovery, his two-year budget for 1979–1981 was not overly austere.

For all its rhetoric about economic recovery, Limann's policies did not really come to grips with the problems of Ghana's rural sector. He clearly understood the need to diversify agriculture and decrease rural exploitation by providing producer price supports and other material incentives. He also planned to encourage the growth of essential food crops (yams and rice) and traditional subsistence vegetable crops, in order to bring down the high cost of living for rural folk. As far as the cocoa industry was concerned, Limann declared:

> We have lost our enviable position as the world's leading cocoa producing country. The factors which have contributed to this situation are many and complex. They include aging cocoa farmers and trees...unavailability of inputs...The most crucial factor, however, has been the decline in the number of cocoa farmers actually working the land...we cannot pin our hopes indefinitely on migrant labor to maintain our role as the leading cocoa-producing

> country. We must therefore institute measures immediately to ensure that we tend cocoa farms ourselves. This requires an integrated approach to the whole concept of rural development which will encourage our own labor and man-power to remain in the rural areas...[64]

What was surprising was that Limann's words were not accompanied by appropriate targeted actions in the cocoa industry to accomplish his goals. On the other hand, plans for rice, sugar cane, and palm oil projects were developed. Out of C283.6M set for the agricultural sector in the 1981/2 budget (C217M of which was to remove bottlenecks in the agricultural sector), the following special programs were funded:

The Upper Region Agricultural Development Project (URADEP) —C20M
The Volta Region Agricultural Development Project (VORADEP)–C10.5M
The Northern Regional Rural Integrated Project (NORRIP) ———C32.2M
Two-Year Agricultural Crash Program ————————————C20.M

There were no special targets for the south, except for the bilateral USAID Midas program in Brong Ahafo, which targeted crops such as rice. It appears that for political purposes, and perhaps because of antagonism toward Akan cocoa producers,[65] the PNP focused more on northern areas than on southern ones. Neither Limann nor his planners sought strategies for dealing effectively with those labor problems they had identified which handicapped the cocoa industry. There was no evidence that they understood that the earlier crisis in the cocoa industry had driven away many male farmers as well as northern laborers, and that now Akan women were the critical labor force in cocoa. As early as 1975, women constituted the bulk of laborers available to work on southern cocoa and food farms.[66] But because this fact was not sufficiently recognized, government planners could not attempt to devise plans that addressed Akan women as autonomous, stable farmers—persons capable of making solid agricultural decisions.[67]

In a widely heralded decision, the PNP did raise the producer price of cocoa to beyond the international market price, so as to encourage production.[68] However, this could not be sustained, given the lack of income-generating activity within the economy, and because it did little to halt the social structural decay that had depleted the rural labor force. Almost no attention was paid to the woeful lack of rural economic and physical infrastructure. The result, despite a brief agricultural production spurt in 1981, was that none of the PNP plans succeeded in increasing the rural labor supply, either in stimulating overall agricultural production or in generating significant government support in cocoa farming areas.

In the short space of two years, it became clear that Limann's economic plans were failing. The government had raised the minimum wage, not by really addressing constraints on southern farmers and thereby increasing agricultural production, but by increasing taxes.[69] Inflation rose to over 100 percent. Since the government refused to devalue the currency, ordinary folk resorted to smuggling and profiteering to make ends meet. In August 1980, the situation had reached crisis proportions. The average daily wage was only C7, but a single egg cost C11 in Accra! Buying the ingredients for a simple meatless meal took the equivalent of several days' salary. Without backyard gardens, workers and even civil servants could not afford to eat.

Transportation between towns and rural areas for food as well as cocoa was drastically reduced because of insufficient gasoline. When there was gasoline, vehicles could not run because of the lack of spare parts. There were other problems: entrepreneurs attempted to create a monopoly on the transportation of food in order to control the profit, and farmers were not enthusiastic about selling produce at discounted prices when this was their only means of livelihood.

Once again, the rural people of Ghana, now joined by urbanites, sought a livelihood outside the country. Some went to Ivory Coast, now made richer by smuggled Ghanaian cocoa. Thousands went to oil-rich Nigeria. However, their reception in these places was often greatly affected by Ghana's recent stigma as a woebegone state which could not care for its people. Many Ghanaians came as illegal immigrants, since they had few marketable skills; the skilled ones were perceived as taking jobs belonging to indigenous folk, or as desperate unemployed folk who further lowered the wage rates. Without adequate police protection, prostitutes and illegal traders were occasionally victimized, and fishermen were killed in "the Black Hole" of Abidjan; in Nigeria there was agitation for the expulsion of Ghanaians.

However, equally as important, the PNP had failed to recognize the public desire for greater participation in the political process. As a result of this failure, it was not possible for a dialogue to begin regarding how to achieve economic balance and parity. The level of conflict and corruption, which had decreased under Rawlings' AFRC, rose as a result of PNP policies and omissions. There was even violence[70] and conflict on the university campus at Legon. Thus, there was urban upheaval to match the rural dissatisfaction.[70] Faced with this turmoil, Limann became more repressive and criticized the diverse opposition groups (including the military), thereby hardening public sentiment. Once again, political failures and economic woes affected the morale of Ghanaians. By failing to rehabilitate the economy, the PNP had failed to find an alternative to cocoa, and thereby save the country. It was only a matter of months before the second Rawlings coup.

Rawlings: New Global, State and Urban-Rural Relations

The second Rawlings coup on December 31, 1981, brought a more pragmatic man to power in Ghana than the one who had taken rule in 1979. Rawlings still had many strong and idealistic notions about remolding economic and political relationships within the state, about "Pan-Africanism," and about revolutionizing relations between the state and the global economy. But primarily, his Provisional National Defense Council government (PNDC) actively sought to answer a number of questions as well: Was it possible to revive the cocoa economy, and if so, on what basis? Where would one acquire the labor and input, as well as individual incentives necessary to do so? How should one create the political base and the popular initiative which could support the desired economic restructuring? What kind of guarded relationship with western economic powers could be negotiated which would create the least dependency within the Ghanaian economy? However, for Rawlings, Ghanian nationalism was primary. There was little evidence that Rawlings understood that the major concerns were with finding those approaches which would create and mediate linkages between levels—local, national and global.

Rawlings's actions upon assuming leadership revealed his ideological commitments, but also reflected his uncertainty about how to answer many of the above questions or how to affect the numerous distorted facets of Ghanaian public life. He arrested several former politicians (including Limann), quickly halted the military license which accompanied the coup, and again declared war on corruption.[71] Rawlings suspended the 1979 constitution, and promised "sweeping changes" which would introduce a "people's government" in place of the failed western political institutions of Ghana's past. He also promised a close examination of foreign involvement in Ghana's economy, with a view toward encouraging Ghanaians to invest at home.[72] However, there were two major pieces of evidence of his populist and nationalist bent. One was his promise to establish people's tribunals around the country, which would provide a new legal code to try the crimes committed against the community and the country. The second was his vow to develop mechanisms for assisting farmers in moving the country's cocoa crop from rural areas to the docks, so that both they and the country could prosper. Implicit in his statements was the assertion that through a process of indigenization and self-regulation, Ghana would begin to turn its political economy around. Rawlings himself declared that "I ask for nothing less than a revolution..."[73]

It was, however, twelve days before appointments were made to the PNDC, and Rawlings appeared to be having difficulty finding people who shared his ideals and had no connection with the former governments. People appreciated his nationalism, but were unclear about his ideological leanings. The announcement of the PNDC's composition appeared to coincide with the renewal of relations with Libya, and the establishment of a Libyan People's Bureau.[74] Angered by the perceived leftist movement in the PNDC, the western press referred to him as a "muddled idealist." On the other hand, students initially proclaimed that "Jerry is for the people," while ordinary folk expressed skepticism about whether *another* military government would really resolve Ghana's problems.[75] Aside from Rawlings's rhetoric and his appreciation for Fanon, Castro and Qaddafi, there was surprisingly little that could be construed as socialistic in Rawlings' early approaches, except for his attempts to pull ordinary people into the operation of institutions, or to create alternative mass institutions—and this was populist, rather than socialist. For example, in a masterful move, he drafted university students and assigned them to the countryside for a few weeks to evacuate cocoa (some of which had been stored for months) and get it to Tema for shipping. Although there were students who complained bitterly of such plebian work, most applauded his forthrightness. There was urgency in his actions: Ghanaians were consuming 30 percent less food than they had 10 years before, with domestic food supplies expected to run out by mid-1982. Although Rawlings tried unsuccessfully to obtain food assistance from abroad, and did succeed in obtaining money for food from Libya, he fully intended to begin the trek towards Ghanaian food self-sufficiency. He said, "There is no excuse for our food crisis...Why should people go hungry when large tracts of fertile land lie idle and fertilizers also lie wastefully at [the] ports?"[76]

Rawlings's populist approach bore fruit. Although there were sporadic skirmishes as the military was pulled back into the barracks, this was more than offset by the swiftness with which People's Defense Committees and Workers' Defense Committees sprang up in urban neighborhoods and industries, in rural villages and on university campuses. Although the populace had been exhausted by the political convulsions of the past decade, they were energized by Rawlings's promise to return power to the grass roots. They became vigilant in bringing former politicians and tax evaders to justice. Such popular support made it possible for him to take other strategically difficult actions, such as recalling 50-Cedi notes to the banks in exchange for vouchers for new currency.[77]

Nevertheless, many were critical of the pace at which Rawlings was moving. Entrepreneurs proclaimed him too radical in some areas, such as in setting government control prices for anything from food and clothing to taxi rides, and then prosecuting taxi drivers, flogging market women, or executing black-marketeers caught breaking the law. They felt that this zeal did not stop *kalabule*, and was therefore responsible for the increased, rather than decreased, shortages of essential commodities. His assaults on "capitalist profit making" by the elite troubled them, and many entrepreneurs fled the country in response. On the other hand, the foreign monetary community judged him too slow in devaluating currency so as to reduce inflation and stabilize prices.[78] Others said that his slow, measured pace was an attempt to bring about change while warding off a possible coup. What was evident by the end of 1982 was that many Ghanaians were assuming a wait-and-see attitude regarding Rawlings and the PNDC.

The year 1983 was significant in a number of ways: it tested Rawlings's ingenuity, it gave him the public mandate to act in several crisis situations that Ghanaians faced, and it gave him a new understanding of what kinds of rural policy decisions were necessary in order to begin revitalization of both cocoa and food crops. The drought of 1983 was the first major event with which Rawlings dealt. Although shortages of food had reached almost crisis proportions in urban areas, the spread of drought conditions near the end of 1982 meant that now even overpriced local food was unavailable. Chickens and goats died for lack of water, and the remaining chickens simply couldn't lay eggs. Money meant little to prosperous urbanites if they couldn't *find* sufficient high-calcium food to prevent teeth from beginning to rattle. People along the coast or in the Akwapim Hills could survive by consuming dried fish for protein, but conditions were worst in inland rural areas where *kwashiokor* and hunger caused the emigration of more than half the population of many small villages. In addition, bush fires raged across many parts of the central, Ashanti and Brong-Ahafo regions, destroying homes and other buildings, decimating the forest as well as cocoa farms. The farm ecology of the area was considerably altered by this single event.

Paradoxically, the massive rural mobilization effort which was needed to rebuild communities and supply the labor force for rural production was complicated by the emigration which had occurred. Rawlings's approach was to encourage rural people to help themselves by participating in local cooperative work groups, or *nhoboa* as they were traditionally known. This was not a new approach; in fact it was something that had been advocated by several former governments to ease the rural labor problem. However, it was the first time that the government attempted to reward groups who organized in this fashion with publicity and needed tools or input. It was also the first time that rural production absolutely could not have occurred without this effort. The traditional aspects of *nhoboa* was emphasized by the fact that the groups were usually composed of elderly farmers who could not have worked their farms by themselves, and of chiefs who wished to set an example for their own areas.

Nigeria's expulsion of Ghanaian nationals in February 1983 provided the stimulus for Rawlings's second, more ingenious approach to rural mobilization. The Ghanaian nationals in Nigeria were a problem for Shagari, since he was trying to deal with an oil economy in decline,[79] fight charges of corruption within his party, and convince his constituents that he was attempting to reverse the economic decline. As part of Shagari's bid for re-election in 1983, he took drastic action against "aliens" who were perceived to be a drain on Nigeria's economy. However, Ghana was unprepared for the thousands off its citizens who stood waiting for the opening of the Ghanaian borders following the expulsion. Ghanaians who had stayed were hostile about the returnees, and embarrassed at their public disgrace. For Rawlings, there was the problem of what to do with so many relatively young and unemployed citizens; the cities could not absorb them. Rawlings's public recommendation was for the Ghanaians to return to their home villages and farms, thus causing the population of many villages to double almost overnight. Not all of the returnees remained. Many simply began the trek "back to Agege" and the lure of any possible employment in Nigeria. But for those who remained there was the problem of what to do with them in the village—how to organize village populations that had been so traumatized by local devastation and international disgrace. Rawlings's solution was to create a National Mobilization Program (NMP) which recruited local people to perform needed construction of schools, roads, clinics, etc., in their local communities. It was designed to fit into the regional administrative machinery, but also to encourage local originality and enthusiasm; it was closely associated with the People's Defense Committees, about which more will be said. Of major importance, however, was his expansion of the NMP to include the "mobisquads" composed primarily of young men, both literate and semi-literate. Many would say that this action reflected that Rawlings was starting to come to terms with the economic realities of the country, and to utilize his charismatic appeal and intuitive understanding of indigenous social behavior to design populist grass roots approaches to the rural crisis.

The mobisquads were ingenious in conception as well as in the intricacy of their "fit" into the social structural conditions of rural Ghana in 1983. Apparently, the first step in their construction involved meeting with local groups of returnees, and systematically recruiting people as volunteers. Oral accounts say that people were housed in temporary places, and fed with supplies directly from Accra before being assigned to perform various labor functions on cocoa and food farms in the area.[80] In addition to the cameraderie or camp spirit which developed, volunteers were rewarded with clothing or bags of rice, thus making it possible for volunteers to make a contribution to the maintenance of their families in the area. In this way, mobisquads became attractive labor groups for rural males during 1984, and it was possible for the PNDC to shift much of the financial responsibility for them from the central government to the regions and local areas. The feeding of the mobisquad was subsequently shifted onto the local group of elderly and female farmers who had solicited their help, and they were given a small token sum of money each time the squad went out.

However, as they have matured, the labor of the mobisquad has lost its voluntary aspects, and now involves direct compensation. Since the cocoa farmers are elderly and unable to maintain the farms, the mobisquads have increasingly been able to ask for portions of the cocoa crop as compensation and in some cases, portions of the land. Of note is the fact that this trend was rationalized by reference to the traditional *abusa* labor category which existed, and which required the farmer to give one-third of the cocoa crop to the overseer who worked the farm.

The mobisquads thus provide a mechanism by which aspiring young rural men can become economically stable, if not upwardly mobile. As a result of compensation from local cocoa farmers, the mobisquads have come into possession of farms which they work cooperatively, and from which they derive revenue. Both this revenue, and relationships which individual men have been able to cultivate with a particular farmer, have made it possible for them to begin small scale individual food farms as well. Therefore, the demographics of farm owners in Brong-Ahafo, for example, should be undergoing a shift as these young men become established.

For a number of reasons, young women are not greatly represented in mobisquad membership. Perhaps this is because the initial thrust of the PNDC was to return young men to rural involvement; but the mobisquad members claim that women do not like to work so hard, and mainly work as cooks for the group unless they are trying to follow their menfolk.[81] The result is the persistence of a sexual division of labor among the rural young, despite the fact that young men have returned to agricultural work. The pressure on females to contribute agricultural labor is lessening as the economy improves. However, one impact of mobisquad development may be that farm ownership is again being solidly identified with males, rather than females.

The institutionalization of the mobisquads reflects only one facet of the PNDC's rural policies. There is now greater penetration of the Cocoa Marketing Board (or COCOBOD) and its component unit the Cocoa Services Division, into the professional and social lives of rural people. The emphasis of COCOBOD has been on reviving agriculture through the rationalization and diversification of cocoa and food farming, without using technical or capital intensive approaches which would eliminate the small farmer. Because the drought and bush-fires destroyed many older cocoa farms, the Cocoa Services Division had a unique opportunity to start from scratch in many areas.[82] Trained CSD technical assistants were called in to educate farmers who were about to replant fields, so that they could plant heartier and more disease-resistant Bonsu varieties of cocoa, which produced at an earlier age than the Tetteh Quashie, Amazon or T-14 varieties. When older, non-diseased trees remained, then farmers were encouraged to diversity types of cocoa planted on a single plot. However, equally as important was that they also introduced new varieties of food trees (palm nuts, for example) that could be intercropped on cocoa farms. in many cases, CSD advised farmers to plant other crops on part of the land, so varieties of swamp rice were being grown around Sunyani. CSD supplied farmers with needed cocoa seedlings free of charge, often from nurseries which were tended by mobisquad members. The farms in the area have generally been grouped into 3000-acre service units, with one central point in the unit (usually the produce buying station) chosen to house the extension services. One field assistant and 4 workers are assigned to service all farmers within the unit, and the buying agency is now attempting to provide motor cycles for them to reach each farmer personally.

In an attempt to upgrade services to farmers, the PNDC had embarked on a plan to provide both inputs and essential commodities to farmers in a standard "farmers package" (lantern, cutlass, cloth, insecticide, soap) which was distributed by mobile units throughout the district. Even the machines needed for spraying cocoa trees are available within villages, although they are not generally owned by individual farmers. The PNDC aims to make these supply units stationary, so that farmers can obtain all kinds of essential commodities in CSD mini-stores throughout farming areas. In general, essential commodities are readily available and consistently priced throughout the south now, so it would appear that the PNDC's goal is mainly to convince farmers of its concern for them. In farming villages around Chiraa and Odumasi, CSD staff were known, approachable, and trusted, perhaps because of the extent to which they were willing to mingle and become a part of the community. Despite the fact that roads to Sunyani and surrounding towns remained hopelessly pot-holed and driving was difficult, there is still a feeling among farmers that the PNDC was contributing to the quality of rural life. Likewise, it was CSD staff who knew the important people in Sunyani town, whether older traditionalists or young mobisquad members.

It is clear that the operations of the Cocoa Services Division and the National mobilization Program has provided a political base for the PNDC in rural areas. Aspiring literate young men soon rise from squad leader to regional office representative—not divorced from rural work, but now involved in links between the mobilization programs and the PNDC. Thus, NMP employment is providing the kind of economic and political training that the Cooperative Society secretary-receivers obtained in the 1950s, and that the Produce Buying Association secretaries received in the 1960s and 1970s. The young men are keenly aware than Accra must be constantly reminded of their successes in acres of land "brushed and planted," numbers of projects completed, numbers of members recruited; they enjoy any news story which projects them in an active relationship with the PNDC. Although the NMP is not an official part of the Regional

Administrative complex, they have a strong working relationship with the regional political structure. Whatever else Rawlings has or has not achieved, he has managed to stop the process of rural disengagement which was evident under Acheampong and Limann and, in fact, to engage the rural farming community on his behalf. Thus, the National Mobilization Programs continue to expand in most regions, drawing strength from rural farming communities.

At an earlier point in the PNDC's development, there was danger of overenthusiasm on the part of rural youth as they rallied for the mobilization programs and in favor of newly established People's Defense Committees (PDCs). After Rawlings came to power in 1982, the PDCs were established all over the country to protect communities from cheats, swindlers and vandals. Thus, they patrolled markets and called unscrupulous traders into question. Because of the recent political chaos, but also because the government wanted to involve local people, the committees were able to oust local politicians from their decision-making functions. In the Sunyani area, the PDCs took it upon themselves to decide land cases, for example, and often rendered questionable judgments. They often used violence and abuse, especially against women traders. However, as local criticism of the PDCs peaked and as the national political climate changed, the PDCs were sharply limited by Accra, particularly from exercising any legal functions. The PDCs were transformed into Committees In Defense of the Revolution (CDRs) and thus acted as watchdogs and advisory groups, referring cases to the local tribunals when there was a possibility of prosecution. Older Sunyani people seemed to feel that the CDRs were no longer defending the community, but defending a political idea, and many of them wanted to keep their distance from this form of politicking.

By 1984, there was a need to consolidate the rural gains which were being made. Rawlings had begun to make overtures to the International Monetary Fund for assistance, and in an attempt to meet IMF requirements, the PNDC increased the producer prices of cocoa, rice and maize. There was also a gradual phasing out of subsidies on agricultural inputs such as fertilizers and sprays, which were thought to have assisted large farmers rather than economically strapped farmers in the past. Northern rice cultivation had risen from its all-time low in 1979 to near what rice production had been in 1975, but this still only met one-third of national need.[83] Under a three-year investment program, it was assessed that allowing greater competition in the marketing and distribution of agricultural inputs and outputs would result in lower agricultural costs, increased availability of materials in rural areas and ultimately even greater incentives for farmers to produce.[84] Cocoa farms had been replanted, goods were back on the shelves in urban markets (albeit at high prices), and the brain drain from the country had been brought to a standstill.

It had also become clear that economic pragmatism was replacing Rawlings's earlier idealism about the gains to be made from grass roots populist approaches. Rawlings was working on "feeding the nation" through rural regeneration, but it would be some time before foreign reserves from cocoa could again fuel the engine of state. The IMF loans which were granted for 1985 appeared to bring results as growth was stimulated within the economy, and inflation fell to 20 percent. Based on this initial economic success, the IMF granted another loan for $513 million for 1986. Rawlings's Secretary of Finance responded to questions about the PNDC's changing economic approaches by saying, "We have had to make tactical compromises as conditions have dictated...We are not talking about utopianism.."[85]

Increased rural integration and the semblance of economic stability encouraged Rawlings to begin to consolidate the political power of the PNDC, and to attempt real political change as well as institutionalization. The major challenge was to consolidate the urban support base—to make the National Mobilization Program, the Committees in Defense of the Revolution, the National Service program and the Public Tribunals function as well in urban areas as they did in the rural areas—and to draw women into the political support base.

The urban response to the component programs of the PNDC has been quite different from the rural ones, and again reflects many of the urban-rural contradictions which Ghana has experienced. The urban population is more varied, has a larger elite sector, has been more intimately involved in the workings of various governments over the years, and has developed a degree of cynicism. In Accra, elites and long-settled urbanites were confused about the National Mobilization Program. They were nonchalant about its projects, which typically involved cleaning of streets and gutters. The response from immigrant northern or *zongo* communities was considerably greater. What worried elites was that in many cases, the soldiers or quasi-military personnel of the NMP enforced unneeded roadblocks and inspected passing cars. They were suspicious because the NMP seemed to possess an importance out of proportion to the functions they performed. On the other hand, the National Service Program (NS), which required a one-year internship for secondary school or college graduates, received generally positive reviews, and most people recognized the value of service to the country. Working-class families had few objections, since the chances of continuing schooling were few, and (despite the low salary) it gave their children employment. Many aspiring middle-class families viewed it favorably, since it gave their children who were secondary school graduates the opportunities to acquire work experience that nepotism in previous governments may have prevented them from acquiring. Their young people aspired to work in the Ministry of Finance or in Foreign Affairs, although being posted to the Northern or Upper Region was a tolerable inconvenience. Favoritism in assignment of NS positions was one problem which faced Rawlings by 1985. The established middle-class often viewed NS as an interruption of an otherwise assured professional life. Therefore, they delayed the internship until completion of college or professional training, then tried to exercise their influence to keep their children posted in urban rather than rural areas. Despite these problems, National Service internships provided many rural areas with professional agricultural, medical and technical assistance which they had long needed.

Urban reaction to People's Defense Committees largely depended upon social class and the degree of economic vulnerability which people felt. Jerry Rawlings was still widely perceived as a "people's man." Manual laborers and lower-level workers, occasion workers or unemployed persons were often enthusiastic about the PDCs because they were given an opportunity to become politically involved for the first time. Workers were adamant about starting a branch within their place of employment, often against the wishes of higher-level staff. Workers then used these groups to search out corruption and fiscal mismanagement that could be referred to a tribunal. Alternatively, they wanted to silence professionals who were critical of the government. The attempt to bring a PDC onto the campus of the University of Ghana-Legon was criticized by faculty and higher-level staff, but the discussion was silenced when the government warned that opposition would be viewed as political resistance. Although university professors viewed this kind of "political cheerleading" as unscholarly, many students had been active supporters of the PNDC during the early phases of the government. Some of them enthusiastically participated in the "confiscation of property" (cars, etc) to be used "in the interests of the people;" this kind of zeal had to be contained by the PNDC. By 1985, PDCs were becoming institutionalized, and student enthusiasm had lessened.

Reaction to the public tribunals was also divided. Naturally, the PNDC construed these tribunals as examples of "people's justice." Paradoxically, defendants literally quaked in their shoes when asked to appear, because there was a presumption of wrongdoing that was often difficult or impossible to disprove. Normal western legal standards of justice did not apply in the tribunals, although trained lawyers were frequently present to counsel the defendants. Merchants, entrepreneurs, managers of government offices, or local politicians might be called in front of the tribunal to explain how and why they made so much profit within any given year; or to explain the source of goods which were unaccounted for through import licenses; or to explain questionable expenditures within government offices. Lay members of the community who served on the tribunals often used the opportunity to vindicate previous grievances against public figures; or they used the position to become politically recognized themselves. Even legitimately earned revenues or property were often confiscated and placed at the disposal of the NMPs. It was not uncommon for bribes to be offered by the accused so that the case would be dismissed. Increasingly, the

PNDC tried to employ lawyers within the tribunal itself, in an attempt to reconcile populist and western standards of justice. However, the Ghana Lawyers Association strenuously objected to their members appearing at tribunal proceedings, and it was rather the "renegade" lawyers who appeared there. Despite this, some lawyers were so incensed at what they perceived as a miscarriage of justice that they voluntarily represented certain classes of political clients. In Accra, people predicted the end of contemporary standards of legal justice if, as they suspected, the PNDC aimed at replacing the courts of law with the public tribunals.

From the urban responses, it seems that some PNDC institutions do not yet have broad-based political support. Leaving aside the military, which will be considered more fully later, there were basically two other important constituencies that were not yet sufficiently integrated to guarantee the PNDC stability over the next few years. These are (a) women and their organizations; and (b) intellectuals, who desire to play a greater role in the construction of government social policy.

The first constituency, women, has been a problematic one for Rawlings even during the 1979 period. That difficulty has not decreased, although the PNDC has made overtures to women. With the growth of the National Council on Women and Development (NCWD) under Acheampong in 1975, there was for the first time an organization which had a mandate to investigate conditions for women all across the country. NCWD was a government body, so members were appointed by the president, with responsibities for coordinating the women-related activities within the various ministries of government. Therefore, it was not autonomous, although in its approach it tried to maintain distance from specific government policies and assume an advocacy and coordination function.[86] They coordinated a number of internationally and locally funded women's projects in the various regions, but at the height of the political confusion between 1975 and 1980, their primary role was that of "crisis management." When accusations were made that women traders were hoarding imported items, NCWD mediated between the groups and the government. Major problems occurred as the government tried to confiscate "hoarded" goods, because the soldiers were hard on women, accusing even elderly ladies of hoarding the wax prints they had saved through the years as security. But NCWD established a mechanism for returning excess items to government stores, thus not exposing women to abuse and violence.[87] Then, as essential commodities like soap became unavailable, NCWD began to train rural women in alternative ways to produce things, using local materials. By 1981, NCWD's crisis mediation approach had managed to win the confidence of women all over the country.

In rural areas like Brong-Ahafo, NCWD's work was often that of educating and advising women about the various service functions that were available—for example, legal assistance if widows were being denied maintenance from cocoa farm proceeds by the deceased husband's heir; or if they were being evicted from a residence which they had shared with the husband.[88] Most women knew nothing about legal rights which they might have. However, Sunyani women also faced considerable hostility from Committees in Defense of the Revolution, because their trading activities were perceived as "profit oriented." If there were conflicts in the markets, the likelihood was that the case would be referred to the CDR and the women labeled as "troublemakers." Much of this antagonism existed because women hesitated to join the CDRs or other organizations affiliated with the PNDC.

The Brong-Ahafo regional representative was particularly interested in helping women to understand the function of belonging to cooperative bodies, since this might decrease their victimization by larger groups and assist them in more efficient economic activity. Nevertheless, the history of women's cooperative organizations in the region was not a bright one. Marketwomen, bakers as well as farmers, were often suspicious that they would be cheated by others in the organization, who would work less but share equally in profits; or they feared to relinquish control over limited individual resources because it was their single security. For all these reasons, experiments with cooperative food farming, food processing, or pottery making often folded soon after the subsidized period ended, and before the women could turn a profit.[89] Although these rural women had developed confidence in their regional representative, they instinctively resisted participation in national political or economic associations.

There was a problem of how to integrate both urban and rural women politically and economically, since many women did not see PNDC efforts as sincere. There were education and literacy projects, economic generating projects, and maternal health projects[90] carried out by NCWD in most regions, and these appeared to have government support. However, it was hard to ignore the many newspaper articles which appeared castigating market women, fishmongers, and female government employees for not doing enough to support the economy, to better social conditions, or to guarantee the stability of the PNDC.[91] There was, however, evidence that the PNDC was concerned about the absence of women in many of its organizations. The December 31st Women's Movement, for example, constantly worked to recruit and grow, and the indication was that it aimed to become the major women's movement in the country. Nana Agyeman-Rawlings (the President's wife), president of the December 31st Movement, was anxious for this group to become a major women's organization, and as such, more central to PNDC activities. Her advice to participants at a CDR conference in Sunyani in July 1986 was "not to ignore women in their activities because they constitute a formidable target group in many areas of their operations." She urged them to help with the liberation of Ghanaian women so that "women would take their rightful position in the current transformation process."[92] Critics claim that the 1986 government action to dissolve the National Council on Women and Development was politically motivated to increase the membership of the December 31st Movement by eliminating alternative allegiances which might limit women's participation in PNDC organs.[93] However, another popular response is that NCWD had fulfilled its function years ago, and that proposals were now needed to allow "women to participate on equal terms with men in all spheres of our national life."[94]

Intellectuals represent another constituency which Rawlings and the PNDC have yet to sufficiently integrate. Unlike rural groups, intellectuals have seen little improvement in their quality of life as a result of Rawlings's programs and policies. True, food and imports are now available, but salaries for intellectuals have not risen as fast as for those in government service. The recent across-the-board government salary increases only made it possible for them to survive and pay school fees, but it remains difficult for them to engage in the type of academic exchange, research and writing that scholars in other countries take for granted. They fight the urge to go abroad for work. However, the major concern is that the PNDC has adopted a guarded attitude towards intellectuals, not often allowing them to participate directly in formulating policy. Economists, agriculturalists and political scientists at the university, who are knowledgeable about government project areas, have often been carefully avoided rather than consulted. The scholars say that those who make economic policy, for example, have little practical knowledge—a sure formula for disaster.

Since 1982, Rawlings has experienced some success at his two initial goals, the creation of alternative justice institutions and the restructuring of rural production relationships. In doing so, the locus of problems temporarily shifted away from the rural areas where it had been concentrated since the Acheampong period, and began to be centered in the urban arena. Rawlings began to be concerned about consolidating a political base for the PNDC military government, and creating institutions (primarily urban ones) through which this can occur. However, Rawlings has not been an autonomous actor; he must not take all the responsibility for this shift. The shift has taken place in large part because Rawlings has became convinced of the power of the international economic system, which he originally had vowed to avoid. He was systematically shown that Ghana's economy could not develop further unless he made overtures to the entrepreneurial sector, opened the economy to foreign investment, and guaranteed a stable climate within which economic activity could occur. It is possible to argue that these are temporary measures—that as soon as cocoa again becomes the major export crop, Ghanaian dependence upon diverse economic players will be reduced. One wonders whether (as under Nkrumah) the prescription for development will ultimately have side effects; and whether, in order to salvage the state, we will again witness the gradual deterioration of rural conditions as marketplace dynamics recreate the "bias against agriculture."

Notes

1. Bjorn Beckman, "The Agrarian Basis of the Post-Colonial State," in Judith Heyer, Pepe Robert and Gavin Williams (eds.), *Rural Development in Tropical Africa*, New York: St. Martin's Press, 1981, 143–167.
2. Dennis Austin, Ghana Observed: Essays on the Politics of a West African Republic, Manchester: Manchester University Press, 1976,111–112.
3. Lieutenant General J.A. Ankrah headed the NLC regime from 1966–1969. According to Pellow and Chazan, it was a tripartite military-bureaucratic-chiefly alliance, which had broad support and which was mainly concerned with administration rather than with political reform. What its supporters shared was an anti-Nkrumah stance, and a commitment to return the country to civilian rule. See Deborah Pellow and Naomi Chazan, *Ghana: Coping With Uncertainty*. Westview Press, 1986, 47–8.
4. Austin, 1976, 123. Austin notes that the ethnic conflict was exaggerated because Busia, an Akan, was challenged by Ebedemah, an Ewe.
5. N.O. Addo, "The Alien's Compliance Law of 1968," *Ghana Journal of Sociology*, 1969.
6. Niara Sudarkasa (ed.), *Migrants and Strangers in Africa*, African Urban Notes, series B, no. 1, East Lansing, MI: Africana Studies Center, Michigan State University, 1975.
7. Ernst Dumor, "Women in Rural Development," *Rural Africana*, East Lansing, MI: Michigan State University, 1983, 77.
8. Robert Price, "Neocolonialism and Ghana's Economic Decline: A Critical Assessment," *Canadian Journal of African Studies*, vol. 18, no. 1, 163–194.
9. Pellow and Chazan, 1986, 56.
10. Pellow and Chazan, 1986, 48–9. Acheampong's government shared the tripartite military-bureaucratic-chiefly support structure, although civilians were overtly subordinate to military officers in the authority structure. Although Acheampong's government has been described as "the most ethnically balanced cabinet in independent Ghana" (p.49), Acheampong focused more on administrative restructuring than on economic reforms, to his detriment.
11. The kinship dynamics which limited women's cocoa production possibilities have already been discussed in Chapters 4 and 5.
12. Okali and Kotey, 1971.
13. Dorothy Dee Vallenga, 1977, 202–203.
14. Prudence Woodford-Berger, 1981, 11, 15.
15. Robert M. Price, "Neo-colonialism and Ghana's Economic Decline," *Canadian Journal of African Studies*, 18, no. 1, 1984, 175.
16. Bjorn Beckman, "The Agrarian Basis of the Post-Colonial State," in Judith Heyer,

Pepe Roberts and Gavin Williams (eds.), *Rural Development in Topical Africa*, New York: St. Martin's Press, 1981, 154.

17. George Benneh, "Ghana's Agricultural Development and the Impact of Government Policies Since the Sixties," unpublished, 1979. Library of Congress Paper, Africana Section.
18. Peter Garlick, *African Traders and Economic Development in Ghana*, Oxford: Clarendon Press, 1971, 49–50.
19. J. Campbell, "Ideology and Politics in the Markets of Ghana," *Canadian Journal of African Studies*, 1985, v. 19, no. 2, 426.
20. Mikell, 1975, 78.
21. Bjorn Beckman, 1981, 157.
22. Op. cit., 1981, 154.
23. Eleanor E. Zeff, "New Directions in Understanding Military and Civilian Regimes in Ghana," *African Studies Review*, XXIV, no. l, March 1981, p. 54.
24. Grier, 1981, 41–2.
25. Pellow and Chazan, 1986, 58.
26. *Daily Graphic*, 4 Feb. 1978, "Clear Goods From Tema Port, Or..."
27. Ibid., 3 Jan. 1978, "Sell Direct to Butchers."
28. Ibid., 26 Feb. 1978. "Distribution of Essential Goods: New Rules Out." Also, 1 March 1978, "Consumer Goods: Market Women to Get Them Direct."
29. Ibid., 11 Feb. 1978.
30. Ibid., 2 Jan. 1978, "One Month for a Change;" also 4 Jan. 1978, "Four Traders get Four Months."
31. Ibid., Feb. 1978, "Brong-Ahafo Workers Support Unigov." The Sunyani rally was also vocal in condemnation of the People's Movement for Freedom and Justice, led by Lt. Gen. A.A. Afrifa and Mr. K.A. Gbedemah.
32. Pellow and Chazan, 1986, 70.
33. Joseph Hanlon. "Ghana: Science Hangs on Amid Economic Chaos," *Nature*, vol. 279, May 1979, pp. 182–3. More than 4,000 teachers had left the country between August 1977 and September 1978. Even university professors found it "impossible for any member of [the] staff to live on his salary. He must have some other source of income."
34. Maxwell Owusu, *The Uses and Abuses of Political Power*, Chicago: University of Chicago Press, 1970, 368–9.
35. Peter Osei-Kwame and Peter J. Taylor, "A Politics of Failure: The Political Geography of Ghanaian Elections, 1954–1979." Paper presented at African Studies Association meeting, Los Angeles, 1984.
36. Mikell survey of Sunyani Area cocoa farmers, 1973. Responses were given to questions about who the farmers would approach regarding a problem in the region; and about whether they felt they should approach the chief, the local council or the regional commissioner.
37. Osei-Kwame and Taylor, op. cit., 26.
38. Merrick Posnansky, "How Ghana's Crisis affects a Village", *West Africa*, 1 December 1980, pp. 2418–2420.
39. Andrew Shepherd, "Agrarian Change in Northern Ghana: Public Investment, Capitalist Farming and Famine," in Judith Heyer, Pepe Roberts and Gavin William

(eds.), *Rural Development in Tropical Africa.* New York: St. Martin's Press, 1981, pp. 168–192.

40. Ibid., 174–5.
41. Fred Hayward, "Perceptions of Well-Being in Ghana: 1970 and 1975," *African Studies Review*, vol. XXII, no. 1, April 1979, 109–125.
42. Prudence Woodford-Berger, "Women in Houses: The Organization of Residence and Work in Ghana," *Anthropologiska Studies*, No. 30–31, pp. 3–35.
43. J. Ofori-Atta, "Income Redistribution in Ghana: A Study of Rural Development Strategies," *Ghana Social Science Journal*, #5, May 1978. pp. 1–25.
44. Merrick Posnansky, "The Ghanaian Drought of 1982–3: The Village Perspective," n.d.
45. "Modern Attitudes toward Matrilineal Inheritance: A Survey in a Kumasi Suburb—New Tafo." Long Essay by Patrick Kofi Aboagye, Department of Sociology, University of Ghana-Legon, 1979.
46. Agnes Klingshirn, *The Changing Position of Women in Ghana: A Study based on Empirical Research in Larteh*, Ph.D. thesis, University of Marburg, Lahr. 1971. Klingshirn argues that African women with viable alternatives would not choose to remain in agriculture because of the low economic returns (p. 166).
47. John Campbell, "Ideology and Politics in the Markets of Ghana," *Canadian Journal of African Studies*, vol. 19, no. 2, 1985, 427.
48. Clare Robertson, *Sharing the Same Bowl: A Socioeconomic History of Women and Class in Accra, Ghana.* Bloomington: Indiana University Press. 1984, 75–122. See also Robertson, 1985, "Response to John Campbell," in Debates and Commentary, *Canadian Journal of African Studies*, vol. 19, no. 2, pp. 431–2.
49. Margaret Peil, "Female Roles in West African Towns," in J. Goody (ed.), *Changing Social Structure in Ghana: Essays in Comparative Sociology of a New State and an Old Tradition.* London: International African Institute. 1975: 75. Also Deborah Pellow, "Work and Autonomy: Women in Accra," Library of Congress, Africana File, 1977.
50. Note that the pattern for Ga women traders (who are traditional residents of Accra) would have been somewhat different than the Akan, given Ga residence patterns of separate male-focused and female-focused households. Nevertheless, household composition or urban residents in Accra was likely to change considerably over both the male and female life cycle. See Leith Mullings, "Ga Women and Socio-Economic Change," in N. Hafkin and E. Bay (eds.), *African Women and Social Change*, Stanford, CA: Stanford University Press, 1976. Also Roger Sanjek, "Female and Male Domestic Cycles in Urban Africa: The Adabraka Case," in Christine Oppong (ed.), *Male and Female in West Africa.* Allen and Unwin, 1983.
51. William. F. Steele and C. Campbell, "Women's Employment and Development: A Conceptual Framework Applied to Ghana," in E. Bay (ed.), op. cit., 1985.
52. Audrey Smock, "The Impact of Modernization on Women's Position in the Family in Ghana," in Alice Schlegel (ed.), *Sexual Stratification: A Cross-Cultural View*, 192–213.
53. Christine Oppong, *Marriage Among a Matrilineal Elite*, Cambridge University Press, 1974, 41, 71, 83.
54. Clare Robertson, op. cit., 1985: 431.

55. Akwasi Arhin, "Prostitution Among Ghanaian Women in the Ivory Coast: A Case Study of Mantoukoua," Long Essay, Department of Sociology, University of Ghana-Legon. March 1981.
56. *Newsweek*. Feb.14, 1983.
57. Dorothy Dee Vallenga, "Attempts to Change the Marriage Laws in Ghana and the Ivory Coast," in Zolberg and Foster (eds.), *Ghana and the Ivory Coast*. 1971: 125–150.
58. Donald Rothchild, "Comparative Public Demand and Expectation Patterns: The Ghana Experience," *African Studies Review*, vol. XXII, no. 1, April 1979, 127–147.
59. Pellow and Chazan, 1986, 59.
60. Barbara Harrell-Bond and Ann Fraker, "Women and the 1979 Ghana Revolution," American Field Service Publication, #4, 1980.
61. Although Ghanaians had rather mixed feelings about the executions, the negative reactions from neighboring countries such as Nigeria were unequivocal. International organizations such as the IMP preferred not to deal with Ghana (Pellow and Chazan, 1986, 60–62).
62. Ministry of Information, "Ghana: 1979-1981," p. 60.
63. Ibid.
64. In the 1978 elections which brought Limann to power through the PNP, the Akan had backed the Popular Front Party (PFP), while the United National Convention (UNC) drew the Ga, Ewe and coastal votes.
65. Christine Oppong, Christine Okali and Beverly Houghton, "Women Power: Retrograde Steps in Ghana," *African Studies Review*, 18, no. 3, 1975.
66. Kathlene Staudt, "Women Farmers and Inequities in Agricultural Services," in Edna Bay (ed.), *Women and Work in Africa*, 225.–248.
67. K. Ewusi, "The Economy of Ghana: Recent Trends and Prospects for the Future." University of Ghana-Legon, 1981.
68. Pellow and Chazan, 1986, 63
69. *West Africa*, Nov. 2, 1981, 2608.
70. W. Ofuatey-Rudjue, "The Challenges of the Third Republic," address given before the People's Rights Protection Society, Accra, Ghana, 1981.
71. "Ghana Skeptical of New Regime's War on Corruption," *Los Angeles Times*, Jan. 24, 1982.
72. "Ghana's New Leader Pledges Sweeping Changes in Society," *The New York Times*, Jan. 6, 1982.
73. "New Rulers in Ghana Return to Leftist Path to Cure Nation's Ills," *The Washington Post*, Feb. 17, 1982.
74. "Ghana Restoring Its Ties to Libya," *The New York Times*, Jan. 12, 1982.
75. "Ghana waits for a muddled idealist to show the way," *Financial Times*, Jan. 2, 1982.
76. "Ghana's Rawlings, 34, Is Admirer of Qaddafi," *The Washington Post*, Feb. 17, 1982.
77. *Washington Post*, Feb. 17, 1982.
78. "Ghana's Economy Sinks Into Quagmire as Rawlings Temporizes on Solutions," *The Wall Street Journal*, April 26, 1982.
79. G. Mikell, "Ghanaian Females, Rural Economy and National Stability," *African Studies Review*, vol. 29, #3, 1986.

80. Interview with R.K.M. Britwum, Director, Cocoa Services Division, 28th and 29th July, 1986. Interviews were conducted with National Mobilization Program officials, and the Mobisquad leaders in Sunyani, Brong-Ahafo during August 1986.
81. However, they mentioned an exceptional mobisquad in one village: it had 30 male members plus all their wives...at least 60 in number, therefore a perfectly balanced mobisquad.
82. Interview with R.K.M. Britwum, Director, Cocoa Services Division, Sunyani on July 28th and 29th, 1986.
83. "Women Want More Control," *West Africa*, August 1985.
84. *Ghana: Policies and Programs for Adjustment*, World Bank Country Study, 1984, Washington.
85. Quote from Kwesi Botchwey, in George Packer's article, "Mirror Images of Ghana and Togo," *The Nation*, March 8, 1986.
86. Interviews with Professor Frances Dolphyne, Department of Linguistics, University of Ghana-Legon (July and August, 1986). She functioned as head of NCWD until its structural revisions by the PNDC in 1986.
87. Although the government agreed to buy back many items at control prices, these were lower than what traders had originally paid, so many defiantly dumped flour and sugar in the street and poured water over it, rather than sell it to GNTC at considerable loss.
88. Interview with Mrs. Yaa Anima Tufour, Brong-Ahafo Regional Director, Women in Development Office, Regional Administrative Complex, Sunyani, July 28, 1986.
89. In the Volta Region, there is an experiment with cooperative gari-processing which has drawn a fairly positive response. in this area, women claimed to be unable to participate unless husbands were involved as well. This and other experiences have led to attempts to transform the project from a licensed cooperative to a group-owned facility which individual members utilize at a nominal rate and which outsiders pay a more substantial fee to use.
90. "Veterans' Wives Set Up Gari Factory," *Ghanaian Times*, August 6, 1986; "Prampram Women's Mill Commissioned," *Ghanaian Times*, August 4, 1986; "Upper Region Women to Launch Literacy Drive," *Ghanaian Times*, July 21, 1986; "Anfoeta Dec. 31, "Women Grow Cassava, Beans," *Ghanaian Times*. July 17, 1986.
91. "Koforidua Fishwives To Be Banned, if...", *Ghanaian Times*, July 4, 1986; "She Heads the District," *People's Daily Graphic*, June 26, 1986.
92. "Cadres told to include women in their activities," *Ghanaian Times*.
93. However, at a five-day workshop of the international bureau of the National Council on Women and Development, which was hosted by the Ghana NCWD, the bureau reports stressed the need for a national machinery to coordinate women's programs and produce an internal development plan, so that "unstable political forces and change" cannot intervene. Such comments seemed to imply that Ghana might be reassessing its evaluation of NCWD, and might want to retain it. Later government comments reinforced this position. "Women's Bureau Plan for the Future," *Peoples' Daily Graphic*, July 17, 1986.
94. "Comment: In the Interest of Women," *People's Daily Graphic*, July 11, 1986, p. 2.

9

Cocoa and Chaos: Global, National and Local Relations

The role of cocoa in the transformation of the societies of Ghana is a disturbing example of the difficulties of modern socio-cultural change. Surpassing gold as the resource that made the Gold Coast valuable to the British Crown, cocoa was later viewed by the leaders of independent Ghana as providing the engine for national development and a weapon in the liberation of Africa from European rule. Instead, cocoa turned out to be an important factor in the chaos that was to overcome the peoples of Ghana.

What this study of cocoa and chaos in Ghana demonstrates is that fixed conceptions of how western capitalist institutions and processes should operate often flounder on the shoals of national and local realities. Often ignored is that the Portuguese, Dutch, Danish, French and British who established early trading and colonial relations with the Gold Coast were continually forced to reassess and adjust to local socio-economic conditions. Often when these strangers accepted local realities, they reified them, thus misinterpreting local socio-cultural systems and losing track of their adaptive ability. The reification of the chieftaincy, of traditional patron-client relations, and of lineage and male-female relations are but a few examples. However, when there was an attempt to introduce or shape capitalist relations based on western notions of appropriate social processes, disjuncture often resulted.

Strangers were not the only ones to make such mistakes. Enthusiastic Gold Coast elites who returned home after acquiring educations in Britain, France or the United States were occasionally guilty of reification. These "returnee" intellectuals (as well as home-grown ones), entrepreneurs and politicians often had to be systematically reeducated before they were capable of really addressing local needs. Those among them fortunate enough to belong to strata or classes whose positions gave them insights into indigenous initiatives could become positive influences in social change. They often contributed insights into how global economic and political challenges could be held at bay by the force of local initiatives, and they could spearhead new phases in African nationalist development. Nkrumah's identity as an Nzima meant that other ethnic groups did not view him with the skepticism that they would have reserved for an Akan, and his adamant anti-colonial and Pan-African stance permitted him to play a creative role in the Gold Coast nationalist movement. Nevertheless, his lengthy absence from Ghana and his education abroad blinded him to some of the economic contradictions within Ghana, and helped bring about the very chaos he would have wished to avoid. Having neither witnessed nor sufficiently understood the struggle for non-manipulative representation by chiefs within the colonial context, the impact of cocoa on indigenous customs, or the struggle of rural folk against the European cocoa-buying monopolies in the 1930s, some of his officials often had difficulty giving adequate interpretations to local realities.

It was easy for both colonial rulers and nationalist leaders who valued cocoa production to underestimate the extent to which rural folk were capable of reacting against the exploitative economic and political relations in which they had historically been involved. When the British spoke of moving the Gold Coast towards democracy, they obviously underestimated the uneven development of the country and hoped for a gradual process by which educated and enlightened urbanites would convince the nation of the viability of a western parliamentary system. For ordinary rural people, however, democratic participation was measured as much by the role of commoner leaders as it was by the spread of economic well-being among the general populace. This fact only occasionally penetrated British consciousness, usually when mass disturbance and rioting disrupted the normal flow of life, as in 1948. It was only at these high points of crisis that they were grudgingly willing to work for policy reforms that reduced the inequalities between segments of the Gold Coast population—ethnic and racial, rural (cocoa-producing) and urban, civil servant and laborer. However, this consciousness was seldom enduring. It has also been difficult for modern Ghanaian leaders to reconcile the initial public enthusiasm for "democracy" with the fact that the public was intolerant of the disequilibrium between economic and political sectors in those societies. They have failed to understand the depths of dissatisfaction with the contrasts between political promises and economic realities, and this has proved the Waterloo of many Ghanaian politicians.

Developments in Ghana have finally reached a point where continuing radical disparities between sectors, particularly those which favor urban and national constituents at the expense of rural people, have repercussions which immobilize the entire state structure. In the 1970s, the culmination of historically unequal rural-national relations was the virtual abandonment of the cocoa industry by Ghanaian farmers. Now, for the first time, leaders such as Rawlings have no choice but to attempt to devise national policies which address the disparity, and which bring the nation back from the brink of economic chaos.

Rural-National Stratification and Integration

There is no doubt that twentieth-century cocoa production helped to create the most fundamental divisions ever experienced by the political economies and the populace in the Gold Coast (Ghana) forest area. With respect to the problem of political economies, if we consider the entire period between the 1800s and the demise of those governments which succeeded Nkrumah in the 1970s, it is clear that these were being largely modified during this early period. Weberian notions of "patrimonial" as well as "feudal" sentiments[1] were readily identified within nineteenth century Ashanti. There were, for example, extreme differences in social status, economic wealth, and political participation, but these were substantially modified by the overwhelming and necessary emphasis upon personal allegiance and overlordship. People's abilities to acquire the necessities for survival and economic productivity depended upon recognition of the traditional "rights in persons" which Ashanti superiors acquired over subordinates. On the other hand, the drafting of men into the *asafo* units to which they had both affiliational loyalties and military responsibilities was a double-edged sword. Although *asafo* recruitment often provided elites with a means of acculturating and pacifying the foreign or unfree while they fought on behalf of the nation, there was the danger of increased social consciousness among these *nkwankwaa*. However, during the transitional phase in the late nineteenth century, the dependency which had cloaked unequal economic relations and prevented much overt reaction to real social and economic divisions within society was being cast aside.

Perhaps the major difference between the old and new divisions in Gold Coast societies developed during the cocoa phase, which gave people additional economic autonomy and freed them from numerous former dependencies. Cocoa created new familial and global dependencies, to be sure; but for the first time many exploitative relationships—urban/rural, ethnic, elite/commoner, and gender—lost their traditional support and took new shapes within colonial and post-colonial contexts. Nevertheless, the Durkheimian contrast between primarily agrarian, cohesive, superficially stratified and communally-focused traditional societies on the one hand, and the contemporary modernizing societies fraught with class, ethnic and geographical conflicts on the other, is a dichotomy difficult to sustain when examined in the light of detailed African sociological and historical facts.[2]

Neither in the 1600s, when the disparate clan-based Akan societies were expanding across the forest area,[3] nor in the 1700s and 1800s when the preeminence of Kumasi provided the coercive force for unification,[4] was there ever the "collective consciousness"[5] approximating an indigenous "nationalism" described by Durkheim for early traditional societies. Despite the Ashanti ideological emphasis on assimilation, far too many external and internal tensions existed to allow for cohesion.[6] The social divisions were often glaring. The bulk of the unfree or servile groups were concentrated in rural areas where they performed agricultural work on plantations owned by the aristocracy and elite, in order to produce the cassava, maize, guinea-corn and yams needed by town dwellers.[7] Thus, the division between rural inhabitants and those in towns always existed in Ashanti history, culminating in stigmatization of the rural population such as described by Arhin.[8] Much as local leaders attempted to respond to rural dissatisfaction by strengthening organizational bases for political representation (such as the *asafuakye* positions), these attempts were perceived by the aristocracy and elite as detrimental to the prerogatives of royals to demand allegiance and service from the people. Rural people's initiatives were capable of challenging the premises by which they were controlled.

Historical perspective becomes all-important for an understanding of the intra-societal reactions to changing social stratification and national integration due to economic factors. From the Asantehene's viewpoint, greater control over the component strata of Ashanti society was essential, indeed functional, if Muslim traders, aggressive European merchants and wealthy cocoa farmers were to be held at bay. If one described the results in Weberian terms, one could say that the Ashanti bureaucracy emerged by the 1700s in order to separate the new, appointive bureaucratic offices from the jural control of traditional lineage groups. Thus the building of a centralized bureaucracy, based as it was on the religious legitimacy as well as political power of the Asantehene, meant that Ashanti bureaucrats now derived their authority from the center. Nevertheless, traditional authority was not destroyed; it was supplemented by the legal authority of the state and the administrative functions which officeholders performed. Bureaucrats now exercised new controls over rural populations, and inadvertently became the foci of additional tensions between social strata. Occupants of bureaucratic positions grew wealthy from the stipends or booty they received and, as patrons, they enlarged the size of their free and servile client pool. In many areas, bureaucratic exploitation of rural folk stimulated rural dispersions, and where that was impossible, rural resistance.

Accompanying these bureaucratic tensions within Ashanti were other problems generated by the changing nature of socio-economic and/or market forces between the mid-1600s and the mid-1900s. Cocoa was simply the latest and most powerful resource to figure into these increasingly capitalistic relationships. Moreover, cocoa transformed them in ways that earlier resources such as gold, oil palm and rubber had not. Ashanti political centralization had brought a shift from dispersed elite control over rural labor and resources, to the superior claims of royals to surplus or tribute generated by local and regional resources. Imported western commodities and coastal wage employment, along with the growing desire of chiefs, bureaucrats and *sikafo* to accumulate wealth, triggered new aspirations for pure money and a market economy unfettered by traditional feudal relations. Gold, which had been held mainly under royal control, became a point of contention in the late 1800s. Wealthy persons intrigued to move it from the royal into the public arena, where they could use it for exchange and investment, as much as for a standard of value. However, by attempting to retain traditional economic relations and prevent the "rationalization" of the emerging capitalist economy, the Ashanti state unwittingly created the conditions for the alignment of its bureaucrats and *sikafo* with the colonial economy. The successful extension of colonial control over Ashanti in 1896 swept away much of the former elite control over persons and their products (slavery, pawning, etc.), and paved the way for the blossoming of the cocoa economy.

One aspect of the relations of production which had not been fundamentally altered before the cocoa period was usufruct in land. Although chiefs had come into local control of land, land relations had not been monetarized in most Gold Coast communities prior to 1900. Indeed, in the wake of the excitement over acquiring mining concessions, the early educated African elite had waged a battle to prevent abusive control of land by chiefs, or its transfer to government control.[9] Again, while there had been a thriving "market in towns and villages"[10] in the eighteenth and nineteenth centuries, these transactions were among the aristocracy, with profits ultimately going to the Asantehene as "owner of the land." What was more important for the aristocrats than the actual land, was the rights of control over producers who lived there. For ordinary folk, usufruct rights to land were vested in their "jural" lineage membership, and personal access to land did not really emerge as an issue till the rubber exporting period of the 1880s and 1890s. At that time, land access was easily handled by rental fees imposed by chiefs on entrepreneurs who operated on public lands.

It was the spread of the cocoa industry during the 1900s, involving as it did most of the southern rural public in producer, transporter or marketeer relations of production, that stimulated interest in private, as opposed to corporate, ownership of land. Nevertheless, whether operating under private land rights or lineage-based corporate land rights, the cocoa industry stimulated concern over private control of the "farm" and its product, as distinct from the land. The product of the farm could be alienated, and its owner made wealthy or reduced to poverty. Stratification, then, was not solely tied to land control, but was also affected by the size of familial and patrimonial labor forces, as well as positions in the old traditional status hierarchy. People in need of money often pledged their farms in order to maintain their status positions. Chiefs, although affected in this way, were less prone to pledging farms, and so retained political and affective control over their citizens, thereby enhancing their economic potential. This power was clearly seen in the role which chiefs played during the "cocoa hold-ups" of the 1930s. Nevertheless, the global capitalist depression combined with these new types of control over property and labor engendered new patterns of rural stratification. Rural producers were increasingly divided from those entrepreneurs more deeply entrenched in regional, national and global economic relations.

At virtually no point have Ashanti and Gold Coast identities and political-economic and cultural features developed in isolation from broader and ultimately global processes. Long before European capitalist penetration, the integration of indigenous societies into long-distance trade was generating economic interdependence and tensions within local African societies. Between the mid-1600s and the mid-1800s, Ashanti leaders of the forest zone deliberately kept at bay the Muslim traders and clerics with whom they had important economic and cultural relations, thus preventing them from threatening the dynamic growth of their state. Only in the peripheral Gyaman-Banda areas was there an early amalgamation of indigenous populations, Akan newcomers, and Muslim traders.[11] In much the same way (but with greater difficulty) did the Ashanti attempt to hold the Portuguese, Dutch and British to the coastal areas, using intermediaries to establish needed trade and political relations. Despite preventive measures, it was the economic growth after 1800 which brought with it the increasing transformation of rural populations, as well as increasing social integration (of Muslims and Europeans) and stratification (of producers from entrepreneurs). The pressures were often greatest on the peripheries of the Ashanti state, where economic and political exploitation in the interest of Kumasi was greatest, and where people became disgruntled. Therefore, it is not surprising that the political and military activities necessary to control the rebellion in the periphery repeatedly cost the Ashanti dearly. During each historical period, pressures from the outside triggered a developmental transformation in both the polity and economy of Ashanti and the Gold Coast. But, it was the post-World War II pressures—the rise of nationalism, the chaos in cocoa-producing areas, and the recent rural disengagement—that dramatically affected the lives of contemporary Ghanaians.

From a theoretical perspective, the divergence between rural interests and urban/national interests is an old problem which bedevils both archaic and modern states, whether western or African. It is possible to describe rural areas and their populations in an Ibn Khaldunian or Gluckmanian, cyclical fashion. Frontier or rural dissenting elements seek to escape the tyranny of the emerging or established state at "time-point one," and then become transformed into that irrational, disengaged but essential labor force whose products bolster the stability of the state at "time-point two."[12] However, at "time-point three," rural elements at the dynamic peripheries, weary of exploitation by the center, exhibit the creative energy necessary to break out of restraining central social, cultural and productive relations. This Ibn Khaldunian/Gluckmanian model, while instructive, fails to come to grips with the fact that the constellation of social groups in rural areas are also a reflection of changing socio-economic processes throughout the entire society. Therefore, the three sequential processes outlined above could take place at one and the same time, at disparate parts of social systems. As the developments within the cocoa industry in Ashanti indicate, the culmination of contradictions contained in rural relations may have demanded a reordering of all significant social relations—whether local, national or global; both political and economic.

Class-Stratum Conflicts: Chiefs, Politicians and Farmers

Cocoa was responsible for creating conditions under which a significant part of the traditional legitimacy supporting Ghanaian chieftaincy was replaced by the legitimacy of wealth, modern education and political office. While this was not the first such transformation of the political order, it was the first in which the rural public rather than aristocrats and elites played the decisive roles. The bureaucrats and chiefs of the eighteenth and nineteenth centuries relied upon the Asantehene for their legitimacy. In contrast, early twentieth century chiefs and queen mothers had constituents who insisted upon judgments in the public interest. There was no inclination to remove the institution of chieftaincy, or to strip it of authority, but merely to make it more responsive. The public now possessed a degree of power largely unknown in earlier times; therefore, they expected to participate more fully in the naming of chiefs and people to fill public positions. This expectation in itself was not revolutionary, but it was combined with a view of rural towns as prosperous places filled with farmers who now paid taxes out of profits from cocoa, and who therefore were equal to any other citizen—royal or otherwise.

Throughout the 1920s and 1930s in Brong and Ahafo areas, chiefs and queen mothers faced vocal factions which refused to allow the enstoolment of candidates whose views were unacceptable. Other conflicts were created as people insisted upon payment for services which earlier they would have felt duty-bound to perform for their chief. These developments also represented a disjuncture and a challenge to colonial/national relations, since local representation through the vulnerable Joint Provincial Council of Chiefs marked their only means of political participation.[13] This challenge forced the chieftaincy to new levels of literacy, modernity, and political aggressiveness in order to continue playing their roles as representatives of their changing traditional constituencies. This new consciousness of the role of chiefs was certainly evident in the defense of chiefs made by Nana Afori-Atta in the 1920s and in the response of chiefs during the cocoa hold-ups of 1938.[14]

Initially, it was not militancy or political consciousness which accounted for the mounting peasant pressures on the chieftaincy. Rather, rural people applied pressure as soon as they became more conscious of structural resistance to their economic needs, and as their desires for individual upward mobility increased. Only when these two aspirations were stifled did the pressures seem to lead to the actual challenge of the office and of chieftaincy.

As it turned out, the new mobile segments—such as Gold Coast cooperative farmers—were more interested in obtaining a fair price for their products and stymieing European monopoly than in challenging representation through chiefs. Therefore, in response to the booming post-war economy, Gold Coast peasants made economic demands just as other groups did, and logically chose leaders with capitalist profit-making capabilities. It is worthy of note that Brong cocoa farmers first attempted to include the chief in their cooperative organizations, but pulled away as chiefs tried to control these organizations, thereby blocking the development of grass roots initiative. Nevertheless. it was the attempt of chiefs to prevent well-known commoner cocoa farmers and educated offspring of cocoa farmers from being chosen as representatives to town councils, along with the attempts to discourage a growing local "Brong" identity that alienated people from the institution of chieftaincy and weakened the ties between chiefs and the state. Peasants made increasingly sophisticated political demands as they perceived the links between nationalism and economic resources. Gold Coast peasants were, therefore, not cut from a more radical piece of cloth than that which fashioned the peasantries of Latin America, the Caribbean or Europe.[15] Rather, Gold Coast cocoa farmers were pulled, by nature of the relationships surrounding the crop which they produced, into the midst of the chaotic stratification and political consciousness generated by single-crop production in a capitalist economy.

That cocoa producers were destined to clash with almost each successive head of state in independent Ghana should have been anticipated. The pattern was set long before independence, as cocoa farmers' organizations struggled to organize in the central and eastern areas; as cocoa middlemen operated as agents of the European cocoa monopolies in the 1920s; and farmers engaged in the "hold-ups" and boycotts of the 1930s. The power of the producers' organizations was recognized by Nkrumah for what it was: a double-edged sword which could be as much a major political asset as it could be an economic and political liability. The key, he thought, lay in undercutting the capitalist of the peasantry, and replacing it with a socialist and pan-Africanist one; and in integrating peasants into an all-encompassing party-controlled (UGFCC) structure within which they would gain a sense of national political priorities. But Nkrumah misunderstood the extent to which peasants were rooted in the traditional order despite their capitalist aspirations. To rural folk, control over their land, their produce, and their home towns became as significant a reflection of local citizenship as their feeling that the chief should reflect their local political reality. To a citizen farmer, the mark of success was the ability to construct a building or otherwise make an investment or contribution to his village or town of origin. Nkrumah could tamper with the institution of chieftaincy by hierarchical promotions and demotions without affecting local political loyalties and legitimacy; but to place national CPP leaders above local chiefs and in many cases to preempt the local decision-making prerogatives of local chiefs and farmers was a serious affront.

Post-Nkrumah leaders appear to have been more careful in the methods they used to penetrate the local levels of the political system. Few attempted the kind of comprehensive penetration which Nkrumah used to control the political economy of the country. Nevertheless, most later heads of state continued to misjudge the extent to which the welfare and autonomy of rural producers was a prerequisite for national political cooperation. As the pace of military coups and civilian changes of governments increased, chiefs had less ability to make their voices heard above the din. The more cynical chiefs sided with various parties as a means of obtaining local payoffs. Nevertheless, the rural wish was not stifled since farmers have effectively manipulated their single guaranteed means of representation—their ability to produce, or not produce, cocoa.

Political Legitimacy, Ethnicity and Coups

The period of greatest political consensus in the Gold Coast, and therefore greatest political legitimacy entrusted to the state, came in the early 1950s as Ghanaians elected Nkrumah and the CPP to head the drive for independence. However, economic, regional, ethnic and ideological conflicts rapidly erupted, fragmenting political loyalties. While many of these conflicts were based on social divisions of the past, they were energized by modern stratification patterns and generally crystallized around the split between the cocoa vs. non-cocoa constituencies in the Gold Coast. To the extent that historical political control in this area lay in the Ashanti-dominated forest zone, one overwhelming gauge of political legitimacy was the extent to which Nkrumah could transcend the obligations to leaders in the cocoa belt of the forest zone. If we view Nkrumah's promises to the Brongs against the backdrop of Ashanti opposition to unitary independence, and the threat this posed to the entire nation, then it becomes clear that Nkrumah did effectively transcend economic and ethnic obligations. By this means, Nkrumah managed to claim the lion's share of "legitimate authority," a feat which allowed him to rule Ghana.[16] Most Ghanaians credited Nkrumah with building the most non-ethnic-conscious institutions and bureaucracies to exist in the post-colonial period. Nevertheless, Nkrumah's concern about overcoming neo-colonialism and utilizing Ghanaian assets to build a strong Africa exacerbated the domestic political problems of the CPP. As Nkrumah's economic and political policies were challenged by the elite after independence, and as his willingness to repress mass dissent grew, his legitimacy steadily decreased.[17] Ironically, it was an external factor—the manipulation and crash of the international price of cocoa—that occasioned the unrest which precipitated the coup that brought Nkrumah down.

The question remains as to what bound the Ghanaian body politic together prior to 1966, and what was responsible for the deterioration of the entire political structure in the period that followed. Historically, Ashanti domination was the force which unified the forest and coastal zone prior to British control, and this rose and fell in response to fluctuations in local aggressiveness and weaponry. First gold, and then cocoa figured prominently in the British fight to preserve their colonial control over the Gold Coast; it was the southern forest economy which provided the economic glue which held the Gold Coast together in the twentieth century. In the immediate post-World War II period colonial domination, as well as bureaucratic control, maintained the status quo, but these also generated reactions which unified nationalists in their quest for independence. Perhaps the major element of change was the articulation of interests by those disparate socio-economic strata which had developed in response to colonial needs, but which colonial power had formerly kept submerged.

The presence of deeply rooted socio-economic conflicts, often ethnic in origin, have sometimes contributed to coups in Africa. The historical and colonial experiences which resulted in the military being the primary source of upward mobility for those who in the past had been marginal made the coup one of redressing grievances.[18] Using the Gold Coast military as an example, we know that coastal men and northerners or Muslims predominated in the Gold Coast army until World War II. It is noteworthy that these groups generally came from areas which had been marginal to the prosperity generated by the cocoa economy. Yet ethnic or regional tensions in the military were not significant. The military only became occupationally and sentimentally important during the First

World War, when the exigencies of the conflict necessitated British liberalization so that even Ashanti men were allowed to enlist. Nevertheless, for the most part local or ethnic interests remained muted. These would only emerge in open stratum or class conflict in the period surrounding and following independence when there was competition between broader political constituencies. While relatively quiescent immediately after independence, such factionalism increased during the economic turbulence of the post-Nkrumah period. In the 1960s and 1970s those military cadres from marginal areas (Ewe, Northern) were often disgruntled by their relative lack of mobility or their exclusion from the political center.

True, some military officers from these groups had steadily risen from marginality to greater educational or technical competence, but they did not yet feel sufficiently rewarded for their efforts. Resentment felt by Ewe and Volta area officers increased, given the alleged "Ashanti favoritism" accompanying the Busia regime; it smoldered during the Acheampong period, and burst into the open again after the "northern backlash" which brought Limann to power. Nevertheless, the ethnic tensions within Ghana's military were low in comparison to places like Nigeria or Uganda.[19] The military provided only one example of political fragmentation; exaggerated regionalism and party competition were the major manifestations. That this political fragmentation rapidly disintegrated into a succession of coups and coercive takeovers of government has caused great concern.

Was it sheer political distortion which fed coups, or was it distortion in the post-colonial political economy which explains the resulting trauma? Political scientists tell us that in the absence of those stable, structural elements which mark the legitimacy of political relationships, a state relies upon coercion and force to maintain social relations.[20] After 1966, the military in Ghana seized authority by possession and control over the means of force; but with the exception of the early phases of the NLC coup and those coups engineered by Rawlings's forces, the military seldom succeeded in obtaining popular approval. In Ghana, one of the reasons was the military's few traditional antecedents. Despite male recruitment into the military within pre-colonial Ashanti, and that many political leaders in the Ashanti state did emerge from the army, these persons derived their legitimacy from the religious authority of the Asantehene and from the civilian bureaucracy. The Ashanti problem with the *Asafuakye* and with the *Nkwankwaahene*[21] for example, was how to keep the temporary military authority from being transformed into persisting political influence. It was the shifting political economy of late nineteenth to early twentieth century society which provided the context for this threatened political transformation of the *nkwankwaa*.

It is the collective memory of this period that has led many contemporary

Ghanaians to suggest that the use of the military to oust unpopular leaders is not alien to their society. Owusu, for example, has argued that "political behavior in Africa...remains predominantly rooted in customary law,"[22] and that the modern Ghanaian coup does not represent a departure from this. He is essentially correct, since traditionally there were occasions (such as the Ashanti New Year)[23] when a leader could be challenged, insulted, and informed of his transgressions without the complainer being subject to reprisals. People could also abandon a leader who abused power, and leaders feared becoming "chiefs without people." One notes that most modern actions for destoolments and coups have been accompanied by a reaffirmation of the principles of traditional leadership and public office.[24] In fact, during the 1920s, destoolments instituted against unpopular chiefs who were colonial supporters were often based on stereotypical documented actions which were "unbefitting a chief." Yet it should be noted that even in the 1920s the majority of actions were stimulated by economic abuses which chiefs perpetrated, and to which the populace was powerless to respond except by the withdrawal of legitimacy from the chiefs. The problem is whether the withdrawal of legitimacy from rulers is the same as traditional sanctions. In contemporary Ghana, self-selected military personnel who operate within crisis situations generated by the machinations of the political economy assert that they have the right to change the government. One is left with the impression that while the military coups may be a reassertion of mass rights to confer political legitimacy, many Ghanaians are clearly tired of these cyclical and violent military seizures of the political institutions.

In the face of this feeling, it does appear true that military coups have been triggered by drastic economic downswings in the performance of the primarily cocoa-based Ghanaian economy. In 1966, the NLC understood that its ability to govern even temporarily was dependent upon the relief which it could offer to cocoa farmers, and through them to the rest of the economy. Consequently, producer prices for cocoa rose slowly but consistently. Subsequent leaders have grappled with the same problem although, as cocoa production declined, their attention turned to manipulation of urban wages, internal food production, and limits on imports as a means of stymieing coups. Nevertheless, coups persisted, and their repetitiveness in Ghana has indeed become a cause for alarm. People have asked whether imitation of previous military action within the country or in other African countries, or indeed in Latin American countries, explain the recurring phenomena. The Ghanaian situation seems to suggest that once the process of military intervention was begun, it did offer a previously unavailable means of bringing disjointed social relations back into alignment. However, both the public and the military seem to tire of the lapse of democratic participation in the political process. The fact that on several occasions the military voluntarily withdrew and restored civilian rule suggests that even the military did not consider itself either monolithic or omnipotent.[25] Internally, the military was also beset by many of the economic, ethnic and class conflicts which plagued the rest of the society, and much of this is still reflected in the split between junior and senior officers which continues to affect Rawlings's government.

Tensions within the military, as among other groups in Ghanaian society, are ultimately linked to the problem of political legitimacy. Akan control over the cocoa crop, and previous Ashanti attempts to use this to secure national political control, stimulated resentment between regions and constituencies. Increasingly, after 1957, Ashanti communities viewed themselves as victimized, unfairly eliminated from power positions within government; Ewe or northern communities saw themselves as having to be ever-vigilant to ensure that Ashanti political and economic domination did not again occur. However, the fact is that strong political communities are located within the cocoa belt and politicians ignore them at their own peril. Severe contradictions ensue when national politicians make overtures to the rural constituents, soliciting their votes and promising economic policy changes, while attempting to exclude traditional leaders, local elites and entrepreneurs viewed as threatening. As coups occurred, the loci of tensions shift in correspondence to the particular ethnic groups at the center of power, and resentment builds up about nepotism and economic favoritism which goes to that particular region. Thus, under Limann, the resentment towards the north grew as the rice economy prospered and cocoa declined. Now, under Rawlings, resentment against the Ewes is increasing.

The irony is that effective political control necessitates broad support and policies divorced from ethnic, regional or economic favoritism. Rawlings's awareness of corruption and nepotism in previous governments has encouraged him to surround himself with an ethnically diverse group within the PNDC government. The previous Ashanti versus Brong disputes over land, allegiance and tribute have receded into the background as the power of Ashanti chiefs declined in direct proportion to the declining economic value of cocoa. Undeniably, the recruitment of government officials from among the Ga, Adangbe and Ewe led many to accuse Rawlings of beginning a pattern of ethnic favoritism. This initially was a difficult charge to substantiate, given the care with which Rawlings had courted various ethnic constituencies and the attention he has paid to a broad rural development policy. On a personal level, Rawlings attempted to build ethnic good will by emphasizing the irrelevance of ethnicity in constructing a strong Ghana. His Ashanti wife has been a most effective ambassador for him, and in speaking before groups she has emphasized his refusal to fall back on "ethnic strategies," as previous leaders have done. Nevertheless, Rawlings's inter-ethnic domestic situation is a positive factor when he has to deal with Ashanti constituents. More recently, problems occurred as corruption or ethnic coup plots required tribunal actions and executions. Increasingly, Rawlings's appointees to replace those removed from office were fellow Ewes whom he felt he could trust. Now it seems that the political pot is being stirred, and there is the chance that ethnic hostilities may rise to the surface.

There is no doubt that while attempting the social, ethnic and economic unification of the country, the Rawlings military government has tried to alter the basis of its original mandate from the Ghanaian people. True, it came to power through military force with a goal of achieving moral government. However, along the way it has indicated that it is convinced that the country is not yet ready for civilian rule, and that a return to civilian government would allow a collapse into corruption as has occurred several times in the past. Branding the multi-party system a "western conception" which simply "institutionalized opposition," the PNDC claims to be seeking a national consensus which leads to a "truly democratic system."[26]

Although many of the PNDC's actions to guarantee political stability have alienated sectors of its original constituency, the PNDC has persistently pursued a number of routes by which it may become institutionalized.[27] In addition to its 1983–1984 economic reforms raising wages, instituting price controls, and increasing agricultural producer prices, the Rawlings government has attempted the transformation of militant organizations such as the People's Defense Committees and the Workers' Defense Committees. Rawlings has changed these organizations into Committees in Defense of the Revolution (CDRs); he has invited highly placed lawyers, professionals and women's representatives to become members of the Cabinet and the PNDC, and he has tried to transform the December 31st Women's Movement into an organization supportive of the government. The bid for rural grass roots support has included overtures to local chiefs, the Asantehene and the clergy, as well as the recruitment of these persons into regional advisory committees. In attempting to broaden the base of support, Rawlings and the PNDC hope eventually to receive a mandate quite different from that of seizing power. As of now, these mechanisms to achieve legitimacy have been viewed cynically, and have not yet been particularly effective.[28] Political legitimacy could prove quite difficult for Rawlings to achieve.

Ghanaian history offers a lesson to those who seek to understand the reasons for political upheaval and the military coup. The Ghanaian populace continually seem to be groping toward economic rationality and growth before conceding legitimacy to the state. Unbridled political power—particularly when used in its raw form, as military or police coercion—alienates the populace and triggers a counter-movement. But the Ghanaian public has also become more cynical about change which comes about through force, and which political leaders later seek to legitimize. This was true in pre-colonial Ashanti, and remains true of contemporary Ghana. Although Rawlings appears to be moving toward economic stability, there remains one major question with which successive Ghana governments appear to have difficulty: What kind of long-term relationship should be built between the rural sector and the state, in order to maintain a political economy within which legitimate dialogue and negotiation occur between the various interest groups making up the state?

Sexual Complementarity and Economic Well-Being

For a number of historical, economic, social and political reasons, the role of women in many societies of Ghana has been an important one. This gender dimension, though often submerged in the analysis of many social processes, cannot be ignored in Ghana, because of an important matrilineal dimension in cocoa production. Matriliny was always a factor in Ashanti, conjugal relations, reproduction and production. The Ashanti forest zone always required a great deal of agricultural labor, and this became even more true when British conquest encouraged the development of western market relations. Concern with polygyny and the sexual division of labor became exaggerated in the opening years of the cocoa economy, and the question arose as to whether gender complementarity had changed to female inequality. These concerns declined somewhat with prosperity, rural wage-labor employment and then recession in the 1920s, but was heightened as economic contraction in a declining cocoa economy destroyed the possibilities of sufficient wage-labor employment. However, sexual complementarity vs. inequality in labor and in familial structures has relevance beyond the local domestic and familial contexts within which it is usually discussed. In the 1960s and 1970s, radical female inequality had repercussions on food and cocoa production, on the viability of rural communities, on massive emigration, and on social problems in urban communities. All of these necessitated policy intervention on the national level. The obvious question is the extent to which the cause of this sexual inequality, as opposed to complementarity, was due to the rigorous demands of the cocoa economy, or to inflexible indigenous kin structures.

The impact of capitalist economic relations and the other attributes of Western culture on rural matriliny shifted kin dynamics so that males increased control over the labor and property of females and their offspring, without a compensating shift in male responsibilities for these persons. Thus, private capitalistic relations were slowly altering traditional corporate matrilineal relationships. In conjunction with economic prosperity, husbands established conjugal households as a means of facilitating the development of their cocoa farms, but they also retained obligations to many matrilineal kin. These obligations limited the extent to which they could pass on cocoa property to sons and wives, since personal property was ultimately destined to become lineage property. Fraternal cohesion also increased as brothers passed on cocoa farms, as lineage property, from one to the other, with sisters seldom being included in this group. Even female-generated property often passed to males rather than to the daughters of these women. From the mid-1900s onward, the vulnerability of women and children within matrilineages increased and reached crisis proportions in the 1960s and 1970s as the cocoa economy declined.

The disability of women was clearly visible in the 1960s, given the rapid impoverishment of female cocoa farmers in contrast to male cocoa farmers. Many Ashanti women complained about the irresponsibility of husbands in caring for the conjugal family. As the legal expulsion orders and then recession removed the northern and Muslim immigrant rural wage-labor force, women's ability to maintain families largely depended on the extent to which they could replace migrant brothers and husbands as wage earners and work the remaining cocoa farms. But on a more personal level, the kinship trauma was equally seen in the increased fragility of Akan marriages. Partners usually remarried, but opted for low-status types of marriages that did not obligate their lineages should another divorce occur. Many Akan young men attempted to avoid marriage, since it was too expensive, unnecessary for female companionship, and generally a bother. Akan schoolgirls facing unwanted pregnancy risked abortion, rather than be tied down with children whom no one was able to support. Thus, the matricentric household within the male-controlled matrilineage became a common rural phenomenon in the 1970s. This problem has never been addressed by the national government and has scarcely been recognized, since there is an operating assumption that rural lineages continue to support their members, including dependent women and children.

This level of disorganization in sexual and familial relations has often been associated in the public mind with impoverished migrant populations in western urban areas, rather than with matrilineal populations in "traditional" areas. The stereotype was the shattered patriarchal family which Lewis identified in Latino urban areas,[29] or the matricentric family among impoverished urban U.S. blacks and hispanics,[30] In the western hemisphere, it was the destruction of the rural economy and resulting urban migration, or racism and male unemployment, which fed the cycle of economic desperation and familial disintegration which occurred. Despite Lewis's suggestions that we systematically investigate the economic factors in the social adaptation of the Latino poor, it was not until considerably later that scholars acknowledged that the fragility of the kin structures themselves was linked to social problems, and began to see the structural relations as adaptive responses.[31] Fortunately, few scholars have attempted to analyze changes in Ghanaian matrilineal family structure in terms of the western "pathology" models, but a number of younger Ghanaian authors have started to discuss the overt male-female friction as aspects of contemporary Ghanaian life.[32] Some of these persons question whether sexual and familial relations can be reconstructed in the face of the economic problems facing Ghanaian families.

The debate about whether Ghanaian matriliny could survive, given advancing capitalist relations, continues. Whereas Aberle and others felt that matrilineal systems were maladapted to modern economic change and destined to give way to patriliny, Douglas had argued that matrilineal structures can prosper in an expanding economy.[33] In Ghana, the problems facing matriliny escalated even at the "boom" phases of cocoa developments, although these became much more severe as the cocoa economy collapsed. Perhaps the issue is not simply whether the economy expands or contracts, but whether matriliny is a crucial component in the economy in that particular matrilineal area. In Ghana, export-oriented production of cocoa did challenge matrilineal cohesiveness. However, in parts of rural Zambia where education and not agricultural products provide the route to post-independence economic mobility, the matrilineal system is thriving as both mothers and fathers attempt to hang onto their matrilineages and receive the benefit of resources generated by educated lineage offspring. In contrast to the Ghanaian situation, the rural Zambian father also strives to remain within the conjugal orbit and prevent divorce, in order to be a beneficiary of familial resources. Nevertheless, there are contrasts even within a nation-state, and between different historical periods as well. In contemporary Lusaka, where the earlier colonial emphasis on employment in copper mining has been changed, both women and men received primary and secondary school educations which prepared them for clerical or other technical employment. Therefore, semi-educated or educated females from matrilineal groups migrate to seek employment in Lusaka. Here, tensions between the sexes have influenced lineage dynamics.[34] Males are opting to delay marriage or deny responsibility for children and, as the number of births outside marriage increase the female-headed household has become a reality which Zambian policy-makers have yet to confront. Matriliny definitely poses problems and faces challenges here.

The Rural Economy and State Policy in Sub-Saharan Countries

Finally, this study of cocoa and chaos in Ghana throws important light on the problem of rural economies and state policies in independent Africa. The condition of the Ghanaian economy at independence was similar to that in many other states—the country was highly dependent upon agricultural producers (and often monocrop production) to generate the resources necessary for national development. Despite efforts to create a state industrial sector with surplus drawn from agriculture, this development took place at the expense of the local, communal and private sectors. In addition, these initiatives foundered as the monocrop commodity fell prey to the real as well as engineered declines in commodity prices within the international marketplace. Post-Nkrumah leaders often labored under the conviction that lack of rural commitment to production was the problem, and cited as evidence the steadily increasing migration of rural folk to the cities. However, pleas for food production and diversification beyond cocoa production had only marginal success because of the lack of state supports such as price incentives, or subsidization of agricultural inputs and living wages for rural laborers. Producer prices for cocoa failed to keep pace with rising real prices. Moreover, available state subsidies and inputs were used to "buy off" the often volatile urban dwellers at the expense of the peasant group which produced most of the country's resources.

Here again, Ghana's dilemma with its political economy is similar to that faced by many African and other developing countries.[35] Urban populations doubled within the space of the twenty years from 1960 to 1980, yet food production had declined.[36] During this same time, drops in the international prices paid for export commodities triggered declines in the rural standard of living, which resulted in further decreases in export commodity production. Tanzania, Nigeria, Uganda, Malawi and Ghana all chose different political and economic routes, yet the results in terms of the standards of living of rural inhabitants have been woefully similar. This has led some analysts to suggest that neither free-market economies, mixed ones, nor socialist ones have made any difference for most post-colonial African countries. The issue of whether African countries must of necessity pursue a route to development which is different from that of the West is still not yet resolved. Nkrumah's, Nyerere's and Sekou-Toure's disparate approaches failed dismally, but the Ivory Coast appears to have been relatively successful using a free-market approach.[37] Some say that the greater level of export diversification within the Ivory Coast economy (with coffee as well as cocoa) may have given it greater flexibility than Ghana. Whatever else one might say about the Ivory Coast economy, Houphouet-Boigny never forgot that he emerged as a leader of an African agricultural movement. He has continued support for agriculture, and despite significant export price fluctuations and some problems over the past five years,[38] the so-called "Ivorian miracle" has maintained itself. Malawi, on the other hand, with a thriving free-market export sector based on a highly stratified smallholder peasantry, is plagued with high infant mortality, disease and starvation. Malawi's price for a successful free market appears to be degenerating peasant conditions.[39]

Two economists have led the debate about development in Africa: Samir

Amin and Eliot Berg. Amin has held that because of the relationship of dependency that exists between African economies and the capitalist global system, the capitalist route to African development is doomed to failure.[40] He believes that colonial extraction of surplus made it virtually impossible for African countries to engage in the kind of "primitive accumulation" which would have provided a secure base for capitalist development. By paying lower wages and prices for production to people in the periphery, western capitalists shifted the dynamic of development to the center.[41] Thus, rural production was continued, but it also rendered these countries vulnerable. According to Amin, African nations were powerless to prevent their own rural exploitation when involved in capitalist relations, and were handicapped because of inequality in global economic exchange. Finally, Amin implies that it was therefore impractical for African countries to engage in economic relations on a national basis, and that regional alliances for exchange and production should be the strategy for economic recuperation. His suggestion is that African countries should essentially "unplug" from the capitalist system; build their own economic community as well as capital; exchange goods through barter or currency agreements; and gradually build up technology appropriate to their own economic requirements and developmental levels. Reentry into relations with the capitalist world, when and if it should occur, would then be on a more equal basis. Amin's ideas are not unique, to be sure: Nkrumah was on record as an advocate of a West African economic community,[42] despite his willingness to have western participation in sectors of the Ghanaian economy. However, Amin's proposals go further in suggesting the severance of relations with Western economic institutions.

In contrast, Berg insists that the problems in African economies were linked to the weakness of their ties to the international export economy.[43] Recognizing the dependence of African economies on agriculture, Berg assesses the problems as cutting across several levels. At the grass roots level, many local producers of both export crops and food crops had reduced production in the 1960s and 1970s because they did not receive sufficient producer price incentives. This created a problem for the increasingly large urban population which faced high prices for the limited amount of food produced. At the national level, governments exacerbated the problem by overtaxing farmers in order to gain revenue for industrial development. This misuse of both capital and human resources is viewed by Berg as posing innumerable difficulties for the African economies. He recommends immediate increases in producer prices for all agricultural commodities, increased attention to agricultural research and crop development and greater provision of inputs to farmers. Berg believed that since governmental control of services and inputs had failed, a more competitive, free-market approach to supplying the needs of the agricultural sector was in order.

Both Amin's and Berg's approaches have been proven to be problematic. It has become quite clear since the 1970s that, while the African states have suffered from the strong links between their economies and the capitalist system, Amin nevertheless overestimated the ability of these states to achieve internal development through unplugging.[44] Tanzania's policies of *ujamaa* produced innumerable problems with ethnic/class stratification, rural production, village relocation, land relations and familial distortion.[45] Nyerere's subsequent decision to pursue a different route to development—one more closely integrated with such western economic institutions as the IMF—was met with local as well as global approval and, despite some problems, has led to optimism about development possibilities. In Ghana, both Acheampong during the SMC period, as well as Rawlings under the PNDC government, toyed with the notion of rejecting recommendations from the World Bank, IMF and other international economic agencies. However, these notions of going it alone, or "unplugging," generally triggered internal economic chaos and massive popular upheaval, as urban folk reacted to the scarcity of imported food and the skyrocketing prices of locally produced food. Food riots became so common in Ghana (as well as many other countries),[46] that the heads of state were forced to reconsider isolationist policies that required intense manipulation of the availability of local food and other commodities. That Rawlings eschewed the isolationist path was clearly seen during the drought of 1983, when he began to make overtures to international agencies. By 1984 he began serious dialogue with the World Bank and devalued his currency, thereby freeing the marketplace.[47] In general, these actions attracted capital investment in the Ghanaian economy, and alleviated the crisis of availability of goods in the marketplace. Consequently, inflation and the size of the black market sector have both decreased.

Berg's competitive, free-market approach to increasing export production has not yet yielded fruitful results. The Lagos Plan of Action (an economic development strategy of the African states),[48] while advocating increased agricultural production and exchange of commodities among African states, was quite critical of Berg's "export-led" development approach. The Africans insisted that, given the continent's environmental and fiscal difficulties and the need for crop diversification in many African countries, any development strategy which encouraged dependence on the one or two existing export crops would be dangerous. They felt that "to expand production of items whose relative price is falling, or whose demand is inelastic, is to cause even further deterioration of the terms of trade."[49] This has turned out to be all too true. Even a country such as Ivory Coast, which has long used an export crop-oriented strategy—becoming in the process the world's third largest coffee producer—now faces problems as falling commodity prices leave it unable to pay its debts.

Obviously, it is much more than simple participation in a free market which will encourage rural and national economic stability in African countries.

Nevertheless, it still remains unclear whether these free-market policies will be able to prevent a recurrence of economic decline, or have long-term salutary effects on Ghana's rural areas. Countries such as Ghana and Zambia, which have risked currency devaluations, cut the size of the civil service bureaucracy, and opened their markets to capital investment[50]—thereby often engendering popular dissatisfaction—may in the long run benefit from increased economic activity in rural areas. But such increases in food and commodity production often may not be sufficient to stop the economic decline, since global recession and depressed prices for commodities have often caused drops in Africa's export earnings.[51] Thus, in Ghana, food production was up and cocoa production had increased by June 1985, but international prices paid for cocoa weakened.[52] Likewise, Zambia has been forced to curb its drastic socio-economic reforms in order to ensure that its population can continue to survive.

Conclusions

There is a growing indication that despite the increases in food, cocoa, and other agricultural production, dependence upon external market institutions remain. Therefore, there are other policy decisions which the PNDC must make in order to have a lasting positive impact on the rural production sector. What appears to be needed are policies which explicitly recognize that rural vibrancy contributes to national stability, by (1) making it a national priority to decrease the disparity between rural and urban populations, and stem rural migration through voluntary measures; (2) allowing local agricultural organizations to address local socio-economic needs as well as facilitate national economic linkages; (3) establishing rural labor policies which encourage a sexually balanced rural labor force; and (4) encouraging diversity in the export-oriented crops produced, while increasing the reliance upon domestic rather than imported food supplies.

Although most previous Ghanaian governments have experienced the repercussions of rural imbalance, they have considered it sufficiently significant to work to eliminate the "urban bias." Despite the fact that Rawlings, with the assistance of the World Bank, has created conditions for stimulating agricultural growth, the national policies have not yet addressed the quality of life in rural areas. Regional centers like Sunyani in Brong-Ahafo have come alive as their aging farmers begin again to earn a living from farming; the agricultural success is convincing young people who have few educational possibilities to remain in farming rather than migrate to try to find non-existent jobs. However, conditions in Sunyani are considerably worse than they were in the early 1970s. Clean piped water and electricity are luxuries which are sporadically available, but not reliable by any means. The push to rehabilitate Ghana's roads did not include those roads to distant rural towns such as Sunyani; therefore, roads which were once well tarred have disintegrated, making travel over 40 miles a challenging endeavor. Given these conditions, many aspiring young people still seek out the quickest route to the city. There are those who argue that the investment in southern agriculture has occurred only because of the link to the export economy, and that there is still no significant shift in the "urban bias," especially when one examines northern communities.

Previous experience with the UGFCC and the cooperatives indicates that considerable attention must be paid to the nature and type of economic organizations within which peasants function, and the degree of relative control which peasant, as opposed to the state, exercise over them.[46] Historically, cocoa farmers have tended to relate to these organizations first in terms of the opportunities they provided for local-level leadership, second in terms of opportunities for local-level resource investment, and third and last in terms of national economic contributions. Given the national focus on controlling and extracting profits from the cocoa organizations, this contradiction often led to antagonistic relationships between the cocoa organizations and the national party. Perhaps the period since the 1970s which saw the collapse of the cooperatives and the near collapse of the cocoa industry will have altered these priorities by focusing peasant consciousness on national and global factors in economic success. Certainly the cohesiveness of rural communities, and of the class of successful cocoa farmers who provided leadership of agricultural organizations and who mobilized local consciousness, will have been greatly weakened by the post-1975 national economic decline.

The recent revival of the rural economy signals a possible renewal of local dynamism (and unfortunately stratification). However, unless there is a consistent effort on the part of the PNDC to reinforce national consciousness by involving rural producers in other significant national issues in which they have a stake (such as investment of resources in building the rural areas), the withdrawal of peasant enthusiasm from existing local agricultural organizations is a possibility. At present, COCOBOD is making significant investments in the cocoa sector. Notably, the current Produce Buying Company and Cocoa Services Division strategy of creating geographical/functional units, within which cocoa is sold and services or inputs to farmers provided, does not allow for the kind of politicization and social mobilization that occurred in the cocoa cooperatives. Nevertheless, whether the need for local involvement can be satisfied through these arrangements is still an open question. While Rawlings's agricultural policies have earned him the support of Akan and other southern rural producers, this does not yet translate into unqualified political support for such institutions as People's Defense Committees or the PNDC. What is still missing is the linkage mechanism that would draw in the elite from these agricultural areas into a dialogue about national priorities.

At present, the composition of the rural labor force is somewhat skewed, as more females than males remain in agricultural labor. The return of refugees from Nigeria and Ivory Coast between 1983 and 1985 caused temporary swells in the male population, but it was the new agricultural policies and the "mobisquads"of the PNDC which caused a return to the present male-female ratios in rural areas. The mobisquads move men rather than women towards capital accumulation resulting in farm ownership. One major challenge for the PNDC will be to devise strategies for lucrative gender-free rural wage-labor opportunities which will encourage women's participation; or alternatively to devise gender-specific but equal wage-labor and capital accumulation opportunities. Such opportunities would then allow for male and female farmers to begin investing in agriculture in much the same way as they were willing to do in earlier phases of cocoa development.

Many of Ghana's problems have resulted from the monocrop nature of production, and are likely to be resolved only through diversification in export crops. The need for several resources to bring in foreign exchange has been demonstrated, but the question is how and where such crops can be developed. The northern areas present particular difficulties with population size and distribution, and variation in water availability, both of which affect production possibilities. At present, state policies support rice production, but the rice is targeted for domestic consumption rather than export. The combination of smallholder production and limited state subsidization appears to be the solution that Ghana is finding most workable. However, the remaining challenge for the government in Ghana is to find northern export crops which will supplement cocoa production. These crops, while satisfying an international demand, must be low in technological and organizational requirements; they should create labor demand which will provide employment for large numbers of people in the north. It appears that only such geographically distributed agricultural diversification will relieve rural producers from the pressure of state expectations, demands and exploitation which southern cocoa producers have experienced. Hopefully, it will be possible, after all, for Ghana to find a way out of the cycle of rural exploitation and national chaos.

Notes

1. Richard Bendix, *Max Weber: An Intellectual Portrait*, New York: Doubleday-Anchor, 1962, 360–381.

2. Mitchell, Marion M. "Emile Durkheim and the Philosophy of Nationalism," *Political Science Quarterly*, vol. XLVI, 1931, 87–106.
3. Ray A. Kea, 1982, 92–3. Kea follows Wilks' (1977, 511–17, 522–26) earlier argument by suggesting that the exogamous matrilineal system, *mmusa-kese*, evolved out of labor groups organized by *obirempon* and elite families, for the purpose of assimilating people of unfree or servile status.
4. I. Wilks, 1975, 126–165.
5. Emile Durkheim, *The Division of Labor in Society*, New York: The Free Press, 1933.
6. I. Wilks, 1975, 86.
7. R. Kea, 1982, 44–45.
8. Kwame Arhin, "Peasants in Nineteenth Century Asante," *Current Anthropology*, vol. 24, 1984, 471–75.
9. For actions of the Aborigines' Rights Protection Society, see Metcalfe, 1964, 539, 542–3, 600.
10. I. Wilks, 1975, 106.
11. K. Arhin, *West African Traders In Ghana in the Nineteenth and Twentieth Centuries*, 1979.
12. M. Gluckman, "The Utility of the Equilibrium Model in the Study of Social Change," *American Anthropologist*, 70 (2), 219–237.
13. David E. Apter, *Ghana in Transition*. New York: Atheneum, 1968, 196–7.
14. G.E. Metcalfe, *Great Britain and Ghana: Documents of Ghana History, 1807–1957*. London: Thos. Nelson & Sons, 1964, 605, 607–9, 617–20.
15. Peter Worsley, *The Three Worlds*. 1985.
16. Jon Kraus, "Arms and Politics in Ghana," in Claude Welch (ed.), *Soldier and State in Africa*. Evanston: Northwestern University Press, 1970, 154–221.
17. Claude E. Welch, Jr., "The Roots and Implications of Military Intervention," in Welch (ed.), op. cit., 1970, 21–22.
18. Ali Mazrui and Donald Rothchild, "The Soldier and the State in East Africa: Some Theoretical Conclusions on the Army Mutinies of 1964," *Western Political Quarterly* XX, 1967, 82–96.
19. Edward Feit, "Military Coups and Political Development: Some Lessons from Ghana and Nigeria," *World Politics*, vol. 20, no. 2, Sept. 1968, 184.
20. Aristide R. Zolberg, "The Structure of Political Conflict In the New States of Tropical Africa," *American Political Science Review*, LXII, no. 1, 1968, 73–77.
21. Op. cit., chapter 3, p. 13.
22. Maxwell Owusu, "Custom and Coups: A Juridical Interpretation of Civil Order and Disorder in Ghana," *Journal of Modern African Studies*, 24, 1, 1986: 69-99.
23. Benjamin C. Ray, *African Religions: Symbol, Ritual and Community*, New Jersey: Prentice-Hall, 1976.
24. Ibid., p. 81.
25. Claude Welch, Jr. "Cincinnatus in Africa: The Possibility of Military Withdrawal from Politics," in M. Lofchie (ed.), *The State of the Nation: Constraints on Development in Independent Africa*. University of California 1971, 215–237.
26. Justice D.F. Annan, member of the PNDC and chairman of the National Commission

for Democracy, as quoted in the interview by Achim Remde, "Traditional Values," in *West Africa*, March 10, 1986, pp. 507–10.

27. Jon Kraus, "Ghana's Shift from Radical Populism," *Current History*, vol, 86, no. 520, May 1987, 205–208, 227–228.
28. Kraus, op. cit., 1987, 205. Kraus states: "It is doubtful that any government could have launched economic reform programs like [Ghana's] if there had been democratic rule; previous governments have shied away from devaluations and budget cuts in the face of popular dissent. But the Rawlings regime must permit free debate again and needs to allow wider political participation if it wishes to be regarded as ruling effectively."
29. Oscar Lewis, "The Culture of Poverty," *Scientific American* 1966, 215: 4: 19–25; *La Vida: A Puerto Rican Family in the Culture of Poverty—San Juan and New York*, New York, Random House, 1966.
30. E. Franklin Frazier, *The Negro Family in The United States*, University of Chicago 1969; and *Black Bourgeoisie: The Rise of a New Middle Class*, The Free Press, 1957. Daniel Patrick Moynihan, *The Negro Family: The Case For National Action*, Washington, DC: U.S. Department of Labor, 1965.
31. Charles Valentine, *The Culture of Poverty: A Critical Reevaluation*, 1968; Elliott Liebow, *Tally's Corner*, Boston: Little-Brown, 1967; Carol Stack, *All Our Kin: Strategies for Survival in a Black Community*, New York: Harper and Row, 1974; Robert Hill, *The Strengths of Black Families*, 1974.
32. Asante-Darko, and S. Van der Geest, "Male Chauvinism: Men and Women in Ghanaian Highlife Songs," in Christine Oppong (ed.), *Male and Female in West Africa*, London: Allen & Unwin, 1983.
33. Mary Douglas, "Is Matriliny Doomed?" in D. Forde and P. Kaberry (eds.), *Man in Africa*, New York: Doubleday, 1971, 123–137.
34. Ilsa Glazer-Schuster, *The New Women of Lusaka*, 1979.
35. Frederick Cooper, "Africa and the World Economy," *African Studies Review*, vol. XXIV, nos. 2–3, 1981, 49–51.
36. Lester R. Brown, "The Limits to Growth of Third World Cities," in *Annual Editions: Urban Society*, Dushkin Publishers, 2nd ed., 1982, 36–41.
37. David B. Ottaway, "Shultz Lauds Ivory Coast as a Model for Africa," *The Washington Post*, Jan. 14, 1987.
38. "Africa's Poor on the Brink: 12 Nations in Severe Debt Crisis," Blaine Harden, *The Washington Post*, June 7, 1987, pp. Al, A25.
39. Blaine Harden, "West's Capitalist Credo Costing Lives in Malawi," *The Washington Post*, December 31, 1986.
40. S. Amin, "Self-Reliance and the New Economic Order," in A.W. Singham (ed.), *The Non-Aligned Movement in World Politics*, Westport, CT: Lawrence Hill & Co., 1977: 145–157.
41. Samir Amin, *Accumulation on a World Scale: A Critique of the Theory of Development* (trans. Brian Pearce), New York, 1974.
42. Kwame Nkrumah, *I Speak of Freedom: A Statement of African Ideology*, New York: Praeger, 1961, 33, 153, 168.

43. Eliot Berg et al., "Accelerated Development in Sub-Saharan Africa: An Agenda for Action," Washington: The World Bank, 1981.
44. See Cooper, op. cit. 1981, for a discussion of Amin's theoretical position.
45. James Brain; "Less than Second Class Citizens: Women in Ujamaa Villages in Tanzania," in N. Hafkin and E. Bay (eds.), *Women in Africa: Studies in Social and Economic Change*, Stanford University Press, 1976.
46. G. Mikell, "African Women Within Nations In Crisis," *TransAfrica*, vol. 2, Summer 1983, 21–35.
47. "Ghana: A Sub-Saharan Test Case," *West Africa*, July 8, 1985.
48. *Lagos Plan of Action for Economic Development of Africa, 1980–2000*, Organization of African Unity, Geneva: International Institute for Labor Studies, 1981.
49. Robert S. Browne and Robert J. Cummings, *The Lagos Plan of Action vs. the Berg Report: Contemporary Issues in African Economic Development.* Monographs in African Studies. Washington: African Studies Program, Howard University, 1984, p. 216.
50. Nii K. Bensi-Enchill, "Better pay, fewer staff," interview with PNDC Secretary for Labour and Social Welfare, Mr. Ato Austin, *West Africa*, 17 March 1986, 554. Donald H. May, "Early Costs Test African Economic Reform," *The Washington Times*, Jan. 13, 1987.
51. "Food Production in Africa Outstrips Population Growth," *The Sun*, Jan. 3, 1987.
52. "Commodities: Cocoa," *West Africa*, 24 June 1985, 1284; also, 17 June 1985, 1238.

Glossary

Abirempon	Plural of *obirempon.*
Abusa	A category of sharecropping labor primarily on cocoa farms. Such persons received compensation which was one-third of the crop harvested.
Abusua	A corporate matrilineal family group, a part of a matrilineage, tracing descent from a senior female ancestor (plural *mmusua*).
Abusua-kese	A matrilineally based, residential and political unit which was traditionally under the control of the class of *abirempon* who established it. Commoners gained land rights through membership in these units (plural *mmusua-kese*).
Acha	A local rice, reddish in color, and less nutritional in content.
Adosoa	Baskets or bundles belonging to women, in which they kept valuables.
Adwadofo	African retail agents or representatives of trading establishment.
Afahene	Plural of *ofahene.*
Ahenfo	Office holders.
Akan	The predominant linguistic and cultural group found in central and southern Ghana, and composed of smaller sub-ethnic units such as Akwapim, Ashanti, Brong, Fanti, etc. Originally migrant from more northern areas, this group tends to be matrilineal in structure.
Akoa	A person who is a subject of someone; a dependent commoner (plural *nkoa*).

Amanhene	Plural of *Omanhene*.
Amantoo	All of the major traditional political divisions of Ashanti, whose chiefs are traditionally subordinate to the Asantehene.
Antihumanifo	The poor, and usually service, commoner citizens of Ashanti.
Aseda	A ceremonial public thanks for some deed performed or thing received.
Asafo	Plural of *osafo*.
Asafuakye	Identical to *Safohene*. These are leaders of the *asafo* units through Akan areas. Popularly chosen young male leader who is not a part of the group of lineage elders of a village.
Asante	Name of the traditional political empire in central Gold Coast. This term is synonymous with "Ashanti," and refers also to the people and cultural aspects of the Ashanti area and traditions.
Asantehene	The king and supreme chief of the Ashanti empire, who ranks higher than the other clan chiefs of Ashanti.
Awunnyade	Death-duty imposed on the estate of an Ashanti, which made the resources in question the property of the state.
Caboceers	Administrative officials within coastal towns who had responsibilities for guaranteeing conditions conducive to good trade relations. Although appointed by chiefs, they might also receive stipends from European traders.
Dambas	A gold weight; 384 of these were said to equal one ounce troy weight. It was commonly used in Portuguese trading transactions between 1482 and 1700.
Fufu	A starchy staple food made of mashed yam and plantain, which was served with soup.
Futuo	Containers such as chests or leather bags in which men usually kept valuables like gold dust.
Kalabule	Economic corruption, usually involving blackmarketeering or the sale of goods above the state's control price.
Kenkey	A starchy staple food made of manioc which was sometimes fermented; it would be eaten with soup, meat or other foods.
Klaploppere	Danish word used in reference to African representatives of merchants.
Kra kuduo	A metal container belonging to men, which contained valuables and ritual items.
Kumasihene	Head of the Kumasi division, and the chief who was elevated to the status of Asantehene.
Lancados	Portuguese traders who lived inland on the upper Guinea coast.
Manilhas	Brass bracelets used as standards of value in early European trade.

Mantiase	The conquered and incorporated towns, whose chiefs were not originally part of Ashanti.
Mmammadwa	Sons' stools; appointed, non-traditional positions created by the Asantehene, which passed father-to-son rather than through matrilineal inheritance.
Mobisquads	Rural work groups organized by Jerry Rawlings, and made up primarily of young men. While originally emphasizing nationalism and communalism, they have gradually incorporated more profit-making aspects.
Mogya	The "blood" group. The group of persons related by matrilineal blood.
Moshi	Normally given to a person of northern or Mossi origin, but also sometimes indicating their origins in non-centralized societies or slave origins.
Mpena Awadie	A low status form of marriage, which is variously defined as "common-law" or "lover-marriage." Since no *tiri nsa* or bridewealth is paid, the husband is not entitled to damages should adultery occur.
Nhoboa	Traditional, local self-help groups, usually composed of neighbors who joined together to work on each others' farms as needed.
Nkoa	Dependent commoners in traditional Ashanti society.
Nkotokuano	A category of labor primarily on cocoa farms. Such persons were paid a set sum for each load of cocoa harvested.
Nkramo	Muslims.
Nkwankwaa	The military retinue of "young men" within Ashanti. Their populist leader, who was not one of the elders, was known as the *nkwankwaahene*.
Nkwasefo	Villagers; rural inhabitants.
Nnonum	Akan captives and slaves.
Ntoro	The ritual connection between father and offspring, which is passed on through sons. There is a spiritual (totemic) identification that father and children share, which must be respected by certain dietary restrictions and ritual sacrifices (*ntoro* is synonymous with *ntron*).
Obaa-panin	Old lady or matriarch the family; the male head of the family is the *Opanyin*.
Obirempon	Wealthy commoners who were considered synonymous with aristocrats. They were involved in trade and usually controlled land and clients (plural, *abirempon*, or *abrempomma* for females).
Odikro	The headman of a village (plural *adikro*).

Odonko	(also *donkor*) Slave; person of non-free origin (plural *nnonkofo*).
Ofahene	A royal office-holder within the Ashanti bureaucracy (plural *afahene*).
Ohene	Traditional lower-level chief (plural *ahenefo*) who possessed a stool signifying a right to rule.
Okonkofo	Entrepreneurs, usually employed by the Asantehene to engage in business (plural *akonkofo*).
Oman	The Akan political unit, made up of lineages at the lowest level; or made up of divisional chiefs, their stools, and their affiliated lands at the national level.
Omanhene	The divisional chief within Ashanti (plural *amanhene*).
Patrifiliation	A tendency for social structures and social relations to be inclined toward favoring males and control by males; but it does not involve public challenge to matrilineal structures, or a change to patrilineality.
Sikafo	Wealthy, privileged persons.
Stool	The ritual symbol of political office or chieftaincy within Akan areas. It is generally a small wooden stool, the authority of which is passed down to the next office holder. Divisional and higher level chiefs have more elaborate stools; the Asantehene has a golden stool.
Tiri Nsa	A ceremonial payment given by the husband to the family of the wife which legitimizes marriage and gives rights of sexual control to the husband. It is popularly known as the "headwine."
Yamfunu	A segment of a matrilineage formed around a sister who traces to the same maternal ancestor as the remainder of the *abusua*.
Xarife	Name given by the Portuguese to the local trade official, usually representative of the chief or king.
Zongo	A place of residence for strangers, most of whom were of northern or Islamic origin.

Abbreviations

ABASCO	A short-lived organization formed by Ashanti, Brong-Ahafo and Sefwi cocoa farmers, in an attempt to retain their former cooperative-society structures within UGFCC, the new state cocoa buying agency formed by the CPP government in 1961. Nkrumah rejected the farmers' proposal.
AFRC	Air Forces Revolutionary Council. Government established after the abortive military coup of Jerry Rawlings in 1979 and after the popular uprising which brought him to power. This government ruled from May to September 1979.
ARPS	Aborigines' Rights Protection Society. Organization established by the indigenous Gold Coast professional elite in the 1890s to protect the property and political rights of Africans vis-a-vis colonial and merchant interests.
BKF	Brong Kyempim Federation (or BKC). The organization primarily of Brong chiefs and people of northwest Ashanti, which fought for regional autonomy from the Ashanti region between 1951 and 1961.
CDS	Cocoa Services Division. A branch of COCOBOD which provides sprays, technical service and advice to cocoa farmers.
CMB	Cocoa Marketing Board. The cocoa purchasing organization established by the colonial government in 1947, which operated under Ghanaian state control from independence until the beginning of the Rawlings government in 1981.
CDR	Committees for the Defense of the Revolution. Local populist

	organizations established by Rawlings in 1984 by transforming the old PDCs and WDCs, so that ordinary citizens could participate in fighting corruption and in supporting the politics of the government.
COCOBOD	The state agricultural purchasing agency established by the PNDC which serviced cocoa farmers and food farmers after 1981.
CPP	Convention People's Party. The nationalist organization founded by Gold Coast people in 1948 to fight for self-government and independence.
CPC	Cocoa Purchasing Company. The organization established by the nationalist party for purchasing cocoa in 1952, which later functioned as a state-owned monopoly company until its dissolution in 1957.
NCWD	National Council on Women and Development. Founded in 1975 as a part of the national decade of women's activities, and functioned to coordinate activities on women through the various ministries in Ghana.
NLC	National Liberation Council. The alliance government of military, civil service and chiefs which assumed power after the overthrow of Nkrumah, until the election of Busia's PP government.
NLM	National Liberation Movement. An Ashanti-based organization formed by economic elites as a challenge to the political authority of the CPP. Its goal was economic and political autonomy for the Ashanti region.
NRC	National Redemption Council (Supreme Military Council I). Military government of Ignatius Acheampong, which ousted Dr. Busia's PP government in a coup in 1971.
NS	National Service Program. Under Rawlings, this program required secondary-school leavers and professionals trained in Ghana to spend one year in health, technical, bureaucratic, or agricultural service for the government.
OFY	Operation Feed Yourself. Movement started by the Acheampong government in 1971 as an attempt to stimulate food production through grass-roots level initiatives.
PDC	People's Defense Committees. Organizations established by Rawlings in 1982, which operated in neighborhoods to stimulate coordinate services and handle local development.
PNDC	Provisional National Defense Council. Government established by the second Rawlings coup of December 31, 1981.
PNP	People's National Party. Government of Hilla Limann which was

	elected in September 1979 and functioned until December 31, 1981.
PP	Progressive Party. The government of K.A. Busia, elected to power in 1969.
SMC II	Military government of Lt. General Akuffo, which demanded that Acheampong step down as head of state. It planned a return to elected, constitutional government, but was overtaken by corruption and overthrown during the first Rawlings coup and popular uprising in May 1979.
UGFCC	United Ghana Farmers' Council Cooperatives. Originally organized as the UGFC (United Ghana Farmers' Council) by Nkrumah, it was transformed in 1961 into a state-owned cocoa purchasing organization and was given the monopoly by the CPP government.
UNIGOV	Political referendum undertaken by the Acheampong military government, in response to growing demands for elections and democratic political participation. While it sought voter approval for continued government control, protests against it resulted in Acheampong's removal.
WDC	Worker Defense Committees. Organizations established in workplaces in 1982 to establish policy and fight corruption.
WID	Women In Development. Regional projects within the District Administrative Offices, which coordinated women's health, educational and development activities within each region.

Index

Note: Page numbers in italics indicate tables.